Edmond Malone (1741–1812) was the greatest early editor of Shakespeare's works, the first historian of early English drama, the biographer of Shakespeare, Dryden, and Reynolds, and a relentless exposer of literary fraud and forgery. His dedication to discovering the facts of literary history through manuscripts and early editions laid the foundations for the scholar's code and the modern study of literature. Yet he was also a gregarious man, attracting many friends – and enemies – among his contemporaries. This first modern full-length biography of Edmond Malone illuminates in a unique way both the intensely private world of the scholar and the highly public world of the late eighteenth-century artistic, intellectual, and political elite, including Samuel Johnson, Edmund Burke, Sir Joshua Reynolds, Sarah Siddons, and James Boswell.

CAMBRIDGE STUDIES IN EIGHTEENTH-CENTURY
ENGLISH LITERATURE AND THOUGHT 25

Edmond Malone

CAMBRIDGE STUDIES IN EIGHTEENTH-CENTURY
ENGLISH LITERATURE AND THOUGHT

General editors
Dr HOWARD ERSKINE-HILL LITT. D., FBA, *Pembroke College, Cambridge*
Professor JOHN RICHETTI, *University of Pennsylvania*

Editorial board

Morris Brownell, University of Nevada
Leopold Damrosch, Harvard University
J. Paul Hunter, University of Chicago
Isobel Grundy, University of Alberta
Lawrence Lipking, Northwestern University
Harold Love, Monash University
Claude Rawson, Yale University
Pat Rogers, University of South Florida
James Sambrook, University of Southampton

Some recent titles

17 *Literary Transmission and Authority: Dryden and other Writers*
edited by Earl Miner and Jennifer Brady

18 *Plots and Counterplots*
Sexual Politics and the Body Politic in English Literature 1660–1730
by Richard Braverman

19 *The Eighteenth-Century Hymn in England*
by Donald Davie

20 *Swift's Politics: A Study in Disaffection*
by Ian Higgins

21 *Writing and the Rise of Finance*
Capital Satires of the Early Eighteenth Century
by Colin Nicholson

22 *Locke, Literary Criticism, and Philosophy*
by William Walker

23 *Poetry and Jacobite Politics in Eighteenth-Century Britain and Ireland*
by Murray G. H. Pittock

24 *The Story of the Voyage: Sea Narratives in Eighteenth-Century England*
by Philip Edwards

A complete list of books in this series is given at the end of the volume.

Edmond Malone. Oil by Sir Joshua Reynolds, 1779

Edmond Malone
Shakespearean scholar

A literary biography

PETER MARTIN

CAMBRIDGE
UNIVERSITY PRESS

PUBLISHED BY THE PRESS SYNDICATE OF THE UNIVERSITY OF CAMBRIDGE
The Pitt Building, Trumpington Street, Cambridge, United Kingdom

CAMBRIDGE UNIVERSITY PRESS
The Edinburgh Building, Cambridge CB2 2RU, UK
40 West 20th Street, New York NY 10011–4211, USA
477 Williamstown Road, Port Melbourne, VIC 3207, Australia
Ruiz de Alarcón 13, 28014 Madrid, Spain
Dock House, The Waterfront, Cape Town 8001, South Africa

http://www.cambridge.org

First published 1995
First paperback edition 2005

A catalogue record for this book is available from the British Library

Library of Congress cataloguing in publication data

Martin, Peter, 1940–
Edmond Malone, Shakespearean scholar / by Peter Martin.
p.   cm. – (Cambridge studies in eighteenth-century English literature and
thought; 25)
Includes bibliographical references and index.
ISBN 0 521 46030 1 (hardback)
1. Malone, Edmond, 1741–1812.   2. Great Britain – Intellectual life – 18th century.
3. Literary historians – Great Britain – Biography.   4. Shakespeare, William, 1564–1616
– Editors.   5. Biographers – Great Britain – Biography.   6. Editors – Great Britain
– Biography.   I. Title.   II. Series.
PR2972.   M3M37   1995
820.9–dc20
[B]
94-19822
CIP

ISBN 0 521 46030 1 hardback
ISBN 0 521 61982 3 paperback

For
Maynard Mack
and in memory of
James Marshall Osborn

Constant employment is, I believe, the true philosopher's stone, and contributes more to the happiness of life, than all the splendid nothings for which half the world are contending.

(Edmond Malone, 1777)

Contents

Illustrations

12. *James Boswell*. Oil by Sir Joshua Reynolds, 1785. 30 × 25 in. Courtesy of the National Portrait Gallery.
13. *Edmund Burke*. Oil by Sir Joshua Reynolds, for Streatham, 1774. 30 × 25 in. Collection: National Library of Ireland. Courtesy of the National Portrait Gallery.
14. *Mrs Hester Thrale* (afterwards Piozzi). Oil by Robert Edge Pine. 1781. 27 × 23 in. Courtesy of Courage, Barclay and Simonds Ltd.
15. *Thou art a Retailer of Phrases*. English School, 1800. Courtesy of the National Portrait Gallery.
16. *Revising for the Second Edition*, 15 June 1786. From *The Beauties of Boswell*. See Boswell's *Journal*, 2nd edn., p. 527. Courtesy of the Lewis Walpole Library, Yale University. *British Museum Catalogue of Political and Personal Satires*, no. 7041.
17. *The Biographers*, 1786. Shows Hester Thrale Piozzi, Courtenay, and Boswell. The bust of Dr Johnson looks down on them, displeased. Johnson also appears as a bear in Boswell's *Journal of the Tour*, in which Boswell is writing. *British Museum Catalogue of Political and Personal Satires*, no. 7052. Courtesy of the Lewis Walpole Library, Yale University.
18. *Titianus Redivivus; – or – The Seven Wise Men consulting the new Venetian Oracle, a Scene in ye Academic Grove*, 1797, no. 1. Courtesy of the Lewis Walpole Library, Yale University.
19. *Joseph Farington*. Drawing by George Dance, RA, 1793. Courtesy of the National Portrait Gallery.
20. *Dr Charles Burney*. Drawing by George Dance, RA, 1794. Courtesy of the National Portrait Gallery.
21. *Fanny Burney*. Drawing by her cousin E. F. Burney in the Brooklyn Museum Collection, n.d. Courtesy of the National Portrait Gallery.

Preface

If a scholar 'who [has] passed his Life among his Books' may be, as Samuel Johnson put it, a fit and useful subject for biography, Johnson's contemporary Edmond Malone is an especially apt choice. For to his minute and multifarious labours during a literary career of four decades, we owe much knowledge not only about Shakespeare but also about Johnson, Boswell, Dryden, Reynolds, Pope, and Goldsmith, as well as English stage history and early English poetry, that without him would have been lost for ever or delayed until the birth of university literary study in this century.

Young 'Neddy', as Malone was affectionately called by his family, could not in the remote Ireland of his birth and upbringing easily have imagined his later career at the heart of London social and artistic life. Many highly educated Irish felt far removed from the artistic and intellectual energy of England, an energy centring in London, Oxford, and Cambridge. And while a young literary Irishman might think it possible to study some day at one of those centres of learning, he could see himself there only as a foreigner who must inevitably return home to feel, more than ever, his sense of separation. A recurring theme in the correspondence Malone received in London from Irish friends like Bishop Thomas Percy, one of the most eminent men of letters of the day, and the Earl of Charlemont, Irish statesman, was the consciousness that they were living on the fringe of European culture. Continually they asked Malone for literary and political news, periodicals, and publications which they feared they would receive either unbearably late or not at all. The thought of being out of the mainstream was inevitably demoralizing.

It was, however, possible to feel the penalties of remoteness without loss of national pride. During the decade before he settled in London Malone felt such emotions as keenly as anyone, and he frequently despaired afterward at what he interpreted as Irish insularity; but he never lost his love of country. He maintained an astute – though at times exasperated – interest in Irish politics, was faithful to his old friends, and returned frequently to visit them and his closely-knit family.

As a scholar–collector, editor, biographer, and critic, Malone based his writing and editing on facts, painstakingly discovered. His thoroughness

and rigorous insistence on accuracy remain exemplary. Today we take this
for granted as part of the scholar's method, but in Malone's day it was
uncommon. He took nothing on faith. His second home was the British
Museum library. He wrote constantly to friends, asking them to ransack
libraries, old repositories, and family collections for the elusive fact, date, or
name that would lighten the quickly darkening pages of literary history.
Malone felt his work was crucial, that he was racing against time; too much
had been lost already. He had little use for those, like Bishop William
Warburton, who he felt passed up rare and privileged opportunities to
preserve literary facts.

Malone embarked on his scholarly career at a propitious time in English
literary history. Cultural and political circumstances were such that what
he had to offer was especially valued. These included: the growth of
antiquarianism and biography; a relish for comprehensive histories of
English poetry on the part of a larger and broader reading public; and the
solidifying consciousness of national identity, accelerated by the French
Revolution, which propelled the discovery and recovery of national authors
to set against the ancients. Shakespeare was at the centre of this patriotically
celebrative mode, but Chaucer, Spenser, Jonson, Dryden, and Pope, to
name a few, bearing the standard of national pride, were also scrupulously
edited in splendid editions, commented upon, and firmly placed in a
national pantheon of poetry. And when Thomas Warton emerged in the
1770s as the defender of national pride, as Lawrence Lipking has put it, in
writing the first history of English poetry, it was clear that the English
search for their own literary traditions had finally come of age. It mattered
less to his countrymen that Warton's *History* was an uncompelling and
uneven compilation of diverse material, than that it was a monument of a
national heritage. All of this sketches the context within which the
astonishing worship of Shakespeare as the national poet climaxed in the
second half of the eighteenth century. So when Malone decided to put his
research talents at the service of Shakespeare, he was eagerly welcomed into
the exclusive pale of leading Shakespeareans by George Steevens – then at
work on a second edition of the *Johnson–Steevens Shakespeare* – with little
more to recommend him than a successful university career, some editorial
and biographical work on Goldsmith, and an evident enthusiasm to roll up
his sleeves and get to work in the archives.

There was something both heroic and obsessive in Malone's approach to
his work. 'When our poet's entire library shall have been discovered, and
the fables of all his plays traced to their original sources', he wrote in 1790,
'when every temporary allusion shall have been pointed out, and every
obscurity elucidated, then, and not till then, let the accumulation of notes
be complained of.'[1] Two centuries of Shakespeare scholarship have

[1] Preface, *The Plays and Poems of William Shakspeare*, ed. Edmond Malone, I, i (1790), p. lvi.

vindicated his zeal, although several of his contemporaries mocked him for it.

Throughout his career, he rarely was free of critics who accused him, sometimes correctly, of numbering the streaks of the tulip. Even Sir Walter Scott, who relied heavily on Malone's considerable discoveries about Dryden, thought his *Life of Dryden* marred by an embarrassment of riches that made it dull. Malone also made enemies by not suffering fools gladly. He could be arrogant and was a terror to forgers. But the weight of critical and literate opinion was heavily on his side. He counted among his close and admiring friends Johnson, Boswell, Burke, Reynolds, Goldsmith, Windham, Priestly, Horace Walpole, Banks, Burney, and Burney's daughter 'Fanny'. He was at the centre of this world, epitomized by the vigorous part he played in the life and progress of the famous Literary Club. The Club, in fact, plays a large part in this biography.

In 1860 James Prior published a biography of Malone, but it is not scholarly rigorous. Samuel Schoenbaum, in *Shakespeare's Lives* (1970; revised 1991), explains the need for a new Life:

James Prior was no doubt an excellent naval surgeon, and his *Life of Malone* qualifies as an agreeable exercise in piety, but it is not an authoritative study of one of the ornaments of the Johnson circle and one of the greatest of all Shakespearian scholars. Yet a more up-to-date biography has not superseded Prior's, despite quantities of untapped manuscript material at the Bodleian Library, the British Library and elsewhere.

In my biography I have tried to offer a fuller picture of Malone, in the full range of his literary activities, than Prior did or than other shorter and more recent studies do, by concentrating on particular aspects of his impressively diverse career. Indeed, that diversity makes Malone a difficult subject. His biographer must follow him into Renaissance and Shakespeare studies, Dryden and Restoration drama, the history of the English stage, Pope, Boswell, Johnson, and the intellectual and social world of late eighteenth-century English letters – epitomized by The Club. It is a large arena.

What I hope emerges in this biography is a clear idea of Malone's enormous contribution to Shakespeare studies. I have tried to put this into perspective by examining the extent of his influence on readers and students of Shakespeare since he left his mark. How lasting was it? How has his work measured up to Shakespeare scholarship since? Much recent writing on Malone's editorial and critical work has been theoretical and deconstructionist. It argues that both Malone's work and the traditional scholarship based on documentary evidence that it heralded was restrictive and distorting. Malone is supposed to have re-created Shakespeare in the image of the archival documents that he painstakingly tracked down.

Historical facts become the potential enemies of the truth. By striking at him, the progenitor of modern scholarship, this theoretical criticism strikes at the heart of the value of historical literary research. In the course of explaining Malone's methods and successes, I hope without being polemical, I try to counter this recent critical tendency. Two other dimensions of my narrative of Malone's scholarly activities are how they helped shape the scholar's code from his day to ours and what this tells us about the direction of literary studies in this period.

Malone the biographer is also a theme, as is his intimacy with Boswell. Nothing shows Malone's personality so clearly as his collaboration with Boswell on the *Life of Samuel Johnson*. It is a very human story, replete with anxieties and frustrations, success and disappointment, and – ever at the core of Malone's work – principles and tenets of how facts should be presented and history told. His especially close relationship with Burke and Reynolds, as well as his hostility towards literary adversaries like Joseph Ritson, his fiery opposition to Jacobinism in any shape or form, and his almost neurotic pursuit of literary forgers also help reveal Malone's complex personality – his uneasy mix of mild-mannered sociability and professional aggressiveness.

Another emphasis in this biography, however, is the current of unfulfilment in Malone's life, personally and professionally. It was always a source of sadness for him that in his early thirties his scholarship took him away, more or less permanently, from his family in Ireland. Bachelorhood pained him even more. He does not fit the mould of the Aubrey-like, self-sufficient, retiring, dusty scholar blissfully sequestered among his books and happy to let the events of the world take whatever course they will. In spite of his respect and fondness for women, and in spite of several efforts to marry, his unwanted lot was a life of domestic solitude. His inability to make himself attractive enough to the women he wished to marry was (as one of his friends put it) his own personal devil.

As a scholar, sometimes he showed a similar inconclusiveness. He loved hunting for archival information more than arranging and writing it up, so that several of his projects were either delayed far too long or never completed. When he did complete a study, he found his gratification too often dimmed by the previous deaths of scholars and friends whom he respected and whose commendation he had eagerly sought. It sometimes seemed to him that the most voluble survivors waiting to greet his publications were carping critics determined to cut him down to size. Add to this his fierce political frustrations over the French Revolution, Irish affairs, and Jacobinism that at times surfaced in his writings and won him few friends; and it becomes easy to see that for him the scholarly life was no ivory tower existence; not infrequently, it was a blend of toil and trouble.

In an effort to make this book accessible to the non-specialist reader, I have provided background to Shakespearean and other literary and historical scholarship whenever useful. Personalities are identified when they are first introduced, literary issues are explained, and political background is clarified. I have not, however, modernized eighteenth-century spelling and punctuation except for bracketed emendations.

I have accumulated debts in the course of writing this biography. First and foremost, to Maynard Mack, who suggested the idea one afternoon in Stratford-upon-Avon rather more years ago than seems possible, who read several drafts and guided me with wisdom at many turns. I dedicate the book to him as well as to the memory of James Marshall Osborn, who intended to write a biography of Malone but died before he could do so. His collections of Maloniana in the Osborn Collection at the Beinecke Rare Book and Manuscript Library, Yale University, have been crucial to my work, and I am extremely grateful to Stephen Parks, Curator of the Collection, for permission to cite from it so extensively. My very great thanks, too, to G. Blakemore Evans, Arthur Sherbo, and Paul Korshin for reading portions of the manuscript and offering invaluable suggestions for revision, as well as to David Fleeman who advised me on the Boswell chapters.

I also wish to thank the following repositories for permission to use manuscript material: Sterling Library and the James Marshall and Marie-Louise Osborn Collection at the Beinecke Library, Yale University; British Library; Folger Shakespeare Library; Bodleian Library; Cambridge University Library; the Trustees of the National Library of Scotland; John Rylands Library, Manchester University; the Victoria and Albert Museum; South Kensington Museum; Library of Congress; the [Donald and] Mary Hyde Collection (Somerville, New Jersey); the Arthur O'Neill Collection, National Library of Ireland; Durham University Library; Huntington Library; the Record Office and Library at the Shakespeare Birthplace Trust, Stratford-upon-Avon; the Shakespeare Institute of the University of Birmingham; Sheffield City Libraries; the Trustees of the Boston Public Library; the Henry W. and Albert A. Berg Collection (New York Public Library); Edinburgh University Library; Pierpont Morgan Library; University of London Library; Petworth House (Sussex); West Sussex Record Office; and Houghton Library, Harvard University. My debts to smaller and private collections are acknowledged in the notes. A Fellowship from the National Endowment for the Humanities in 1986 enabled me to spend an entire academic year on research for this book, as did a sabbatical leave from the British Campus of New England College. A grant from the Gertsch Fund at Principia College enabled me to include illustrations in this book that otherwise I would have had to exclude. I am also indebted to Laetitia Yeandle at the Folger, Dr Iain Brown (Assistant

Keeper of Manuscripts) at the National Library of Scotland, Eric M. Lee
at the Beinecke, and Francis O. Mattson (Curator of the Berg Collection)
at the New York Public Library for extensive help at those repositories.
Margaret Birkinshaw, Librarian at New England College, helped me
frequently to obtain books I needed; Eileen Brocklehurst supplied Latin
translations; and Lionel Moon provided vital last-minute help with the
preparation of the manuscript. Finally, as ever, my thanks to Cynthia, my
best, my ever friend, for her encouragement and support.

Abbreviations

BL Add. Ms.	Additional Manuscripts, British Library
Attempt	Edmond Malone, *An Attempt to Ascertain the Order In Which the Plays Attributed to Shakespeare Were Written*, first published in vol. I of the *Johnson–Steevens* edition (2nd edn. 1778); revised for Malone's Shakespeare editions in 1790, 1821.
Beinecke	Beinecke Rare Book and Manuscript Library, Yale University.
B–M Corr.	*The Correspondence of James Boswell with David Garrick, Edmund Burke, and Edmond Malone*, eds. Peter S. Baker, Thomas W. Copeland, George M. Kahrl, Rachel McClellan, and James M. Osborn. *The Yale editions of the private papers of James Boswell, research edition: Correspondence*, vol. 4, 1986.
Boswell 1778–82	*Boswell: Laird of Auchinleck 1778–82*, eds. J. W. Reed and F. A. Pottle, 1977.
Boswell 1782–85	*Boswell: The Applause of the Jury 1782–85*, eds. Irma L. Lustig and F. A. Pottle, 1982.
Boswell 1785–89	*Boswell: The English Experiment 1785–89*, eds. Irma L. Lustig and F. A. Pottle, 1986.
Boswell 1789–95	*Boswell: The Great Biographer 1789–95*, eds. Marlies K. Danziger and Frank Brady, 1989.
Bronson, *Joseph Ritson*	Bertrand H. Bronson, *Joseph Ritson, Scholar at Arms*, 2 vols. Berkeley, 1938.
Burke Corr.	*The Correspondence of Edmund Burke*, ed. T. W. Copeland, 9 vols. Cambridge, 1958–70.
DPW	*The Critical and Miscellaneous Prose Works of John Dryden ... and An Account of the Life and Writings of the Author*, ed. Edmond Malone, 3 vols. 1800.
DF	*The Diary of Joseph Farington*, eds. Kenneth Garlick and Angus Macintyre (vols. I–VI), ed.

	Kathryn Cave (vols. VII–XVI continuing). New Haven and London, 1978–.
Everyman *Life*	Boswell's *Life of Johnson*, ed. and intro. by Sir Sydney Roberts, 2 vols. New York and London, 1960.
F&P	James M. Osborn, *John Dryden: Some Biographical Facts and Problems*, 1940.
Fettercairn	Fettercairn Papers (Acc. 4796) deposited in the National Library of Scotland.
Folger	Folger Shakespeare Library, Washington, DC.
Hebrides	*Boswell's Journal of a Tour to the Hebrides with Samuel Johnson, LL. D.*, 1973, ed. F. A. Pottle (1961).
Hill-Powell	James Boswell, *The Life of Samuel Johnson, LL. D.* ed. G. B. Hill, rev. edn. L. F. Powell, 6 vols. 1934–64.
HMC	*Reports of Historical Manuscripts Commission.*
Inquiry	Edmond Malone, *An Inquiry Into the Authenticity of Certain Miscellaneous Papers … Attributed to Shakespeare, Queen Elizabeth and Henry, Earl of Southampton*, 1796.
J–S	*The Plays of William Shakespeare, with Notes by Samuel Johnson and George Steevens.* 2nd edn., 10 vols. 1778; 10 vols. 1785; 15 vols. 1793; 21 vols. 1803, 1813.
Malahide	*Private Papers of James Boswell from Malahide Castle, in the Collection of Lt.-Colonel Ralph Heyward Isham,* eds. Geoffrey Scott and F. A. Pottle, 18 vols. 1974.
Malone–Jordan	*Original Letters from Edmond Malone, the Editor of Shakespeare, to John Jordan, the Poet, now first printed from the autograph manuscripts preserved at Stratford-upon-Avon,* ed. J. O. Halliwell, Esq., 1864.
M–D	*The Correspondence of Edmond Malone, the Editor of Shakespeare, with the Rev. James Davenport, D.D., Vicar of Stratford-on-Avon,* 1864.
Ms. Malone	Malone manuscripts in the Bodleian Library, Oxford.
NLS	National Library of Scotland.
OFB	Osborn Files, Beinecke Rare Book and Manuscript Library, Yale University.
P–M Letters	*The Correspondence of Thomas Percy & Edmond*

	Malone, ed. Arthur Tillotson. Baton Rouge, Louisiana, 1944.
PP (1790)	*The Plays and Poems of William Shaksepare*, ed. Edmond Malone, 10 vols. in 11, 1790
PP (1821)	*The Plays and Poems of William Shakspeare*, eds. Edmond Malone and James Boswell Junior, 21 vols. 1821.
Prior	Sir James Prior, *Life of Edmond Malone*, 1860.
Reynolds, *Works*	Sir Joshua Reynolds, *Works* ... [*with*] *An Account of the Life and Writings of the author*, ed. Edmond Malone, 2 vols. 1797; 2nd edn., 3 vols. 1798.
Schoenbaum, *Shakespeare's Lives*	Samuel Schoenbaum, *Shakespeare's Lives*. Oxford, 1970; rev. edn. 1991.
Shakespeare Verbatim	Margreta de Grazia, *Shakespeare Verbatim: The Reproduction of Authenticity and the 1790 Apparatus*. Oxford, 1991.
Smith, *Eighteenth Century Essays on Shakespeare*	D. Nichol Smith, *Eighteenth Century Essays on Shakespeare*, 1963; first published in 1903.
Supplement	*A Supplement to the Edition of Shakespeare, Published in 1778 by Samuel Johnson and George Steevens*, ed. Edmond Malone, 2 vols. 1780.
Walpole Corr.	*The Yale Edition of Horace Walpole's Correspondence*, ed. W. S. Lewis, 48 vols. New Haven, 1937–85.

1

Irish beginnings

1

The Malone family name, Malone told his kinsman Charles O'Conor in December 1787, derived from some ancestor with a bald head: '*Moil* I know is bald, but I know not the Irish for head; and rather suspect that the gentleman's name was *Owen*, and that he was called ... *Moil Owen* which was afterwards easily corrupted into *Malone*.'[1] The extensive Malone lands in County Westmeath, many of which were still in the family in Malone's lifetime, had been won by the Kings of Conaught in their wars with the Kings of Meath towards the end of the eleventh century. From that time on, Malone stated in the *Irish Peerage* of 1789 for which he wrote the history of his family, 'the family have continued possessed of the lands, where they were originally settled, a period of more than six hundred years.'[2]

In his account of his family history, it was the oratorical brilliance of his relatives that appealed to him most. His grandfather, Richard Malone, whose father had established the principal family seat at Baronston in the late seventeenth century, was like most of the Malones a successful, even celebrated, lawyer.[3] His son, Anthony, the great family political success story, matched his father in fame as an orator but won even greater distinction as an Irish patriot in the British House of Commons. Lionel Cranfield Sackville, first Duke of Dorset, it was believed, had compared Anthony Malone favourably with two of the greatest speakers in the realm: 'the three ablest men I have ever heard were Mr Pitt [the Elder], Mr Murray [subsequently Lord Chief Justice], and Mr Malone; for a popular assembly I would choose Mr Pitt; for a Privy Council, Murray; for twelve wise men, Malone.'[4]

Malone's father, Edmond Senior, also chose the law. He was educated at

---

[1] Letter to Charles O'Conor, 12 December 1787, fols. 2–3, Huntington Library, STO 816.

[2] John Lodge's *Peerage of Ireland*, ed. M. Archdall, VII (1789), pp. 280–93. See J. K. Walton, 'Edmond Malone: An Irish Shakespeare Scholar', *Hermathena*, XCIX (1964), 5–26; and James Woods, *Annals of Westmeath* (Dublin, 1907), pp. 292–303.

[3] On Richard Malone's diplomatic and legal achievements, see W. J. A. Taylor, *History of Dublin University*, p. 394.

[4] Cited by W. E. H. Lecky, *The History of Ireland in the Eighteenth Century*, I (1896), p. 463, n. 1.

Oxford and the Inner Temple in London and called to the English Bar in 1730, but in 1740 his English practice failed and he was compelled to return to Ireland where, by contrast, he was distinctly successful and eventually entered politics. It was perhaps Malone's mother, though, who accounts most for his having turned his gaze, at an early age, toward a career in England. Formerly Catherine Collier, daughter of an Essex family, she was the niece of Robert Knight, whose wife was Henrietta Knight, Lady Luxborough, half-sister of Alexander Pope's close friend Henry St John, Viscount Bolingbroke, and the poet William Shenstone's correspondent and patroness.

Malone himself was born in Dublin on 4 October 1741,[5] a second son, the year after his parents had taken up residence at their country estate, Shinglas, in County Westmeath, a beautiful though modest Georgian house that still stands today in extensive rolling acreage. Virtually nothing is known of his childhood and adolescence except that in 1747 he was sent to Dr Ford's preparatory school in Molesworth Street, Dublin, where his brother Richard had already been enrolled for two years. In July 1757, not yet sixteen, Malone entered Trinity College, Dublin, where a year earlier his father had received an honorary LL D.[6] Again, his brother had preceded him by two years but would leave the next year to study at Christ Church, Oxford – a privilege that financial constraints brought on later by his mother's illness denied to Malone. He turned out to be an exemplary student, naturally diligent, consistently at the top of his class. In his very first examination at Christmas, the first of four in the academic year, he shared top honours with James Drought, subsequently Fellow and Professor of Divinity at the College, and John Kearney, later Fellow and Provost and lifelong friend. He also earned the first of several premiums: books stamped with the College Arms.[7] We know little more about his undergraduate career than that he wrote some poetry and, more noteworthy, some literary history, including a manuscript translation in prose of *Oedipus*, 'To which is prefixed an Essay on the Origin and Progress of Tragedy & on the Office & Advantages of the Antient Chorus.' The translation is accompanied by surprisingly erudite annotations and explanatory notes, while the essay (some twenty pages) includes both a brief comparison of Sophocles and Euripides and an enthusiastic argument in favour of the restoration of the Chorus in modern drama. 'The motive which induced the author to undertake this work', he writes in his preface, was his desire to explain the origins of tragedy to 'those persons who have not studied the Antient Poets.' After a few pages, he apologizes for not continuing with his comparison of the two tragedians and launches into an analysis of 'the

---

[5] Malone's birth is registered as 1 November 1741 in the Register of St Peter's Church, Dublin.
[6] See *Alumni Dubliniensis*, 1756.
[7] See Walton, 'Edmond Malone: An Irish Shakespeare Scholar', 7–9.

Antient Chorus', which he says 'has been entirely rejected by all the modern tragick writers', with the result that 'few but those who converse more with the dead than the living, have any ideas of its use & advantages.'[8] Though he never pursued his argument for choruses, these pieces are early signs that he already had a taste for conversing with the dead.

We also know from the letters of John Chetwood, his friend and classmate at Trinity, that as an undergraduate he was not a little romantically inclined. In the next few years the two young men would find themselves exchanging poems and confidences over their romances, real and imaginary. His teasing letters to Chetwood – now lost, we know of them only through Chetwood's replies – during the summer holidays, either in 1761 or 1762, were full of the latter's having fallen in love with a young 'Eliza' known to them both who they were convinced would soon prove fickle. In one of his replies, which alludes to Malone's prior statement that a mutual friend was about to steal Eliza from him, Chetwood hints that Malone too has been in love and apparently with someone who did not return it: 'How cou'd you be so cruel as to blast all my present bliss with such a prophetick, such a deathful Sound: ... In short, wou'd it not my Dear Ned (for you can inform me) deaden & damp my spirits, & convert my attention from present Enjoyment to the thoughts of future Misery?'[9] It is a pity we have only Chetwood's side of the correspondence at a time when Malone's thoughts of love were young and hopeful, not yet disillusioned. Chetwood's phrase, 'for you can inform me', seems to imply that Malone experienced some early disappointment, but his general good cheer during these last days at Trinity signals confidence. Four years later, that confidence would be shattered, and his thoughts about himself and his future would be correspondingly darkened.

2

The only shadow in Malone's otherwise bright and successful under-graduate career was his mother's health. It had been deteriorating for some time and she increasingly found it difficult to walk. Since a favoured eighteenth-century treatment for almost all forms of malaise was a change of air, it was decided a stint in England might be tonic, and so in the summer of 1759, midway through his Trinity days, Malone accompanied his mother and father to London.

His brother had been at Oxford for a year by then, but it was his own first visit to London and, notwithstanding the alarming reason for the trip, certain to be impressive. Here was the intellectual centre of Europe, and he was about to enter it. Unfortunately, no letters survive from that visit, nor

---

[8] Ms. Malone 40, fol. 92. See also James Prior, *The Life of Edmond Malone*, 1860, p. 6; and Ms. Malone 40, fols. 63–68, 90–109. Most of Malone's exercise books and juvenilia have been lost.

[9] BL Add. Ms. 147. Probable date for this letter is 1761.

did he and his father stay long once they had deposited his mother at Highgate, moving on soon to the Midlands where his father had business. We may infer there was time to visit the London bookshops, however, to pick up needed volumes difficult to come by in Dublin; time also, one may guess, for theatres and coffee-houses, where he and his father might catch sight of eminent theatrical, political, and literary figures. They left for home in October, too late for him to resume his studies in the winter term.

His mother soon removed from Highgate to Bath, from where on 15 November she wrote the first letter we have to Malone, her 'dear nedy':

I received a letter from you on sunday last which gave me great pleasure & for which I thank you [;] it gives me also great pleasure to hear you are safe in Dublin after so long a journey & so dangerous a voyage as the Irish one is at this time of year [.] I wish you had been more particular as to your sickness[,] company[,] & fears but that will serve for another letter.

Drinking the supposedly health-giving waters 'constantly', brought to her at her lodging because she 'almost allways [*sic*] got cold' at the Pump Room, does not appear to have done much good yet, but she assures him she will persevere. She has done a 'heroick action' by telling Richard at Oxford that he need not visit her until the entire family joins her for Christmas. Why did he not write about Harriet and Kitty, his sisters? 'I long to see you', she concludes, 'but what signifies wishing[?] It cannot be but the time will I hope come when we shall all meet & till then shall never injoy [*sic*] perfect hapiness ... '[10]

Alone in Ireland, father and son consoled themselves with each other's company at Shinglas until the new year, while Malone occupied himself with studies. In January, he was back at the University, a step which in deference to his dejected father he very nearly did not take. It was the right thing to do, however, as his father urges in a January letter 'from this lonely place', where he was doing a bit of farming and living in one room plus his bedroom and eating some simple mutton every day. 'I often wish for your company', he writes, 'but at the same time am glad that you made the choice you did, of sitting down to read for next examinations, as you will by that means soon recover the time lost by our English expedition last summer.' He assures his son that if it ever comes in his power to reward him for his academic diligence, he would show him 'all the affection and kindness the most deserving child can expect. But as human events are so precarious, there is no trusting to that chance. Continue, therefore, my dear child, the same course of industry you are in, in order to qualify you to get your own bread, and to make your own way in the world.' Since God had been pleased to endow him 'with a good understanding', he cannot fail.[11]

[10] Arthur O'Neill Collection. See also *Faulkner's Dublin Journal*, 28 August 1759.
[11] Prior, pp. 8–9.

It probably did not occur to either the son or his parents at this point that he might make his way in the world in any other profession than the law. The expenses at Bath left little money to spare, and the family legal practice presented the best route to a secure future.

During the spring, the news from Bath was worrying, although his mother's letter on 11 March brought some happy if temporary relief: 'I just begin to use my limbs with a can[e] after very near 3 months confinement', she writes; 'If I have many more such fits they will soon wear me out ... I shall not repine at a severe one provided I have you & *all* my children with me.'[12] One piece of news that eased the financial strain came on 2 June when, after a special examination, Malone won a scholarship at Trinity, becoming a Scholar of the House.[13]

3

Malone took his final examination at Trinity in Michaelmas term, 1761, and received his BA degree at the first Commencement after that on 23 February 1762.[14] He had finished, distinguishing himself as one of only three to earn the top mark, *valde bene*. He also knew where he was going next. He had long since decided to follow his uncle's, father's, and grandfather's footsteps to the Inner Temple in London to become an Irish barrister. The preceding year he had been given 'Admittance into the House' on payment of £3 6s 8d. By a coincidence which literary historians cannot fail to wonder at, the Inner Temple records show that he was admitted the same year as James Boswell.[15] Since he did not intend to begin his law studies until the following year, he decided to remain in Dublin and read – possibly law although probably also literature[16] – a useful thing to do at home as his father was away on the legal circuit for much of the time and he was in total command of his own time.

If Malone learned from his father's example and distaste, the prospect of becoming a barrister and travelling for long periods as a circuit judge through the countryside may have preoccupied him at this time. His father had always dreaded leaving family and home, enduring the vagaries of weather and transport together with fatiguing and often unpleasant legal business. It was the sort of duty from which he was often grateful to return undamaged: 'I got safe home, my Dear Ned, yesterday, after a long circuit, without any ill accident to myself, or to my chaise & horses ... '[17] But the

---

[12] Catherine Malone to Edmond Malone Senior, Arthur O'Neill Collection.
[13] This was announced in *Faulkner's Dublin Journal*, 3 June.
[14] He signed the Trinity College Registry of Degrees on that date.
[15] Inner Temple Records, 14–20 November 1761, pp. 88, 133.
[16] He quickly applied to become a Reader of the Trinity Library, a privilege not normally accorded to undergraduates. See J. K. Walton, 'Edmond Malone: An Irish Shakespeare Scholar', 8.   [17] 11 April, Add. 9.

family finances were still tight and a barrister could earn a respectable income; moreover, the opportunities for political activity were always available. It was best to proceed along that course.

He entered the Inner Temple probably in the new year, 1763. Little survives for the years in London that followed. Except for his father, his family apparently saw little reason to keep his letters, though surely one of them must have recorded the events of that exceptional day (10 May 1763) when he was 'invited to come to the bench table' in Commons.[18] To become a 'Bencher' was comparable to becoming a Warden in a Guild – within the student body it was a governing elite who were awarded the right to nominate their successors. From that day until the autumn of 1766 he remained in London except for brief visits to Bath to see his ailing mother.[19] In order to be called to the Bar, a law student had to 'keep' (or attend) twelve terms. There were only four terms per year, each three weeks long, so that a barrister's curriculum extended over three years.[20] That left plenty of time for other things, but what they were in Malone's case we can only guess except for several fugitive satirical articles that he published on Irish politics and the abuse of the English language, and his corrections of a new edition of Swift's correspondence.[21] It stretches the imagination that even the young Malone would while away the hours correcting the text of Swift's correspondence for his own amusement. Someone must have asked him to do it, but who or why is unknown.

He had rooms in the Inner Temple and doubtless took most of his meals in the Commons as they were both excellent and cheap. Though he failed to meet his fellow matriculant Boswell who was soon off to study law in Utrecht, his rooms were only a stone's throw from Samuel Johnson's lodgings on Inner Temple Lane, and on an unspecified day in 1764, when he was twenty-two, the old moralist and the young Templar met. As Malone later wrote in his copy of Johnson's *Prayers and Meditations*,[22] Edmund Southwell, the father of his good friend Thomas, took Malone along to Inner Temple Lane and introduced him. The Southwells were a prominent Anglo-Irish family well known to the Malones. This was probably the most important meeting of Malone's life. For the rest of his days he became an ardent follower of Johnson's and, Boswell excepted, the most enthusiastic defender and celebrator of Johnson's writings and life.

[18] Inner Temple Records, p. 155.
[19] See his mother's letter to his father on 11 December 1764 about her deteriorating health (Add. 11).
[20] Robert J. Blaekham, *Wig and Gown: the Story of the Temple, Gray's, and Lincoln's Inn* (1932), pp. 163–64.
[21] See Prior, pp. 470–71; Ms. Malone 41, f. 70; *St. James's Chronicle*, 883 (28–30 October 1766), 2.
[22] 'This Edmund Southwell first introduced me to Dr. Johnson in 1764, when he had chambers in the Middle Temple Lane', Malone wrote in his copy of *Prayers and Meditations* (cited courtesy of Mr W. R. Batty).

As in Boswell's case, Malone's first meeting with Johnson led to others. We can only speculate about what they discussed. Literature, almost certainly, and more than likely, Shakespeare, came into play for Johnson was just then finishing the great edition which he had begun in 1756. What is regrettable is that Malone, though he wrote of his meetings with Johnson in letters to John Chetwood and perhaps to others – none of which have been found – failed to keep a record of their conversations. It is perplexing as well as regrettable that even in later years he never wrote down his recollections of these early encounters with the greatest author of the age – although he did make notes about his meetings with Johnson in the late 1770s and early 1780s.[23]

He was, nevertheless, in his own way, already becoming one of Johnson's intimates. Returning to Ireland from a visit with Malone in 1765, Chetwood envied his friend's 'Intimacy with the Editor of Shakespeare, & the opportunities you have by your Situation in London of collecting books. I wish you have sufficient influence over Mr Johnson to urge him to continue his writings.' Chetwood had trouble crediting Malone's discovery that indolence was one of Johnson's personal devils: 'You amaze me by accusing him of Indolence; I imagin'd from the perusal of his Dictionary, that his Application was at least equal to his Abilities.'[24] At about this time, in the autumn of 1765, his Shakespeare edition complete, Johnson resolved to study law with a view to rousing himself to a new sense of purpose.[25] To this end, he was about to start work as private secretary to William Gerard Hamilton, whose writings, together with unpublished notes on the Corn Laws that Johnson compiled for Hamilton at about this time, Malone would publish in 1809 under the title, *Parliamentary Logick*. For years Hamilton had employed Burke as his private secretary, but Burke had resigned and Hamilton again needed someone who, as Malone was later to write, would 'furnish him with sentiments on the great political topicks that should be considered in Parliament.' Johnson's project to study law can only have made Malone additionally interesting to him both because of Malone's legal training and because of his Irish connections. For years Hamilton had been an eminent Irish politician and still was Chancellor of the Exchequer for Ireland. Malone was thus well placed to give Johnson information. Given the brief experience Malone had already had in politics and his lifelong interest in the subject, he would also have been impressed with the idealism shown by a major literary figure who wished to have a positive influence on political thinking in his time. Johnson's example stayed with him for the rest of his life.

He was also well placed to pass on to Trinity College information about

---

[23] See Malone's note about Johnson's household in this early stage of their friendship, Everyman edition, I, p. 260 n.2.   [24] Ms. Malone 38, fols. 180, d-e.

[25] Bate, *Samuel Johnson* (1977), p. 408.

Johnson, though it is not known whether he had anything to do with Trinity's awarding Johnson an honorary Doctor of Laws in July of 1765. Boswell in his *Life of Johnson* sees this surprising and 'unsolicited mark of distinction' as joining well with what he calls Johnson's 'temporary fit of ambition, for he had thoughts of both studying law and of engaging in politicks.'[26] But Malone knew better. 'Mr. Boswell was certainly mistaken in this respect', he wrote about thirty-five years later in his edition of the *Life of Johnson*.[27] From first-hand experience, he knew that Johnson was not studying to go into politics and that the honorary degree was a totally unrelated expression of Trinity College's esteem. Whether the award was a surprise to him as it was to Johnson Malone failed to say.[28]

4

Two events occurred early in 1765 that shattered the Malone family. The first was that Catherine Malone died in January. Owing to her continued invalidism in Bath, it is unlikely that members of the family had held out much hope; nonetheless, her death deeply demoralized them. The other shock was that an expected legacy from a relative named Mrs Weaver did not materialize; she had died in March without leaving them a penny. 'We may bid adieu to the prospect of any share of her personal fortune', Malone informed his father on 26 March.[29] The father was equal to the disappointment: 'By not suffering the events of life to affect us', he told his son, 'we shall by degrees become superior to all calamities. I well know that one thousand pounds a-piece to my children would have been a great benefit; but after all, their happiness depends more on the wisdom and virtue of their own minds than on that or any other sum. So let us, my dear child, think no more of it.'[30]

5

Always interested in politics, English as well as Irish, Malone throughout his life took pleasure in reporting the most recent political events in London to his father and friends. Like most young men with political and literary interests who were new to the city, he quickly made a habit of spending hours at a coffee-house where he could make the acquaintance of 'the town'. It was indispensable that a young man be aware of the latest political, stage, literary, and social gossip. Malone picked up much of what he needed to know at his favourite coffee-house, The Grecian in Devereux Court, whence in April 1766 he regaled his father with news of Pitt's

---

[26] *Boswell's Life of Johnson, LL. D., together with Boswell's Journal of a Tour to the Hebrides*, eds. George Birbeck Hill, rev. and enl. by L. F. Powell, I, p. 489.   [27] Ibid., p. 520.
[28] One of the signatories of the honorary LL D. was Michael Kearney, a lifelong friend.
[29] Adam Collection, University of Rochester, J. R. 2.228.   [30] Prior, p. 12.

misfortunes with the gout, adding perhaps boastfully: 'I am at present writing in a coffee-house, in the midst of so much noise and bustle – the celebrated anti-Sejanus (Mr. Scott) on one side and Mr. [Charles] Macklin [the actor] on the other – that I can't add anything more at present.'[31] He was also now scribbling verses and composing essays. More than anything else about Malone in these early years, Chetwood admired his 'poetic' fire. On 26 November 1765, he referred feelingly to the rival demands of law and literature between which he supposed, probably on good evidence, Malone was torn. A 'Man of imagination, possess'd with a Passion for the Nine', he told him, 'shou'd never be licentious in the indulgence of either if he means to be deeply learn'd in the Intricacies of Law. Such is the severe tax upon you, & the Ingenious of your Profession.'[32]

In a letter just ten days earlier, Chetwood also alluded to several of Malone's poems. He wishes he could see him, if for no other reason than 'to examine the recesses of your escritoire.' 'That warm brain of yours', he added, 'can never find enjoyment in inaction. The forms of beauty, either moral or personal, solicit it too strongly to suffer it to be at rest.' There is little in the legal world, as Chetwood prophetically saw it, to content a mind like his: 'No law jargon, no collection of statutes, not all the Pandects in the world, can ever avail to extinguish the passion for the muse when she has taken legal possession.' If Malone insisted on suppressing his poetic compositions, then 'Shakespeare's curse attend you.'[33] Shakespeare's curse aside, perhaps wisely Malone suppressed all his poetry.

In the summer of 1765, staying in the English countryside near Chester, Chetwood tried to pry Malone away from the city, where he felt he was becoming too sedentary. 'The Situation of this place', he wrote on 30 July, 'wou'd inspire you with that exalted Enthusiasm, that a fine rural scene so naturally suggests. But You have been so long an Englishman, that the hanging Grove, the opening Lawn, the winding River, the distant Sea, are Objects that perhaps from their frequency have lost their force upon you.'[34] Perhaps, perhaps not, but clearly the city had cast a spell on Malone and he was reluctant to leave it. Chetwood even wrongly suspected that a new love affair was detaining his friend: 'some happy fair one, possess'd of all the Beauties, Accomplishments ... enslav'd my friend's Affections'. He knew Malone's soul was 'as impregnated with fire as the Flint, & that both when struck are equally prone to produce flame', but he misjudged him this time.[35]

[31] Prior, p. 23.   [32] Ms. Malone 38, fol. 180.
[33] 15 November 1765, Osborn Files, Beinecke Rare Book and Manuscript Library, Yale University.   [34] Ms. Malone 38, fols. 180b-c.   [35] 13 August, OFB.

6

We have it from Chetwood that Malone had neglected his correspondence in the first half of 1766. His father thought so, too. With his mother now dead for more than a year, his father ached to see and hear from his sons: 'I can't express to you, My Dear Ned', he wrote in June, 'the uneasiness I am under at not hearing from you or Dick for so long a time; you are both now the principal objects of my affection & attention...' Malone was completing his studies at the Inner Temple and his father had to know his plans for the summer as well as when Dick was returning from his own excursion to France. Something also was in the wind regarding an improvement of the family's fortunes. A meeting between Malone Senior and Lord Worthington would soon decide whether the former would receive a judgeship. 'I can with great truth say', he added, 'my children are more essentially interested in the event, than I am myself; for I want very little for myself; my great anxiety is, for the present easy support of my children.'[36] Perhaps with the new confidence that sprang from the likelihood that his father would be appointed Judge of the Court of Irish Common Pleas, Malone found himself quickly winding up his affairs in London during the summer and preparing for an entirely new experience: an autumn sojourn in the south of France with his close friend Southwell and Southwell's father Edmund, who had introduced him to Dr Johnson.

They travelled first to Paris and then continued on to Avignon, arriving in early November.[37] After one month in Avignon, which he disliked – 'old, straggling, ugly' – Malone with a heavy heart heard from his father that the prospects for the judgeship were dimming. His bitterness was tempered by philosophy: 'It shall be a lesson to me, never to believe in any great man's word, unless coupled with performance, & to aspire by every truest means at the greatest blessing of life, independence.' 'I mean to go next week', he added, 'for a few days to Marseilles, with a gentleman of this town, who has offered me a place in his chaise.'[38] At last, towards the end of the month, he received the happy news in Marseilles, that his father had in fact succeeded to the bench.

While he was in France, Malone began to have second thoughts about a legal career. His correspondence with his father hints at some emerging tension between them over the matter. Finished at the Inner Temple, he still needed further study for the Irish Bar. Could he muster the enthusiasm for that, especially since at the end of it, and very soon, lay the dismal prospect of leaving London? In a letter describing Marseilles, he tried to

[36] Add. 13–14.
[37] Malone took with him a set of instructions in French telling what should be done in case of a fever. They have survived in Malone's handwriting, Ms. Malone 39, fol. 378.
[38] Bodleian, Ms. 31753, d.3, fol. 2.

reassure his father as well as himself: 'Though I did not carry any of my law-books with me, yet I can't say I was wholly idle at Marseilles.' He had drawn up a codicil to Lady Macclesfield's will, who had just arrived in Marseilles. That was useful to be able to report.[39] Then after returning to London in February, without the Southwells, he announced his fresh determination to proceed with law: 'I am very glad I happened to find chambers [at the] Temple, as I find you wish I shd be in town. It is my firm resolution to apply as closely as possible till I go to Ireland, to the study of law, & the practice of the Court of Chancery:... I hope soon to make up the time I have lost.'[40] The die, then, was cast. A few more months remained to him in London; then it would be farewell to the great literary world of Johnson, coffee-houses, theatre, newspapers, and politics.

7

Back in Ireland, Malone was called to the Irish Bar in late 1767.[41] Such evidence as there is suggests that the next two or three years were less than happy partly because he missed London, partly because he fell in love with Susanna Spencer, an enigmatic figure about whose background nothing is known. With her he seems to have experienced such an intense few months in early 1769 that when the relationship crumbled for reasons now unclear he suffered what we might call today a nervous collapse: he lost the will to read, to join in family activities, to practise law.

The cause of this mysterious disappointment may have been family disapproval, but we know so little about the woman in question that it is difficult to guess what could have been objected to. Just possibly status. Status, at any rate, was on Malone's mind when he wrote on 14 April, possibly to Southwell. Referring to a girl known to them both, who had been forced to marry a wealthy man against her wishes, he denounced the injustice of it and describes his own recipe for conjugal bliss: 'From the Person, parts & address of the young Lord, I thought the poor Girl payd dear enough for his Estate & title ... I hope no child of mine will ever stoop to be exalted on such terms; domestic enjoyment in comfort & mediocrity has a thousand superior charms.'[42] Either in reply to this or another letter, Southwell wrote in May from Avignon: 'I have turned and re-turned all the words and expressions of your letter, in order to get some insight into the cause of your distress, but am still as much in the dark as ever ... Would to God I were near you! Perhaps I might comfort you, or give some counsel, or hit upon some expedient to extricate you from this distress.' Nonetheless,

---

[39] 28 January 1767, Prior, pp. 27–28.   [40] 18 April 1767, Ms. Malone 26, fols. 138–39.
[41] See the list of attorneys in *Wilson's Dublin Directory* (1792).
[42] This letter, now lost, was sold by Sotheby's, 1 May 1917 (see *American Book Prices* for that period). Cited from a transcript in the OFB.

he could guess the problem was 'something of a love affair which you have not been able to bring about … I hope there is no disagreement with your father'[43] – possibly a shrewd guess.

Malone could not get over his unhappiness. Retreating for the better part of the summer to Spa with his brother did little good. His sisters, who had been away at school for years but now were living with their father at Shinglas, also joined in the effort to cheer him. Henrietta ('Hattie') pleaded with him in August to recover his spirits for his friends' benefit as well as his own: 'I own it is a very hard task, but the greater the difficulty, the more merit you will have in conquering it.' She recommended the 'dissipation' of recreation, entertainment, and a diverting social life on the grounds that although in his present frame of mind it could not bring any real 'amusement', it is 'the best remedy against low spirits.'[44] His younger and favourite sister, Catherine ('Kitty'), also wrote in September to the same end. None of this was to any avail. When a few months later his boyhood friend William Jephson, who was staying with the Malones, wrote to him, the tone of the entreaties had become impatient, even irritable: 'We talk of you like true lovers; begin generally by abusing, and assuredly end by praising you. Why will you not enjoy the affection that is lavished upon you, and manfully slight that which you cannot obtain or ought to scorn?' Could he not take heart from the love his family lavished on him and recover his old self? 'And such sisters, my dearest Ned! But I have done with this. I never throw away the hope of seeing you one day or other think and act like yourself.'[45]

His dejection lingered on for at least another two years. Finally, arrangements had to be made to see Susanna Spencer out of the country – to America, to which Chetwood, discreetly not mentioning her name, alluded in September, 1771: 'I cannot … resist my inclination to entreat that you will give me the solid satisfaction of informing me of the departure of ____ to America as soon as you know it. I never wish that person to be in the same quarter of the globe with you; for as long as that is the case, I see plainly that you are not master of one atom of resolution.'[46] As it turned out, she did not leave. So instead, perhaps on the suggestion of his exasperated father, who if he could not understand his son's attraction to this woman, certainly could understand London's, Malone took his leave of the Munster legal circuit, which he had been on since 1769, and sometime after March 1772 travelled to London, where he remained an indeterminate time. We know nothing of his doings there.

---

[43] Prior, p. 34.   [44] Prior, p. 34.   [45] Prior, p. 35.   [46] Prior, p. 35.

8

Once back in Ireland he persevered with the Munster Circuit, though he took no pleasure in it; nor was he attracting the legal briefs which register success in that field.[47] He acknowledged his boredom on the circuit to Chetwood, who was quick again to deplore the 'soporific influences of law' and sound the clarion of the Muses.[48]

But Malone was not deaf to the Muses. On 27 September 1774, partly to honour the memory of Goldsmith who had died the previous April, he fell in with a production of *She Stoops to Conquer* at Knoctopher, the country seat of Sir Hercules Langrishe, a member of the Irish House of Commons who also wrote on behalf of Irish rights. It was a memorable social occasion with Irish political overtones, for two of the other players that evening were Henry Flood and Henry Grattan, both politically active Irish patriots. Malone played two parts and wrote an excessively long epilogue of eighty-two lines, with several allusions that suggest his literary tastes.[49] The poem is a pastiche of ready-to-wear eighteenth-century phrases and heroic couplets more workmanlike than might have been expected. It celebrates Shakespeare, touches on Irish politics in deference to the actors Flood and Grattan who have paused 'to moralize in Shakespeare's school', and concludes with a panegyric on the stage urging this small company of friends to continue to tread Shakespearean ground:

> Long may you play these polish'd pastimes o'er,
> And cull the choicest flowers of ancient lore!
> Mix grave and gay – the pathos and the jest –
> The tragic robing, and the motley vest!
> Solicit comedy with playful leer
> To blunt the dagger and to break the spear;
> Now with Jack Falstaff frame the merry lie,
> And with illustrious Brutus learn to die;
> Now stride in transport o'er a tyrant's tomb;
> Now melt in softness at the maiden's bloom;
> With blushing Pistol sometimes strut and swagger
> Now clutch the airy vision of a dagger.

In these urgings, he probably reflects the ambivalence of his own impulses, torn as he was between his love of literature, the stage, and scholarship, and the obligations of his profession and his responsibilities as an educated Irishman to the welfare of his country.

Studies in the history of poetry also took his mind off the law and lifted his spirits. One of his more exhilarating moments this same year was a

---

[47] On Malone's early scholarship with Irish statutes, see Prior, p. 38.
[48] Prior, p. 38 (no date).   [49] Ms. Malone 41, fols. 66–67.

literary discovery of some significance. On a visit to Dr Thomas Wilson, Senior Fellow of Trinity College, he had the curiosity (and presumably the permission) to look through several filing drawers, finding in one of them several of Pope's papers which Henry St John, Viscount Bolingbroke, as the poet's literary executor, had taken up as 'sweepings' from the poet's study after his death. One of the papers was a working manuscript in Pope's hand of his unfinished poem, 'One Thousand Seven Hundred and Forty', until then unknown. Malone carefully transcribed the manuscript, following closely all Pope's 'interlineations, corrections, alterations' and producing 'a *facsimile* in every respect except the handwriting which I have not attempted to imitate.'[50] But he failed to publish his find. As the manuscript has disappeared, the less reliable version we now have of the poem we owe to another source.

Apart from literature, Irish politics started to absorb more of his time. He began to write for the newspapers, and eventually this led to his being nominated to the Irish Parliament as a member for the University of Dublin. Among the political publications to which he may have contributed in 1772 was a volume titled, *Baratariana*, written largely by Sir Hercules Langrishe and augmented with 'Letters', mostly by Flood and Grattan, attacking the government in the style of Junius, the pseudonymous Whiggish author of a series of political attacks that appeared in the *Public Advertiser* from 1769 to 1772. One or more of these 'Letters' may have been by Malone. According to Prior, several of his (now missing) letters refer to articles, 'paper squibs and crackers' written against the government. One in particular was a weakly ironic piece in which he lamented the Irish consumption of millions of eggs every year when a little restraint could yield more substantial food in the form of chickens.[51]

Another of his anti-government forays was an article he wrote with William Jephson, published in 1775 in the *Freeman's Journal*, predicting that Flood's strategic joining with the government that year as Vice-Treasurer, in order to push for the independence of the Irish Parliament from within the government, would fail and that he would return to his proper opposition 'home'. When Flood did just that in 1782, Malone reminded Lord Charlemont that he had predicted it seven years earlier. He also resolved 'to arrange all the curious matter that he [Flood] has collected on that subject' – the independence of the Irish Parliament – and publish it: 'After his three hours speech ten years ago, upon it, I endeavoured when I went home to put as much of it upon paper as I could recollect, and I still have the copy by me…'[52] Nothing came of the idea.

[50] On Malone's discovery of the poem, see Prior, 'Maloniana', pp. 364–65. See also, *Twickenham Edition of the Poems of Alexander Pope*, gen. ed. John Butt, IV (1939), pp. 330–31.
[51] On *Baratariana*, see Lecky, *History of Ireland in the Eighteenth Century*, I, chap. III, p. 105.
[52] *Reports of the Historical Manuscript Commission*, XIII, 10, p. 394.

9

On 22 March 1774, Malone's father died suddenly, leaving him, his brother, and his two sisters with modest incomes and the modest independence that came with them. They had spent little time with their father since their mother died in 1765, but they had always been, and would still remain, devoted to each other, writing frequently about family news and taking an active interest in each other's lives as fully as the distance between them allowed. Not much was changed for the girls; still unmarried, they remained at Shinglas while Richard divided his time between his legal practice and the management of the estate.

But for Malone life changed dramatically. With his increased independence from the drudgery of a barrister's life, and the increased confidence that went with it, he promptly proposed himself that summer to the electors of the University as their parliamentary candidate in their constituency. The notion got about, however, that as the nephew of Anthony Malone, who like Flood had accepted government office years earlier and eventually been turned out, he would be an inappropriate representative of a university firmly opposed to the autocratic Irish policies of Townshend's corrupt government.

Malone confronted this charge in a speech to Trinity's electors in the autumn of 1774, dismissing the idea of his being the wrong man for the job as petty 'electioneering artifice' and praising his uncle as a man of principle instead of mere party. The speech anticipates the moral indignation and flair for invective that would surface frequently in years to come when he attacked his literary adversaries. Whatever the faults of his uncle, he declared, he acted on principle, for 'no man perhaps ever supported the administration so disinterestedly, or got so few favours from Government either for himself or his connexions.' With some stridency, he then rounded defiantly on the self-seekers who opposed reform for fear of losing their places at the public trough:

the seat of a lord-lieutenant of the kingdom is besieged by men ... who, in addition to great present emolument, grasp at future and numerous reversions; who, not content with the highest offices in their own line, invade the offices of other men, thrust themselves into every department, civil, military, and ecclesiastical, and into stations for which the whole tenor of their lives and studies has rendered them wholly unqualified; who accumulate place upon place, and sinecure upon sinecure; who are so eager to obtain the wages of the day before the day is well passed over their heads, that they have emphatically and not improperly been styled ready-money voters ... [53]

On the strength of such sentiments, Malone won the nomination, but he did not keep it for long. A few days before the election was held in May

[53] This speech has survived only in Prior's *Life*, 'Maloniana', pp. 467–69.

1776, his uncle Anthony died, leaving to Malone's brother Richard his entire estate at Baronston and to Malone himself a comfortable annual income of about one thousand pounds, comparable roughly to thirty thousand pounds today. In that speech to the University electors, he had made much of the small independence which his father's legacy had afforded him. He was no man's slave, he announced, 'for a few months ago I obtained, at too high a price indeed, an honourable independence; nor shall any motive upon earth induce me to forfeit that independence.' Now he had at his disposal a much greater sum for the rest of his life. He was free to do what he had wanted to do ever since his student days in London. He gave up the nomination and without too much reflection decided to turn his back on the law as a profession. Instead, he would pursue a life of scholarship and become a man of letters. The road at last was clear.

10

His uncle's legacy immediately freed him to contribute to an edition of Oliver Goldsmith's works, a project he had had in mind ever since a couple of years earlier a group of publishers decided to bring out a new edition. Malone had known Goldsmith, who died in April 1774, either in Dublin or more probably (perhaps through Johnson) in London in the 1760s. Goldsmith had attended Trinity with Burke before Malone's time there. To contribute to an edition would be an act of both friendship and patriotism. With this objective, he took ship for London sometime soon after May 1776. It was his first visit there in almost eight years.

There was another reason, too, for going to England. Susanna Spencer had somehow managed to get there. Time had neither healed his emotional wounds nor killed his affection for her and, in spite of all advice from friends and family, he sought her out in London. The letter he wrote to her has disappeared, but her reply survives:

Why need you Edmond put so ill natured a construction on my silence as to tell me it proceeds from contempt. I have never felt any such sentiment in my heart. I always have had the most sincere and heartfelt friendship for you. You at least that have been made acquainted with every throb of that heart know that I have twice almost sacrificed my life to try if it were possible to make your happiness & [you] shou'd not accuse me so unjustly[.]

The impediment to their relationship, we may infer, continued to be their class differences. Had she not tried everything to 'remove impossibilities'? All has been to 'little purpose'. The only reason she had not written was that he had resolved to forget her, and 'Providence ought to restrain me from undoing in a moment what you had been doing to accomplish a thing so much to be wished for your Peace and tranquillity.' Her own comfort was now unimportant, although he should know that 'there is no person more wretched' than herself. Knowing his emotional state, she concludes, 'You'll scarce be able to read this, and its [*sic*] with the greatest difficulty I write it. I wish you happy, be assured, and if I cou'd make you so wou'd gladly do it.'[54]

This letter threw him into emotional disarray all over again, but at least he was in London once more and there were many other things to think about. There were books to buy, old friends to meet, plays to see, and research to do. If his plans for a literary career were to be launched by work on Goldsmith, this was the time and place to talk to people who knew him, find issues of the periodicals to which he contributed, and round up fugitive pieces. Still, we know nothing of the six months or so he spent in London. After he returned to Ireland in February 1777, suffering from his first attack of rheumatism, his anxieties about Susanna were renewed by another letter. She knows he is ill and is alarmed at his remedies: 'Surely its [*sic*] a Cruel way to Cure you to have you Plunged in Cold water this weather.' As for herself, the bitter weather is agony – her 'Pot freezes by the fireside ... I have never been well Since you left England, one Cold upon another, but my Situation was so Wretched I kept myself up as long as I cou'd[.] I at last was obliged to be Carryed up to my bed ... ' The most worrying part of her letter is her account of her deep depression: 'I cannot get up my Spirits at all. I have Such violent fits of Crying Seise [*sic*] me that it almost overpowers me.'[55] Her financial problems remained severe, though he was already helping her with a regular allowance. What must have distressed him most was that from so far away he could do little else to relieve her.

11

Malone must have put at least some of his time in London to good use because in the spring, 1777, shortly after his return to Ireland, *Poems and Plays by Oliver Goldsmith* was published in Dublin,[56] with his eight-page memoir of Goldsmith and his notes to the poems and plays. Based on Glover's 'Authentic Anecdotes' (1774),[57] supplemented by first-hand information he had obtained from Dr Wilson at Trinity and other sources[58], Malone's method in the memoir combines the ethical and anecdotal, the same strategy that Boswell would bring to high art in his *Life of Johnson*. Anecdotes enable him to sketch the nuances of Goldsmith's personality. Well-chosen scenes and incidents, quoted conversation, glimpses of Goldsmith's personal manner, and several undisputed facts give the work

[54] Ms. Malone 39, fol. 376.   [55] 27 January 1777. Ms. Malone 39, fols. 372–73.

[56] *Poems and Plays by Dr. Oliver Goldsmith, to which are prefixed, Memoirs of the Life and Writings of the Author* (1777); London edition, 1780, with Malone's memoir slightly altered.

[57] Glover's anecdotes were published in *The Universal Magazine* in May 1774, and reprinted in the *Annual Register* the same year.

[58] See Wilson to Malone, 24 February, Ms. Malone 42516, fol. 90.

its sympathetic and sensitive character. He does not ignore Goldsmith's personal weaknesses, but neither does he dwell on them, as he felt too many contemporary critics tended to. He does not attempt literary criticism, although almost nobody except Johnson and one or two others in Goldsmith's time had said anything significant about his writing. All he offers regarding the quality of Goldsmith's poetry, for example, is the lame observation that he was 'happy in the selection of his images, in the choice of his subjects, and in the harmony of his versification.' Instead, he sees the value of what he is writing mainly in its accuracy and authenticity. This, not literary analysis, was to be the hallmark of his scholarship for the rest of his life. While there had been no scarcity of biographical accounts of Goldsmith during the preceding two years, he writes, his anecdotes are 'all founded upon facts' because they were collected by Glover, 'who lived with him upon the most friendly footing for a great number of years, and who never felt any sorrow more sensibly than that which was occasioned by his death.'[59] The biographer's job is to discover and record what he decides has the highest claim to truth while it is still deliverable. There lay the originality of his contribution to Goldsmith studies. In later years, as the greatest scholar of his day, he would have returned to Goldsmith to do an edition and complete Life had not Bishop Thomas Percy staked out the territory beforehand.

12

The Goldsmith edition evidently whetted Malone's appetite for literary history. That he now knew which way his life was turning may be surmised from his seeking out George Steevens, then the greatest Shakespearean commentator of the age, on a brief visit to London in the late summer or early autumn of 1776. Steevens had made his reputation in 1773 with his triumphant ten-volume edition of Shakespeare, the first of the great scholarly variorum editions that have influenced the course of Shakespeare textual history to the present day. Johnson, who published his own edition in 1765, had called on Steevens to produce the 1773 edition as a follow-up to his edition, recognizing the need for a more scholarly treatment of Shakespeare's text and realizing he did not have the energy, eyesight, or inclination to do the research himself. It was Steevens' road to fame.

When Steevens met Malone, he apparently read his promise as a scholar quickly and he made two decisions that proved immediately helpful to Malone and launched his career in Shakespeare studies. The first was to lend Malone his precious, annotated copy of Gerard Langbaine's comprehensive catalogue, *An Account of the English Dramatic Poets* (1691), to take back with him to Ireland. Langbaine's *Account* was an indispensable reference at the time for anyone working with Shakespearean texts,

[59] Goldsmith, *Poems and Plays*, (1777), p. viii.

especially useful for anyone interested in the sources of the plays. Steevens' copy was especially valuable because he had copied into it a wealth of useful annotations that William Oldys, biographer and antiquarian, had inserted in his own copy in the first half of the century. To these Steevens had added his own annotations, making it a gold mine of dramatic history. It is a measure of Malone's scholarly seriousness that he sat down and transcribed the entire volume. He kept the transcription for the rest of his life, adding others' notes to it in addition to many of his own. At the end of the fourth volume of his interleaved and bulging copy, he wrote: '30 March 1777. I finished this transcript of Steevens & Oldys notes to Langbaine.'[60]

Steevens' other, more astonishing, decision was to invite Malone to help him complete his second edition of the 1773 *Johnson–Steevens Shakespeare*. An honour, indeed, even though Steevens did not have in mind anything like the prestigious co-editorship that Johnson had bestowed on him. Malone accepted. It was an arrangement that galvanized his decision to give up law for literature and embrace London as his permanent home. He returned home, glowing with pride, to settle his affairs, but he did not dally there. One can imagine with what exhilaration he wrote the following modest sentence at the end of his transcriptions of the Steevens and Oldys notes to Langbaine, 'I left Ireland, May 1st, 1777.'[61] He may not have been surprised, though he certainly was disappointed, to find while he was home that his family and friends did not welcome the news. Even after he had returned to London, they tried to persuade him to reconsider. When his university friend Denis Daly heard that he was feeling remorse again over Susanna Spencer's plight, he wrote to him from Ireland, 'For God sake, if you dont like your situation where you are, Come hither, where tho' you should not be quite happy yourself you will be sure to make your friends so.'[62] Not a very convincing argument, Malone must have thought. It was his brother Richard who put the case against his new life most forcefully. Their mutual friends regretted his having 'quitted the kingdom' at a time when the opportunities at the Irish Bar were never better. Even a seat in Parliament 'might easily be obtained', to which end he is even ready to pay the election expenses. If Malone is concerned about the embarrassment of returning home with his tail between his legs, Parliament would provide the perfect explanation for their friends. Why not come home and think of London as a place 'ultimately to retire to' should 'a homecoming to Ireland prove disastrous'?[63]

Richard Malone completely misjudged his brother. There was no turning back from his new life and what his closest of friends, James Caulfield, first Earl of Charlemont, in his first known letter to Malone, called Shakespeare 'lucubrations'. Charlemont's friendship was a godsend

---

[60] Ibid., p. viii.   [61] Malone's annotated copy of Langbaine is now in Ms. Malone 129.
[62] Ms. Malone 129.   [63] September 1777, Add. 20.

to Malone from the start. A prominent cultural and political figure in both Dublin and London, Charlemont was, among other things, an ardent collector of books, for which obsession Malone became a blessing to him. He resided in London between 1764 and 1773, where he cultivated a wide circle of literary friendships, so that he was able to give Malone much valued introductions to the literary and artistic world of the city. This first letter of his to Malone, both affectionate and encouraging, characterizes their relationship over the next twenty years. 'That some wise ones may smile at your lucubrations, I doubt not', he reassures him. 'But let them smile, there is nothing more despicable than their censure. For surely that wisdom may be accounted folly which would cut off one principal source of amusement from a state which seems to stand in need of every such assistance to render it tolerable.' His scholarly undertaking needed no apology, for the 'history of man' is 'the most important study of the human mind.'[64]

[64] See Charlemont to Malone, August 1777, *HMC*, XII, 10, pp. 338–39.

2

'Shakspearomania'

1

When Malone said goodbye to his surprised and mildly disapproving family in May 1777, he was in the enviable position of not having to work for his living. In the ranks of Shakespeare commentators, editors, and literary historians, this independence gave him a distinct advantage since most other men of letters held salaried positions that consumed much energy and time. Indeed, this partly explains his rapid rise to fame over the next three to four years. It also helped that he brought with him both the enthusiasm of a newcomer and the confidence one normally associates with a seasoned scholar.

One thousand pounds per year endowed Malone with the freedom to immerse himself completely in English literary history and meant also that he could freely purchase books and build a useful library. Good public research libraries were improving when he arrived in London, but they were still scarce. London was certainly better than Dublin, but the British Museum, founded in 1753, had only recently become the haunt of scholars. Although Malone made it his second home, he found either he had to rely on contacts at the Bodleian and Cambridge to transcribe what he needed or he had to travel there when he could for a few days' visit. Any scholar, if he had the means, had to build his own private library as a basic resource. Malone did not do this by half-measures. Once his annual income began, he started to spend huge portions of it on books, causing himself financial embarrassment in later years. After almost a quarter of a century of buying books in London, in August 1800, he scribbled a note to himself about his library: 'I had, when I came to London in 1777 between three and four hundred pounds [*sic*] worth of books: and many of the books which I have purchased [especially] within these fifteen years, are become much more valuable than they were when I bought them: so that my Library, I imagine, is now worth two thousand Pounds.'[1] The value today of that sum is about sixty thousand pounds, but even the value of what he brought with

---

[1] Ms. Malone 34, fol. 178.

him in 1777 is close to twelve thousand pounds – no small achievement for a young man of thirty-five.

2

He found a house for himself and his books right away, but not in London. Perhaps Steevens, who himself lived away from the city centre in Hampstead, persuaded him, although his choice of 'Sunning Hill' (now Sunninghill) in Staines was much further than Hampstead from London – an odd choice for one who had pined for London life and planned to use the British Museum regularly. In his first invitation to Steevens to visit him, he was at pains to explain to him that his home was not as distant as it might seem and would not impede their collaboration on the correction of printer's sheets: 'This place is but three hours drive from London, and the post comes in every night but monday, so that you may easily have a sheet sent to you.'[2] Steevens may have thought of a three-hour drive as long enough. There were rural pastimes, such as horseback riding – 'I was just going out on horseback when I received your letter', he told Steevens on 5 October.[3] Lord Charlemont, with whom Malone now begins to correspond regularly, suspected the incompatibility of scholarship and Staines. 'Don't let Sunning Hill', he warned on 18 August from Dublin, 'seclude you too much from the world. Retirement is a good thing but certainly too large a dose of it is not suited to your contributions.'[4] Denis Daly remarked more plainly, 'If you were determined to be a Hermit, I dont think you had any occasion to leave Ireland ...'[5] For the time being, however, he decided to stay where he was and even hired an annoyingly dilatory carpenter to build badly needed bookshelves, as he told Steevens on 3 August: 'In the delay of my Cabinet Maker (who is as tedious as an Emperor and bestows it all on me) I am in great disorder at present. When I am a little more settled, I shall hope to prevail on you to make an excursion to my little retreat.'[6]

3

The first known mention of the work Malone had in hand comes from Charlemont: 'What is your chronological account of the writing of Shakspeare other than the history of the progress of the greatest genius that ever honoured and delighted human nature?'[7] The editors of the First Folio, Malone would write, 'manifestly paid no attention to chronological arrangement';[8] indeed, neither they nor the producers of the three following folios in the seventeenth century included dates for any of the plays, grouping them instead as comedies, histories, and tragedies.

---

[2] 3 August 1777, Folger, uncatalogued
[3] To Steevens, 5 October 1777, Folger, uncatalogued.   [4] *HMC*, XII, 10, p. 339.
[5] September 1777, BL Add. Ms. 20.
[6] To Steevens, 3 August 1777, Folger, uncatalogued.
[7] August 1777, *HMC*, XII, 10, pp. 338–39.   [8] *PP (1790)*, II, p. 451.

Eighteenth-century editors like Nicholas Rowe, Pope, and Edward Capell had thought it would be useful to know the chronology of the plays as a tool for measuring Shakespeare's artistic development and progress, but nobody except Capell – a couple of years before Malone began to tackle the problem – had done anything about it. All eighteenth-century editions, including the 1773 *Johnson–Steevens* edition, had followed the arrangement of the plays in the First Folio. Steevens, though, had come to see the importance and urgency of such a study. His own second edition might benefit immmediately from Malone's work if he could avail himself of the younger man's findings as soon as they were available. And who knew what else of use to him Malone might turn up as he threw himself into his research at the British Museum.

When Malone began hunting for evidence on the chronological order of Shakespeare's plays, he inaugurated a new stage in the succession of eighteenth-century Shakespearean editors. The preceding stage, which embraced the work of Theobald, Warburton, Capell, Johnson, and Steevens, had ended with the *Johnson–Steevens* edition – the last of the major editions since Rowe's to be published under the auspices of the Tonson publishing house.[9] Much had been achieved, especially by Capell and Steevens, to rescue Shakespeare's plays from the impressionistic and refining treatment of the text by Rowe, Pope, Hanmer, Warburton, and others;[10] but much remained to be done, not only to base the editing of the text on documentary evidence and make it faithful to the original printings, but to correct Rowe's unfactual and undocumented biography of Shakespeare that had appeared in 1709 and been slavishly followed and accepted for about seventy years. The public still wanted much more than it had been given, especially about Shakespeare's life. With his already extensive knowledge of early English drama, relish for digging into archives, and lawyer's training in examining and testing documentary evidence, Malone was well placed to satisfy this demand. His approach, from first to last, was to search for documents from Shakespeare's age. With them he could claim that anything he wrote about the poet was authenticated fact.

4

Both the public demand and Malone's eventual success in satisfying it must partly be seen in terms of the insatiable appetite for factual history, biography, anecdotes, and antiquarianism in the eighteenth century – an Enlightenment zeal for objective truth in the world of letters. It must also

[9] On pre-Malone editors of Shakespeare, see Ronald B. McKerrow, 'The Treatment of Shakespeare's Text by his Earlier Editors, 1709–1768', *Library of Shakespearean Biography and Criticism* (1933; reprinted in 1970).

[10] Peter Seary reassesses Theobald's Shakespearean scholarship, in *Lewis Theobald and the Editing of Shakespeare* (1990).

be understood in terms of the emerging idolatry of Shakespeare (Bard-olatry), especially after 1730.

Throughout the eighteenth century, there was a growing preoccupation with individual historical and literary personalities for the light they could throw on public events, literary works, and the manners and culture of an age. This focus on character, which shaped much of the historical writing of the period, emanated especially from a fascination with memoirs, anecdotes, journals, and diaries. As historians turned more and more to such archival material, they discovered that a wealth of it abounded in repositories of one kind or another: the British Museum, Oxford and Cambridge college libraries, muniments rooms of country houses, records offices of towns and cities, and private collections. Since the sixteenth century there had always been an interest in collecting materials for local history, but in the second half of the eighteenth century it is the sheer volume of detailed historical and literary research, the relentless pursuit of documents, and the inclination to allow well authenticated particulars into histories – even if they threatened to interrupt narrative coherence and lead the reader into interesting but possibly irrelevant byways – that characterize scholarship.

The taste for such research, and the urge to retrieve documents, could lead to pedantic antiquarianism – many examples of which can be found in the pages of the *Gentleman's Magazine* – which satisfied little more than the idle curiosity of an amateur researcher, who was frequently a cleric. As one literary historian has put it, 'the English countryside swarmed with inquisitive parsons whose love of antiquities was often their most sincere profession.'[11] Horace Walpole observed, however, that specific, erudite historical investigation, uncovering facts about common lives and manners such as the contents of a wardrobe or the property investments of a poet, could lead the historian into little eddies that 'are preferable to a thousand vague and interested histories.'[12] Walpole's own *Anecdotes of Painting in England* (1762–71) illustrates this historical approach, as do Edward Gibbon's *History of the Decline and Fall of the Roman Empire* (1776–88) and Thomas Warton's *History of English Poetry* (1774–81). Warton's *History* lacks a coherent narrative precisely because he opts for details about poets and poetry rather than settle for a general and bland survey of schools. Like Malone's later biographical and textual work and his study of English stage history, the *History* turns out to be a history of manners, or cultural history, as well as an account of English poetry.

[11] Lawrence Lipking, *The Ordering of the Arts in Eighteenth-Century England* (1970), p. 141.
[12] *Historic Doubts on the Life and Reign of King Richard III* (1768); cited in John Butt, *The Mid-Eighteenth Century* (ed. Geoffrey Carnall), Oxford History of English Literature, VIII (1979), pp. 217–18. Malone's copy of Walpole's book on Richard III, with his copious notes, is in the British Library (10805.ee.5).

The enthusiastic pursuit of archival documents ushered in a new era of scholarship. The Shakespearean studies of Capell, Farmer, Steevens, and (especially) Malone were thoroughly and profoundly affected – even 'revolutionized' – by discoveries of documents that they said enabled them to get closer to authentic texts of the plays. Malone would seek them everywhere, often in places where nobody else had thought of looking. Indeed, much of what he found has remained basic to the study of Shakespeare up to the present day. It is important to mention in this context, however, that some recent scholarship has radically attempted to reassess the significance of Malone's scholarly procedures – and traditional (post-1750) scholarship in general – by interpreting his attention to historical documentation as a distorting factor instead of a virtue. In her critical study on Malone's scholarship and the apparatus in his 1790 edition of Shakespeare, Margreta de Grazia urges that by redefining 'authenticity' as that which can be proved by external (documentary) evidence instead of that which was accepted as true by consensus or authority, Malone 'worked to stabilize the preparation of Shakespearean materials' and at the same time rejected and misunderstood the 'contributions which had been received and passed down over the generations linking his period to Shakespeare's.' By returning to 'original and unmediated' documents, he 'lost sight of the successive traditional treatments which formerly endowed the study of Shakespeare with purpose and meaning.'[13] Malone's commentaries, prefaces, and histories reveal abundantly that he was aware of what earlier Shakespeareans and literary historians had done, as well as what himself was doing. He insisted that 'mediated' documents – ones that had been sifted through generations of critical treatments and had picked up apocryphal baggage along the way – endowed Shakespeare study with 'purpose and meaning' only if they were objectively verifiable. Otherwise, such meaning had to be re-examined and perhaps discarded. Far from freezing Shakespeare within his (Malone's) rigid documentary and factual criteria, as de Grazia suggests, he was committed to liberating him and his plays from the obfuscating and romantic effects of changing taste and fashion. From the start, this was his method. Malone was like the architectural historian who in order to evaluate and restore the original style and character of an existing Jacobean building must strip away the contributions of later periods, regardless of how beautiful they may be. The 'mania' in this chapter's 'Shakspearomania' was his obsession with finding authentic sources. There was, however, nothing irrational about the obsession.

To follow Malone in his new project of dating Shakespeare's plays, we

---

[13] Margreta de Grazia, *Shakespeare Verbatim: The Reproduction of Authenticity and the 1790 Apparatus* (1991), pp. 50–51.

need to catch something of the flavour and excitement of Shakespearean idolatry. The revival of Shakespeare after the closing of the London theatres from 1642 to 1660 began in the Restoration uncertainly through the staging of certain favourites, mainly the major tragedies and a few audacious adaptations such as John Lacey's *The Taming of the Shrew*, Nahum Tate's *King Lear*, and Sir William Davenant's *Macbeth*. Such adaptations, which appealed to Restoration audiences even if they distorted Shakespeare, added and removed characters, altered the action, and rewrote the text. They increased in number throughout the Restoration period and continued into the eighteenth century, when they were joined by newer adaptations by actors such as Thomas Betterton and Colley Cibber. Thus Shakespeare was revived at the same time as a need was created for him to be restored to himself.[14]

But what *was* the real Shakespeare? For most playgoers at the start of the eighteenth century it was difficult to know, not only because of the popularity of adaptations and the infrequency with which several of Shakespeare's histories and comedies were performed – his tragedies, chiefly responsible for his new popularity, were acted most often because few original tragedies were then being written – but also because of the scarcity of accessible editions. No new Shakespeare edition had been published since the bulky 1685 Folio and that was not easily available. What was needed was a new marketable, multi-volume edition.

When Jacob Tonson, the already highly successful bookseller and publisher of Milton's and Cowley's works, satisfied that demand with Rowe's six-volume edition in 1709, he inaugurated a series of editions that would be published by his house over the first three-quarters of the century and provide editorial authority for the apotheosis of Shakespeare. Rowe also included in his edition a biography of Shakespeare, which alerted the public for the first time to the poet's individuality, as distinct from whatever bibliographical identity he had via the sequence of seventeenth-century folios. The biography was short, about forty-five pages, and most of it consisted of stories passed on to Rowe by the actor Thomas Betterton, who had gone to Stratford to gather any intelligence he could. Very few of the stories Rowe spun out about Shakespeare from Betterton's information turned out to be verifiable, but that was less important than the effect they had on the public's dawning curiosity.

By the 1730s, Shakespeare had become a very marketable product in the book trade, which in turn, together with influences like the newly formed and energetic 'Shakespeare Ladies Club' and theatre rivalries, encouraged theatre managers like Henry Giffard and John Rich to include more

---

[14] On Shakespeare's revival in the Restoration and early eighteenth century, see Gary Taylor, *Reinventing Shakespeare: A Cultural History From the Restoration to the Present* (1989), chaps. 1–2.

Shakespeare in the repertory. In 1710 only about ten per cent of all plays staged in London were Shakespeare's; by 1740 one-quarter were his, and that included not just the traditional small nucleus of tragedies but several of the histories and (especially) comedies that had never before been acted in the eighteenth century.[15] Far fewer of these, too, were adaptations. While several adaptations lingered on, like Tate's *King Lear* and Cibber's *Richard III*, the average playgoer, now more familiar with the texts, increasingly expected to see the plays in their authentic state. Shakespeare was well on his way to becoming a theatrical and cultural icon.

The most powerful boost to Bardolatry, however, came with Garrick in 1741. In that year Shakespeare's large monument, designed by William Kent, was dedicated in Westminster Abbey, quickly becoming something of a national shrine, a sort of saintly focus of patriotism. That was in one temple. In the other, the theatre, Garrick turned Shakespeare into a national demigod. His acting brilliance became synonymous with the distinctly English naturalness, irregularity, and power that the public associated with Shakespeare. He also had a scholarly interest in Shakespeare that manifested itself in one of the largest eighteenth-century collections of quartos of his plays and of early English drama in general.[16] To some extent, he and Shakespeare became one, a merging that the iconography of the period supports.[17] He even boasted to a Frenchman in 1765 that Shakespeare was 'the God of my Idolatry.'[18]

In his tenure as Manager of Drury Lane from 1747 to 1776, Garrick produced no fewer than twenty-six of Shakespeare's plays. Also influential in the shaping of Shakespeare's apotheosis was the spectacular – at least it would have been spectacular had it not been for the torrential rains – Shakespeare Jubilee that Garrick arranged in Stratford-upon-Avon in 1769. Although a fiasco, the effect of its publicity on the public was what Garrick intended: it completed the identification of Shakespeare as the National Poet, a particularly serviceable icon later when the French Revolution challenged English patriotism.

When Garrick died, he fittingly was buried at the foot of the monument in the Abbey. Years later, Malone summed up his contribution to Bardolatry in this way:

[15] However, as a recent historian of Bardolatry has written, the Tonson genealogy of great (and expensive) Shakespeare editions – Rowe–Pope–Theobald–Warburton–Johnson–Capell–Steevens – did not promote the poet's popularity outside aristocratic circles nearly so much as did the cheaper reprints or so-called 'stage editions' of the individual editions. These were the editions people actually read. They permeated the cultural consciousness of the reading and playgoing public. See Jonathan Bate, *Shakespeare Constitutions: Politics, Theatre, Criticism 1730–1830* (1989), pp. 22–24.

[16] On Garrick's scholarship and library, see George M. Kahrl and George Winchester Stone, *David Garrick: A Critical Biography* (1979), chap. 6.

[17] See Bate, *Shakespeare Constitutions*, chaps. 2–4.

[18] Garrick, *Letters*, ed. D. M. Little and G. M. Kahrl, II (1963), p. 463.

[his] good taste led him to study the plays of Shakspeare with more assiduity than any of his predecessors. Since that time, in consequence of Mr. Garrick's admirable performance of many of his principal characters, the frequent representation of his plays in nearly their original state, and above all, the various researches which have been made for the purpose of explaining and illustrating his works, our poet's reputation has been yearly increasing, and is now fixed upon a basis, which neither the lapse of time nor the fluctuation of opinion will ever be able to shake.[19]

The veneration that prevailed when Malone began his revolutionary work on Shakespeare's text, life, and age continued to develop into the nineteenth century, becoming more and more entrepreneurial. Although Malone would do his part to promote it, Shakespearean commercialism complicated his work because it muddied all sorts of streams. From iconography, to forgeries, to Shakespearean relics, to unreliable Stratford legends disseminated by self-appointed local historians, to bitter editorial rivalries, the country was awash with erroneous, unreliable, or misleading information. One of the tasks Malone took upon himself from the beginning was to stem the flow, or at least to purify it with facts. It became part of his life's work.

5

From the beginning of his career, Malone believed that in this era of Bardolatry the reader who tried to understand what Shakespeare said and meant had a difficult job. He maintained throughout his career that scholars like himself, therefore, had an important service to perform for their times and were not mere pedants. A corrupt text, deceptive spellings, mystifying punctuation, words no longer in use, words in use but with wholly changed sense, and ambiguous phrasing – all this needed to be put on a firmer, historically based footing. It was a very serious business. The modern reader may gain a proper perspective of these editors' labours by reading a few commentaries on particular passages by a succession of scholars.

Taking up, for example, Othello's line, 'Put out the light, and then put out the light' (V.ii), in his first complete edition, Malone writes a long explanatory note disagreeing with Warburton's textual reading and agreeing with Farmer's and Steevens'. Warburton preferred the reading, 'Put out the light, and then – Put out the light' – that is, Othello says he is going to put out the light and is about to say he will then murder Desdemona, but he stops short at the horror of the thought and instead simply says again he will put out the light, which unlike Desdemona's life can easily be relit. But Malone says he agrees with Farmer that Warburton 'gives a spirit to the passage that was not intended. The poet, I think, meant merely to say, – "I will now put out the lighted taper which I hold,

[19] 'Historical Account of the Rise and Progress of the English Stage', *PP* (*1821*), III, p. 294.

and then put out the light of *life*"; and this introduces his subsequent reflection and comparison, just as aptly, as supposing the latter words of the line to be used in the same sense as in the beginning of it, which cannot be done without destroying that equivoque and play of words of which Shakespeare was so fond.' He adds that few images occur more frequently in Shakespeare's plays than the candle, gives examples, and then concludes: 'The question is not, which regulation renders the passage most elegant and spirited, but what was the poet's idea.'[20]

In a less well-known and important passage from *Romeo and Juliet*, 'Ladies that have their toes / Unplagu'd with corns' (I.v), Malone restores 'toes', as found in all the early editions, in place of 'feet', which Pope had substituted: 'The modern editors, following Mr. Pope, read, with more delicacy, their *feet*. – An editor by such capricious alterations deprives the reader of the means of judging of the manners of different ages; for the word … undoubtedly did not appear indelicate to the audiences of Shakespeare's time, though perhaps it would not be endured at this day.'[21] Pope's use of 'toes' was followed by Theobald, Warburton, and Steevens.

Modern scholarship has supported Malone's positions on these two passages; on others it has not. The point here is that such animated disagreements, even if housed in an unobtrusive footnote, were at the centre of Shakespearean criticism in the eighteenth century. They are also behind a few of the bitter quarrels between Malone and Steevens.

6

There are signs, even in 1777, that Malone doubted Steevens' conscientiousness about accuracy and suspected him capable of indulging in sly tricks. He must have known something of his reputation for mischievousness at the expense of other scholars – William Gifford called Steevens the 'Puck of Commentators'. It was near this time, in April 1778, that Topham Beauclerk said to Dr Johnson about Steevens: 'You, Sir, have a friend (naming him) who deserves to be hanged; for he speaks behind their backs against those with whom he lives on the best terms, and attacks them in the news-papers. *He* certainly ought to be *kicked* …. He is malignant.' But Johnson did not quite agree: 'No, Sir; he is not malignant. He is mischievous, if you will. He would do no man an essential injury; he may, indeed, love to make sport of people by vexing their vanity.'[22] It was too early for Malone to make up his own mind, although in October he did notice at the printer's, and did mildly object to, a minor liberty Steevens had taken in his preface. 'Have you yet printed *your preface*.'? he asks; 'In the end of it, as well as I recollect, you have said something about my

---

[20] *PP (1790)*, IX, pp. 620–21.   [21] Ibid., p. 46.   [22] Hill-Powell, III, p. 281.

undertaking [an edition of] *B[eaumont] and Fletcher*; I dont know whether I shall ever do anything in the business and at all events should not chuse to be tied down to it by a publick engagement of this sort; and therefore request you will expunge what relates to those authors.'[23] Already aware of a potential rival, was Steevens trying to divert him from Shakespeare by urging him to take up Beaumont and Fletcher? Such chicanery as then informing the public that Malone would be doing just that was not beyond him.

Astonishing in an unknown barrister just come from Ireland is Malone's confidence. By way of dating the plays, for example, he conjectured that Shakespeare rhymed more frequently in the early plays than in the later. 'I am not at all sure', he said to Steevens, 'that the argument which I have founded on Shakespeare's rhymes, has any weight, but such as it is, you have not, I think, given it quite fair play.'[24] Or take this passage in a letter to Steevens on 12 September 1777, disagreeing with Thomas Tyrwhitt's dating of *Romeo and Juliet* from the Nurse's mention of an earthquake – a highly respected scholar and critic, Tyrwhitt was author of *Observations and Conjectures upon Some Passages of Shakespeare* (1766):

It seems to me very unlikely that Shakespeare when he was writing Romeo and Juliet should have computed back with such precision, as Mr. Tyrwhit [*sic*] supposes, to the date of [the] earthquake – so as to fix the action of the play in 1591 – which, all [Shakespeare's] novels told him, happened thirty or forty years before – It strikes me as only one of those characteristic traits, by which he has so strongly marked all his old women, who delight to comment on a multitude of minute circumstances though they have no relation whatever to the business in hand. Shakespeare probably enough remembered this earthquake and thought it might serve for the nonce as Mantua.[25]

Throughout the hectic months approaching publication, he sent Steevens a stream of addenda and corrections for the latter's commentary, pointing out at least twenty-five errors in the printer's copy for his first six volumes, of which he made, for Steevens' convenience, 'a table of errata'. He also questioned the wisdom of Steevens' plan to publish by January: 'I am every day more and more convinced of the propriety of not being too hasty in putting the *Essay* to press; for three or four new observations have occurred even since I wrote to you last.'[26] Nevertheless, the second *Johnson–Steevens Shakespeare* was published in January 1778, with Malone's own contribution appearing in volume one. It was cautiously titled, *An Attempt to Ascertain the Order in which the Plays attributed to Shakspeare were written.*[27]

[23] 5 October 1777, Folger, uncatalogued.   [24] August 1777 (Hyde Mss.).
[25] 12 September 1777, Folger, uncatalogued.   [26] 31 August 1777, Folger, uncatalogued.
[27] The *Attempt* was published in the first volume of *Johnson–Steevens* edition, 2nd. edn., 1778, pp. 269–346.

The *Attempt* commanded special attention in Steevens' new edition; and Malone anticipated that it would have to be defended because of its extensive and potentially tedious detail and because only Capell before him had deemed it worthwhile to do anything substantial of the kind. Rowe had written in 1709 that he would have liked to know which play was Shakespeare's first: 'it would be without doubt a pleasure to any Man, curious in Things of this Kind, to see and know what was the first Essay of a Fancy like *Shakespear's.*'[28] Unconvinced, however, that a chronology would reveal much about Shakespeare's genius, which was an instrument of Nature, he never did anything about it. Pope showed some interest, but only in order to illustrate his neo-classical idea that Shakespeare's plays became more correct 'in proportion to the respect he had for his auditors', not as a way of evaluating his art.[29] In his 1765 preface to his edition, Johnson acknowledged that Shakespeare experienced 'gradations of improvement' throughout his career, but did not take the matter further because 'the chronology of his works is yet unsettled' – and he knew he was not the man to settle it.[30] Capell, who had quietly done some excellent and original research into the dating of the plays and composed an undated 'Scheme of their Succession', would not get around to publishing until 1780 in his *Notes and Various Readings*, by which time the gloss on the project had been dimmed by Malone's work.

Since Malone did not meet Capell until after publication of the *Attempt*, it is unlikely that he benefited from Capell's research on chronology except for what he had read in his 1767–68 edition. One passage, though, in Capell's introduction could well have articulated for the younger scholar a rationale for his eventual career as Shakespeare's biographer. 'How much is it to be wish'd', Capell wrote, 'that something equally certain, and indeed worthy to be intitl'd – a Life of Shakspeare, could accompany this relation [the "Origin of Shakspeare's Fables"], and complete the tale of those pieces which the publick is apt to expect before new editions.' Capell also complained that 'the critick and the essayist swallow up the biographer, who yet ought to take the lead in them', adding that while 'the occurrences of this most interesting life (we mean, the private ones) are irrecoverably lost to us', it was still possible to reconstruct the poet's 'publick' life as a dramatist: 'When he commenc'd a writer for the stage, and in which play; what the order of the rest of them, and (if that be discoverable) what the occasion; and, lastly for which of the numerous theatres that were then subsisting they were severally written at first, – are the particulars that should chiefly engage the attention of a writer of

---

[28] Smith, *Eighteenth Century Essays on Shakespeare* (1903; 2nd edn. 1963), p. 4. More recently, see Margreta de Grazia, *Shakespeare Verbatim*, pp. 141–51.

[29] Preface to 'The Works of Shakespear' (1725), Smith, *Eighteenth Century Essays on Shakespeare*, p. 47.   [30] Smith, *Eighteenth Century Essays on Shakespeare*, pp. 127–28.

Shakspeare's life.'[31] It was into this biographical maze that Malone entered when he wrote the *Attempt*.

Malone called his study an *Attempt* because he recognized that nobody could ever be completely sure of the plays' order. Still, he added, it was a worthwhile topic because though much had been done lately towards 'elucidation' of the plays, 'very few particulars have been recovered, respecting [their author's] private life, or literary history.' Reiterating Johnson's biographical–critical premise that Shakespeare increased 'his ideas, like other mortals, by gradual acquisition' and 'grew wiser as he grew older', Malone urged that it was therefore 'no incurious speculation, to mark the gradations by which he rose from mediocrity to the summit of excellence; from artless and uninteresting dialogues, to those unparalleled compositions...'. Without a firmer basis of fact, there would continue to be an almost universal indifference to how the events of the day and the poet's life relate to the plays.[32]

There are signs of the emerging biographer, then, in these preliminary remarks. He is already linking criticism with biography and history, an approach supported by the growing eighteenth-century fascination with biography, which climaxed in Johnson's *Lives of the Poets* (1779–81) and Boswell's *Life of Johnson* (1791). In the preparation of the latter, in fact, Malone would himself play a significant part. And he was the first in the study and presentation of Shakespeare to develop an explicitly biographical method. The effort would unfold a new range of critical possibilities, at last enabling one to trace the development of the poet's mind as well as his art. A couple of years later, against a good deal of critical opposition from Steevens and others, Malone decided to edit and publish the Sonnets and narrative poems partly for the same reasons. His historicist perspective guided him away from a sustained evaluation of the plays themselves, their merits and defects, into a new mode of looking at the progression of Shakespeare's art from 'mediocrity to excellence' – the first instalment of a more comprehensive portrait he would later delineate of Shakespeare's improvement of status, material as well as artistic. In deploying any factual information he could lay his hands on as he dated the plays, Malone did not limit his argument, as Margreta de Grazia has suggested, to a temporal notion of the 'internally impelled expansion' of Shakespeare's art, in the process slighting external factors such as the status of the audience, popular taste, economics, and personal experience. She writes that by substituting a chronological scheme for the First Folio grouping of the plays into three

[31] Capell, *William Shakespeare, His Comedies, Histories, and Tragedies* (1767–68). More than a decade later was published Capell's *Notes and Various Readings to Shakespeare*, ed. John Collins, 3 vols. (1779–83).
[32] *An Attempt to Ascertain the Order in which the Plays Attributed to Shakespeare Were Written*, *J–S*, I (1778), pp. 269–70.

dramatic kinds, Malone 'committed the plays to a history of individual and finite creation rather than one of collective and indefinite production on stage and in print.'[33] Malone is supposed to have obscured the non-authorial contributions the First Folio made to the study of Shakespeare, by reorganizing the plays. But he, as we shall see, included more, not less, in the historial, biographical, and textual equation. Rather than isolate Shakespeare within his own developing genius, Malone's method forces us to see the poet more completely in his own person and in his own age.

In dating the plays, Malone relied on allusions in the plays to contemporary events, which to him often suggested Shakespeare's personal responses to these events; and entries in the Stationers' Register recording the publication of books that from internal evidence he judged Shakespeare to have known or read. He also based much of his reasoning on the simple point, stated as a strong probability but not certainty, that of the nineteen plays not published in Shakespeare's lifetime, all but four were 'late' – that is, composed in the last ten years of his career. Of the sixteen 'genuine' plays printed in the poet's lifetime, he continued, thirteen were written before 1600. He gave two reasons why the later plays were not published until after Shakespeare's death – both biographical:[34] first, that the public did not, before Shakespeare died, have as long as it did with the earlier plays to call for publication; second, that after the poet became one of the shareholders of the Globe Playhouse in 1603, it was in his and the theatre's interest not to publish, 'manuscript plays being then the great support of every theatre.' Malone stresses that Shakespeare exercised greater control over these later plays because he wrote them exclusively for his own company, the King's Men, whereas previously he had written for several theatres which therefore possessed manuscript copies, prompt copies, and other sources to draw on in any publishing ventures.[35]

Malone's biographical principle in dating the plays is also evident in his discussion of the plays themselves. When did Shakespeare begin to write for the stage? If he wrote as early as the late 1580s, why then did not contemporary writers like George Puttenham in *The Arte of English Poesie* (1589) and Sir John Harington in his *Brief Apologie of Poetrie* (1591) mention him? In his commentary on the three parts of *Henry VI*, he took up Tyrwhitt's identification of Shakespeare as the 'upstart crow, beautified with our feathers', to whom Robert Greene had angrily and jealously alluded in 1592 in his *Groatsworth of Wit*. This illustrates convincingly, he argued, that Shakespeare had written some drama at least by 1592; it

---

[33] See de Grazia, *Shakespeare Verbatim*, pp. 147–48, 150–51.

[34] In his 1821 edition, he adjusted his first attempts to date the plays, but he did not also reconsider these two arguments.

[35] Malone later proposed the 'fallible criterion' that the more rhymes in a play, the earlier the play (*Attempt, J–S*, 1778, I, pp. 280–81).

further suggests that the poet's earliest dramatic efforts, the second and
third parts of *Henry VI*, were probably reworkings of old plays. He went
about these conjectures lamenting, as frequently he would when writing
about literary figures even as recent as Pope, that biographical detective
work must always be cast as probability, not certainty; for 'The silence and
innacuracy of those persons, who, after [Shakespeare's] death, had the
revisal of his papers, will perhaps for ever prevent our attaining to any thing
like proof on this head.'[36] At the other end of Shakespeare's career, we have
Malone's biographical conjectures regarding the poet's retirement. Accepting Tyrwhitt's idea that because of allusions in *The Tempest* it must have
been written in 1614, he disagreed with current thinking that Shakespeare
wrote no plays in his Stratford retirement. His Muse, he said, would not
have allowed him to rest.[37]

In evaluating Malone's success, we must remember that this was
pioneering research.[38] There were few people he could profitably consult.
Left on his own, he did remarkably well, although he was uncompromising
with himself in assigning to each play a specific year instead of (as is the
present practice) of a two- or three-year range. For twenty-three of what he
thought to be the thirty-five definitely 'genuine' plays, his dating is by
present standards either correct or within one or two years of the figure
generally accepted today. For twelve plays he miscalculated by three or
more years. In 1790, when he tried again, slightly altering and expanding
his arguments, he adjusted the dates of seven plays, each closer to modern
estimates. A reviewer in the *Monthly Review* of September 1793, observed
that this new research mostly confirmed Malone's earlier *Attempt*, with only
two plays 'much removed from their former dates' – *The Winter's Tale*
(moved back ten years to 1604 – still six to seven years earlier than modern
scholarship has dated it) and *The Taming of the Shrew* (moved forward
twelve years to 1594, which agrees with modern estimates).[39] Finally, in a
third survey, inserted by James Boswell Junior into his *Life of Shakespeare* in
the 1821 edition of the plays (the so-called third variorum), he altered
seventeen dates, not in every instance in the right direction, but on the
whole establishing the order of the plays as it is accepted today.[40]

In his conclusion to his essay, Malone reminded his readers that this was

---

[36] *Attempt, J–S* (1778), I, pp. 275–78.
[37] In 1808, he argued that it was written earlier (*An Account of the Incidents From Which the Title and
Part of the Story of Shakespeare's Tempest were Derived, and Its True Date Ascertained*).
[38] A review of Capell's *Notes and Various Readings of Shakespeare* in January 1794, noted something
'familiar to Mr. Malone's ingenious Essay, attempting to ascertain the order of the several
dramas', but it did not suggest Malone had borrowed from Capell (*Monthly Review*, LXX, 22).
[39] *Monthly Review*, LIX, 71–72.
[40] His most glaring errors in 1778 were: *The Tempest* 1614; *Henry VIII* 1601; *Taming of the Shrew*
1606, which he correctly adjusted in 1790; and *Othello* and *Julius Caesar* seven or eight years too
late. After his last attempt, published in 1821, he erred significantly only with *Henry VIII* and
Julius Caesar.

only an 'attempt' to date the plays and said he hoped it would encourage others to similar research. In the event that it did, he wrote, he would be 'happy to transfer the slender portion of credit that may result from the novelty of this undertaking, to some future claimant, who may be supplied with ampler materials and endued with a superior degree of antiquarian sagacity.'[41] Though this sentiment rings a little false since he failed to credit Capell, he had indeed cornered this area of research. Nobody else in his lifetime attempted seriously to date the plays.[42]

In 1778 this was a conspicuous beginning. It won him more attention than he received from the notes he had been writing for Steevens' second edition, though for the present he was happy in such work as the edition went to press. With his confidence unchecked and growing by the day in a widening circle of eminent friends and acquaintances, he was gratifyingly in his element.

7

After a few months in Ireland at the end of 1778, Malone was back in London picking up with Steevens where he had left off. The main change in his personal life when he returned was that he abandoned Staines. Sometime before leaving for Ireland, he had finally moved into London, first briefly to a house in Marylebone Street, and then permanently to a house he rented at 55 Queen Anne Street East (today called Langham Gardens). Located in a quiet residential area at the back of Oxford Street and a few steps off Portland Place, the house (which still stands although the ground floor currently houses the scruffy offices of a small international clothing firm) was just a twenty-minute walk from the British Museum. From this time on, Malone increasingly became an urban character, rarely leaving London for prolonged periods. He identified himself with the city social life as fondly as did Boswell. And he became especially popular as a dinner guest of the leading wits and personalities of London, taking pleasure himself in offering dinner parties at Queen Anne Street East. By 1779 his life had assumed a pattern that remained virtually unchanged for thirty-three years.

In February 1779, Malone also began to have his portrait painted by Sir Joshua Reynolds, thereby beginning one of the dearest friendships of his life. To ask Reynolds to paint him was an act of confidence by a man who knew he had a great future as a scholar. It was also expensive because for a face and shoulders Reynolds was then charging thirty-five guineas. Reynolds' engagement book shows that Malone sat for his portrait no fewer than ten times between 23 February and 10 July. He kept good

---

[41] *J–S* (1778), I, p. 346.
[42] See James Hurdis's *Cursory Remarks Upon the Arrangement of the Plays of Shakespeare* (1792); and R. Sill (under the pseudonym Charles Dirrill), *Remarks on Shakespeare's Tempest, containing an Investigation of Mr. Malone's Attempt to Ascertain the Date of that Play* (1797).

company in the waiting room, for Reynolds records that on several of these days he also painted Gibbon, the Duke of Marlborough, Dr Johnson's friend Mrs Hester Thrale, and (on 28 April and 17 May) the King himself.[43] Malone's portrait, which now hangs (or is concealed) in the basement of the National Portrait Gallery, where one can see it only with permission, pictures him as the mild and polite gentleman many said he was. Nothing about the conventional portrait suggests that Malone was a scholar: no books, parchments, shelves, study. In fact, the background is a landscape scene, rather out of character with the urban bibliophile Reynolds knew. The round, soft face is that of a young man in his mid-thirties, without the wrinkles and creases, the weariness of the flesh, brought on by intense study. There are signs in the face, however, of the ambivalent personality of this scholar–gentleman. His features are soft and pink, nothing dramatic; the forehead is broad, suggesting the intellectual; the nose is long and elegant and chiselled, suggesting dignity. But his brown eyes have a piercing look about them, almost a fierceness of concentration that would make someone think twice about disagreeing with him. The mouth is thin-lipped and set very firmly. There is not the faintest suggestion of frivolity of manner or appearance, although there is more than a mere hint of good humour.

Either before or soon after publication of the 1778 *Johnson–Steevens* edition, Steevens invited Malone to push on with the *Supplement*. The original idea was to include in it several apocryphal plays – at times attributed to Shakespeare because the Stationers' Register had listed them with the poet's name or initials and included them in the Third Folio – but not attributable with any confidence to his canon. Later, Malone decided to include the narrative poems and Sonnets, a decision Steevens opposed but grudgingly accepted, though in his own third edition of 1793 he refused to include them.

Malone's decision to include the poetry would make the *Supplement* a more significant publication, for it would thereby become the first authoritative critical edition of the poetry, complete with a full textual apparatus. None of the preceding eighteenth-century editions of Shakespeare's plays, except Bernard Lintot's in 1711[44] and a quarto edition of the

[43] See Sir Joshua Reynolds 'MS Ledgers 1760–1792'. 2 vols., II, fol. 46; William Cotton, *Sir Joshua Reynolds' Notes* (1859), p. 98; and Prior, 'Maloniana', p. 383. Schoenbaum says that the portrait was painted in 1774 (*Shakespeare's Lives*, (rev. edn. 1991), p. 111), but references in Reynolds' engagement book to Malone's payment of £36 13s 1d on 12 May 1774 (*Walpole Society* (1970), 42, 158) and of £36 15s 0d on 3 July 1778 (*Walpole Society*, 42, 159) as a second instalment on the portrait painted in 1774 are for a portrait of his uncle Anthony; the latter amount is identified as 'Remaining for Chancellor Malone'. Reynolds does not appear to have recorded Malone's payment.

[44] Lintot's one-volume edition of the poems in 1709 included only *Venus and Adonis*, *The Rape of Lucrece*, and *The Passionate Pilgrim* of 1599. He added the Sonnets and other poems in the 1711 edition, *A Collection of Poems*, vol. II.

poems published in 1726 to match Pope's edition, included the poems
because – remarkable as it may seem to us – the editors did not think much
of them. Edward Capell was a singular exception in that he did much work
on the poems, marking up a copy of Lintot's 1711 edition towards an edition
that he never published. It seems likely that Malone saw and used Capell's
marked up copy before he published his own edition of the poems in 1780
because several notes in his edition that are signed 'C' are almost certainly
by Capell. Apart from that cryptic attribution, however, he scarcely
acknowledged help from Capell.[45]

Steevens knew he could rely on Malone for a scrupulous job of editing in
the *Supplement*. Although he had differed with him on many matters of
interpretation, and said so, in his new edition he had publicly announced
his admiration for Malone's chronology: 'By the aid of the registers at
Stationers' Hall, and such internal evidence as the pieces themselves
supply, he has so happily accomplished his undertaking, that he only leaves
me the power to thank him for an arrangement which I profess my inability
either to dispute or to improve'[46] – sweet praise, indeed. The stage was set
for Malone's second important contribution to Shakespeare studies.

He was now in charge of the *Supplement*, though he and Steevens saw
much of each other and worked closely together, and Isaac Reed, Steevens'
eventual heir to the *Johnson–Steevens* editorship, helped out with a few notes.
On Sunday, 18 February 1779, Steevens invited him for work and 'to eat
your Roast Beef...putting at the same time your night-cap in your
pocket.'[47] They wrestled together over the question of whether or not
Shakespeare wrote all of *Pericles*; and Steevens was particularly interested
in making a case against Shakespeare's authorship of *The Life and Death of
Thomas Lord Cromwell*, which had been entered in the Stationers' Register
on 11 August 1602 under the initials, 'W. S.', and published in the Third
and Fourth Folios. Both were to be included in the *Supplement*. Some
unexpected but generous assistance also came from Sir William Blackstone,
the first Professor of Law at Oxford and author of *Commentaries on the Laws
of England* (1766), for many years the best historical account of English law.
In what must have been Blackstone's last literary effort (he died in 1780),
he gave Malone, possibly at Steevens' urging, the notes on Shakespeare he
had written too late for inclusion in Steevens' edition; he was also writing
new ones. 'All his notes will be ready in about three weeks' time', Steevens
reported on 24 March.[48] Malone and Blackstone quickly became friends.[49]

Malone mentions Blackstone's help, as well as Tyrwhitt's, in a long letter

[45] On Malone's and Capell's work on the Sonnets, see H. E. Rollins (ed.), *The Sonnets*, 2 vols.,
Philadelphia, II (1944), pp. 36–39.   [46] *J–S* (1778), I, p. 268.
[47] 18 February 1779, Folger Y.c. 1434 (15). See also Steevens to Malone: 3 June (Beinecke); 16
June Folger Y.c. 1434, (17); 8 September (Beinecke); and 7 December Folger Y.c. 1434 (18).
[48] 24 March 1779, Folger Y.c. 1434 (16).
[49] See Blackstone's letter to Malone, 22 May 1779, Add. 21.

to Charlemont on 5 April about his 'Shakspearomania' – 'These you see
are all great names', he remarks, with a touch of politic false modesty.[50]
Dated April 1779, this is the first of a series of superb letters over the years
to his friend, brimming with news about books, politics, writing, and
scholarship, as well as about his personal life. An Irish statesman and a
cultured man of letters who became the fourteenth member of Dr Johnson's
Literary Club in 1783, Charlemont was also one of the early members of the
Dilettanti Society, founded for the encouragement of the arts in 1734. He
was one of the great connoisseurs and patrons of architecture, painting, and
the arts in general, having travelled widely in Italy and Greece and
popularized the taste for Greek antiquities. He was the perfect correspondent for Malone.[51] 'Lord Charlemont is the politest man I have ever
seen', Malone writes in 1783. 'In him politeness is no effort. It arises
naturally and necessarily from his warm and affectionate heart.'[52] There
was nobody, inside or outside his family, in whom he confided more than
Charlemont:

My Shakspearomania still continues strong upon me, and has now engaged me in
a work with which I think you will be pleased. I mentioned, I believe, to you that
I intended to publish a Supplement to the late edition – but I have now enlarged
my scheme, and mean to print, at the same time, the sonnets – the 'Tarquin and
Lucrece' [*The Rape of Lucrece*] – the 'Venus and Adonis' – and the seven spurious
plays.

Even if these two poems are spurious, he adds, as contemporary works they
will be 'not entirely without their use in the edition.' He probably had in
mind their usefulness for cross-referencing, a technique of first importance
that Malone introduced into Shakespeare editing, whereby the meaning of
words in one play or poem could elucidate their appearance in other texts.

8

Malone still had not met Capell, formerly Deputy-Inspector of plays, who
now lived most of the time reclusively in the Temple on a sinecure from the
Duke of Grafton. He had recently left his remarkable collection of
Shakespeareana, together with the useful catalogue that for decades he
meticulously kept,[53] to Trinity College, Cambridge, after his own college,
St Catharine's, declined his offer. It was possibly the best such private
collection in England at that time. Malone was on the verge of completing
his law studies in London when in 1767–68 Capell published his six-volume

[50] *HMC*, XII, 10, pp. 342–45.
[51] Malone was introduced to Charlemont by William Jephson (*HMC*, XIII, 8, p. 222) or met him
at Stephen's Green (Prior, pp. 40–41).   [52] Prior, 'Maloniana', p. 357.
[53] The catalogue was transcribed and privately printed by George Steevens as the *Catalogue of Mr.
Capell's Shakespeariana*, presented by him to Trinity College Cambridge, 1779 (privately
printed), ed. W. W. Greg (1903).

edition of Shakespeare, demonstrating the value of the early 'good' quartos and the need for an editor of a literary work to decide on a 'copy-text', a basic text taken from the edition judged to be most representative of the author's intentions. In a sense, as a foremost textualist has suggested, Capell was the first 'modern' editor because his was a completely new and 'pure' edited text derived from extensive collating of sixteenth- and seventeenth-century quartos and folios.[54]

In spite of Malone's fundamental respect for Capell's textual work on Shakespeare and his commentary on the poet's sources, both he and Steevens (and others) over the next few years belittled in print the older scholar's work and neglected to acknowledge properly their debt to him. When John Collins, who edited and brought to press Capell's *Notes and Various Readings* (1779–83) posthumously, defended him in his dedication to the first volume of the work, his main charge against editors like Steevens and Malone was that they had stolen from Capell by 'a regular system of plagiarism.'[55] Malone never replied to this charge. But it is true that after Capell's *School of Shakespeare*, containing extracts of Shakespeare's sources, came out in the final volume of the *Notes and Various Readings*, it offered him much material for his 1790 edition – material he used but inadequately acknowledged. In his notes he was also keenly critical of Capell's scholarship.

Aspects of Capell's work were certainly eccentric. He had difficulty writing crisp straightforward English, and it became something of a joke to make fun of his archaic style. Dr Johnson, on seeing some of Capell's Shakespeare criticism in 1780, remarked: 'If the man would have come to me, I would have endeavoured to "endow his purposes with words"; for, as it is, "he doth gabble monstrously".'[56] Furthermore, Capell's long delay in publishing his notes and commentary to his 1767–68 edition prevented the public and perhaps even Malone from properly appreciating the originality and significance of his research. By the time his *Notes and Various Readings* was completely in print in 1783, Malone and Steevens had long since anticipated and borrowed from him, so that few people took the publication seriously. John Colman in the *Monthly Review*, alluding to Johnson's remark that Capell had 'thrown away a life on Shakespeare',

[54] See G. B. Evans, 'Shakespeare's Text', *The Riverside Shakespeare* (1974), pp. 33–34; and 'Shakespeare's Text: Approaches and Problems', in *A New Companion to Shakespeare Studies*, ed. Kenneth Muir (1971). See also de Grazia, *Shakespeare Verbatim*, pp. 54–56; Alice Walker, 'Edward Capell and his Edition of Shakespeare', in *Studies of Shakespeare*, ed. Peter Alexander (1964), pp. 132–48; Taylor, *Reinventing Shakespeare*, pp. 141–44; Hymen H. Hart's informative (unpublished) dissertation on Capell, University of Illinois; and Sailendra Kumar Sen, *Capell and Malone, and Modern Critical Bibliography* (1960).

[55] On Malone's debts to Capell, see Alice Walker, *Textual Problems of the First Folio*. See also G. B. Evans, *The Riverside Shakespeare*, p. 33; and John Mair's portrayal of Malone as a vindictive persecutor in *The Fourth Forger: William Ireland and the Shakespeare Papers* (1938).

[56] Hill-Powell, IV, p. 5.

succinctly observed that while Capell was 'working his way under ground, like the river Mole, in order to emerge with all his glories', a 'host of literary ferrets' like Malone, Steevens, Farmer, and Percy 'burrowed into every hole and corner of the warren of modern antiquity, and overrun all the country, whose map had been delineated by Edward Capell.'[57] This was the climate of opinion within which Malone could deride and borrow from his predecessor with impunity.

Consider, for instance, Malone's attack on Capell in a note to *Julius Caesar* in his privately printed pamphlet, a *Second Appendix* to the *Supplement* (1783): 'A modern editor, (Mr. Capell) who, after having devoted the greater part of his life to the study of old books, appears to have been extremely ignorant of antient English literature … His work exhibits above *six hundred* alterations of the genuine text … capricious and unwarrantable.' Warming to the assault, he continues:

This editor, of whom it was justly said by the late Bishop of Gloucester, that '*he had hung himself up in chains over our poet's grave*', having boasted in his preface [introduction], that 'his emendations of the text were at least equal in number to those of all the other editors and commentators put together', I had lately the curiosity to look into his volumes with this particular view. On examination I found that, of three hundred and twenty-five emendations of the antient copies which he has properly received into his text, *two hundred and eighty-five* were suggested by some former editor or commentator, and *forty* only by himself.

The 'innovations and arbitrary alterations', Malone continues, totalled six hundred and thirty-three.[58]

In another note on *Twelfth Night*, Malone ungenerously remarks that Capell 'appears to have been entirely unacquainted with our antient language.'[59] Malone uses this language about one who was, after all, the most progressive Shakespeare scholar in the middle of the eighteenth century, but he nonetheless appropriates several of Capell's notes, identifying him vaguely as a 'modern editor'. Only once, when he credits Capell for 'properly' consulting the early texts, does he say a positive word about him by name. His behaviour may be explained by the factors mentioned earlier, and perhaps especially by his envy that Capell anticipated him somewhat as a revolutionizer of Shakespearean editorial tradition, but his conduct remains an unpleasant anticipation of his later subsequent appropriation of Joseph Ritson's notes. Almost twenty years later in a scathing and biased pamphlet, George Hardinge would cite his depreciating use of the notes of people he did not respect as a feature of 'the essence of Malone'.[60]

[57] *Monthly Review*, December 1783, 484–85.
[58] *A Second Appendix to Mr. Malone's Supplement to the Last Edition of the Plays of Shakespeare* (1783), p. 38.   [59] *Second Appendix*, p. 19.
[60] George Hardinge, *The Essence of Malone* (1800) and *Another Essence of Malone, or, The 'Beauties' of Shakspeare's Editor* (1801).

Capell's introduction also called for new biographical work on Shakespeare, and this Malone took to heart in his work on stage history. Such study, Capell had remarked, could 'rise quickly to a volume; especially, with the addition of... a brief history of our drama, from its origin down to the poet's death; even the stage appear'd on, it's [*sic*] form, dressings, actor's [*sic*] should be enquir'd into, as every one of those circumstances had some considerable effect upon what he compos'd for it.'[61]

As rival book collectors, too, Malone and Capell experienced some awkward moments with each other. In February 1779, Malone made one of those rare 'finds' that all collectors fantasize over and that made Capell pulse with envy. He purchased from a bookseller a 1607 copy of the *The Taming of A Shrew*, which he thought was a 'bad' or unreliable quarto of Shakespeare's play, originally published in 1594.[62] He wrote on the back of the title page: 'Bought from Mr Wagstaffe bookseller in Feby 1779, at the exorbitant price of Two Guineas. This is the only copy that I have seen, except that in the possession of Mr Steevens, and perhaps these are the only two now extant.' He added, with a typical collector's flourish, 'Mr Capel [*sic*] for 30 years searched for one in vain.'

When Capell heard that Malone had found this volume, he tried to persuade him through Wagstaffe to relinquish it to him. He wrote three letters to Wagstaffe, the first on 21 March, offering Malone what he was certain he could not refuse: 'Could Mr Malone be prevailed upon to accept of two or even three 4o Shakespeares, of elder date than his "*Shrew*", in exchange for that one? I have duplicates by me, and he shall take his choice if he will honour me with a call. If that must not be, a sight of it would be an obligation to him in granting... it.'[63] Malone's answer was cold and business-like:

Mr M will not dispose of the play on any account, as he considers it a very great curiosity and believes it to be one of the scarcest pieces extant. But if Mr Capell wishes to peruse it, and will be so good as to favour Mr Malone with the loan of *Romeus and Juletta* by Arth[u]r Brooke, which he wishes much to see, the *Old Shrew* shall be delivered to the messenger who brings the other. Mr M. will take the greatest care of the poem and hopes Mr Capell will be equally careful of the play.[64]

Capell accepted the offer and an exchange was made before the month was out. Malone's ironic comment on this little contest in a letter to Charlemont a few days later is somewhat disarming: 'I paid, a few days ago, two

---

[61] Capell, *William Shakespeare, His Comedies, Histories, and Tragedies*, introduction, I, pp. 49–74.

[62] Scholars now generally believe that this so-called 'old' *Shrew* is a memorial reconstruction of an earlier, probably Shakespearean, version of the play. The book is now in the Beinecke, Malone 152. Scholars also now see the 1594 quarto either as Malone did or as a pirated and inaccurate version of Shakespeare's play.

[63] See Malone's letter, pasted in the volume (Beinecke, Malone 152).

[64] This letter also he pasted into Beinecke, Malone 152.

guineas for the old "Taming of A Shrew" (not Shakspeare's) and Mr. Capel [*sic*] was so miserable about it, that he wrote three letters to the bookseller that sold it, requesting to let him have a sight of it, a circumstance which, you know, adds a great value to these sort of things. I really now begin to consider it as a very useful and necessary piece of furniture, and wonder how I did without it so long.'[65]

It is impossible to say what Capell, after the *Attempt* was published, really felt about this newcomer to the ranks of Shakespeare scholars. He was not as ambitious as Steevens and therefore not as likely to feel threatened. But he appeared to fear, with some clairvoyance, that Malone might not properly acknowledge any help he received. When Malone asked, in early May 1779, the favour of seeing a few of his old Shakespeare quartos, his response was lukewarm: 'Mr. Capell is not a little distress'd how to forme an answer that shall satisfy a gentleman he is so much oblig'd to as to Mr. Malone; nor can he do it without many words, and without desiring entire credit to the worth of those words.' He said the chief obstacle was that he had donated his collection of 'Shakspeareana' to the Trinity College library, which was presently binding it 'uniformly'.[66]

That summer, undeterred, Malone journeyed to Cambridge with Steevens to examine Capell's collection and toured the university, visiting a number of eminent dons, especially Dr Richard Farmer, of Emmanuel College, whom he had met a few times in recent months at the British Museum and who was then at work on his important study of the authorship of the three parts of *Henry VI*.

9

Soon after the Cambridge trip, about half-way through work on the *Supplement*, in mid-1779, a rift between Malone and Steevens first appears. Steevens' mistake was to mention Susanna Spencer. What seems to have happened is that Steevens patronizingly mentioned that Malone's Shakespeare work was a device to keep him busy and his mind off her. Malone was offended just by the reference, but beyond that annoyed by Steevens' dismissal of his work as a type of hobby. He replied curtly that Steevens had misjudged him: the work on the *Supplement* had, in fact, revealed to him the need for an entirely new edition, more scientifically and methodically edited than the *Johnson–Steevens* edition was ever likely to become. He had, therefore, decided to produce a new edition on his own.

[65] Among other items he acquired at that time were the 1609 quarto edition of Shakespeare's Sonnets – the sole authority for the text – and the first quarto edition (1594) of *The Rape of Lucrece* (to Charlemont, 5 April, *HMC*, XII, 10, pp. 342–44).
[66] Photostat, OFB. See Malone's note in Steevens' edition dated February 1781 (Beinecke, Malone 143).

Steevens was stunned. Suddenly, his supremacy among Shakespeare
editors seemed in doubt. His jealousy from then on would sour their
friendship and make Malone's life difficult. His reply was not a study in
tact:

I received your favour last night, and am sincerely sorry at being inform'd that you
commenced annotator for any reason less flattering than your own mere
amusement. I recommended your present task to you, because you seem'd to like
it, because you were well qualified to succeed in it, and because few things more
essentially contribute to our happiness, than to have some one object constantly in
view, – some standing dish in our larder which we may have recourse to as often as
we are in want of a literary meal.

Malone, to say the least, did not warm to the notion of his Shakespearean
researches resembling a 'standing dish'. He intended to make the poet a
regimen for life. Steevens assured him he would never again mention
Susanna Spencer, a subject which tends to 'revive ideas which you are
studious to forget.' 'Before I seal this', he added, 'I shall throw both your
letters into the fire, that no memorial of this slight misunderstanding
between us may remain in my possession.' The rest of his letter is distinctly
cold and businesslike and, regarding some of his own annotations, he
snapped, 'You may without ceremony reject any of my observations which
do not, on recollection, coincide with your own opinion.'[67]

10

Coming up to publication of the *Supplement* in April 1780, there was the
usual rush of last-minute additions, corrections, and emendations.
Blackstone's sudden illness and death early in the year prevented most of his
notes from reaching Malone on time, although many of them found their
way into his next edition. Dr Samuel Henley, who had just published some
'ingenious' annotations on Shakespeare in the *Gentleman's Magazine*, also
sent a few notes as, to quote Malone, 'a deposit in the literary Shakespeare-
Bank.'[68] He also heard from Thomas Percy, one of the most highly
respected men of letters of the age, whose *Reliques of Ancient English Poetry*
(1765) had won him fame almost overnight.[69] Malone first met Percy in
1775 and corresponded with him, off and on, until the latter's death in
1811. Percy, like Charlemont, after his removal to Ireland, depended on
Malone for literary news from London, and Malone's letters to him are
mines of information. With the first known letter between them on 13

[67] Photostat, OFB. See Dewey Ganzel, *Fortune and Men's Eyes: The Career of John Payne Collier*
(1982) on the bitter enmity between Malone and Steevens (p. 84).
[68] 4 February 1780, fol. 1, Boston Public Library; see also Malone to Henley, 10 February 1780,
Boston Public Library.
[69] See Bertram H. Davis, *Thomas Percy: A Scholar-Cleric in the Age of Johnson* (1989).

November 1779, Percy sent Malone 'a parcel of Notes' on Shakespeare –
a 'bushel of Chaff', as he put it, in which he hoped Malone could find '2
or 3 good grains.'[70]

In the meantime, Steevens became more sensitive to Malone's corrections
of his commentary, as is evident in this remark of 16 February 1780: 'I do
not wish you to make the smallest change in any of your remarks; and hope
I am not unjust or weak enough to be offended at such ... freedom or levity
as I myself have often used. I hope you will throw away that thought.'[71]
Malone's aggressiveness acutely irritated Steevens; and since he kept up
and increased the pressure, it is no surprise to see Steevens' ire blossom as
publication day drew near. There is a touch of naivety, or idealism, in
Malone's expectation that Steevens should take all this correction and
criticism with dignity for the sake of Shakespeare. Steevens may have asked
himself, with justification, how Malone would respond when he was on the
receiving end.

When they were published in late April 1780, the first of the two volumes
of the *Supplement* contained Malone's account of the Elizabethan theatre,
his reprint of Arthur Brooke's translation of the Italian *Romeus and Juliet* –
borrowed from Capell – used by Shakespeare as source – and the Sonnets.[72]
The second volume housed the seven apocryphal plays that had been
included in the Third Folio.

The Sonnets and the apocryphal plays had been edited previously, but
with the elaborate textual and explanatory annotations Malone gave them
he was able to argue convincingly (and for the first time) the question of
authenticity.[73] He argued that except for *Pericles* and the second and third
parts of *Henry VI*, none of the plays was Shakespeare's. In the process, as has
recently been pointed out, he introduced to Shakespeare studies the
distinction between internal and external evidence: stylistic evidence from
the poems and plays being either validated or invalidated by documentary
evidence obtained from the Stationers' Register and other sources.[74] As
Malone had already explained in his *Attempt*, almost the only argument
ever given in favour of Shakespeare as author of these plays was that his

---

[70] *The Correspondence of Thomas Percy & Edmond Malone*, ed. Arthur Tillotson (1944), p. 1.

[71] To Steevens, 16 February 1780, Folger, Y.c. 1434 (19).

[72] The poems were *Venus and Adonis*, *The Rape of Lucrece*, the *Sonnets*, *The Passionate Pilgrim*, and *A Lover's Complaint*. The plays were *Pericles*, *The Lamentable Tragedy of Locrine*, *Sir John Oldcastle*, *London Prodigall*, *Thomas Lord Cromwell*, *The Puritaine*, and *A Yorkshire Tragedy*.

[73] Charles Gildon's edition of the Sonnets appeared in 1710, as part of Rowe's edition in 1709, vol. VII. Thomas Evans edited the poems in 1775. See Hilton Landry's critical estimate of Malone's edition, 'Malone as Editor of Shakespeare's Sonnets', *Bulletin of the New York Public Library*, 67:7 (1963), 435–42. See also Rollins (ed.), *The Sonnets*.

[74] See de Grazia, *Shakespeare Verbatim*, pp. 109–10. She argues that Malone's use of his factual criteria was not 'appropriate' because the spurious plays, like legends about Shakespeare's life, were not fraudulent 'impositions' like forgeries (p. 110). See also Schoenbaum, *Internal Evidence and Elizabethan Dramatic Authorship: An Essay in Literary History and Method* (1966).

name or initials had appeared on the title pages of quarto editions entered
in the Stationers' Register.[75] Overall, his analysis reflects the antiquarianism of his age and anticipates subsequent Shakespearean criticism.

11

Malone was mostly well pleased with the reviews. The reviewers were
generally happy about the scholarly treatment of the theatre and the
appearance of the poems and the seven rare plays in a modern edition.
There were particularly complimentary reviews in the *Gentleman's Magazine*,
already noted, and in the *Monthly Review*. The latter praised him for his
'laborious and critical' efforts and judged that although his work 'doth not
place itself on an equal footing with the last edition of Johnson and
Steevens, yet it merits a place next to it: and the admirers of Shakspeare will
esteem themselves indebted to Mr. Malone for the pains he hath taken to
gratify their curiosity.' One especially striking feature is the *Monthly Review*
reviewer's sense of a growing competition between Malone and Steevens.
After stating Malone's thesis, for example, that the 'machinery' of the stage
was very simple before Shakespeare's time, that 'it seldom went beyond a
painted chair, or a trap-door', he adds: 'Mr. Steevens, however, is of
opinion that the machinery of the stage in the time of Shakspeare was not
so simple and scanty as Mr. Malone supposes.'

Towards Malone's additional notes or 'Supplemental Observations' on
the plays, the reviewer grows critical, perhaps in deference to Steevens' own
claims of thorough annotation in his last edition: 'Some of them are of very
little consequence' and serve only 'to enlarge the catalogue of *parallel*
passages, already sufficiently numerous in the preceding volumes.'[76] This
complaint, in fact, would become pervasive over the next two decades, as
the public grew impatient with the fertile textual commentary spawned by
rivalries between Malone, Steevens, Reed, Ritson, and others.

When he came to the poems, especially the Sonnets, the reviewer was
noncommittal. He acknowledges that the 'species of poetry adopted by
Shakspeare in his "Sonnets", is differently estimated by Mr. Steevens and
Mr. Malone; the former calling it "the contrivance of some literary
Procrastes" [*sic*]; and the latter, though not its professed champion, yet is
so far interested in its credit, as to think it is worth his while, to bestow some
little pains in rescuing it from the contempt thrown upon it by the former.'
The disagreement is left unresolved: 'though Mr. Malone hath the last
word (being the Editor), we have reason to think that Mr. Steevens is
disposed to adhere to his own opinion.'[77]

[75] *PP (1790)*, preface, I:i, pp. lix-lx.
[76] *Monthly Review*, LXIII (October 1780), 249–55. See also *Gentleman's Magazine* (August 1780),
375–77.   [77] *Monthly Review*, LXIII (October 1780), 256–57.

Steevens was clearly not in the mood to be converted, certainly not by Malone. When he published his fourth edition in 1793, he remarked quarrelsomely:

We have not reprinted the Sonnets, &c. of Shakspeare, because the strongest act of Parliament that could be framed, would fail to compel readers into their service; notwithstanding these miscellaneous Poems have derived every possible advantage from the literature and judgment of their only intelligent editor, Mr. Malone, whose implements of criticism, like the ivory rake and gold spade in Prudentius, are on this occasion disgraced by the objects of their culture.[78]

Steevens appeared to miss the point, which Malone was the first (in print) to grasp, that the fame of Shakespeare's plays need not rule out an edition that included his poems. Otherwise, he expressed the prevalent bias of his age, that the sonnet was an inferior form of poetry. In his *Dictionary*, Johnson had defined 'sonnetteer' as a word spoken 'in contempt' to describe 'a small poet', and added that the sonnet was 'not very suitable to the English language.'[79] Steevens, apparently irritated by Malone's stubborn independence in including the Sonnets in the *Supplement*, became the 'laughing-stock of later commentators and critics' by contributing notes to Malone's edition that severely attacked Shakespeare's language in them. Steevens once remarked that Malone had little ear for poetry, but his own notes, referring to Shakespeare's 'miserable conceits' and 'studied deformities of style', appear to imply a critical and aural infirmity inherited from several preceding generations of Shakespeare's editors.[80]

Though Malone shows his independence from Johnson, Steevens, and the general critical opinion of his age by including and defending the Sonnets in his 1780 edition, and again later in his 1790 edition of Shakespeare's complete works, he does not (as the reviewer for the *Monthly Review* noted) value them as we do today. 'As it appears to me that they have been somewhat underrated', he writes, thinking of Steevens, 'I think it incumbent on me to do them that justice to which they seem entitled.' He faults them, to be sure, for their 'want of variety' and extravagant conceits. On the other hand, he admires their smoothness and harmony, their 'perspecuity and energy'. Their beauty will 'strike every reader', he observes, whose poetic tastes allow him to appreciate other sorts of verse and versification than the conventional heroic couplet and blank verse of the current age.[81]

One wishes he had gone further. Nathan Drake, one of the earliest and staunchest defenders of the Sonnets, wrote in 1817 of 'the absurd charge

[78] *J–S*, I (1793), p. vii. See Rollins (ed.), *The Sonnets*, I, p. 38.
[79] On eighteenth-century sentiment against the sonnet as an art form, see Rollins (ed.), *The Sonnets*, II, pp. 336–53.
[80] *Supplement*, II (1780), p. 685. See Rollins (ed.), *The Sonnets*, II, 336–37.
[81] *Supplement*, I (1780), p. 83; I, pp. 684ff.

against, and the inadequate defence of, sonnet-writing, brought forward by Messrs. Steevens and Malone', although he attributed the 'depreciation' of Shakespeare's Sonnets chiefly to Steevens.[82] A more balanced judgment must allow that Malone helped nudge contemporary sentiment in Drake's direction by giving the Sonnets a thoughtful hearing. 'Steevens' view was the general one', Robert Graves wrote in 1927,[83] 'and if Malone by his emendations, which have become the accepted Shakespearian text, had not overridden the general critical opinion of the *Sonnets* and presented them fileted [*sic*] to the plain man, the plain man of to-day would undoubtedly be unaware of the existence of the *Sonnets*.' Even without Malone, modern scholarship would long ago have made the Sonnets available to the 'plain man', but otherwise Graves' tribute stands.

By including the Sonnets and narrative poems, Malone made widely available for the first time images of Shakespeare as private individual and non-dramatic poet as well as public dramatist. He was the first to identify Shakespeare with the first person singular of the Sonnets, and the first to suggest that Sonnets 1–126 were written to a man and the following twenty-eight to a woman. In other words, he highlighted their biographical character by matching passages in them with certain events in the poet's life, in the process inaugurating critical controversies about the Sonnets that still persist.

The Romantics were particularly grateful for this more personal and lyrical self-portrait of the poet. For in Malone's hands the Sonnets unfolded complex and varied images of a restless and enquiring poetic self, and he showed also that the narrative poems were among the finest Elizabethan and Jacobean 'smaller pieces' of their genre. For the new age about to open, he hastened the awakening to Shakespeare as individual genius.[84]

Recent theoretical criticism, however, sees in these achievements and their influence on later generations of Shakespeare readers less to applaud. Gary Taylor, for example, notes Malone's 'unabashedly biographical' approach to Shakespeare in iconoclastically overturning traditional stories about him and bringing his biography into commentary on his works. Taylor appears to urge that this is something to apologize for, but beyond his own polemic against historicism and Malone's commitment to the authority of the documented past he is not clear why. Rowe, Taylor writes, felt it would be a pleasure to know which was Shakespeare's first play, and he and his successors had some relevant information at hand to look into the matter, but he successfully resisted this 'confessedly idle curiosity'. The fact is Rowe and his successors had but a fraction of the factual information on

[82] Drake, *Shakespeare and His Times* (1817), II, p. 74.
[83] Robert Graves and Laura Riding, *Survey of Modernist Poetry* (1927), p. 78 (cited in Rollins, ed., *The Sonnets*, II, p. 366).
[84] See Gary Taylor on Malone's influence on the Romantics, *Reinventing Shakespeare*, pp. 156–61.

this subject that Malone turned up. They did not pursue the chronology of the plays because they were unable to, not because they concluded it was an 'idle curiosity'. Taylor laments 'this conjunction of the temporal and the personal', this interest in the development of a poet's mind and art that characterizes Malone's work on the chronology and Sonnets, because of its profound influence on the Romantics and their influence on the subsequent reading of Shakespeare. Even poor Hazlitt, who resisted 'the fashion of late to cry up our author's poems, as equal to his plays', fell prey to this biographical urge.[85] Malone, who limited himself rigorously to what he could discover about Shakespeare's artistic development from historical documents, is thereby blamed indirectly for inducing the Romantics to study Shakespeare's spiritual evolution. The argument is proleptic and distorting: Malone is being judged on the basis of what happened after him.

De Grazia is more specific. Her point is that in emphasizing Shakespeare's self-portrayal in the Sonnets, 'deducing sentiments and senses of words from documents he read and parallel passages he found in the plays', Malone 'further sequestered Shakespeare from the reader, ensconcing him in an introspective space of his own.'[86] But after Malone elucidated patterns of autobiography in the Sonnets with objective external evidence, all of it documentary or bibliographical, Shakespeare's persona and its relationship to his age was never before clearer and more vivid. To the reader unaccustomed to thinking of Shakespeare the man as having a separate identity from his works, which was increasingly common as one went back in the century, Malone's research drew back the curtain on a new and wider stage. Shakespeare was less 'sequestered' than ever. If Malone could discover, for example, what was Shakespeare's sense of words, rather than just the collective sense of words – although he did that, too, with authority and objectivity – the poet's individual artistry would emerge, whose calling was, after all, the subjective use of words, ideas, and experiences. Anchored by the objective discovery of the subjective or private, Malone had far less need to be conjectural in his commentary than previous editors. The 'inventiveness' of past commentators was, in fact, anathema to him. When he did venture into the realm of conjecture, it was only after he had considered the available objective evidence, most of which in the biographical vein he himself had brought to light.

Biographical discoveries aside, it was to the text of the poems and Sonnets that Malone contributed most. Using the 1609 Quarto printing of the Sonnets instead of the 'spurious' 1640 version 'pirated' by Benson, he corrected the text systematically for the first time in a century and a half. He rejected the Benson edition because of its attributions and arrangement of the Sonnets, restoring their cycle structure of the 1609 edition and

---

[85] Ibid., pp. 156–57.   [86] De Grazia, *Shakespeare Verbatim*, p. 152.

removing individual titles that in 1640 had been tacked on to them by Benson. De Grazia has objected to Malone's treatment of the Benson edition because information about the 'productive network' of the publication has shown that there was 'nothing transgressive' about it. There was nothing deliberately spurious and misleading about it; it was just that collections of this sort in the middle of the seventeenth century treated details of authorship – authenticity of text, selection of poems, arrangement – as only one of several factors in book production.[87] Malone, however, was more familiar than most scholars with the bibliographical realities of producing a book like Benson's. The point is he never thought of the collection as a deliberate forgery. He came close to using some invective in describing its lack of authenticity and perpetuation of inaccuracy, but the bite to his criticism was inspired by the uncritical adoption of Benson by a succession of eighteenth-century editors. For blatant forgeries he reserved an invective in which anger and disgust played a more prominent part. It is naive and misrepresentative to suggest that in his pursuit of authentic documents he lost sight of the historical, bibliographical, and social forces behind the transmission of Shakespeare's works in the seventeenth century.

Malone's influence on later editors and editions – until the Globe and Cambridge editions of 1864 and 1866,[88] – is forcefully put in the variorum edition of the Sonnets (1944):

His effect on the text was immense: for the majority of editors before 1864 he left little to do except to insert (or omit) an occasional hyphen, to change a period or comma here or there, to modernize some archaic spelling. No nineteenth-century or twentieth-century editor has done textual work at all comparable in importance to Malone's; few have surpassed him as an annotator; and dozens have taken credit for details borrowed from him without acknowledgment. Truly, one knows not whether to marvel more that he in that misty time could see so clearly, or that we in this supposedly clear age walk so stumblingly after him. He will be praised of ages yet to come.[89]

Although this paean must be qualified with the reminder that several of Malone's emendations of the 1609 Quarto were either misguided or too self-assured, and that he left syntactically difficult passages unexplained or, when he attempted explication, wrongly explained, it is well to remember that it was as an annotator, not interpretive critic, that he saw himself. Throughout his career as a Shakespearean, he adhered to the principle that an editor's role was to provide a scientifically based reading of the text and any auxiliary information he could identify from documents, Shakespeare's

---

[87] Ibid., pp. 165–73. De Grazia judges Malone's attacks on the Second Folio and earlier biographers of Shakespeare on similar grounds. See also Josephine Waters Bennett, 'Benson's Alleged Piracy of *Shakespeare's Sonnets* and of Some of Jonson's Works', *Studies in Bibliography*, 21 (1968), 235–48.   [88] Edited by W. G. Clark and W. A. Wright.

[89] Rollins, *The Sonnets*, II, pp. 38–39.

works, and English literature in general that could 'illustrate' passages.[90] He provided, for example, excerpts of passages in the poet's works illustrating similar usage of the Sonnets' words and phrases and thus supplied the raw materials for later criticism. His intimate knowledge of English literature as well as his legal mind qualified him superbly for this task.

With the help of the Sonnets, he made his first significant point about Shakespearean biography[91] – a matter that produced a memorable disagreement between him and Steevens. At Sonnet 93, which opens with the lines, 'So shall I live, supposing thou art true, / Like a deceived husband', Malone disagrees with William Oldys that in this and the preceding Sonnet Shakespeare was probably addressing his wife, Anne Hathaway, whom he suspected of infidelity. He insists that these poems were not even addressed to a woman, but what interests him most – and this became typical of him, ever on the alert for unexpected discoveries of 'lost' knowledge – is the possibility that Oldys based his mistaken theory on something he knew about Shakespeare's marriage that never found its way into print. This leads Malone to speculate about the poet's will. By leaving Anne Hathaway only his 'second best bed' and nothing else, was he repaying her for infidelity?[92] And was it Shakespeare's jealousy that inspired his portrayals of that emotion in such plays as *Othello* and *The Winter's Tale*?[93]

Steevens, to whom Malone sent the note, was unimpressed. This was idle conjecture, he thought; and in a note that he added in reply at the end of the first volume – the sheets containing the poem and its notes were already at the press – he disingenuously played the sceptic. There is very little we know about Shakespeare, he wrote, and very little we are ever likely to know, so it is better not to waste good ink and paper in dreaming up sensational possibilities. Still more important, he felt it was critical folly to regard the plays as reflections of the dramatist's emotional life, or to use them as biographical sources.[94]

In understanding what lay behind Steevens' note, one needs to remember that at the time all sorts of popular traditions circulated about Shakespeare's life with scarcely a scrap of evidence to back them up. Steevens could not foresee Malone's later efforts on behalf of Shakespearean biography; to him it seemed that Malone was indulging in literary gossip and contributing to unfounded legends which people dearly wished to

[90] See Landry, 'Malone as Editor of Shakespeare's Sonnets', 438.
[91] Schoenbaum takes note of Malone's important new contribution to Shakespearean biography in his *Supplement* (*Shakespeare's Lives*, pp. 173–75).
[92] It is now generally accepted that Shakespeare did not slight his wife in his will. The second-best bed was the marriage-bed.
[93] *Supplement*, I, p. 463. See de Grazia on Malone's five-page note to Sonnet 93 as a new way of reading Shakespeare 'as the engaged poet who observed himself' (*Shakespeare Verbatim*, p. 159).
[94] *Supplement*, I, p. 654.

believe in the absence of solid fact. Malone did not see it that way. He included Steevens' note in his edition, but his own forceful reply seeks to explain what might lie behind Shakespeare's bequests: 'His wife had not wholly escaped his memory; he had forgot her, – he had recollected her, – but so recollected her, as more strongly to mark how little he esteemed her; he had already (as it is vulgarly expressed) cut her off, not indeed with a shilling, but with an old bed.'[95] One of Shakespeare's recent and foremost biographers has observed that in the realm of Shakespearean biography, this statement 'would become profoundly influential – more influential than any other single statement he would ever make.'[96]

One reviewer of the *Supplement* in the *St. James's Chronicle* cavilled. Given Steevens' financial interest in the paper, which Malone's friend Joseph Haslewood called 'the literary pin-basket of the day',[97] it is not unlikely he wrote the reviews himself or convinced someone else to write them. In early May, anonymous and trifling notes began to appear in the *St. James's Chronicle* which niggled at minor points, textual and factual.[98] Their general criticism of Malone's liberal 'Censure on the Inaccuracy of Former Editors'[99] must have particularly rankled. What Steevens particularly disliked about Malone's work was his appropriation of the role of Shakespeare's foremost editor. Three years later, he wrote to his and Malone's friend, Thomas Warton, former Professor of Poetry at Oxford and, after 1785, Poet Laureate, bemused by the spectacle of sprouting editors in the Shakespearean 'Mash tub' and sneering at Malone, who 'intends to froth and lime at a little snug booth of his own construction.' Snug booth or not, Malone through his example convinced Steevens that his time was up as the reigning editor of the day. In the same letter, Steevens told Warton he was giving up his 'licence' or editorship of the *Johnson–Steevens* edition to Isaac Reed.[100]

[95] Ibid., p. 657.　　　　　　　　　　[96] *Shakespeare's Lives*, p. 174.
[97] Haslewood, *Some Account of the Life and Publications of the Late Joseph Ritson, Esq.* (1824), p. 17n.
[98] *St. James's Chronicle*, 9–11, 11–13, 13–16, 16–18 May (nos. 2989, 2990, 2991 and 2992).
[99] 16–18 May.
[100] 16 April 1783, cited from J. Wooll's *Biographical Memoir of … Joseph Warton* (1806), pp. 398–99.

3

Dr Johnson and The Club

1

By the early 1780s, Malone had begun to move comfortably at the centre of London literary life. He was dining out regularly with, among others, Dr Johnson, Steevens, Reed, Reynolds, Farmer, Walpole, John Nichols, and John Henderson, who owned a large library and was regarded then as second only to Garrick on the stage. Malone was not a sparkling conversationalist, and never would be, but people valued his clubbability and mild manner. Still, by 1782 Malone did not see people like Burke, Boswell, Gibbon, Dr Burney, Banks, Windham, Fox, Samuel Dyer (the translator and supposed 'Junius'), and John Wilkes frequently enough to satisfy him. He especially wanted to see Dr Johnson more often.[1] By joining Dr Johnson's Literary Club, a new and more expansive world opened up for him.

The Club, as it was more simply known, was Reynolds' brainchild, who had proposed the idea to Johnson in 1764. Originally, it had eight members who included, in addition to Reynolds and Johnson, Burke, Goldsmith, the Hon. Topham Beauclerk, and Bennet Langton, a dear friend of Johnson's and an eminent Greek scholar. At first, they met at the Turk's Head in Gerrard Street, Soho, over a light supper, one evening per week at seven, continuing their conversation, as Boswell put it, 'till a pretty late hour.' Ten years later, with a slightly expanded membership, they dined together more lavishly every other Tuesday during the sitting of Parliament. After their number inflated to twenty-six in December 1777, the members passed a resolution in November 1778, limiting membership to thirty and another on 3 May 1780 expanding it to thirty-five.[2] By then membership had become a much coveted honour.

Malone was well placed to apply for membership. He had, in addition to Johnson, the backing of Reynolds, with whom he had become friendly in

---

[1] On Malone's friendship with Johnson, see J. M. Osborn, 'Edmond Malone and Dr. Johnson', *Johnson, Boswell, and Their Circle* (1965), pp. 1–20.
[2] Malone's notes on The Club, which contain these and many other facts, are in Ms. Malone 36.

the course of having his portrait painted in 1779.[3] But as he admitted on 5
April 1781 to Charlemont, who already was a member, he had failed in his
first two or three attempts to 'get into your club.' Garrick's death in 1779[4]
had created a vacancy, but Malone heard from the grapevine that out of
respect for Garrick's memory the members had decided not to elect anyone
in his place for some time. This attitude perplexed an impatient Malone
since, as he explained to Charlemont, the more 'agreeable' Garrick had
been, 'the more need there is of supplying the want by some substitute or
other. But as I have no pretensions to ground even a hope upon, of being
a succedaneum to such a man – the argument was decisive and I could say
nothing to it.' But he had not given up. Others also wanted to get in, and
as The Club again had 'some thoughts of enlarging their numbers',
'perhaps we may be all elected together.' Eager as he was, Malone wryly
observed, he was 'not quite so anxious as Agmondisham Vesey, who I am
told, had couriers stationed to bring him the quickest intelligence of his
success…'.[5]

Charlemont naturally supported Malone's application but in Ireland
could do little to promote it. He wrote back promptly, 'For my own sake,
I wish you every success in your endeavours to get into the Turk's head
club. Why am I not in London to vote for you?'[6] It was no use, in any case,
for he and the others all failed again, receiving the dreaded blackball with
which any single member could anonymously and instantly kill an
application. The members stuck to their decision regarding Garrick's
memory and no new member was elected until 5 February 1782. On that
day, the memory of Garrick having dimmed sufficiently, Malone at last was
admitted into this august company, receiving the good news from Gibbon.[7]
His enthusiasm and organizational skills quickly made him indispensable
and it was not long before he became The Club's first Treasurer and,
according to The Club's historian, held the office 'till his death … the only
one connected with it, for the President, or Chairman, as he is now called,
[was] changed at every meeting.'[8] He attended his first meeting on 19
February.

2

Johnson had only about two years left to live. Malone did not see him at
The Club until 2 April, when Johnson presided; and after that, not again
until 2 December. Nevertheless, he now saw him more often at other times,
mostly at the latter's house, and he began to keep a journal recording their

---

[3] Reynolds' engagement book records that Malone sat ten times for Reynolds between 23
   February and 6 July.
[4] Malone recorded in his journal in 1789 Reynolds' account of how Johnson responded to
   Garrick's desire to join The Club (Prior, 'Maloniana', pp. 392–93).
[5] *HMC*, XII, 10, pp. 344–45.   [6] Ibid., p. 349.
[7] [Donald and] Mary Hyde Collection.   [8] M. E. G. Duff, *The Club* (1905), p. 7.

conversations. The journal proved useful years later when he added notes
to the several editions of Boswell's *Life of Johnson* he saw through the press.[9]
Nobody, apart from Boswell, would defend Johnson's life and achievements
as tenaciously as he in the years ahead. Boswell once referred to him as
'Johnsonianissimus'.[10] John Courtenay, later a member of The Club and
good friend of Malone's, composed a poem honouring Johnson in which he
praised Malone for studying Johnson so faithfully:

> And you, MALONE, to critick learning dear,
> Correct and elegant, refin'd, though clear,
> By studying him, acquir'd that classick taste,
> Which high in Shakspeare's fame thy statue plac'd.[11]

While Johnson was publishing his *Lives of the Poets*, Malone had the chance
to help him with them by providing facts for the *Life of Pope* as well as for
a Life of Goldsmith that he wanted him to write.[12] At the same time, though
he venerated Johnson, he was not blind to the limitations of the *Lives of the
Poets*. He regarded thorough biographical research as crucial to Johnson's
project, but Johnson had not shown himself to be a diligent researcher.
Johnson admitted this. 'Sometime in March [1781] I finished the "Lives of
the Poets"', he told Bennet Langton, 'which I wrote in my usual way,
dilatorily and hastily, unwilling to work, and working with vigour and
haste.'[13] When the first batch of the *Lives* appeared, which included
Milton, Dryden, Cowley, and Waller, Malone remarked to Charlemont on
5 April 1779 that while the 'critical parts' of the *Lives* were 'amusing and
instructive', the biographical sections were flawed by 'a want of industry':

He hates much trouble. A man of infinitely inferior parts (Horace Walpole, for
instance) would have collected a great many anecdotes, and made a more
entertaining work. Johnson complains in his preface to Shakspeare that he did not
find the possessors of the old quartos very communicative of them. Yet every one
knew that Garrick allowed every person that asked it to have access to his valuable
collection; and nothing would have displeased Johnson so much as to have had a
cart-load of them laid down in his study.

Malone's point was that Johnson's achievement in these *Lives* was unique,
reflecting his own moral and critical acumen; the humanity and wisdom
that lie behind them could never be matched by a mere accumulation of
facts. Nonetheless, he felt the *Lives* were deficient because they were not

---

[9] The Everyman edition of Boswell's *Life of Johnson* contains more notes by Malone than the Hill-Powell edition, so in the notes below I sometimes cite from the Everyman edition instead of Hill-Powell.   [10] Hill-Powell, I, p. 7, n.2.

[11] John Courtenay, *Poetical Review of the Literary and Moral Character of the Late Samuel Johnson* (1786), introduction by Robert E. Kelley, Augustan Reprint Society, no. 133 (1969), p. 24.

[12] See Boswell on Steevens' and Reed's contributions to Johnson's *Lives of the Poets* (Hill-Powell, IV, p. 37); and Malone's letter to Percy on 2 March 1785 about the abortive Life of Goldsmith (*P–M Letters*, pp. 17–18).

[13] Hill-Powell, IV, p. 34. See Boswell's account of Johnson's reluctance to consult Lord Marchmont on Pope (Hill-Powell, III, pp. 342–44).

factual enough to make them reliable personal records. He also judged Johnson to be guilty of several political 'prejudices' in them, especially concerning Waller and Milton, that distorted his interpretations of character, though he believed that these 'prejudices ... do not appear to affect his criticism, which are [*sic*] in general in my opinion extremely just.'[14] Later, in the 1804 edition of Boswell's *Life of Johnson*, Malone also corrected Johnson's remark in his *Life of Pope* that Lord Marchmont had neglected Pope's papers. Malone told this to Johnson's face, but Johnson never made the correction. In a note to Boswell's passage on the matter in the 1804 edition of the *Life of Johnson*, Malone tactfully explained that Johnson's failure to correct the passage showed only his inattention to biographical detail: 'This neglect ... assuredly did not arise from any ill will towards Lord Marchmont, but from inattention; just as he neglected to correct his statement concerning the family of Thomson the poet, after it had been shewn to be erroneous.'[15] Malone corrected him on Thomson as well.

Malone also attempted some stylistic criticism of the *Lives*. Shying away from interpretive criticism, he did not analyse the prose itself but instead tried to understand how it was formed. He was more interested in how and why a style evolved than in getting into any detail about what that style was like. For example, in his journal, early in 1783, he thought that Johnson's prose in the *Lives* may have been influenced by the energetic and exuberant prose of Richard Hooker and Sir Thomas Browne. The prose 'has all the vigour and energy of the *Rambler*, without so much artificial niceness in the construction of the sentences, and without the hardness of phraseology that distinguishes that work.' Having been a student of Johnson's writing for years, he felt he knew enough to be able to describe how it developed, although he regretted he could not recover specimens of Johnson's juvenilia:

I should be glad to see some of his very earliest prose productions before he came to London, in order to ascertain whether from the first he adopted the style by which he has been so much distinguished ... I imagine there are three periods or epochs in his style. At first he was certainly simpler than afterwards. Between the years 1750 and 1758 his style was, I think, in its hardest and most laboured state. Of late, it is evidently improved.[16]

In February 1782, Malone invited Dr Johnson to his home to meet Dr Farmer, whose work on Shakespeare Johnson had long admired, but he was too ill to come. So far as we know, Johnson never visited Malone at his home. 'I have for many weeks been so much out of order', he wrote to Malone on 27 February, 'that I have gone out only in a coach to Mrs. Thrale's, where I can use all the freedom that sickness requires. Do not,

[14] *HMC*, XII, 10, pp. 344–45.   [15] Hill-Powell, IV, pp. 50–51, and 51, n. 2.
[16] Prior, 'Maloniana', pp. 341–42.

therefore take it amiss, that I am not with you and Dr Farmer. I hope hereafter to see you often.' In the meantime, Malone sent him a copy of his pamphlet on the young Thomas Chatterton's ingenious forgeries of the 'Rowley' poems and received in reply the second of only two surviving letters he had from Johnson.[17] When Boswell published both of them in the *Life of Johnson*, he confirmed 'the regard which Dr Johnson entertained for Mr. Malone, who the more he is known is the more highly valued' and remembered with regret that Johnson 'was prevented from sharing the elegant hospitality of that gentleman's table, at which he would in every respect have been fully gratified.'[18]

It was probably at Johnson's home in Bolt Court that on 15 March 1782 Malone had the conversation with Johnson that he recorded most completely. Boswell was in Scotland at the time, so he asked Malone by letter if he could find out from Johnson what his authority was for an anecdote about Joseph Addison's collection of a one-hundred-pound debt from Richard Steele by serving a legal action on him. Boswell's choice of Malone to query Johnson about a potentially delicate matter of sources suggests the confidence he had in Malone's tact and relationship with Johnson. Malone had no difficulty with Boswell's request, but wishing to draw out Johnson on the subject of biography, he mentioned that 'some people thought Mr. Addison's character was so pure, that the fact [about Steele's debt], *though true*, ought to have been suppressed.' Johnson vigorously rejected the argument. Stressing the ethical uses of biography, he replied that 'if nothing but the bright side of characters should be shewn, we should sit down in despondency, and think it utterly impossible to imitate them in *any thing*. The sacred writers ... related the vicious as well as the virtuous actions of men; which had this moral effect, that it kept mankind from *despair*.'[19]

Malone then turned the conversation to Pope. What would Dr Johnson think of his preparing a new edition of Pope's works?[20] Malone had thought of an edition of Marlowe and Nashe, or another of Shakespeare, and had been walking over to the British Museum almost every day to research Elizabethan and Jacobean drama; but he was tempted to turn his attention instead to Pope by Joseph Warton, Thomas' younger brother, whose just-published second volume of his *Essay on the Writings and Genius of Pope* Malone thought an abominable piece of scholarship.[21] He decided that a

[17] Hill-Powell, IV, p. 141.   [18] Ibid., p. 141.
[19] Ibid., pp. 52–53. See also Osborn, 'Edmond Malone and Dr. Johnson', in *Johnson, Boswell, and Their Circle*, ed. Mary Lascelles (1965), p. 6; and Malone on Johnson as biographer (Everyman *Life*, II, p. 352, n1).
[20] See James M. Osborn's brief note on Malone's interview with Johnson about Pope, *PMLA*, 50 (September 1935), 928–29.
[21] See Charlemont's dismissive remark to Malone about Joseph Warton on 4 October 1782 (*HMC*, XII, 10, pp. 420–21).

good new edition of Pope was needed, with a well researched biographical study. Johnson's *Life of Pope* was a fascinating literary study, but it was not factual enough; he had made little use of Lord Marchmont's recollections of Pope or even of the anecdotes about Pope compiled by Pope's friend Joseph Spence. As for Pope's editor Bishop William Warburton, Malone had little use for his scholarship on any subject, especially on Pope and Shakespeare. Years later, in October 1791, still contemplating the edition of Pope from which he had been distracted by other projects, he wrote critically to Johnson's friend, the Scottish judge and scholar Sir David Dalrymple (Lord Hailes), complaining about Warburton's effect on Pope scholarship.[22] Warburton became a recurring dunce in Malone's own personal book of fools, a prototype of the arrogant dullness which he believed the world of scholarship could well do without.

Johnson's reply to Malone's question turned out to be an important statement on the sanctity of an author's text, though Malone did not enjoy his praise of Warburton: 'He said he thought whatever *Warburton* had done ought to be *retained*. Add as much as you will to his notes but suppress nothing. He supposed that the new arrangement that W. had made of P's works was concerted between them before the death of Pope – & that therefore I had no right to alter it.' As for the correspondence, which Malone thought 'might be better arranged in the order of time', Johnson insisted that as Pope 'chose to class them as written to particular persons', they should remain that way. 'The most you have a right to do', Johnson admonished Malone, 'is by a table to direct how they may be most conveniently read.' His conclusion: 'An author's disposition of his own works is sacred, & an ed[ito]r has no right to vary it.'[23] Malone disagreed with much of this. That an editor should not add authentic works to a poet's canon simply because the poet himself and earlier editors had omitted them, was already anathema to him. He felt that once Pope, or Shakespeare, or Dryden, wrote a poem it became part of literary history and, regardless of the poet's desires, ought to be preserved and published.[24]

While Johnson's remarks cannot have encouraged him much, Malone nonetheless made a good many notes in the early 1780s towards a new edition of Pope. There is a notebook of his in the Bodleian Library devoted almost exclusively to Pope.[25] Many of the comments he wrote in it are responses to Johnson's *Life of Pope* and Warburton's edition. Other projects, however, soon took priority and made him set Pope aside for another time.

[22] 17 October 1791, National Library of Scotland.   [23] Ms. Malone 30, fols. 64–65.
[24] Malone was also sceptical over Johnson's assumptions regarding Pope's plans for his own published works (Pope notebook, Ms. Malone 30, fol. 85v).
[25] Ms. Malone 30. It is likely that Malone made a few of these notes in order to help Johnson with his writing of the *Life of Pope*.

3

Among Malone's earliest journal entries recording conversations with literary figures and noting his own observations on literature are accounts of several of his conversations with Johnson, transcriptions of which he gave to Boswell in the late 1780s. But the notes Malone gave Boswell did not turn up with the great discovery of the Boswell papers in Scotland and Ireland earlier this century, and the journal itself disappeared after James Prior used it for his biography of Malone in the middle of the nineteenth century. Only those portions of the journal that Prior included in his biography have come down to us, but what there is indicates that Malone venerated Johnson more than any other English literary figure. He was determined to preserve the memory of his idol and protect his achievements from the wilful and accidental distortion of a Johnson 'industry'.

One of Malone's earliest remarks in his journal, dated March 1783, concerns Johnson's conversation. Recalling their first meeting, he explains Johnson's brilliance as a conversationalist as well as anyone ever has. 'Dr. Johnson is as correct and elegant in his common conversation as in his writings', Malone writes; 'He never seems to study either for thoughts or words; and is on all occasions so fluent, so well-informed, so accurate, and even eloquent, that I never left his company without regret.' Reynolds had told him, he continues, that early in his life Johnson

laid it down, as a fixed rule, always to do his best *on every occasion* and in *every company*, to impart whatever he knew in the best language he could put it in; and that by constant practice, and never suffering any careless expression to escape him, or attempting to deliver his thoughts without arranging them, in the clearest manner he could, it was now become habitual to him.

Malone adds, 'When first introduced I was very young; yet he was as accurate in his conversation as if he had been talking to the first scholar in England. I have always found him very communicative; ready to give his opinion on any subject that was mentioned. He seldom however starts a subject himself; but it is very easy to lead him into one.'[26]

Malone also describes poignantly Johnson's courage, philosophy, and faith in the face of illness in an entry for June 1783: 'When Dr. Johnson was struck with the palsy a few days ago, after the first shock was over and he had time to recollect himself, he attempted to speak in English. Unable as he found himself to pronounce the words, he tried what he could do with Latin, but here found equal difficulty. He then attempted Greek, and could utter a few words, but slowly and with pain.' Driven to extremities but not forgetting his Maker, 'in the evening he called for paper, and wrote a *Latin*

[26] Prior, pp. 92–93.

Hymn, addressed to the Creator, the prayer of which was that so long as the Almighty should suffer him to live, he should be pleased to allow him the enjoyment of his understanding; that his intellectual powers and his body should expire together.' Malone's conclusion: 'a striking instance of fortitude, piety, and resignation!.'[27]

Since Johnson had been ill for some time and was not easily able to get out, he eagerly awaited the visits of his friends. He disliked being alone almost as much as he feared death. One winter day, Malone happened in on him hunched over some local history of Birmingham in front of his fire, before which apples were laid. When Malone asked him if the apples 'were preparing a medicine', Johnson replied, '"Why, no, sir; I believe they are only there because I want something to do. These are the solitary expedients to which we are driven by sickness."'[28]

4

Research trips and a visit to Ireland prevented Malone from attending The Club during the autumn and early spring of the next year, after which he and Johnson saw each other only three more times at Club dinners.[29] He did not record any of these, though at Johnson's last Club dinner on 22 June Boswell noted his 'manly fortitude' in not troubling the company with 'melancholy complaints', for he was in obvious pain and had to drag himself to get there.[30] The members who were present had no way of knowing, of course, that this was Johnson's last appearance at The Club.

When Johnson died on 13 December 1784, Malone promptly wrote a long, eulogistic obituary for the *Gentleman's Magazine*, the most detailed and accurate that appeared in any of the London papers. Linking Johnson and Shakespeare, he describes the former as 'a man of the most stupendous mind, (for no weaker epithet is adequate to its powers) that has appeared in this century, or perhaps will appear for a century to come. His writings, like those of Shakespeare and a few others will certainly be read with admiration as long as the English language shall remain.'[31] Two days after Johnson's death, Malone received a letter from his friend John Byng, passing on an account of Johnson's last hours which he had been given by William Windham's servant. This letter is the best surviving record of Johnson's last night, and it must have been gratifying to Malone that Boswell, to whom Malone showed it, decided to include it in his *Life of Johnson*.[32] Another sign of Malone's intimacy with Johnson and complete

---

[27] Prior, 'Maloniana', pp. 359–60.
[28] Prior, p. 7; cited also in Hill-Powell, IV, p. 218, n. 1.
[29] These dinners were on 27 April, 25 May, and 22 June 1784.
[30] Hill-Powell, IV, p. 326.   [31] *Gentleman's Magazine*, LIV (December 1784), 899–911.
[32] Hill-Powell, IV, pp. 418–19.

acceptance into his circle is that in the funeral procession to Westminster Abbey he, Burney, and Steevens rode in the first coach after the one carrying Johnson's executors.[33]

As a postscript to Malone's veneration of Johnson, second only to his idolatry of Shakespeare, I may cite the lady who visited him around 1804 and remarked:

Next to Shakspeare, Dr Johnson appeared to be the great object of his admiration. He had often visited him in Bolt Court, and in a morning's stroll took me to view the exterior of the house. On one occasion, the doctor, during the decline of his health, proving unusually silent, Malone rose to retire, believing him to be in pain or his presence inconvenient. 'Pray, sir,', [sic] said Johnson, 'be seated. I cannot talk, but I like to see you there.' On two or three occasions, also, he [Malone] had managed the breakfast tea-kettle when Levett [one of the longtime residents in Johnson's house] was absent or otherwise engaged. Mr. Malone had several engravings of Dr Johnson in his study.[34]

As the years passed and fewer of Johnson's friends remained to recall their conversations with him, Malone became increasingly nostalgic. The house in Bolt Court and other Johnsonian sites took on for him an almost sacred character and became shrines in his literary imagination.

Long before Johnson's death, Malone had made up his mind to do what he could to sustain and perpetuate the memory of the man, his work, and his wisdom.[35] His subsequent aid and encouragement to Boswell was part of his commitment, and he defended Johnson in the press, corrected misrepresentations and distortions whenever they appeared in the several biographies, and became the most energetic supporter of The Club. He also supervised the raising of a monument to Johnson's memory. He wanted it to be the Enlightenment's complement to the Shakespeare monument dedicated in Westminster Abbey in 1741. He organized the subscriptions and design for the statue and saw to it that the inscription on it reflected Johnson's (especially literary) achievements. The lengthy process of setting up the monument turned out, however, to be in many ways agonizing and disappointing.

5

Soon after Reynolds, in the spring of 1785, proposed the idea of a monument to be set up in Westminster Abbey, he asked Malone to help him raise the money for it.[36] But few except Club members were willing to

---

[33] On the funeral, see the *Gentleman's Magazine*, LIV (December 1784), 947.

[34] Prior, pp. 90–91.

[35] See Malone on the Johnson 'industry' two months after Johnson's death, which included Steevens who 'loves bush-firing' (*P–M Letters*, pp. 18–22).

[36] On the monument, see Peter Martin, 'Edmond Malone, Sir Joshua Reynolds, and Dr Johnson's Monument in St Paul's Cathedral', *The Age of Johnson*, ed. Paul Korshin, III (1989), pp. 331–51. See also Hill-Powell, IV, Appendix I, pp. 464–72.

contribute. 'Though two years have elapsed since Dr Johnson's death', Malone complained to Percy in September 1786, 'and a subscription was immediately opened for the purpose of erecting a monument for him, and the Club fixed the subscription at the low sum of *two* guineas, yet not a single subscriber but two has appeared (except the members of The Club themselves) tho' the proposals were hung up for some months in three or four great booksellers shops.' This should not have surprised him, he added, since he had met with little success outside The Club in raising subscriptions for a new edition of Goldsmith that Percy was then planning – 'so difficult is it to extract even a small sum out of people's pockets for any object whatsoever.' Two years later, to get things moving, Reynolds favoured a benefit play, but Malone liked the less public and more 'honourable mode' of each Club member procuring five subscribers at two pounds each.[37] Malone's idea prevailed, but Reynolds' may have been better, for the money merely trickled in and after four years only two hundred pounds had been received.

By 1789 Club members began to disagree about the sort of monument the sculptor John Bacon should be asked to create. In February, Malone indignantly told Banks: 'To answer all the cavils that may be made either with respect to the sum expended on Dr. Johnson's monument or the design of it w[oul]d be a vain attempt. One man w[oul]d have a picture in mosaick; another a bust; another a statue; and a fourth neither bust nor statue, but emblematical figures.' Some thought a full-length statue would be grotesque, but that was silly since 'Johnson's limbs were so far from being unsightly that they were uncommonly well formed, & in the most exact & true proportion.' Even if they were not, 'what would it signify? The scheme is not to set up an Antinous, but to transmit to posterity a true & perfect exhibition of the entire man.'[38] Reynolds, who this time agreed with Malone, eventually carried the day on that point, so that by the end of the year it was agreed that six hundred pounds would be spent to have Bacon produce a full-length statue.[39]

Malone finally solved the financial problem early in 1790. According to Boswell, at a special public meeting at Thomas' Tavern in Dover Street on 5 January 1790, Malone, though in a 'strange agitation', 'pertinently and genteelly' addressed the problem.[40] In a letter to Percy in 1803 Malone recalled what happened. He claimed that the monument would never have been erected had he not 'struck out the scheme of forming a Committee of eight, and directing a circular letter to about 200 persons, selected from all

[37] *P–M Letters*, p. 31. On The Club's plans to raise money for the monument, see Duff, *The Club* (1905), p. 8; and Duff, *Annals of The Club* (1914), p. 32.

[38] Banks Corr., Natural History Museum, Department of Botany, 26 h. 8.

[39] See Boswell's letter of 30 November 1789 to William Temple about the meeting in which this question was resolved, Hill-Powell, IV, pp. 465–66.

[40] *Boswell 1789–95*, p. 28 (*Malahide*, XVIII, pp. 15–16).

the Nobility, Gentry, & Scholars of the Kingdom, who were likely to patronise and forward such a measure.'[41] With Banks, Burke, Reynolds, Malone, Boswell, Metcalfe, and Windham on the committee, its frequent meetings produced, in Boswell's words, 'more good-living than business',[42] but eventually seven hundred pounds were raised from one hundred and sixty persons.

Nevertheless, Malone could scarcely believe how many outright refusals to contribute he had received. Cynically, he remarked to Percy, 'you cannot well conceive, when money is to be got from gentlemen, and the application is to be made *by a gentleman*, how many delays & obstructions there are ... I have somewhere among my papers about 40 letters of *absolute denials* from the band of 200 above mentioned; many of them very considerable names.'[43] He thought one of the most paltry contributions was Mrs Hester Piozzi's, who as the former Mrs Thrale for many years had been an intimate friend of Johnson's and in 1786 translated that friendship into the highly successful *Anecdotes of the Late Samuel Johnson*. Malone and Boswell, among others, were angered by her distortion of many facts about Johnson in the *Anecdotes*, so Malone nurtured some animosity towards her anyway. Initially, she sent two guineas for the monument, but with the subscriptions going so badly over the next few years, Malone increasingly resented what he interpreted as her selfishness. He wrote to her again for more money with thinly veiled contempt, and in February 1790, she replied to him using the stiffly formal third person, justifying herself but sending more money:

Mrs. Piozzi sends her Com[pliment]s to Mr. Malone, assuring him that She has already subscribed two Guineas for this Purpose and has now sent three more to make up five. Mr Cator of the Adelphi who interested himself in their Affairs while abroad, wrote Mr Piozzi word in August 1785 that Sir Joshua Reynolds would accept only two Guineas from any one; and that he had paid it in Mrs Piozzi's Name. – Mr Cator said too that he had sent in the same little Sum for each of the Miss Thrales to whom he is Guardian.

Her letter left him cold. He pasted it in his edition of her *Anecdotes* as more evidence of what he saw as her flawed character and judgment, acidly writing on it, 'The Committeee appointed to solicit Subscriptions for Dr Johnson's Monument, applied, among others, to Mrs Piozzi, who had gained 500*l* by this book, and 600*l* by publishing his Letters. The above was the answer sent to me by this worthless woman, together with the mighty sum of *three* Guineas.'[44]

Mrs Piozzi's contribution aside, this incident highlights Malone's temper, his impatience and anger with people who did not live up to his own ideas

---

[41] Malone to Percy, 8 February 1803, *P–M Letters*, p. 143 (Ms. Malone 26, fol. 60; cited in Hill-Powell, IV, p. 467).   [42] *Boswell 1789–95*, p. 34 (*Malahide*, XVIII, p. 21).
[43] *P–M Letters*, p. 143.   [44] Hill-Powell, IV, pp. 467–68.

of how homage should be paid to great literary figures. Throughout the 1780s, his temper frequently shows in the vocabulary he adopts to put down people with whom he disagrees. At such times, he steps out of character as a mild-mannered and clubbable companion. In his defence, we should realize that he saw Mrs Piozzi, who of all people he thought should have cherished the memory of Johnson, as trifling with one of his two main literary icons.

Reynolds complicated the monument enterprise in March 1791, when Malone was in Ireland, by deciding that the monument should not, as was planned, be erected in Westminster Abbey, which he said was already 'stuffd with statuary' and congested with 'a squeeze of tombs', but in St Paul's. Banks relayed to Malone Reynolds' feeling that St Paul's, on the other hand, 'has hitherto lain fallow for the harvest of the chisel.' The monument would do a greater honour to the arts at St Paul's where it could be bigger, be seen more clearly, and encourage more sculpture. Burke was for the idea, although (as Banks put it to Malone) he waggishly quipped that this would be 'Borrowing from Peter to give to Paul.'[45] Malone's conservatism and trust in the ennobling aura of historical precedents and tradition were evident in his determined opposition to the idea. He wrote to Boswell from Dublin on 14 April: 'A cenotaph in one church, and Johnson's body in another, *in the same town*, is surely a monumental solecism. Besides five centuries will not give St. Pauls the venerable grandeur and respectability that belongs to the old Cathedral.'[46]

If Malone had read Reynolds' *A Journey to Flanders and Holland* (1781), he should not have been surprised by his strong preference for St Paul's. In his 'Account' of Reynolds, which prefaced his edition of the artist's writings in 1797, he took note of Reynolds' lament in his *Journey* over the languishing state of sculpture in England. Reynolds wrote:

Almost the only demand for considerable works of sculpture arise from the monuments erected to eminent men. It is to be regretted that this circumstance does not produce such an advantage to the art as it might do, if, instead of Westminster Abbey, the custom were once begun of having monuments to departed worth erected in St. Paul's Cathedral.

The Abbey was already full, he complained, 'so stuck up in odd holes and corners, that it begins to appear truly ridiculous: the principal places have been long occupied ... '. In the meantime, St Paul's 'looks forlorn and desolate, or at least destitute of ornaments suited to the magnificence of the

[45] See Banks's letter to Malone in Ireland, 27 March 1791, BL Add. Ms. 22549, fols. 1–2; and Hill-Powell, IV, p. 468.

[46] *The Correspondence of James Boswell with David Garrick, Edmund Burke, and Edmond Malone*, eds. Peter S. Baker, Thomas W. Copeland, George M. Kahrl, Rachel McClellan, and James M. Osborn. *The Yale Editions of the private papers of James Boswell, research edition: Correspondence*, vol. 4 (1986), p. 419.

fabric.' The only reason Reynolds had gone along with the original idea of the monument in the Abbey was that Johnson was buried there. Eventually, Malone was converted, as he acknowledges in a note to Reynolds' passage in his *Journey*:

Our author considered the plan which he has here sketched, as likely to be extremely beneficial to the Arts, and was so desirous that it should be carried into execution, that after it had been determined to erect a monument to Dr Johnson in Westminster Abbey, and a place had been assigned for that purpose, he exerted all his influence with his friends, to induce them to relinquish the scheme proposed, and to consent that the monument of that excellent man should be erected in St. Paul's; where it has since been placed. – In conformity with these sentiments, our author was buried in that cathedral; in which, I trust, monuments to him and to his illustrious friend, Mr. Burke, will ere long be erected.[47]

Reynolds' offer to pay for extra costs, not his arguments about the promotion of sculpture in England, persuaded Malone and other Club members to accept St Paul's.[48] Bacon began his work on the monument soon after.

In the meantime, a decision had to be made about an appropriate Latin inscription. This posed problems because of Johnson's varied career and achievements, but the matter was turned into something of a pedantic farce, one that irritated Malone, by Reynolds' choice in 1791, without the committee's knowledge, of Dr Samuel Parr, a pedagogue and schoolmaster, to write it.[49] Parr certainly had the right credentials for the job: he had a great reputation as a writer of epitaphs and as a classicist and student of lapidary verses. But he appeared to nurture a grievance against The Club, conceivably because he had been blackballed in 1786. He unhelpfully tried to force an inscription on the committee that Malone and others believed underplayed Johnson's achievements. The matter was not resolved until 1795 when, in his capacity as principal judge of the inscription and after several blunt letters to Parr, Malone won the day. The monument was at last unveiled to the public in February 1796. Malone at last had his Johnsonian shrine. At the same time as the Johnson monument was being completed, Malone was busy preparing the edition of Reynolds' writings which, after another protracted and frustrating period of fund raising and many wrangles over procedure, he would publish in 1797. The edition would eventually help pay for the artist's own monument, set up near Johnson's beneath the dome of St Paul's.

---

[47] *Works... [with] An Account of the Life and Writings of the author*, ed. Edmond Malone, 2nd. edn. (1798), I, pp. lxv-lxvi.
[48] See the *Public Advertiser* (20 April), Hill-Powell, IV, p. 469; and Malone's remark to Percy thirteen years later (*P–M Letters*, p. 143).
[49] See Warren Derry, *Dr Parr* (1966), chap. VII.

4

Courtship, books, forgeries, and Horace Walpole

1

Malone could not, in spite of his active scholarly and social life, shake off his depression over Susanna Spencer. He was restless: 'I endeavour to employ my thoughts with books and writing, and when I am weary of them fly into company', he confided in Charlemont on 8 January 1782, 'and then, disgusted with that, return back to the other; but all will not do.' He could not get over 'an attachment that has continued with unabated force for thirteen years; nor at my time of life [he is forty-one] is the heart very easily captivated by a new object.'[1] Her whereabouts are unknown during these years, though by 1801 she was living in Grosvenor Square, and by 1805 she was probably at a madhouse in Hoxton. Malone settled an annuity on her,[2] but he seldom visited her. Her condition became progressively desperate; she wrote to him on 1 January 1805: 'It wou'd have been much better had you suffered me to die[.] Do not answer this letter. I hope soon to be better and will then write again.'[3]

In spite of his telling Charlemont that at his age his heart was not 'easily captivated', he was unhappy living alone: 'I am a very domestic kind of animal, and not at all adapted for solitude, and indeed have been peculiarly unfortunate.'[4] He needed a wife. Only a few months after writing to Charlemont about Susanna Spencer, one of his best prospects for marriage presented herself in the person of Sarah Loveday, a charming and beautiful woman from Caversham twenty years younger than he and the daughter of John Loveday the antiquarian and friend of Malone's.[5] They

---

[1] *HMC*, XII, 10, p. 394.
[2] In February 1781, Malone settled an annuity of £100 on Susanna Spencer, which he raised to £750 in November 1801. See his will, 17 November 1801 (PRO, PROB 11/1533, ff. LH 276–RH 277). See also Ms. Malone 37, fols. 24–25.
[3] 1 January 1805, Ms. Malone 38, fol. 177–78.
[4] Malone to Charlemont, 19 November 1782 (*HMC*, XII, 10, p. 421).
[5] I am greatly indebted to Sarah Markham, who has kindly allowed me to use extracts from the Loveday family papers. See her recent book on Sarah Loveday and her sister Penelope in *A Testimony of Her Times* (1991); and her portrait of their father, John Loveday, *John Loveday of Caversham 1711–1789: The Life and Times of an Eighteenth-Century Onlooker* (1984).

probably met on a seaside holiday in Weymouth during the summer of 1782, where he visited for a couple of months or more in the company of the family of John Byng, who later became his close friend and fellow member of The Club. Sarah Loveday was a member of the party. Windham, a good friend of Byng's who had been visiting the Lovedays at Caversham at least since 1774, may have suggested the idea so that Malone could have a complete break from study and rest his eyes for a while.

Byng joined the party on 26 August for about a fortnight, not especially looking forward to the pleasures of Weymouth, for as he put it in his diary for that date, possibly alluding to Malone's presence, the place had become 'the resort of the giddy and gay; where the Irish beau, the gouty peer, and the genteel shopkeeper, blend in folly and fine breeding.' By that time, Malone (whom Byng did not yet know) had fallen under Sarah's spell and a late summer romance had begun. On 28 August, when he first met Malone, Byng was amused by his distraction over her: 'we met Mr M[alone] a very civil gentleman, an attendant on our set, and seeming to have a particular kindness for my charge.' The next day Byng had to escort her on the beach 'to defend my charge (S. L.) from any violent attacks of the Irish volunteer.' Byng took an immediate liking to Malone and appears to have put in a good word for him to Sarah, describing him as 'an Irish gentleman of (strange to tell) diffident, sensible manners; and deeply smitten with our little Sally.'[6]

Sarah Loveday would have been an excellent catch for Malone. Not only was she supremely beautiful – young men used to go out of their way simply to catch a glimpse of her face – and of a family well liked by friends of his, but she was also a gentle girl of twenty-one accustomed to houses with good libraries and relatives with antiquarian interests. The Loveday home in Caversham always seemed full of conversation about literature and history. On the other hand, devoted to his books, spending much of his time in the British Museum, and frequently reading well into the night in his study, he could not be said to have been an ideal husband for her.

In a few verses which he scribbled in his diary on 2 September, Byng described an excursion which the whole holiday party took to a well-known local spring, on which Malone and a Colonel Yorke appear to have been especially attentive to Sarah:

> It is well known
> York, Byng, Malone
> Do lovely Sally bring
> After her dip
> To take a sip
> ... Of Upway's noted spring.[7]

[6] The Hon. John Byng (later 5th Viscount Torrington), *The Torrington Diaries*, ed. C. Bruyn Andrews (1934) I, pp. 87, 89, 92, 94–95, 101–2.   [7] *The Torrington Diaries*, I, p. 96.

But Malone's attentions spoiled the holiday for both him and Sarah. Very happy in her own family, she did not really want to marry. Naturally cheerful and gregarious, she told Malone she had 'no mind to matrimony.' Furthermore, during those first few days at Weymouth he became too ardent. That could explain a so-called 'Irish stare' which, as Windham observed, writing poignantly to Mrs Byng from Weymouth eighteen years later, was one of the reasons he lost her favour:

Here we are breakfasting at the hotel, and looking out upon the beach where you used to figure, if I mistake not, attended by your Major Yorke and other gallants. Poor Malone, too, who by an unfortunate Irish stare, not at all belonging to his character, lost the favour of a woman who might have made him happy, and probably herself too.[8]

Malone's ardour, and the consequent difficulty he had of talking naturally to Sarah, are themes in a poem he wrote to her during their courtship. It seems one of her other suitors, who Malone claims did not love her as deeply as he did, had composed admiring verses to her with ease – verses which Malone dismissed as superficial and shallow. The 'glow' of his own 'real passion' could never be captured by such 'studied phrase', either in verse or conversation. As he implies in the following verses, it is up to her to appreciate and understand that,

> If Waller's Lyre, or Prior's Muse,
> Or tender Hammond's lays were mine,
> The softest, sweetest verse I'd choose
> And Sacharissa's praise were thine.
>
> But artificial was their strain
> No lovely Delia e'er they knew,
> Of what was unreal they complain
> Successful most, when most untrue.
>
> At ease the unimpression'd heart
> In truthful son may sportive deal,
> But vain the Poet's boasted art
> When love's diviner power we feel.[9]

She undoubtedly could tell, from his behaviour if not from these verses, that he was genuinely fond of her and that the 'Irish stare', whatever that was, was uncharacteristic of him. But he was not practised in the art of courtship and pursued her too intensely. He even proposed to her in Weymouth. In order to slow things down, she declined his invitation to some social event. He was, in turn, hurt by her 'guarded caution'. 'How, my dear Miss Loveday', he wrote, 'have I deserved that you should treat me with such

---

[8] August 1800, *The Windham Papers*, ed. the Earl of Rosebery (1913), II, p. 160.
[9] 'An apology for not following the example of a Poet who had address'd some lines to S. L.' (transcribed into a book of verses by Penelope Loveday, who identifies the lines as Malone's; Loveday Family Papers).

marked unkindess?' Had he ever embarrassed her or her friends with
'importunate, unavailing solicitations'? Perhaps their mutual friend Byng
had urged him on her 'with too much partiality'? He asked only to be
treated like a close friend, 'whose only offence has been the aspiring to a
happiness that he did not deserve, who is at least entitled to your pity, and
who, be assured, is sufficiently unhappy without the additional weight that
you have now laid upon him, by making him believe he is the object not
merely of indifference, but of aversion.' Not very gracefully, he signed the
letter, 'the unfortunate E. M.'. She replied with more confidence and grace
that it never occurred to her he could act with anything but 'delicacy' and
good taste. She confessed feelings of the 'head and heart' for him but was
surprised 'to have been *so misunderstood.*' In a second letter to her at
Weymouth, he charged her with 'distinguished coldness'; his affections
were not 'of that commodious and manageable kind that is so often found
in the world.' He added, somewhat pompously one fears, that he had taken
too much of her time, but he knew that, his heart being what it is, his fate
'is decided for life.' She had sentenced him for life to a 'cheerless solitude.'
This self-pitying, humourless letter was not, on the whole, well calculated
to make her change her mind.

Unhappily, then, for Malone, nothing came of his courtship. He visited
Caversham the following year, probably in July, where he may have seen
her again, but it was her elder sister, Penelope, who subsequently saw more
of him than Sarah did at the homes of friends in London.[10] When he died,
Penelope pasted a newspaper account of him into her diary of June 1812
with a passage from Shakespeare that she thought applied to him: 'His life
was gentle, and elements so mixed in him, that Nature might stand up and
say to all the world, "This was a Man"!' In the following retrospective
extract in the year of his death, she explained how such a man could fail to
win her sister:

Mr Malone possessed mild and truly amiable manners; and his flow of agreeable
conversation was enriched by a well stored and accomplished mind. The almost
affectionate degree of cordial and gratifying attention that he shewed me in our too
infrequent meetings, and the sincere esteem I had for his virtues, has made me feel
as if I had really lost a valued relation. Such he would have been to me many years
ago had my sister Sarah consented to accept his addresses. The ardour of his
attachment, and its being so strongly marked out before a large and mixed party
assembled at a sea-bathing place, where they first met, distressed and embarrassed
her extremely, as her positive refusal had not put a stop to his assiduities and
pointed attentions. She therefore felt it absolutely necessary to put a painful force
on her nature, and to maintain a settled reserve of manner to a person whose society

[10] Sarah Markham has supplied me with correct transcriptions of the Malone–Loveday letters,
which were published by Winifred Hoper (inaccurately) in 'Some Unpublished Windham
Papers', *The 19th Century and After* (1919), 86, 673–74. The following citations from the
correspondence are taken from the Loveday Papers.

as a friend would otherwise have been acceptable to her. Under the mistaken impression of her having been unnecessarily frigid, he wrote letters which with her answer she shewed me, and I without her knowledge preserved.[11]

Malone would have only one more good chance to marry. As for Sarah, although she received several offers of marriage, she remained single, tragically becoming an invalid. Indeed, one of the reasons she never married may have been her suspicion that her health would deteriorate. Malone wrote of her in a letter to his sister, Catherine, eighteen years later: Mrs Windham had just visited 'her friend Benwell (Pen. Loveday that was) who was a wife but six weeks,[12] and has been two or three years a widow. Sally lives with her, and is unable to go up or down stairs, or to move in any way abroad but in one of Merlin's chairs in a garden: a martyr to the stone.'[13] She outlived him by many years, however, dying in 1832.

As Windham and Penelope Loveday both testified, the romance did not bear fruit largely because of misunderstandings on both sides, but the episode reveals elements in Malone's nature that sometimes urged him to behave in a manner likely to be misunderstood. Sarah was surprised at his reading of her conduct, but she could not see that he was not one to play coy or engage in social rituals without saying exactly what he thought. It upset him if he imagined others were behaving less candidly than he; hence his letter accusing her of insensitivity and unkindness. It was an uncompromising thing to say, but, in spite of himself, in spite of the tenderness he felt for her, he said it. At a deeper level, well out of sight of his social intercourse, there was an adversarial streak that told him if she was not for him, she must be against him. He concealed this streak far less in the realm of literature and politics; it was not often that he took kindly to criticism, even of a constructive kind. In his scholarly work, he had the self-assurance of right being on his side by virtue of superior knowledge and research. Moreover, any sign of animosity, dishonesty, deception, and misrepresentation mingling in his opponents' criticism would ignite his temper and impel him to say things in society and in print that surprised and confused his critics. The Sarah Loveday episode illustrated that his mild manner could easily turn to aggressiveness if he thought that he, 'the unfortunate E. M.', was the victim of unfairness or injustice. It is perhaps an idle question, though nonetheless an intriguing one, to wonder whether matrimony would have reduced this paranoia and thus had a tempering effect on his relations with other critics.

News of this disappointment at the age of forty-one saddened Malone's

[11] Markham, *A Testimony of Her Times*, p. 101. Sarah Markham has in her possession a copy of Malone's *Biographical Memoir of the late Right Honourable William Windham* (1810), on the flyleaf of which Penelope wrote: 'Written by Mr Malone, my much valued friend.'

[12] She had been married eleven, not six, weeks.

[13] 4 December 1800, Ms. Malone 38, fol. 6.

family. To his sisters Kitty and Hattie, who knew that their brother badly
needed domestic attention – mostly for his health – and wrote regularly
admonishing him to take better care of himself, this was a great chance lost,
perhaps the last chance. He resigned himself to a life of bachelorhood with
as much philosophy as he could muster – and a tinge of bitterness.

2

The regimen that in January 1782, Malone remarked, occupied most of his
thoughts and made his life, before and after Sarah Loveday, less unbearable
included books, writing, and good society. He did not mention the theatre
but that was an oversight, for he had loved it since moving to London, and
even before that on his visits. He attended plays regularly and made friends
with the leading actors and actresses, especially John Philip Kemble and his
sister the tragic actress Mrs Sarah Siddons, successors to Garrick, whose
London careers began in 1782–83.[14]

Malone became acquainted with Kemble and Mrs Siddons in the
autumn of 1781 through his part in preparing *The Count of Narbonne* for the
stage, a tragedy written by his boyhood friend Robert Jephson. Jephson
had already written two plays, one of which, *The Law of Lombardy*, Malone
had helped revise for publication in 1779. Sometime in 1781 or 1782, when
he was supplying Isaac Reed with biographical material on Jephson for his
Biographica Dramatica, Malone recalled Steevens' unkind criticism of *The
Law of Lombardy*, attributing it to jealousy of himself: 'All this abuse of the
Law of Lombardy was written by Mr. George Steevens, for no other reason
but because the author Mr Jephson was my intimate friend.'[15] Malone
arranged for *The Count of Narbonne* to be acted at Drury Lane and for Mrs
Siddons and Kemble to take the leading parts. He also helped revise it and
wrote an epilogue, extravagantly praised by Jephson – 'I do not suppose
there are more than three in the language that come near it.'[16]

An unexpected result of Malone's efforts to get the play staged was the
start of a friendship with Horace Walpole. Walpole had written the
epilogue to Jephson's earlier tragedy, *Braganza* (1775), and found himself
working with Jephson again, not entirely to his liking, on *The Count of
Narbonne*. Jephson, who had borrowed several ideas for his play from
Walpole's *Castle of Otranto*, sought his advice about revisions and ended up
dedicating the play to him. Malone and Walpole therefore became

[14] See *The Diary of Joseph Farington*, ed. Kenneth Garlick and Angus Macintyre, vols. I–VI; ed. Kathryn Cave vols. VII–XVI continuing (1978), XI, p. 4044, for Malone on Mrs Siddons as a better tragic than comic actress. See also Jonathan Bate, *Shakespearean Constitutions*, pp. 34–37, 136–43.
[15] Malone wrote this on a cancelled sheet in Isaac Reed's *Biographica Dramatica* (1782) that contained a sharp attack on the play (vol. 2, p. 185).
[16] Jephson's remark and Malone's epilogue are cited in Prior, pp. 80–81.

collaborators of a sort, though in its early stages their friendship had its awkward moments. To begin with, Malone had written an angry letter (now lost) to Thomas Harris, Manager of Covent Garden, complaining of his excessive haste in presenting *The Count of Narbonne*. It took all of Walpole's tact as peacemaker to keep the resentful Harris from taking the play off. 'My finesse was nearly *derouté* by an Irish head', he told The Revd. William Mason on 13 November 1781, alluding to Malone's Irish temper.[17] Also, Jephson resisted Walpole's proposed revisions of the play as well as his ideas for staging it, and Malone was unwillingly caught in the middle. Not fond of the public aspects of the theatre in any case, Walpole was glad to wash his hands of the play: 'I have been plagued about Mr Jephson's play ... though it has succeeded perfectly, the author is dissatisfied. I had four sides last week, and tonight another letter of eight pages to scold me for letting the statue on the tomb be cumbent instead of erect, in short I do not wonder he is a poet for he is distracted – he shall act his next play himself for me.' 'I brought it into the world', he told a friend after the opening night, and 'was well delivered of it; it can stand on its own legs, and I am going back to my own quiet hill [Strawberry Hill in Twickenham], never likely to have anything more to do with the theatre.'[18] He also told Malone bluntly: 'I confess I think Mr. Jephson too tenacious ... I would not for the world say one thing to you and another to Mr. Jephson ... You have shown yourself so zealous a friend to him, and I hope have found me so too.'[19]

Malone was pleased with Walpole's cordiality towards him. 'I have lately become acquainted with your friend, Mr. Walpole', Malone proudly informed Charlemont in January 1782, 'and am quite charmed with him. There is an unaffected benignity and good nature in his manner that is, I think, irresistibly engaging. He is now employed in reprinting his "Anecdotes of painting", in 8 vo., without plates, the book having become very scarce and extravagantly dear' – to the third edition of that work, on Walpole's request, Malone contributed some historical notes on Van Dyck.[20] Charlemont was delighted: 'I am exceedingly glad that you are acquainted with my very much beloved friend Mr Walpole, as I am sure you must love him, and that consequently a connexion with him must contribute to your Happiness.'[21]

Malone's friendship with Walpole survived Jephson, lasting until Walpole died in 1797 at the age of seventy-nine although it never ripened into intimacy. Not fond of Dr Johnson, Walpole never joined The Club. In his later years, he lived privately at his famous house, Strawberry Hill, a

---

[17] *The Yale Edition of Horace Walpole's Correspondence*, ed. W. S. Lewis, vol. XXIX, p. 26.
[18] 26 November 1781, *Walpole Corr.*, XXIX, p. 167.   [19] Prior, pp. 83–85.
[20] 8 January 1782, *HMC*, XII, 10, pp. 394–95. Walpole acknowledged Malone's help in the edition, *Anecdotes*, 3rd. edn. (5 vols. 1782), II, p. 162.
[21] C. February, 1782, *HMC*, XII, 10, p. 396.

place of iconographic importance on the Thames which Malone visited at least twice, first in 1784 and again with his sisters in 1785. In his journal, Malone conjectured whether Walpole, who was a 'Fribble' – one who behaved frivolously – when he first came to London in 1746, was Garrick's model for Fribble in his play, *Miss in Her Teens*. He then wrote this sketch:

This gentleman (Mr. Walpole) is still somewhat singular in appearance; but it seems only a singularity arising from a very delicate and weak constitution, and from living quite retired among his books, and much with ladies. He is always lively and ingenious; never very solid or energetic. He appears to be very fond of French manners, authors, etc. etc., and I believe keeps up to this day a correspondence with many of the people of fashion in Paris. His love of French manners, and his reading so much of their language, have I think infected his style a little, which is not always so entirely English as it ought to be. He is, I think, a very humane and amiable man.[22]

3

In the early days of his career in London, as he was establishing a reputation, Malone was also actively collecting books, especially early English drama. In doing so, he followed in the footsteps of scholars like Warburton, Capell, Steevens, Reed, and Percy, whose large collections were crucial to their editorial and textual work in Shakespeare and early English literature. He was also following the examples of Langbaine and Oldys, who inspired him bibliographically, and especially Garrick. His appetite for early editions of plays was insatiable, as is evident from his correspondence with Lord Charlemont. And he bought for others as well as for himself, always alert for volumes for, among others, Percy, Windham, Denis Daly, and, especially, Charlemont. He undertook to build a library of sixteenth- and seventeenth-century English drama and poetry for Charlemont, who, like his other Irish friends, could not attend the London book auctions where the most highly prized items came onto the market. Their letters from 1779 tell a fascinating story of enthusiastic and informed bibliophiles with money to spend hunting for rare volumes in an age when excellent private libraries were becoming more common and competition for old books at the auctions was becoming fierce. Malone rarely missed an important auction over the next thirty years, so Charlemont was happy to place large sums at his disposal.[23] Charlemont knew what he wanted, but from the start Malone found far more for him than he had ever thought of buying. It was an expensive business, as Malone was at pains to explain,[24]

---

[22] Prior, pp. 86–87. On Walpole's relationship with Malone, see J. M. Osborn, 'Horace Walpole and Edmond Malone', in *Horace Walpole: Writer, Politician, and Connoisseur*, ed. W. H. Smith (1967), pp. 299–324.

[23] For an account of Malone's book collecting, see J. M. Osborn, 'Edmond Malone: Scholar–Collector', *Transactions of the Bibliographical Society*, XIX (1964), 11–37.

[24] See Malone to Charlemont, 5 April 1779, on the 'exorbitant' prices of books (*HMC*, XII, 10, pp. 342–45).

but by 1780 Charlemont was thoroughly caught up in the passion for collecting, 'a passion which the spleen of wisdom may brand with the title of folly', he told Malone, 'but which I will boldly avow and boast of, since I possess it in common with you.'[25]

The auction of Topham Beauclerk's library, which began on 9 April 1781, was a good example of the fierce competition Malone had to contend with. Beauclerk had been one of Dr Johnson's dearest friends and an original member of The Club. Malone thought him one of his chief rivals as a collector, telling Charlemont on one occasion: 'He is a most formidable antagonist. He stands much in my way and yours also in the purchase of old trumpery. He sends his servant by six or seven in the morning to the booksellers on the day of their sale, and runs away with everything rare.'[26] When he died in 1780 at the age of forty-one, he left about thirty thousand volumes, one of the largest private collections in England. At the auction, which lasted forty-nine days, Malone had a sterling chance to acquire what he had lost to Beauclerk in earlier sales. But he was thwarted again, as he told Charlemont on 18 June, this time by the exorbitant prices created by the current fashion to possess old volumes and by, as he put it, ignorant buyers who threw their money around indiscriminately:

The rage for all sorts of ancient English literature is so great at present that all books of that kind went extremely high. Mr. Garrick having made a collection of old plays, every manager [of a theatre] now thinks it necessary to do the same. Mr. [Thomas] Harris, of Covent Garden, has now commenced collector, and having a great deal of money, and, as it should seem, not much wit, employed a very ignorant fellow to purchase for him, who gave most extravagant prices, and seemed to have no other rule than to bid more than any one else. In consequence of this, I picked up very few plays there, either for you or myself.[27]

The reference to Garrick is apt, for he was the best informed and most extensive collector of early English drama of the age. His example for other actor-managers, including Malone's friend John Henderson, to assemble their own dramatic libraries was considerable; and his collection of Shakespeare quartos, part of the huge gift he left to the British Museum, was the only one that exceeded Malone's at the time of the latter's death.[28] As Malone saw it, Garrick had driven prices up precipitously by making book collecting fashionable.

4

In the world of antiquarian enthusiasm where there could be exciting discoveries of rare books like *The Taming of A Shrew*, which Malone found at

[25] 11 January, *HMC*, XII, 10, p. 337. This letter should be dated c. 1779–80, for Charlemont refers to the *Supplement* as shortly forthcoming from the press.
[26] 29 April 1779, *HMC*, XII, 10, p. 347.
[27] *HMC*, XII, 10, p. 381. The sale earned five thousand and eleven pounds.
[28] On Garrick's book collecting, see Kahrl and Stone, *David Garrick*, pp. 165–99.

a bookseller's, or manuscripts of medieval English poems and account books of Elizabethan playhouse owners, few events caused such a stir as the publication in 1777 by Thomas Tyrwhitt of poems by Thomas Rowley, a monk who was supposed to have lived in Bristol in the fifteenth century.[29] Rowley and his poems turned out to be the imaginative fabrications of the talented young Bristol poet Thomas Chatterton, but many, including Lord Charlemont, needed convincing that they were not authentic after Tyrwhitt's edition had brought the poems to the public's attention.

Published eight years after the first of the Rowley poems had appeared in 1769, the year before Chatterton committed suicide, Tyrwhitt's edition created a controversy. It is not surprising that so many people believed in the poems when one considers their brilliance and the late eighteenth-century intoxication with the past; also that after publication of Percy's *Reliques*, there was a revival of interest in older native poetry. The forgeries took advantage of the new enthusiasm for an indigenous brand of primitivism in the form of antique poems. Chatterton appears to have been encouraged by the example of James Macpherson in the 1760s, who was thought to have forged poetic 'translations' of poems he said were by the Scottish epic poet Ossian (son of Fingal). Macpherson became famous with his fabrications, intoxicating his age with, as Mathew Arnold put it, 'apparitions of newness and power.'[30] He was never exposed, but Chatterton was, and it was Malone who exposed him.

Before turning to Malone's exposure of Chatterton's forgeries, it is useful to comment briefly on the psychology of forgery in this period, as well as on the psychology of its reception and detection. One historian of the subject has written as follows:

Since the value of antiquity was ... for this age almost entirely subjective, imitations, no matter how genuinely and deeply recreative, could earn no higher credit than that of ingenuity or cleverness – *unless* they were downright successful deceptions. Bring to light genuine relics, or supposed relics, and fame and fortune might follow. Bring forth excellent imitations and nothing followed but mild applause. Hence the way of the literary transgressor never looked more tempting, nor, indeed, at its commencement more innocent; and we are treated in consequence with that curious parade of hoaxes, from Ossian to [William Henry] Ireland, that is so marked a feature of later eighteenth-century literary history.[31]

The second half of the century was an age of 'histories' of music, literature, painting, and architecture. In addition to Percy's *Reliques*, the following

---

[29] *Poems, supposed to have been written at Bristol, by Thomas Rowley and Others, in the Fifteenth Century*; first advertised in the *London Chronicle*, no. 3158 (1–4 March 1777).

[30] Arnold, *On the Study of Celtic Literature* (1867), p. 116.

[31] Bertrand H. Bronson, 'Thomas Chatterton', in *The Age of Johnson: Essays presented to Chauncey Brewster Tinker*, ed. Frederick W. Hilles (1949; 2nd printing, 1964), p. 248. The fullest biography of Chatterton is by E. H. W. Meyerstein (1930).

monumental works whetted the public's appetite for ever more re-creations of the vanished past: Walpole's *Anecdotes of Painting in England* (1762–63, 1765), Burney's *History of Music* (1776–89), Warton's *The History of English Poetry* (1774–81), and Gibbon's *The History of the Decline and Fall of the Roman Empire* (1776–88). It was also, as we have seen, an age of biography, in which anything a historian, scholar, antiquarian, or critic could recover about people who lived as recently as half a century earlier took on fascination. Johnson and Boswell and books like John Nichols' *Biographical and Literary Anecdotes* (1782) and David Erskine Baker's *Companion to the Playhouse* (1764), which was edited by Malone's friend Isaac Reed under the title *Biographica Dramatica* in 1782, catered to that taste. There were innumerable studies of the classical world (based on archaeological work) at one end of the spectrum, and local histories at the other.

If this spell of the past had a negative aspect, it was that often it was accompanied by an irresponsible enthusiasm and carelessness, or even urge for deception – and not exclusively on the part of amateur local historians. This tendency accounts for the recriminations and hostile attacks that were whipped up by forgeries. The 'bare fact of antiquity', rather than the qualities of documents, became the critical issue, often generating acrimony between believers and non-believers.[32] Malone was less interested in the qualities of documents than the facts. He was not inclined to be charitable if he scented deception.

Neither Tyrwhitt nor Warton believed the Rowley poems were authentic. Tyrwhitt added an appendix to his third edition of the poems in 1778, arguing against the antiquity of the poems. Warton argued similarly in a chapter devoted entirely to the matter in the second volume of *The History of English Poetry*, published that year.[33] There the matter stood for the time being, while rumours circulated that unidentified pro-Rowleians were preparing a scholarly reply. It came finally in late November or early December 1781, when Jacob Bryant, a classical scholar, published his extensive *Observations upon the Poems of Thomas Rowley; in which the authenticity of those poems is ascertained.* Bryant was convincing because he was so thorough, more so than either Tyrwhitt or Warton, who had been tentative and conservative. A few days later a new, complete edition of the poems was published, edited by Jeremiah Milles, Dean of Exeter and President of the Society of Antiquaries, backing Bryant with historical argument gleaned from the Bristol local records. The onus of argument was, therefore, back on the shoulders of the anti-Rowleians.

This is when Malone entered the fray. It was a topic tailor-made for his scholarly and legalistic skills. His solid grasp of medieval and Renaissance poetry impelled him to send an anonymous 'brat into the world', as he

[32] Bronson, 'Thomas Chatterton', p. 248.
[33] Warton, *The History of English Poetry*, II (1778), pp. 139–64.

described it to Charlemont,[34] in the form of an article signed 'Misopiclerus' for the December issue of the *Gentleman's Magazine* which the editor, John Nichols, may well have asked him to write.[35] A second part of the essay, ridiculing Bryant and Milles, was published in January. At just over ten pages, this two-part piece was a preliminary volley against the pro-Rowleians, written hastily while Warton and Tyrwhitt were composing their own attacks that would not appear until late spring and summer of the next year.

Malone attacked Bryant and Milles rather than Chatterton. It was not a forgery by a young man long dead that angered him; indeed, unlike the Shakespeare forgeries in 1795 which were to incense him, the Chatterton poems were brilliant. As long as the public understood they were not composed in the fifteenth century, they could be appreciated as the wonderful productions of an imaginative though misguided boy. What irked Malone was that two men could use such authority as they had, with inadequate literary-historical knowledge, to mislead. The Rowley question was one over which Malone and Steevens could almost forget their differences. Malone sent Steevens the *Gentleman's Magazine* essay, which Steevens said he liked best for its ridicule, 'for I hold ridicule to be specific in the causes of Mills, Bryant, Glynn, and all who are visited with their disease.' Steevens praised Malone's burlesque in the second part because he felt that the light touch, not scholarly overkill, was the best weapon against the two Rowley champions: 'It is difficult to write seriously on the subject and yet a melancholy consideration is it that so much trouble should be necessary to bring people to proper use of their senses.' He said that Warton's artillery would soon also be aimed at the pair, 'the Dean and the Mythologist' as he called them, but 'both in jest and earnest.'[36] Walpole, however, identifying Malone to Mason for the first time by name, thought Malone should not have attempted the burlesque: 'A Mr. Malone has published some strong criticisms' on Milles and Bryant, 'but unluckily has attempted humour which is not an antiquary's weapon.'[37]

Among other effects, the Rowley controversy deepened Malone's and Walpole's friendship. Walpole's sentiments, Steevens added in his letter, 'perfectly coincide with yours.' Walpole, who had a different stake in this controversy, pretended to be indifferent to it, but an anxiety haunted him dating back to March 1769, when the young Chatterton, the year before he killed himself, sent him a forged essay on painting supposedly by 'T.

[34] 8 January, *HMC*, XII, 10, pp. 393–94. Malone collected a few items on the Rowley controversy; his collection is now in BL, c.39, fols. 11, 12, 20.

[35] *Gentleman's Magazine*, LI (December 1781), 555–59, 609–15. The second half appeared in January.

[36] OFB. On Steevens' own contributions to the Rowley controversy in the *Gentleman's Magazine*, (1782), 276, 288), see *Notes and Queries*, 2nd. ser., X, 282–83.

[37] 7 February 1782, *Walpole Corr.*, XXIX, p. 176.

Rowlie'. For a time, Walpole was fooled and accepted it as genuine, but later suspected a hoax and withdrew his support. Chatterton was bitter with disappointment and when he died the following year the word got around that there was a link between his death and Walpole's alleged treatment of him. Bryant and Milles revived the stigma that had lingered, impelling Walpole to defend himself in 1779 with a 'Letter' to Milles that he printed at Strawberry Hill.[38] It was more gratifying to Walpole than he admitted that when Malone was preparing his own attack in December, 1781, he asked him to see a copy of this 'Letter'. Walpole sent a copy with the comment that he hoped Malone would understand he was forced to write it 'to clear himself from as unjust aspersions as ever were conceived, and not to take part in a controversy to which he is very indifferent.'[39] Malone's essay in the *Gentleman's Magazine* acknowledged, with a deft compliment, his debt to Walpole's unpublished 'Letter', which 'shows him to be as amiable as he is lively and ingenious.' He sent Walpole a copy on 4 February 1782, to which the latter replied on the same day that the essay was 'far too good to be committed only to the few hours of life of a newspaper.'[40]

Walpole's remark struck a chord because, catching his breath in January, Malone hinted to Charlemont that he had a more comprehensive exposure of Chatterton's forgeries in mind. The controversy was 'going on ding-dong', though Bryant and Milles 'have said everything that could be said on their side of the question, and have staggered some.' Warton was preparing his answer, Tyrwhitt planned 'to enter deeply into the business' with a 'vindication' that would not be out for some time, and as for himself, he had been encouraged by Tyrwhitt 'to make a pamphlet' of his essays 'in order to bind up with all the other pieces which that wonderful youth, Chatterton, has given occasion to.' He said he would send him his pamphlet, when it came out, 'notwithstanding your leaning to the other side of the question.' He worked hard on it for the rest of the month and published his sixty-page *Cursory Observations on the Poems Attributed to Thomas Rowley* in early February 1782. He sent Walpole a copy immediately, who was delighted with it. Walpole apologized for his long letter of thanks by citing 'the pleasure your book gave me – in which I fear your kindness to me had a little share too.'[41]

The pamphlet was well received. He had scooped both Tyrwhitt and Warton. Tyrwhitt ended up writing much more than Malone's sixty pages but conceded that Malone's method of comparing Chatterton's Rowley

---

[38] 'A Letter to the Editor of the Miscellanies of Thomas Chatterton'.
[39] C. December 1781. *Walpole Corr.*, XLI, pp. 465–66. Malone's copy of Walpole's 'Letter' is now in the Boston Public Library.   [40] 4 February 1782, *Walpole Corr.*, XLII, p. 1.
[41] *Walpole Corr.*, XLII, p. 3. For a modern edition of *Cursory Observations*, see James M. Kuist, *The Augustan Reprint Society*, 123 (1966). I cite from this edition.

forgeries with his acknowledged poetry provided the most certain evidence
of a hoax. Complimenting Malone's 'ear' for old English poetry, Tyrwhitt
graciously acknowledged that much of what he was going to write had been
anticipated by Malone's pamphlet:

I think it sufficient to refer the reader, who may have any doubts upon this point,
to the specimens of really ancient poetry, with which the verses of the pretended
Rowley have lately been very judiciously contrasted. Whoever reads those
specimens, if he has an ear, must be convinced, that the authors of them and of the
Poems did not live within the same period.[42]

Warton, too, approved. Praising Malone as an 'ingenious author', he
admitted that he 'has been beforehand with me in this sort of tryal.' 'But
mine was made', he added quickly, 'before I had seen his very sensible and
conclusive performance.'[43]

Percy, first among experts on old English poetry, wrote to Malone from
Carlisle on 19 February that his 'ingenious and entertaining publication'
had in many ways proved 'quite decisive of the Question.' Complaining
that far away in Ireland he had seen 'neither the Antique nor modern
composition of Chatterton', he flattered himself that he could have 'offered
some things in aid of your Positions.' Even so, he mentioned certain sources
of Chatterton's, whom he warmly calls 'this Lad', which Malone had
neglected. Percy's letter is typical of the post- mortems on the forgery that
would continue for years. And as these continued, people became more
impressed by the genius of the forger. Percy called him a 'wonderful Boy'
for having 'ransacked' certain sources like Dugdale's *Baronage* for his facts
and thought he had made the commentators look like fools.[44] Someone
with a knack for the burlesque, he said, more likely Steevens than Malone,
ought to write a 'good serio-comic Criticism' for the *St. James's Chronicle* at
their expense.[45]

Malone's exposure of the forgery in the *Cursory Observations* typified his
methods of establishing the history and background of any literary work.
He based his argument on versification, the historical context, and the
physical appearance of the items in question – in this case, parchment
manuscripts. He found that anachronisms abounded, such as Chatterton's
imitations of authors who lived after Rowley. The handwriting, too, was all
wrong, and the parchments were not old enough. But it was the critical look
at the poetry itself, and how it compared with medieval poetry that Malone
cited as well as with other poetry Chatterton wrote, that particularly
impressed critics like Warton, Tyrwhitt, and Percy. Malone also described

[42] Tyrwhitt, *A Vindication of the Appendix to the Poems, called Rowley's*, p. 82.
[43] Warton, *An Enquiry into the Authenticity of the Poems attributed to Thomas Rowley*, pp. 292–93.
[44] See Steevens to Warton, 4 May and 29 October 1782 (BL Add. Ms. 42561, fols. 116, 123).
[45] Hyde Collection; not included in *P–M Letters*. On Nichols' role in the Rowleian controversy as
    editor of the *Gentleman's Magazine*, see *Literary Anecdotes*, VIII (1815), p. 113.

his own credentials as the exposer of the hoax, his 'antiquarian sagacity' as Steevens called it, at the same time inveighing against would-be critics like Bryant and Milles for their relative ignorance: for it is a 'fixed principle', Malone wrote, 'that the authenticity or spuriousness of the poems attributed to Rowley cannot be decided by any person who has not a *taste* for English poetry, and a moderate, at least, if not a critical, knowledge of the compositions of most of our poets from the time of Chaucer to that of Pope.' 'Without this critical knowledge and taste', he continued, 'all the Saxon literature that can be employed on this subject (though these learned gentlemen should pour out waggon instead of cart-loads of it,) will only puzzle and perplex, instead of illustrating, the point in dispute.'[46]

Malone's effort to account for Chatterton's genius by analysing the quality of the verses and the scale of the achievement given the short time the gifted seventeen-year-old had to write them reflects the growing public respect for the boy's amazing abilities. In his pamphlet Malone was even more complimentary to the young poet than he was in his initial essay. After Chatterton's arrival in London, 'if his forgeries had met with any success', Malone writes, 'he would undoubtedly have produced ancient poetry without end.' But he realized that Percy, 'in whom he expected to find at once a dupe and a patron, was too clear-sighted to be deceived by such evident fictions, and that he could earn a livelihood by his talents, without fabricating old Mss. in order to gain a few shillings.' 'It is indeed astonishing', he continues, 'that this youth should have been able to compose, in about eighteen months, three thousand seven hundred verses, on various subjects.'[47]

For all its undoubted scholarly brilliance, the pamphlet nonetheless ends feebly with an ironic 'serious and well-intended proposal' aimed at the nonsensical antiquarianism practised by Bryant and Milles. They and their publishers ought to be padlocked into 'the room over the north porch of Redcliffe church' in Bristol in order to wean them

by degrees from the delusion under which they labour, and to furnish them with some amusement, they may be supplied with proper instruments to measure the length, breadth, and depth, of the empty chests now in the said room ... to ascertain how many thousand diminutive pieces of parchment, all eight inches and a half by four and a half, might have been contained in those chests [according to my calculation, 1,464,578; – but I cannot pretend to be exact].

Malone continues, they should be fed mouldy bread which they may cut with the knife they say illustrates the authenticity of the poems. If after two weeks they are found to be 'entirely re-established in their health, and perfectly composed', they 'may be suffered to return again to their usual employments.'[48]

[46] Malone, *Cursory Observations*, pp. 2–3.   [47] Ibid., pp. 47, 49–50.
[48] Ibid., pp. 58–62.

For that lighter vein, Malone was quickly ridiculed, with Warton, in a pamphlet by Burnaby Greene, *Strictures Upon a Pamphlet entitled, Cursory Observations*. Greene mocked him for his failure as 'a writer abounding in exertions of the risible muscles' and for having the audacity to mock respected critics.[49] When Steevens saw Greene's advertisement for his piece, he warned Warton: 'You have undoubtedly seen Burnaby Greene's advertisement. He is to strike at Malone with his sword; the "wind and whiff" of it will do for you.'[50] Malone was on the receiving end again in the August issue of the *Gentleman's Magazine* when an ironic poem appeared deriding both him and his scholarship and mentioning both Shakespeare and Johnson, the two writers he most admired. One of the stanzas reads:

> Malone, you're petulant and vain,
> Shakespeare has turned your giddy brain,
>   and Johnson scarce can cure you;
>   You'll live an exile from his [Shakespeare's] wit,
> No more your notes will he admit,
>   Nor Steevens now endure you.[51]

They would not be the last time Malone was ridiculed in print.

[49] Greene, *Strictures Upon a Pamphlet entitled, Cursory Observations*... (1782), p. 3. See Kuist, *Cursory Observations*, p. vi.
[50] 27 April 1782 (BL Add. Ms. 42561, fol. 114).
[51] 'Ode Addressed to Edmund Malone, Esq. on his presuming to examine the learned and unanswerable arguments urged by Jacob Bryant, Esq. and the Rev. Dr. Milles...', pp. 379–81.

5

Scholarship and strife

1

About twenty years after Malone died, his friend John Taylor recalled, 'Mr. Malone was quite a gentleman in his manners, and rather of a mild disposition, except when he had to support the truth, and then there were such firmness and spirit in what he said as could hardly be expected from one so meek and courteous; but he never departed from politeness and respect.'[1] His friends in The Club would have agreed about his gentlemanliness and mildness, as would have Susanna Spencer and Sarah Loveday. Rival scholars, on the other hand, would have recognized the truth of Taylor's point about Malone's 'firmness and spirit', although they might have chosen more forceful words to describe this streak in the man. Steevens had already felt the force of Malone's tenacity on behalf of the 'truth' and he did not like it. Neither did Joseph Ritson and a succession of others throughout Malone's career. What Malone's friends saw as justifiable pride and confidence, his rivals saw as arrogance and intolerance.

In choosing his next project after the *Supplement*, Malone had plenty of encouragement from Johnson, Percy, and Warton. From Warton he hoped for more than just encouragement, however, for at Oxford he had ready access to much of the material Malone needed at the Bodleian and Ashmolean Libraries and, presumably, was free from any scholarly commitments since he had just completed *The History of English Poetry*. His first letter to Warton on 14 March 1781, introducing himself, brimmed with literary questions, but it also offered literary gifts: 'Though I have not the pleasure of being personally known to you, I trust the similarity of our pursuits will plead my excuse for the liberty I now take; and in return for the trouble I am going to give you, beg leave to send you some verses by Spenser ... [not] taken notice of in your *Observations*' [on *The Faerie Queene*, 1754].[2] Somehow Warton mistakenly got the impression from this letter that the 'trouble' Malone was going to give him involved an edition of Marlowe and Nashe, not Shakespeare, but the important thing to Malone

---

[1] John Taylor, *Records of My Life*, II (1833), p. 155.   [2] BL Add. Ms. 42561, fol. 104.

was that Warton was ready to help him: 'I am happy to hear that you have undertaken an edition of Marlowe's and Nashe's [sic]; it highly deserves a Revival in form. You may command any Information which you think I can communicate.'[3]

About one year after Warton published the third volume of *The History of English Poetry*, he was attacked harshly in print by a man who would soon plague Malone, too. In October 1782, Joseph Ritson published a slashing fifty-page pamphlet attacking not only Warton's *History* for inaccuracies but also Warton himself for wilful misrepresentation of the facts.[4] Ritson was a highly competent, thorough, and knowledgeable scholar, especially of early English poetry and drama. More of an antiquarian than a literary historian, however, he nourished resentment towards people like Warton and Johnson who attempted to turn facts into interpretive and narrative histories.

At some point in his laborious search for facts about English literature, Warton recognized that he could never learn enough to make his book 'both coherent and scrupulously accurate.' He, therefore, sacrificed the 'antiquarian's dream of perfection and completion' in favour of writing a narrative *History* that was interpretive and evaluative – one 'in which the curiosity of the antiquarian is connected with taste and genius, and his researches tend to display the progress of human manners.'[5] Ritson thought he thereby committed the cardinal sin of sacrificing factual accuracy for narrative coherence. Johnson was, as in so many other ways, the chief inspiration in this new idea of the history of the arts. Any narrative, he wrote, whether fictional, historical, or (especially) biographical, must be a 'specimen of life and manners.' We have seen how his dislike of mere facts affected his *Lives of the Poets* – he would hold out his hand if it rained facts, but he would not go out of his way to search for them.[6]

A late disciple of Johnson's, Malone was one of Warton's men of taste as well as an antiquarian. One of the requirements of admission to The Club was a man's clubbability – that is, his ability to share ideas and facts, consult others' opinions, nurture a taste for generality. Nothing was as likely to get an applicant blackballed as dogmatism or a reputation for pedantry. The important thing was to try to see and express the meaning of things. Although, as Boswell once noted, 'respectable and gentlemanlike

[3] 2 April 1781, OFB 39.206.
[4] See Bronson, *Joseph Ritson: Scholar at Arms*; and J. M. Osborn's review of the biography, 'Ritson, Scholar at Odds', *Modern Philology*, 37:4 (1940), 419–29.
[5] See Lawrence Lipking, *Ordering of the Arts*, p. 84; on the conflict between the antiquarian and historian, see introduction and pp. 82–85. See also R. D. Thornton, 'The Influence of the Enlightenment upon Eighteenth-Century British Antiquaries, 1750–1800', *Studies on Voltaire and the Eighteenth Century*, XXVII (1963), 1601ff.
[6] *Johnsonian Miscellanies*, ed. George B. Hill, I (1897), p. 348.

rather than shining' in company,[7] Malone was capable of elaborating ideas in The Club's spirit of philosophic discovery. He saw himself as a scholar–critic member of an intellectual community. He wanted, above all else, to retrieve facts in order to set Shakespeare in his period and relate the man to his plays – to make him more understandable and approachable to the general public. His example of an antiquarian who aspired to combine the roles of critic, historian, and scholar irritated Ritson eventually even more than Warton did.

Jealousy and frustration also motivated Ritson. He was acutely jealous of Johnson, Steevens, Percy, Warton, Reed, and, increasingly, this newcomer Malone. He believed the Johnsonians had shut him out from the London publishing world, that through the good offices of the booksellers they had cornered much of the literary scholarship in the last forty years of the century. A lot has been made in the past few years, chiefly by Gary Taylor, of this conspiracy theory. Ritson's social background and ideology are supposed to be the main reasons for his isolation from the leading Shakespeareans: his working-class background, radical politics – Horne Tooke, the political agitator whose liberal politics Malone despised, was one of his friends – and anticlerical views. He was 'Citizen Ritson', an apologist for 'low' or popular culture, an editorial revolutionary who must be kept at bay, not a 'gentleman' scholar like Malone, Percy, and his other antagonists. Malone also has been accused of single-handedly 'locking' Ritson out of publishing through his contracts for Shakespeare editions. If Ritson had published an edition of Shakespeare, so this argument runs, he 'may well have created a radical alternative to the conservative tradition epitomized by Malone' – even if his edition proved to be 'wrong as often as Malone's.' His political and social ideas would have evoked a more liberal Shakespeare, one less bound to the prevailing assumptions of his age.[8] The evidence for these claims is, to put it mildly, thin. Apart from his keen competitiveness when he was trying to establish his credentials as a Shakespearean, evidence of an elaborate plot on Malone's part to lock Ritson out of Shakespeare editing is almost non-existent. There is a danger here of adopting Ritson's own neurotic suspiciousness. Furthermore, most of the evidence given of Malone's conservatism is comprised of his anti-French polemics after 1789, which certainly do not permeate his criticism; neither do they satisfactorily explain Malone's antipathy to Ritson. A more probable explanation for Ritson's behaviour is supplied by his friend Joseph Haslewood, who wrote in 1824 that if Ritson behaved acrimoniously, it was because of his 'continual habitude of seclusion, and the painful belief, arising therefrom, of chilling neglect and consequent unimportance, too often the consequence of not mixing actively in society.'[9] Rather than

[7] *DF*, I, p. 174.　　　　[8] Taylor, *Reinventing Shakespeare*, pp. 144–45.
[9] Haslewood, *Some Account of the Life and Publications of the Late Joseph Ritson, Esq.* (1824), pp. 37–38.

attempt to cultivate relationships with the established authorities, as
Malone did when he first arrived in London, Ritson attacked the big
names, his surliness compounding what his biographer describes as 'the
total absence in his mental equipment of a humorous sense of values.'[10]

Ritson made a tactical error in picking on Warton first. By doing so, in
spite of the accuracy and reasonableness of much that he said, he cast
himself in the role of a reviled interloper. Warton's geniality and helpfulness
made him beloved of many, and he was also in 1782 one of the two or three
most highly respected scholars in England. But in a letter to a friend in
August, Ritson revelled in what he called his 'scurrilous libel against Tom
Warton.'[11] Then audaciously he sent Warton a complementary copy and
published a taunting 'letter' to him in the 9–12 November *St. James's
Chronicle* which he began with the scriptural quotation, 'How are the
Mighty fallen', continuing in this vein:

You have long lived the Usurper of the Throne of ancient English Literature. Your
Words are Law, your Nods Decisions in the Empire of Learning – and Woe to the
Wretch who durst dispute your Tribunal. But your Reign is now expired ... your
Altars are demolished, your Molten Images are cast down and broken, and your
Divinity is no more.

The details of Ritson's attack on Warton do not concern us here; it is
enough to say he was serving notice on other scholars, as well, that if they
were not certain of their facts, they had best beware. He would raid their
editions and unsparingly expose their faults in pamphlets and the papers.

Malone appears not to have read anything of Ritson's before, although
he had seen him several times at the British Museum.[12] He wrote to
Charlemont on 19 November about this man 'Wrightson' who was already
planning a sweeping attack on the most prominent Shakespeare commentators. Without knowing if Ritson was going to include him in the attack,
but apparently not too worried, he observed that even if Ritson had 'a good
deal of good matter' in his pamphlet and had 'caught Mr. Warton tripping
pretty often', his criticism was 'spoiled by the petulance and indecency of
the manner.' He had heard that Ritson 'has now in the press a severe
critique on the whole phalanx of Shakspeare commentators', especially
Johnson, 'which is absurd enough, for he undoubtedly did a great deal
well, and his omissions every body knows already, and have been in a good
measure remedied by others going through the drudgery that he could not
submit to.'[13]

---

[10] Bronson, *Joseph Ritson, Scholar at Arms*, I, p. 73.

[11] *The Letters of Ritson*, ed. Joseph Frank, with a Memoir by Sir Harris Nicolas (1833), I, p. 61.

[12] In telling Warton about the attack, Steevens wrote on 29 October 1782, from Emmanuel
College, 'I have often found your assailant at the Museum ...' (BL Add. Ms. 42561, fol. 123).

[13] *HMC*, XII, 10, pp. 422–23.

2

Ritson's great ambition was to publish an edition of Shakespeare based on the best collating of texts that had yet been done. He had little respect for the textual work in the 1778 *Johnson–Steevens* edition. But how could he command the attention of the booksellers, to whom the Johnsonians had virtually an exclusive pipeline? He must somehow put forward his credentials. In May 1783, he published *Remarks, Critical and Illustrative, on the Text and Notes of the Last Edition of Shakespeare*, denouncing almost all other Shakespeareans. By pulling down the others, he hoped to set himself up. Steevens, whom Ritson treated especially harshly, retaliated, as he had earlier on behalf of Warton, by writing some playful burlesques of Ritson under a pseudonym in the *St. James's Chronicle*. It stung him to read Ritson's claim that the *Johnson–Steevens* edition ought to have no future because of its textual flaws: 'From a republication of the last edition nothing is to be expected.' Ritson mocked Steevens' statement that 'the text of this author seems now finally settled!'.[14] A few years later, Malone made the same point about Steevens' text. Malone, too, came under Ritson's fire for his *Supplement*, though some of the worst of Ritson's abusive attack fell upon the sick and elderly Johnson, to whom Ritson astonishingly sent a copy with his compliments. He also sent a copy to Malone.

Steevens was not overly distressed by the way Ritson treated Malone and was delighted when he heard of John Nichols' blunder of sending Malone and Ritson advance copy of their abuse of each other in the *Gentleman's Magazine*, to the obvious discomfiture of them both. On 17 March, two months before Ritson's *Remarks* was published, Steevens savoured the mistake in a letter to Dr Michael Lort, formerly Professor of Greek at Cambridge: 'A pleasant circumstance happened on Saturday. Malone is printing a pamphlet about Shakespeare [his second Appendix to the *Supplement*], and so is Mr Ritson. Nichols by mistake sent Ritson's proof to Malone, & Malone's to Ritson. The first thing Malone discovered was Ritson's disposition to abuse him, & Ritson at the same time, met with Malone's design to forestall him.'[15] To Nichols, Steevens scribbled the note: 'I congratulate you on the happy exchange of proofs you made betwixt Messieurs Malone and Ritson.'[16]

Ritson saw in Malone the next great Shakespearean. Capell had died in 1781, Steevens was bowing out – or so he thought – and Tyrwhitt and Farmer were not as ambitious. He resented, as Steevens was beginning to, Malone's authoritative tone in his writing about Shakespeare. He scoffed

---

[14] Ritson, *Remarks*, p. vi.   [15] 17 March 1783, Folger, Y.c. 1434 (27).
[16] Nichols, *Illustrations of the Literary History of the Eighteenth Century*, V (1817–58), p. 441.

that Malone was 'remarkable for the pertinence, propriety, and real importance of his learned and ingenious remarks.'[17]

It is easy to deride Ritson's manners, but his ideas about textual collation represented an advance on Johnson and Steevens. He accused both of not practising what they preached, of saying they had collated lots of early quartos with the folios while doing so only superficially. He could not accuse Malone of the same thing, although five years later, in another pamphlet entitled *The Quip Modest* (1788), he rebuked him for his distrust of the Second Folio. Malone liked the First Folio 'since the *second* has been the means of detecting so many of his mistakes.'[18] Following Theobald,[19] Ritson understood that the Second Folio corrected many printing errors in the First Folio and that it must have received attention from an 'editor', as distinct from merely a supervisor or printer. He also ridiculed many of Malone's notes, in both the *Supplement* and the 1778 *Johnson–Steevens* edition, as painstakingly silly, trivial, indecisive, neutral, obtuse, unclear, and ignorant. He also derogated several of the people who contributed notes to the *Supplement* – 'mr. Malones mushroom assistants in this notable piece of editorial cookry.' And he declared, in bold typeface, that he was preparing 'THE GENUINE TEXT OF SHAKSPEARE'.[20]

3

Long before he privately printed copies of his *Second Appendix* to the *Supplement* on 29 April 1783, Malone had decided to go ahead with a new edition of Shakespeare in order to forestall Ritson. Though in November he had assured Steevens, 'surely no bookseller will be found absurd enough to contract for a new Edition of Shakespeare after your's [*sic*]',[21] in the spring he entered into agreements with several London booksellers for a new complete edition. What had made him change his mind? Partly, he was determined to anticipate Ritson's own plans for an edition, partly he had been left in possession of the field by Steevens' apparent exit from Shakespearean scholarship.

In the spring of 1783, Steevens was telling everyone that he was done with Shakespeare, ostensibly because he was tired of making money for the booksellers with, as he put it, 'gratuitous' editions. 'Ingratitude and impertinence from several of the booksellers have been my reward for conducting two laborious editions, both of which are sold', he complained. He wanted another, an octavo, edition of the *Johnson–Steevens* edition to

---

[17] Ritson, *Remarks*, p. 177.   [18] Ritson, *The Quip Modest*, p. 15.

[19] On the rival claims of F1 and F2 in Theobald's editing, see Seary, *Lewis Theobald and the Editing of Shakespeare*, pp. 136ff.   [20] Ritson, *Remarks*, p. 237.

[21] Bodleian, Montague d/2, fol. 48.

come out, which would include many of the notes that commentators had written since 1778, but he did not want to have anything to do with it.[22] The preceding November he had told Malone that partly because of Ritson, to whom 'we all may be vulnerable', he dreaded another edition and 'perhaps shall devolve the labour of it, in great measure, on another hand.'[23] By the spring, before he knew of Malone's independent editorial aspirations, he was backing Isaac Reed. Reed himself appears to have hesitated: he would not do it gratuitously, just for the honour of Shakespeare. Steevens urged Nichols to pay him well; if Nichols did, he would give Reed his own material, although 'I pledge myself also not to molest him about my own notes, or even to see a single page of the work before it is printed off and published.'[24]

In early April, Reed agreed to do the edition and Malone made it generally known that he would pursue his own editorial path. Steevens fumed when he learned of Malone's plans. In sending Reed all his material from his 'old shop', as he termed his study, he could not resist a swipe at his former collaborator: 'You will probably inherit all the custom, except Mr. Malone's', who intends to concoct his own brew 'at a new house to which it seems he has got a license.'[25] His feelings are clearer in a letter to Warton on 16 April, in which he uses again the beer metaphor to describe the prospective flow of Shakespeare editions and commentaries:

Whatever the vegetable spring may produce, the critical one will be prolific enough. No less than six editions of Shakespeare (including Capell's notes...) are now in the Mash tub. I have thrown up my license. Reed is to occupy the old Red Lattice, and Malone intends... a little snug booth of his own construction. Ritson will advertise sour ale against his mild... and another, viz. our text without notes (your true critical hops) will also soon be in tap.[26]

Malone explained circumspectly to Steevens why he wanted to produce a new edition, a rival to the *Johnson–Steevens*: '[I] should not have undertaken the work that I mentioned, but that I expect some amusement from it.' The real reason was his conviction that the *Johnson–Steevens*, based on fragmentary collation, was textually out of date. Reed's edition, therefore, posed no threat to his plans since Reed inherited a text that he did not plan to alter significantly – certainly not through comprehensive collation. Malone even told Steevens he was ready to help Reed. 'Be so kind', he wrote coolly, 'to furnish him with the sheets of my Appendix.'[27]

---

[22] See Steevens to Malone, 28 November 1782, Folger, Y.c. 1434 (26).

[23] 20 November, Folger, Y.c. 1434 (25).

[24] Nichols, *Illustrations*, V, p. 442. See Malone to Percy, 30 September, *P–M Letters*, p. 8.

[25] Steevens to Reed, 9 April 1783, Folger, C.b.2, no. 6.

[26] John Wooll, *Biographical Memoir of the Late Rev. Joseph Warton* (1806), pp. 398–99. Steevens wrote a similar letter to Nichols, 20 April, OFB, Box 35, item 16.

[27] 18 April 1783, Henry Hyde Collection.

4

Malone had two Shakespeare editions in mind, to be printed simultaneously: an edition of the plays and poems complete with a new text and all relevant notes, critical apparatus, appendices, and so on; and a duodecimo 'portable' edition that he could publish more quickly. The latter would be a 'useful *family* Shakspeare', not so much for scholars and men of letters as for interested readers and playgoers who wanted Shakespeare without the huge corpus of commentary that had swelled over the last two decades. He informed Percy in September, 1783, when he was visiting his family and friends in Ireland, that the ten-volume portable edition would 'reject all superfluous and controversial notes' and 'explain and support the meaning of words ... to come at once to the true meaning of the passage.' Ritson's declaration in his 'very impudent and scurrilous pamphlet' had given him the idea for it: 'I immediately resolved that he should not deck himself in our feathers, and offered my services without fee or reward to the booksellers, who instantly accepted them. No opposition whatsoever is meant to the larger work to which I shall contribute all such notes as are too bulky for the other.' If after his and others' editions the public still does not 'understand' Shakespeare, he added, 'either they or his editors must be sad blockheads indeed.'[28]

Malone's plans for a compact edition proved a devastating blow to Ritson, who was far from enjoying his rival's enviable position of being able to work 'without fee.' Although he never said so in public, Ritson eventually abandoned his idea and never did publish an edition of Shakespeare. Instead, he spent the next decade producing an edition of songs and ballads about Robin Hood. Indeed, he became even more bitter, his bitterness a few years later bearing fruit in yet another attack he aimed chiefly at Malone.

Malone explained to Percy his editorial strategy for the text. He thanked Percy for the loan of his Second Folio, which he said would come in handy in his textual work, and then articulated a principle that remained central to his editorial approach for the rest of his life:

[Ritson's] principal charge against us, is, that not a single play has ever been duly collated; and that particularly we have all neglected the *Second* folio. Now the truth of the matter is, that the second folio has been the cause of almost all the grand corruptions of Shakspeare; and is so far from being a copy that one ought to consult for the purpose of improving the author by *new* readings, that it ought to be carefully examined with a view to detect the numerous sophistications that its editor has introduced in almost every page.

The editor of the Second Folio, he argued, who understood neither Shakespeare's metre nor the pronunciation of certain words, frequently

[28] *P–M Letters*, pp. 8–9.

added words to complete the metre. Moreover, he never consulted any of the early quartos to check them against the First Folio for omitted words.[29] Such errors were transmitted through the next two folios into all the eighteenth-century editions, and although by checking 'the *only* authentick copies' Capell and Steevens had corrected many, 'yet some still remain.' He seemed to agree in spirit with Ritson that even recent editions 'must stand or fall by their own merit, and are all *equally* void of *authority*', but he argued against Ritson's fondness for the Second Folio, which he felt would make his edition textually worthless. He told Percy that Johnson and Steevens had coaxed him out of attacking Ritson in the papers, the right approach as it turned out, 'for I believe there have not been fifty copies of his book sold.'[30]

In March 1785, when parts of his duodecimo edition were already in the press, he wrote again to Percy about his methods of collation. He had been relying slightly on Capell and others, but in the collation of early editions he was ignoring his predecessors' work and adopting 'a method of collation that I learned in my own [legal] profession, and which cannot err. Before each sheet is printed I make a person read it aloud to me while I hold the first folio in my hand; so that the smallest deviation is easily detected.' As a result, not even 'that shallow caviller, Ritson, can attack me.' He had decided to bring out the portable edition before the larger edition, but even that was painfully slow work, 'partly from my own desire of making the work correct, and partly from the tard[y]ing of the printing House.' He expected Reed's edition to be published in two or three months, but his own, in seven volumes, would not be out, he thought, until the next year.[31] It appeared some time later, though without the first volume.[32]

[29] Gary Taylor over-simplifies Malone's editorial method by saying that he 'equated antiquity with truth' in his preference for the First Folio over the Second (*Reinventing Shakespeare*, p. 146). Malone's use of the early editions to arrive at a text was far more sophisticated than that – by far more sophisticated, as I argue, than anyone had ever been before or would be until the work of the great nineteenth- and twentieth-century editors. He made ample use of earlier quartos to check the authority of the First Folio, and vice versa. He even preferred some readings in the Third Folio. Even if we do not agree entirely with Malone's opinion of the Second Folio, there is no doubt that his antipathy towards it was based on careful reasoning.

[30] *P–M Letters*, pp. 10–11. Gary Taylor has suggested (without evidence) that Malone used his influence with the Johnson circle and others to pre-empt Ritson and blackball his plans for an edition.   [31] *P–M Letters*, pp. 22–23.

[32] The duodecimo edition was titled, *The Plays of William Shakespeare, Accurately Printed from the Text of Mr. Malone's Edition, with select explanatory notes* [edited by *John Nichols*]. *In seven volumes...*, (1790–86). Jaggard wrongly identifies this edition as an octavo (*Shakespeare Bibliography*, 1911). Malone also published *Conjectures Concerning the Date of... Macbeth* in *The Hibernian Magazine* (October 1786).

5

From the start of his scholarly career, Malone showed a keen interest in collecting portraits – 'heads', as he put it – of English literary figures.[33] He regarded them as a crucial part of the biographer's and literary historian's evidence, another form of documentation. A few of these hung on his walls, but most of them he filed away for reference and use in his publications. He and Steevens, himself a collector, found that here was one subject over which, for the most part, they could forget their rivalry. 'I am happy to find that the [John] Skelton was acceptable', he wrote to Malone on 8 May 1782; and on another occasion, when Malone was helping him acquire 'heads' at any price for his collection, Steevens confessed that he had allowed 'the rage of collecting to triumph over prudence.'[34] Malone purchased much of Steevens' collection at auction after his death, who owned one of the largest collections of such engravings and sketches in England when he died.

Portraits of Shakespeare were particularly prized, not just as collectors' items but as historical evidence. Borne along by Bardolatry, rumours frequently circulated about some portrait or other that was supposed to be of Shakespeare. Steevens, sceptical about most of these, once told Malone of a 'pretended original' portrait that had just been sent down from Stratford. As in almost all such cases, he was sceptical: 'You may see it at No. 86 Cheapside. It is a small full length. It could never have been designed as a representation of our Author. If Mr. Walpole saw it, he might possibly know who it was meant for. It is attended by some wretched, worse, painted glass, exhibiting the different implements peculiar to some Months of the Year.'[35] But Steevens could not always be relied upon for objective judgment. James Boaden, an acquaintance of Malone's, who in 1824 published his comprehensive *Inquiry Into the Authenticity of Certain Pictures and Prints ... Offered to the Public as Portraits of Shakspeare*, wrote that Steevens 'was unfortunately a person, who took a very marked delight in ruffling the complacency of others' and who muddied the waters with pronouncements about alleged Shakespeare pictures.[36] Although Boaden

---

[33] Malone made several entries in his journal concerning painters, paintings, and engravings. See, for example, Prior, 'Maloniana', pp. 380–81, 382–83, 385, 389, 393, 397–406, 457–59. See also chapter 11.

[34] 8 and 23 May 1782, Folger, Y.c. 1434 (23). See Malone's letter to Charlemont on 18 June 1781 about 'Hogarthmania' in London and Steevens' obsession with collecting Hogarth (*HMC*, XII, 10, p. 382); and Malone's and Charlemont's correspondence about Hogarth: 29 June 1781, Prior, 'Maloniana', pp. 72–73; 2 and 20 July 1781, *HMC*, XII, pp. 385–86, 386–87; and July 1787, Prior, 'Maloniana', pp. 73–74).

[35] 9 May 1782, Folger, Y.c. 1434 (23). Malone speculated occasionally in his journal about alleged portraits of Shakespeare (Prior, 'Maloniana', pp. 380, 400–1).

[36] James Boaden, *An Inquiry into the Authenticity of Certain Pictures and Prints ... Offered to the Public as Portraits of Shakespeare* (1824), p. 68.

thought that Steevens and Malone 'usually worked themselves up to the feeling of partizans [sic] rather than that of inquirers, and determined to see no marks of authenticity out of the frame of their favourite portrait', he thought more highly of Malone's contributions to critical writing on Shakespeare portraiture than anyone else's.

Throughout the seventeenth century, the only accepted image of Shakespeare was the Droeshout engraving that appeared as the frontispiece to the First Folio. In 1708, a new image appeared when a painting allegedly of Shakespeare came to light in the possession of the actor Thomas Betterton, one that was originally said to have been owned by Sir William Davenant, from whose estate Betterton bought it in a public sale. While Betterton owned it, it was engraved for the frontispiece of Rowe's 1709 edition. It also gained credibility in 1719 by some notes George Vertue wrote on it; he traced its history through documentary evidence further back than any other alleged portrait of Shakespeare. After Rowe, all eighteenth-century editions of Shakespeare included it rather than the Droeshout. As a result, the new portrait, later called the Chandos portrait because it had passed to the Duke of Chandos, became the most frequently copied picture in the eighteenth century.[37] Capell even had a copy that in 1779 he gave to Trinity College, Cambridge. But copies from copies, with slight embellishments added or removed according to the whims or abilities of the engravers, bore little resemblance to the earliest engravings, much less to the original painting which apparently nobody ever thought of consulting. Moreover, the authenticity of the portrait itself was scarcely ever considered, either by Rowe or his successors; it just became another image, accepted and acceptable, like the stories about Shakespeare's life that Rowe published.[38]

Malone was the first Shakespearean scholar to take a serious, authenticating interest in Shakespeare's appearance. Just before he left in the spring of 1783 for several months in Ireland, he decided to seek out the original Chandos portrait and obtain an engraving of it.[39] He did not trust the multitude of copies in circulation. He wrote to the Duke of Chandos in the late spring, asking for permission to see it and have it copied in the public interest:

[37] See Schoenbaum's discussion of the Chandos portrait, *Shakespeare's Lives* (rev. edn. 1991), pp. 202–6. On the role of the Chandos portrait in the individuation and authentication of Shakespeare by Malone and others, see de Grazia, *Shakespeare Verbatim*, pp. 79–86. For more general studies on Shakespearean iconography, see M. H. Spielmann, 'Shakespeare's Portraiture', in *Studies in the First Folio* (1924); Schoenbaum, *Shakespeare's Lives*, pp. 279–94; David Piper, '*O Sweet Mr. Shakespeare I'll have his picture*': *The Changing Image of Shakespeare's Person 1600–1800* (1964), and *The Image of the Poet: British Poets and Their Portraits* (1982), pp. 49–52.

[38] See de Grazia, *Shakespeare Verbatim*, pp. 80–82.

[39] This was one of several excursions Malone took to see Shakespeare-related portraits. See Prior, pp. 458–59. See also Thomas Warton's letters to him, 19 and 30 March, 27 October (Rinaker, pp. 108–10, 113).

The only original Picture of our great poet Shakspeare, is, I understand, in your Grace's possession. Having undertaken the revision of an edition of his works, I wish to ornament it with a faithful Engraving from this picture...

My humble request therefore to your Grace is, that you will be pleased to permit an artist that I shall employ to see this picture, if in town; or to make a drawing from it, if it be at either of your Grace's Seats...

I should add, that I derive no kind of emolument from the work that I have mentioned having solely undertaken it from my veneration for our great and unrivalled poet.[40]

When he saw the painting on 23 June,[41] he immediately liked its 'poetic' informality: the gold earring in the left ear, a long moustache and a short beard, long and rather untidy hair, open collar, and intelligent eyes. It was like seeing it for the first time because of the poor quality of existing engravings. Even Reynolds' copy in 1760 was inaccurate.[42] So with the Duke's permission, he asked his friend the painter Ozias Humphry, who over the years copied for him many drawings and paintings of poets and critics, to draw it. When Malone received Humphry's drawing, he wrote on the back of it, 'This excellent drawing of Shakespeare was made in the spring of 1783 by that excellent artist, Mr. Ozias Humphry, from the only original picture extant, which formerly belonged to Sir William Davenant, and now [is] in the possession of the Duke of Chandos. The painter is unknown.' Humphry's faithful copy was 'invaluable', he noted with a sense of having contributed significantly to Shakespearean iconography, because the original was 'in a state of decay.' He added, 'Mr. Humphry thinks that Shakespeare was about the age of forty three when this portrait was painted; which fixes its probable date to the year 1607.'[43] 'You have made me very happy by the Drawing of Shakspeare', he wrote to Humphry on 17 August from the Duke of Bedford's Woburn Abbey, where he had stopped to look at other paintings on his way to Ireland.[44] He included a not very faithful engraving of Humphry's drawing in his edition of Shakespeare with the conviction that its subject was, indeed, Shakespeare. As has recently been shown, 'unmediated' by the assortment of classical icons that had ornamented previous engravings, it sent the message that this was an image of a real poet, perhaps *the* real poet.[45] Malone always kept Humphry's copy hanging in his study;[46] it now hangs in the Folger Shakespeare Library in Washington, DC.

---

[40] Cited courtesy of the owner of the letter, Mr Eduard Verbeck, Hertogenbosch, Holland. On the Chandos portrait, see Boaden, *Inquiry*, pp. 39–59.

[41] In his copy of Langbaine's *Dramatic Poets* (Ms. Malone 129), Malone noted on 23 June: 'This day... I viewed the original picture of Shakespeare...' (p. 479).

[42] See Malone's notes on this portrait, Ms. Malone 40. Boaden, whom Malone lent copies by Humphry and Reynolds, describes the differences between the portrait and Reynolds's copy in *Inquiry*, pp. 41–42.   [43] Boaden, *Inquiry*, pp. 40–41.   [44] Prior, p. 459.

[45] De Grazia, *Shakespeare Verbatim*, p. 83.   [46] Boaden, *Inquiry*, p. 42.

Steevens was sceptical, dubbing it the 'Daventico–Betterno–Barryan–Keckian–Nicolsian–Chandosan' portrait after all the theories about its history. For him, the subject of the painting exhibited 'the complexion of a Jew, or rather that of a chimney-sweeper in the jaundice.'[47] His raillery was inspired not so much by doubts about the portrait as by rivalry with Malone. Boaden, who venerated Malone and accepted his judgment of the portrait, understanding Steevens' motives, commented that Steevens mischievously 'undertook to depreciate the present portrait.'[48] It was not until later, when he was researching Dryden's life, that Malone discovered what he thought was proof enough to overcome Steevens' doubts. As he wrote in his journal in 1788, 'There was a picture of Shakspeare painted by Sir Godfrey Kneller [between 1683 and 1692], and presented by him to Dryden; but I have never met with it. Perhaps it fell into Congreve's hands. Kneller probably copied the picture which Betterton then had, and which the Duke of Chandos now possesses.'[49] Malone's conviction that the Chandos portrait was of Shakespeare has never been conclusively proved. Today it hangs in the National Portrait Gallery in London.

6

Malone spent the autumn and winter of 1783–84 in Ireland. He had not been home for six years. He saw old friends, especially the Jephsons, and he made a point of visiting Percy and Charlemont; but naturally it was his family who were most delighted to see him again on the right side of the Irish Sea. By then they had given up the idea of persuading him to return to Ireland to live. He had left home uncertainly six years before, abandoning his legal practice, ideas of entering the Irish Parliament, and the prospect of a life as a country house owner at Shinglas. He returned as the editor of the *Supplement*; the critic who had announced the order of Shakespeare's plays; one of the exposers of the Rowley forgeries; the editor of an entirely new, forthcoming edition of Shakespeare; a member of the famous Club; and the established friend of many of the leading literary figures of the age. It was a remarkable success story in six short years.

He had seen his brother Richard in London a few times over the past years, but not his sisters or his brother's wife Phillipa, whom he scarcely knew. So there was much catching up to do and his visit was hectic. 'We have been chiefly employed in paying and receiving visits', he told Percy.[50] His sister-in-law had plenty of time to get to know him because he stayed at Baronston for his entire visit, except when he was in Dublin at his

---

[47] Cited in Schoenbaum, *Shakespeare's Lives* (rev. edn. 1991), p. 205.
[48] Boaden, *Inquiry*, pp. 43–47. On Steevens and the Chandos portrait, see James Boswell Junior's Advertisement, *PP (1821)*, I, pp. xxiv-xxvi.   [49] Prior, 'Maloniana', pp. 380–81.
[50] 30 September 1783, *P–M Letters*, p. 7.

brother's town house on Sackville Street He charmed her: 'he has an uncommon good understanding with the most Humane Gentle disposition I ever saw united with what are allow'd uncommon parts … '.[51]

After attending to his affairs at Shinglas, he helped in his brother's election campaign for a seat in the Irish House of Commons. 'On my arrival here about a month ago', he wrote to Percy, 'I plunged into the midst of a contested County Election, in which my brother was engaged. After a ten days struggle, I had the pleasure to see him come off victorious.' This was the sort of life that but for the grace of his uncle's legacy he might well be leading. It still did not suit him; his brother's victory was 'the only compensation one can have (if indeed it be one) for going through so troublesome a business.'[52] He returned to London in March 1784, eager to return to his work. Six months was too long to have been away from it.

[51] This letter to her aunt in England on 26 October 1783, and others from Phillipa cited below, are taken from a transcription in 1946 by John Sawyer in his notebook, OFB. The manuscripts of the letters have since disappeared.   [52] *P–M Letters*, p. 7.

6

'*O brave we!*'
Helping Boswell with the *Tour to the Hebrides*

1

Returning to London in March 1784 – a journey he broke up with a visit to Oxford to see Warton and the picture gallery[1] – Malone knew that the next few years would be filled with arduous scholarly work. He did not anticipate, in the bargain, spending hundreds of hours with Boswell on projects made urgent by Johnson's death at the end of the year. This Boswellian connection accounted for the divided focus of his work during the second half of the 1780s between Shakespeare and Johnson. Not yet established as a leading Shakespearean with his own edition under his belt, he was nonetheless willing to slow down his own work to help Boswell.

He worked away quietly with his Shakespeare, spending much of his time at the British Museum. He was also in great demand socially. He was frequently a guest at predominantly male dinner parties with Reed, Windham, Burney, Boswell, Reynolds, Burke, John Courtenay, Byng, Banks, and Henderson. On 19 December 1784, for example, he dined at Lord Palmerston's in Hanover Square with Reynolds, Banks, Windham, and Langton – all close friends of Johnson's who attended his funeral the following day. An entry by Windham in his diary suggests the casual and spontaneous nature of many of these dinners, often the result of an accidental meeting at a coffee-house, someone's home, a bookshop, or the theatre: 'Fell in, fortunately, with a dinner at Malone's. Found much satisfaction in such a restoration to better society, with the health of the country to qualify me to enjoy it.' Just as spontaneously, on the other hand, Windham, always the great sportsman, could decide not to go to Malone's – 'I was to have dined at Malone's, but went instead to a boxing match.'[2] Malone continued faithfully to attend the Club dinners; on one occasion in May 1786, the members commissioned him 'to procure a hogshead of Claret from Ireland.'[3] Courtenay, elected to The Club in 1788, a member of the House of Commons, and a voluminous author both in verse and prose

---

[1] He noted the visit in his copy of Gerard Langbaine's *Dramatick Poets*, BL Add. Ms. 45613.

[2] Windham, *The Diary of the Right Hon. William Windham 1784–1810*, ed. Mrs Henry Baring (1866), pp. 123, 84.   [3] M. E. G. Duff, *Annals of The Club 1764–1914* (1914), p. 7.

– although of nothing of importance – became a good friend, as did
Reynolds and Boswell. The four took to calling themselves The Gang.

Malone and Boswell met in 1781, possibly on 14 April when Boswell
records in his journal that they were dinner guests at Reynolds'.[4] They met
occasionally at Club dinners, though they had little chance to get to know
each other well before 1785 because Boswell could manage only a few weeks
in London every year away from Scotland. London is where he wanted to
be, but Scotland had claims on him. He loved his family and hated being
away from them, but he hated the life of a country squire at their estate at
Auchinleck and practising law in Edinburgh. Dejected and fretful, even
morbidly depressed in Scotland, he would come alive the nearer he got to
London. He desperately hoped, against his wife's wishes, to move his family
there permanently. The city fed him energy and creativity.

Malone knew – everyone knew – that for years Boswell had been keeping
notes of his conversations with Johnson, first perhaps simply to preserve his
conversation and then later with a view to writing his biography. After
Johnson's death, the public expected Boswell to publish his biography
expeditiously, but the booksellers commissioned Sir John Hawkins to write
it instead. An original member of The Club and generally disliked for his
rudeness, Hawkins quarrelled with Steevens and on one occasion even
forcibly turned him out of his house; he also insulted Burke. Malone
mentions Hawkins disparagingly in his journal as having helped himself
surreptitiously to a number of Johnson's private papers. He was not alone
in doubting the value of any biography Hawkins could produce, despite his
access to many valuable manuscripts.

Mrs Hester Lynch Piozzi, too, formerly Mrs Hester Lynch Thrale,
decided to write on Johnson. Johnson had met this intelligent Blue
Stocking lady and her husband in 1764 and for a time became almost
domesticated at the Thrale home in Streatham Place. Over the years she
recorded a number of personal anecdotes about Johnson that she promised
some day to give to the public. She also harboured bitter feeling towards
Johnson and his friends that Malone, Boswell, and a number of others
feared might distort her treatment of Johnson. It was time for Boswell to
pull himself together and produce something on Johnson without delay.

Against this background of competition and rivalry, the moment arrived
when Malone and Boswell took special notice of each other. It happened at
Malone's house on the evening of 29 April 1785. Malone invited Boswell,
Mrs Byng, and some other female company for dinner. In the course of the
evening, Boswell must have mentioned the manuscript of his *Journal of a*

---

[4] *Boswell 1778–82*, p. 323 (*Malahide*, XIV, p. 19). See Boswell's mention of Malone in his journal
before they met in 1781: 15 and 30 April 1780, *Boswell 1778–82*, pp. 324, 336; see also 7 May
1781, *Boswell 1778–82*, p. 347). On their first meeting, see Osborn, 'Edmond Malone and Dr.
Johnson', p. 10; and Pottle, *The Literary Career of James Boswell, Esq.* (1929), pp. 162–63.

Tour to the Hebrides with Samuel Johnson, LL.D. that he had brought with him to London in late March, determined to prepare it for the press. Acknowledging it needed a good deal of revision and editing, he must also have confessed that he had done almost nothing about it since he arrived, having consumed his time instead in a regimen of dining, womanizing, and drinking. In the past, Johnson had encouraged and calmed him when his melancholy spirits drove him to such excesses in London. But Johnson, whom Boswell had adopted as one of several substitute father-figures in the vacuum created by his own father's neglect, was no longer there. It began to look as if he would not soon, or perhaps ever, get his manuscript into publishable shape. Malone sized up the problem immediately and they talked well into the night about the *Tour* and Boswell's aspirations of joining the English Bar. 'Sat with him till two in the morning', Boswell wrote in his journal afterwards, 'full of bar scheme, and *was* encouraged.'[5]

Malone knew that Boswell's spirits were mercurial. In company he could be brilliant and animated; when alone, he could fall into depression and despair. His instability had several causes, from his father's disappointment with him to his frustrated ambition to live in London where he hoped either to practise law or represent Ayrshire as a Member of Parliament. He was also ineffective in securing patronage and preferment. Left on his own without the disciplining influences of friends and family, at best he found it difficult to write, at worst he succumbed to wine and women. And yet the *Tour*, not to mention the *Life of Johnson*, would require countless hours of lonely and disciplined work.

What sort of advice could Malone give Boswell and what qualities did Boswell recognize in Malone that attracted him? Boswell needed someone on whom he could depend for regular encouragement and confidence, one to whom he could confess his limitations and sense of inadequacy. Malone was one year younger than Boswell, but he found himself cast in the role of Boswell's stable and wiser brother. He was also, like Boswell, devoted to preserving the public's memory of Johnson; and he recognized Boswell's genius for making friends and recording conversations with a sense of immediacy that made Johnson live again in thousands of ways. Self-assured and self-disciplined, he possessed the editorial judgment, taste, and decisiveness Boswell needed.

Beyond the practical and literary basis of their friendship, they also quickly developed a deep and fiercely loyal fondness for each other, one that survived differences of judgment and opinion as collaborators and continued unabated for ten years until Boswell died in 1795. It was a matter of only a few weeks before Malone was signing his letters to Boswell, 'Yours

[5] *Hebrides*, pp. x–xxi. On the Malone–Boswell friendship, see Osborn, 'Edmond Malone and Dr. Johnson', pp. 10–20; Baker, introduction to *B–M Corr.*, pp. 165–88; Frank Brady, *James Boswell: The Later Years, 1769–1795* (1984), pp. 282–311.

affectionately', a rare formula in eighteenth-century letters.[6] Thus was born one of the most productive partnerships in English literary history – one that produced, as Malone hoped, two great works of literature.

The day after that dinner at Malone's, Boswell began to work with fresh incentive. He spent much of the next day working on the *Tour* – 'In almost all forenoon writing *Tour*' – and arranging with his publisher Charles Dilly and the printer Henry Baldwin to have it come out that year. 'You must *feed* the press', Malone told him. But there were too many distractions in May, and it was not until the end of the month that he threw himself into the project wholeheartedly. He turned to Malone for help. Several times every week they worked together. There were morning, afternoon, evening, and late night sessions, almost daily. They breakfasted, lunched, took tea, and dined over the *Tour*. Boswell's journal for the next four months is full of entries such as the one for 3 June, 'Was almost all the forenoon with Malone revising "Hebrides"'; or the one for 22 June, 'Went to Malone and corrected well.' 'Malone all morning', he noted on 28 June.

There is little evidence in Malone's hand of his proposed emendations of the *Tour* for the first edition, which was published on 1 October, because the two men were constantly in each other's company at Malone's house, going over the journal together. Malone probably read the journal aloud, suggesting revisions as he went along, which Boswell on the spot either accepted, rejected, or modified. Their procedure – based on Malone's tried and tested method in his own work – was to remove a sheet of the journal from Boswell's notebook and make changes directly on it or, if the revisions were so lengthy as to make the text difficult to read, write them out on loose leaves, so-called 'papers apart', cueing them to the text. As a result, they transcribed far less. They then sent these sheets and ancillary papers to Baldwin, whose compositor would decipher the sometimes labyrinthine marginal notes, deletions, and additions and set them in type while the two collaborators continued to prepare the next batch of copy. In this way they were able to 'feed the press.' When it came to preparing the second edition published in December, they would not be this efficient because Boswell was away then from London and Malone had to send him lists of emendations through the post, either to accept or reject. But their correspondence about the second edition gives us a better idea of Malone's suggested revisions and Boswell's responses.[7]

At least twice that summer Malone had to cancel a session with Boswell because he had fallen behind with Shakespeare. On 27 July, Boswell wrote in his journal, 'Malone was busy today with his Shakespeare. So I could not

---

[6] *Hebrides*, p. xviii.
[7] See *B–M Corr.*, pp. 175, 188, 203–65; and Brady, *James Boswell: The Later Years*, p. 286. In the discussion below of Malone's editorial help, I take my examples from his and Boswell's work on both the first and second editions.

get any of his time.' 'I am so much in arrear', Malone wrote to him on 9 August, 'that I must devote the whole of to-morrow to preparing some copy for my compositors, who are at a dead stand-still in consequence of my late neglect; but I will give you the *whole of thursday*; – I shall expect you at breakfast, and we will have a beefstake [*sic*] above stairs.'[8] He was as good as his word, for in his journal for the following day Boswell records a very heavy day's work winnowing out the 'chaff' from his manuscript: 'Malone devoted the whole of this day to me, that we might get forward with my "Tour". I breakfasted, dined, drank tea, and supt with him, and sat till near two in the morning. Yet we did not get a great deal winnowed, there was so very much chaff in that portion of it.' Nothing but the Johnsonian cause and his affection for Boswell could have induced Malone to part with so much of his time. Also, he could see that it was a tonic for Boswell to work under a steady hand. He pressured him to work hard, but he also relaxed with him and praised him. Seldom as happy as when he was with Malone, Boswell had only the highest praise for his collaborator's literary and editorial skills. He wrote to Thomas Barnard, Bishop of Killaloe, on 1 July, giving Malone credit for his progress: 'My *Journal* is revised by Mr. Malone, who I really think is the best critick of our age; and he not only winnows from it the chaff which in the hurry of immediate collection could not but be in it, but suggests little elegant variations, which though they do not alter the sense, add much grace to the expression.'[9]

Malone contributed grace of expression, but his chief objective was to help his friend transform a work that was essentially spontaneous – a record of events composed soon after they occurred – into a piece of more finished and discreet prose. A journal is a private affair, and a feature of Boswell's is that it features his personality as much as Johnson's. Malone's view was that while its details would interest, even fascinate, the public, that does not mean they all ought to be made public. Johnson himself, although he was delighted with what he read of the journal and urged Boswell to publish it, had spoken critically of many people, like The Revd. Kenneth Macaulay whom he called 'the most ignorant booby and the grossest bastard.' But should the public know that? Would Johnson have wanted the public to know that? Such passages needed to be judged individually in light of the feelings of the people described and the dignity of Johnson himself, without at the same time sacrificing the Boswellian colour, spirit, accuracy, and personal energy of the prose.

Even under the influence of Malone's tempering judgment, Boswell got into trouble with friends as well as foes by including remarks that injured feelings and were attacked as inaccurate. Since Boswell felt that his principal strength lay in recording conversations, he often resisted Malone's

[8] *B–M Corr.*, p. 197. See Malone's note to Boswell, c. 23 June, pp. 195–96.
[9] Yale Boswell Papers, C.1880.1.

efforts to eliminate passages he thought were indecorous. It must have been after discussions with Malone about that specific subject that on 16 September he noted in his journal, 'An addition to my "Tour" (defending *my* faculty of writing conversations) occurred to me. So I staid in town and Malone and I laboured as usual.' In the 'Advertisement' to the third edition in August 1786, he defended the 'authenticity' of his recorded conversations: 'I will venture to predict, that this specimen of the colloquial talents and extemporaneous effusions of my illustrious fellow-traveller will become still more valuable, when, by the lapse of time, he shall have become an *ancient*... '[10] Malone knew enough not to try to emasculate this aspect of Boswell's genius, but he also wished to protect his friend from the recriminations he was convinced some passages would provoke.

There were other problems, such as the matter of detail. Close observer that he was, Boswell often recorded minutely what he saw. If he retained everything he had written, the book would be too long, especially in the format of an octavo with the wide margins to which Dilly had agreed. Much of the detail, moreover, was irrelevant and would diffuse the narrative impact. As Boswell's biographer has put it, Malone conformed to his age's neo-classical preference for generality, according to which 'small particulars' (Malone's phrase) in a narrative were thought to interfere with the beauty and coherence of the whole.[11] He recommended surgical paring of detail, deleting, for example, descriptions of villages, local customs, meals, and most descriptions of landscape if he thought they added little to the portrait of Johnson. He did not, in any case, think Boswell was good at describing landscape, and Johnson had already presented a good deal of this kind of description in his own account of the *Tour*.

Boswell seldom disagreed with Malone, even over the latter's excision of Scotticisms. As a Scot, he lacked some confidence in phrasing things acceptably for the English reader, and the last thing either of them wanted to see was the author ridiculed for provincial and 'vulgar' language from the North. 'A wild *muir*', Malone noted in early June, 'I believe is a Scotch word. We call it *moor*.' Drawing attention to the phrase, 'when a man's house falls into *disrepair*', Malone remarked, 'I doubt whether Dr. J. used this word – because, I believe, it does not exist. Perhaps – "decay" may do.' As regards '*worthy-like* Clergyman', 'this is a Scotticism. I don't know what it means & therefore know not how to supply its place.'[12] About what Boswell described as 'some pretty sore rubs' that Burke had received from Johnson, Malone remarked, 'Is not this a vulgar phrase – "smart blows" would be better, though I don't like it much.' Boswell protested against this last one and, momentarily, Malone relented; but after talking it over with

---

[10] Hill-Powell, V, p. 4.   [11] *Hebrides*, p. xi; *B–M Corr.*, p. 198.

[12] Malone included these examples in the first list of emendations (Yale Boswell Papers, C.1880.1) that he sent to Boswell with his letter dated 3–10 June 1785 (*B–M Corr.*, pp. 189–93).

Bennet Langton, who 'said *sore* was certainly unjustifiable and must be a Scotticism', he insisted it be changed, adding: 'A rub cannot be *sore*, though it may make the person rubbed *sore*. So to avoid impropriety, and to keep to your *idea*, it is printed "severe rubs" considering *rubs* metaphorically.'[13]

Even after many such changes, Boswell still was criticized in the papers for his language, as in the 5 November issue of the *Public Advertiser* that Malone, wagging his finger, copied out and sent him: 'The only *deep* Observation of Boswell in his *Johnsoniana* is his remark that a man may *dance* gracefully and *walk* awkwardly. As an illustration, the Scottish authors *speak* as if they were never out of the Isle of Sky [*sic*], and write as anglicisedly pure as a Chesterfield.' Malone had anticipated this kind of criticism. It was, in fact, chiefly Boswell's Scottishness that was attacked in the critical reviews. To underline this again, Malone sent his friend what he called 'a paltry epigram' from the *Morning Post* of 20 October, part of which read:

> And now to raise a little cash,
>   This Quack of Caledonia,
> Crams JOHNNY BULL [with] sickly trash,
>   And calls it the JOHNSONIA.[14]

They learned their lesson. For the next edition, Malone, Courtenay, Langton, Reynolds, and others were ready to ring the alarm over any expression that could be remotely construed as a Scotticism.

Malone also corrected wordiness, inelegant phrasing, and bad grammar. But often he seems fussy and pedantic when trying to refine Boswell's vigorous style. He proposed changing 'a violent quarrel' to 'a warm altercation', for example, not just to lower the temperature of the scene but also to make the sentence sound more elegant. 'Might push the bottle around' became 'urged drinking.' Although he was hunting for wordy phrasing, he sometimes made Boswell more, not less, wordy. In place of Boswell's 'I loved to behold Dr. Samuel Johnson rolling about in this old magazine of antiquities,' he recommended, 'It gave me pleasure to behold ...'. Instead of 'It gives me pleasure that by mentioning his name I connect his title...', he recommended, 'It gives me pleasure that the mention of this gentleman gives me an opportunity of subscribing to the just and handsome...'. Elsewhere, Boswell described a sermon Johnson delivered 'in a boat on the sea... upon a fine, calm Sunday morning'; Malone drew a mist down on the scene by suggesting, 'in a boat upon the sea, which was perfectly calm, on a day appropriated to religious worship.'

---

[13] *B–M Corr.*, pp. 203, 238. They were then working on the second edition.

[14] Malone's extract from the *Public Advertiser* is in the Boswell Papers, Ca. 1892. See *B–M Corr.*, p. 242, note 19, for the epigram and other attacks on Boswell that appeared in the *Post*.

By 20 September, they had finished revising all the sheets, and on that day Boswell composed his dedication of the *Tour* to Malone, without whom there would have been no book to dedicate. A Dedication to Malone was also just the place to make his claims for authenticity, for the public was coming to see in Malone the new apostle of scholarly and historical accuracy. He was also a Johnsonian and, above all, a friend:

As one of those who were intimately acquainted with him [Johnson], you have a title to this address. You have obligingly taken the trouble to peruse the original manuscript of this Tour, and can vouch for the strict fidelity of the present publication. Your literary alliance with our much lamented friend, in consequence of having undertaken to render one of his labours more complete, by your edition of Shakspeare, a work which I am confident will not disappoint the expectations of the publick, gives you another claim. But I have a still more powerful inducement to prefix your name to this volume, as it gives me an opportunity of letting the world know that I enjoy the honour and happiness of your friendship ... [15]

This was totally sincere. They were proud to tell the public they were good friends. Malone, who had insisted that Boswell should not mention him as the author of any passages, must have been highly gratified to have his forthcoming Shakespeare edition mentioned in such a memorable publication.

Boswell was sincere but not entirely accurate when he wrote that Malone had merely 'perused' the original manuscript. It was common practice in the eighteenth century to revise journals heavily for publication. In that spirit, Malone, as Boswell put it, 'adopted' this 'Literary child', sifted through it, and made corrections everywhere, even altering the wording of what people were supposed to have said. Boswell recalled only the main words in Johnson's and others' remarks; he did not have a photographic memory, which is why on 13 October he could, with a clear conscience, reiterate to Malone, who had altered many of Johnson's sentences, '*Authenticity* is my chief boast.'[16] Neither of them saw their alterations as damaging the authenticity of the book, nor as materially altering the portrayal of Johnson.

2

Boswell was not in London to bask in the glow of publication when the *Tour* came out on 1 October. He had lost no time in returning to his family at Auchinleck. Any apprehensions he may have had of how well the *Tour* would sell were quickly dispelled. 'I heartily congratulate you on the astonishing success of your labours', Malone wrote to him on 5 October with the good news; 'there will [be] an immediate call for a second edition,

---

[15] Hill-Powell, V, pp. 1–2.
[16] For Boswell's attitudes towards his collaboration with Malone, see Brady, *James Boswell: The Later Years*, pp. 287–91.

which must be put to press before you return to town.' 'O *brave we!*'
Malone exulted in a letter to Boswell two weeks later, for Dilly had just told
him only 230 copies of the first edition remained in his warehouse. All 1,500
copies printed were sold out within a month and another edition was called
for as soon as possible. Reynolds had already read it twice and was 'very
lavish in its praise', although 'he thinks you do not seem sufficiently warm
& hearty toward Dr J. I cannot say I think there is any foundation for this.'
Courtenay, too, was 'highly pleased.'[17]

Praise of the *Tour* far outweighed criticism – the papers 'have been
living on you ... this fortnight', Malone told him[18] – but there was cause for
concern. Some of the criticism infuriated Malone, who sprang to Boswell's
defence in an anonymous article in the 6–8 October issue of the *St. James's
Chronicle*, signing it, 'An Enemy to Nonsense and Slander.'[19] Suggestions,
complaints, and attacks came in from friends and foes alike. Reynolds,
Courtenay, Windham, Langton, Reed, Burney, Burke, William Gerard
Hamilton, John Wilkes, and others suggested or demanded that certain
parts be changed. There were injured feelings and disagreements, especially
outside the Johnson circle, about what Johnson actually said. Malone was
caught in the middle, mediating as best he could. There were few people
who could be counted on to appreciate, without reservation, Boswell's
honesty in reporting conversation as it really occurred. Boswell was raising
this sort of writing to an art, one almost too boldly original for the times.
Malone was in a unique position: he was closer to Boswell's thinking about
biography than perhaps anyone else living. If anyone could understand, he
could. And yet, with his tact and what Boswell increasingly regarded as
fussiness, he, too, continued to have reservations.

One of the most awkward moments came when Burke, not unreasonably,
conceived a strong dislike of the discussion of his literary style and wit.
Boswell's offending passage was this remark by Johnson on Burke's wit:
'No, sir, he never succeeds there. 'Tis low; 'tis conceit. I used to say Burke
never once made a good joke.'[20] To moderate this comment, Boswell had
inserted a long note arguing that Burke did, in fact, have a good wit, and
providing examples of it. Burke was not alone in thinking that only made
matters worse. Malone, Windham, Courtenay, and Hamilton – 'every one
in short' – liked neither the examples nor the explanation. They 'talk
loudly', Malone told him, 'that the specimens you have given of Burke's
wit are not good ones, that they have more of pun and conceit than of wit
in them. I was, you may remember, apprehensive of this, and thought it

---

[17] *B–M Corr.*, pp. 200–1. See Malone to Warton about the success of the *Tour* and Boswell's plans
for the *Life of Johnson*, 23 November, BL Add. Ms. 42561, fol. 317.
[18] *B–M Corr.*, p. 226.
[19] No. 3836, Thursday 6 October–Saturday 8 October, p. 4. The proof of this article is in the Yale
Boswell Papers, P82.   [20] *Hebrides*, p. 19.

dangerous to stake his character in this point of view on particular instances. Mr. Hamilton, who lived long in great intimacy with him, says, he could have given twenty better.'[21]

In light of Burke's well-known personal sensitivity to the press, it is surprising that during the first set of revisions Malone did not protest more vigorously to this public assessment of his wit. Even as they prepared the second edition, he not only did not throw out Boswell's anecdote, but 'tacked a rider' to it, as if written by Boswell, stating that Burke's wit was only one 'of the many talents he possesses, which are so various and extraordinary that it is very difficult to ascertain the rank and value of each.' It was a long and laboured note (over four hundred words) that Malone hoped would placate Burke and his friends, for (as he told Boswell) it 'pays B. a handsome compliment':[22]

I was well aware, how hazardous it was to exhibit particular instances of wit, which is of so airy and spiritual a nature as often to elude the hand that attempts to grasp it ... it is always dangerous to detach a witty saying from the group to which it belongs, and to set it before the eye of the spectator, divested of those concomitant circumstances, which gave it animation, mellowness, and relief. I venture, however, at all hazards, to put down the first instances that occurred to me, as proofs of Mr. Burke's lively and brilliant fancy; but am very sensible that his numerous friends could have suggested many of a superior quality.[23]

Boswell loved this note's 'rich plumage' and wanted Malone to sign it with his name or 'A Friend.'[24] But Malone declined. Indeed, it may have struck him as absurd for Boswell to attribute this one note to him when the book was full of his notes. He told Boswell that if he wished to tell Burke who wrote the note, he could – 'To this I have no objection – but I will prove to you decisively when we meet that nothing more should be done.'[25]

Boswell did write to Burke,[26] but Burke, who knew his own powers and was apparently in less doubt than Malone of their 'rank and value', was livid when he read the note. He wrote a chilling tongue-in-cheek rebuke to Boswell on 4 January 1786, which was aimed at Malone as well:

I am extremely obliged to you and to Mr. Malone (to whom I beg my best compliments) for your friendly sollicitude [sic] with regard to a point relating to me, about which I am myself not very anxious ... I shall be well content to pass down to a long posterity in Doctor Johnsons [sic] authentick Judgment, and in your permanent record, as a dull fellow and a tiresome companion, when it shall be known through the same long period, that I have had such men as Mr. Boswell and

[21] 19 October 1785, B–M Corr., p. 230.   [22] B–M Corr., p. 230.
[23] Hill-Powell, V, pp. 33–34n.   [24] 27 October 1785, B–M Corr., pp. 247, 251.
[25] 5 November 1785 , B–M Corr., p. 267.
[26] Boswell to Burke, 20 December 1785, B–M Corr., pp. 147–48. On Burke's and Boswell's estrangement, see B–M Corr., pp. 90–92; Hill-Powell, V, p. 32 and n. 3, and p. 465; and Brady, Boswell: The Later Years, pp. 304–5.

Mr. Malone as my friendly counsel in the Cause which I have lost ... I have turned to Mr. Malones [*sic*] Note. It is sound and judicious in every respect, in its general principles; though by his partiality and condescension only, applicable to me.

While this contretemps did not damage Burke's growing friendship with Malone, it did strain his with Boswell. The editor of Burke's letters has wondered, 'how could the usually tactful Malone have compounded the offence?'. Perhaps because 'Boswell (and Malone too) thought Burke beyond the petty vanities of ordinary men.'[27]   But one may wonder whether it was reasonable to expect Burke to forgive an insult in the main text, which everyone would read, because he was praised in a long note, which far fewer would read. In any case, he probably concluded there was no real penitence on Boswell's part since he did not eliminate Johnson's remark in the second or third edition.

John Wilkes was also upset. He told Boswell there was 'a horrid deal of trash' in the *Tour* that would hurt Johnson's reputation. This did not unduly disturb Malone, who thought Wilkes hot-headed, rakish, impetuous, and anarchic. His censure of Wilkes, in the following reassuring letter to Boswell, was largely politically motivated and provides an early sign that his literary judgment was not unaffected by his strong bias against radical thought and behaviour:

Wilkes, I am told, says, 'you have now fired a pocket pistol at Johnson's reputation; presently [with the *Life*] you mean to discharge a blunderbuss at it, and afterwards Madam Piozzi is to stab at him with a stiletto.' Is this in his letter to you, or only oral? – Poor man! how little he knows! But I am sure he has no taste for *good sense*, and would rather have the name of saying a good thing, than benefit mankind by instructing them, if he were capable of doing so; which I believe he is not.[28]

Sir Alexander Macdonald, a large landowner and chieftain on the Isle of Skye, further clouded Boswell's life in November and December. He had entertained Boswell and Johnson at his home on their tour – meanly and cheerlessly, they thought – and was outraged to read Boswll's portrait of him as a man of boorish and cheerless tastes who oppressed his tenants ('a penurious gentleman' and 'a rapacious Highland Chief') and as a man with a grudging sense of hospitality.[29]   Boswell had reconsidered what he wrote about Macdonald in his original draft and tempered it for the first edition by cancelling a leaf and, unfortunately with insufficient help from Malone, rewriting some of it. The revision did not go far enough, at least not for Macdonald. Malone could not resist lecturing Boswell when he heard of Macdonald's wrath:

[27] *B–M Corr.*, p. 92.
[28] 19 October 1785, *B–M Corr.*, p. 235. Malone's irritation is also evident in his letters to Boswell, 19 and 21 October, *B–M Corr.*, pp. 230–31, 242.
[29] *Hebrides*, 1st edn., p. 474; Hill-Powell, V, p. 378.

If we had happened to have laid our heads together on that business, I think we could have made out of your materials, – a short, argumentative, witty and biting piece, which would not have been open to any just animadversion: – but it is now in vain to think more of it.[30]

It was Margaret Boswell's fear that Macdonald might challenge her husband to a duel that alerted Boswell to the gravity of the problem. He told Malone that while he was amazed 'the little we suffered to escape' had infuriated Macdonald, he now was sorry, on Margaret's account chiefly, 'that *any* part of it appears (with his *name* I mean)': 'She has been in sad anxiety lest he should call me out and was going to write to you intreating you would prevent it. I have no great fear of *that*. But why be in any degree a publick executioner?' 'I have the milk of human kindness in abundance', he moaned; 'I have been much disconcerted by my Wife's affectionate fears.' He, therefore, proposed cancelling another leaf and sent Malone his revisions of the damning passages, 'which must be well weighed, when our heads are laid together.' He also asked him to allay his wife's fears if he knows for certain that Macdonald 'does not take it hot.'[31]

But Macdonald did 'take it hot.' He wrote Boswell, who had recently arrived in London, a vitriolic letter on 27 November containing some Latin verses that did little for the latter's peace of mind: 'Damn me if with a heavier weapon [than the pen] I do not tickle your ass's head, till the blood flows down and the bare skull reeks horridly where I have ripped off the hide.'[32] All he wanted to do was make Boswell shake in his boots. He felt that if he could bully him into making revisions in the second edition, the public would believe Boswell had been humiliated under pressure. He succeeded on both counts. Courtenay advised Boswell how to fire a pistol and over the next month he and Malone took turns holding his hand until the quarrel died down. It was bad publicity. Malone's main concern was not Boswell's personal safety, which he never doubted, but the damage Macdonald could do to Boswell's reputation as a writer and, by transference, to Dr Johnson's.[33]

These uncertain days were made more anxious by another indiscretion of Boswell's while he was in Scotland. He wrote a tactless and impulsive pamphlet, *A Letter to the People of Scotland ... Diminishing the Lords of Session*, which had the desired effect of helping to kill a Bill in the House of Commons to reduce the number of Lords of Session by one-third. In it Boswell discoursed in an exaggerated, personal, and patriotic vein about what he saw as the inglorious state of Scottish politics. His most recent

---

[30] 5 November 1785, *B–M Corr.*, p. 271.   [31] 11 November 1785, *B–M Corr.*, p. 279.
[32] This is quoted from Brady, *James Boswell: The Later Years*, p. 308.
[33] On the Macdonald affair, see *B–M Corr.*, p. 295, n.8; *Malahide*, XVI, pp. 221–59; and Brady, *Boswell: The Later Years*, pp. 306–11.

biographer has described the performance as 'a desperate case of exhibitionism.'[34] It also sharply attacked certain eminent political figures.

The pamphlet reminded Malone of his ambivalence regarding Boswell's persona as a writer. On the one hand, he knew that Boswell's prose entertained because it was honest, animated, and self-centred. But his friend was reckless and often risked making himself a laughing stock. The pamphlet angered him because he had invested much energy and time protecting Boswell from a hostile press. It angered him also because what was at stake was Boswell's credibility as Johnson's biographer. Another firm rebuke was called for. 'You cannot imagine how much mischief your own pamphlet has done you', he wrote on 5 November,

and how slow people are to allow the praise of good thinking and good writing to one whom they think guilty of such indiscretion in that pamphlet as a man of sound sense (they allege) would not be guilty of. I venture to tell you this, because perhaps you will not hear it from others; and it proves decisively my doctrine, that a man should in his writings have as few *weak* places as possible. Pray turn this to account hereafter.

Boswell knew that Malone's letter was 'friendly' and in his best interest, and he promised to reform, though not entirely: 'I shall henceforth *to a certain degree* be more cautious to leave as few *weak* places (in the opinion of my friends) in what I publish.'[35]

3

While Boswell was in Scotland, Malone superintended the next edition. As he told Boswell on 5 October, he had 'read the whole once more over, and with great delight.' He kept 'a table of errata, which cover two half sheets. Many of them however are very minute.' Apart from typographical errors, 'which you may safely trust to me, if the second edition should go to press before you return', there were several paragraphs that 'might be improved.'[36] So they were off on three or so more months of revision, leading to publication of the second edition in December. Since they had to write to each other until Boswell returned in mid-November, we have a better record of their working relationship, and their disagreements, this time around. Their letters abound with hundreds of queries and answers.

Boswell generally welcomed Malone's revisions of his Scotticisms, wordiness, and inelegant phrasing. To quote his biographer again, 'one is a little shocked by the absence in Boswell of the jealousy of authorship, his lack of confidence in his own private and natural style.'[37] Nonetheless, he

---

[34] Brady, *James Boswell: The Later Years*, p. 277; see his discussion of the *Letter*, pp. 274–81.
[35] *B–M Corr.*, p. 271; see also Boswell to Malone, (11 November), p. 276.
[36] Ibid., pp. 202–3.   [37] *Hebrides*, pp. xii, xvi.

continued to resist what he saw as Malone's excessive dislike of the colloquial and his taste for more bookish language. Malone scrutinized every sentence for syntax and phraseology. 'Are you not too desireous [*sic*] of perfection?', Boswell protested on 2 November; 'We must make *some* allowance for the Book being a *Journal*.'[38]

Boswell resisted most vigorously Malone's efforts to suppress his intrusion into the narrative or make him reconsider Johnson's remarks on their contemporaries and friends. A sentimental scene between Veronica, Boswell's infant daughter, and Johnson is a good example of what Malone and Courtenay disliked. Boswell had written that Johnson interpreted Veronica's 'little infantine noise' as a sign of fondness, almost as if she divined his greatness, and that Johnson resolved 'she should have five hundred pounds of additional fortune.'[39] Courtenay 'wishes with me', Malone wrote, 'that Veronica had been left quietly in her nursery.' Boswell disagreed: 'I am convinced you are right as to the effect in *general* of weak parts in a Book and that *my way* is no excuse. But to omit Veronica *now* would do no good. It would not be put to *my* credit; Besides I am fond of it. So I insist on retaining it ... To omit it *now* would be to invite attacks, by flying.' In his next letter, he added, 'Veronica is herself so fond of her appearance that she would be much mortified if I should delete her.' As the sheets had already been set up at the printer's by the time he received Boswell's belated reply, Malone had to give in about Veronica; he agreed it 'would be foolish *now* to omit it.' Malone and Courtenay proved to be right, for inevitably the reviews picked up that scene and mocked Boswell for it.[40]

The urgency and pressure of revising the *Tour* had made an impression on Boswell's wife, Margaret, who (against her instincts) pushed Boswell to return to Malone for the final stages of the work. 'My Wife says she wishes I would set out so as to be with you as soon as possible', he wrote on 30 October; she tells him his 'spirits are like brandy set on fire. If not constantly stirred the flame will go out.' 'It is strange that Scotland affects my spirits so woefully', he wrote on 8 November; 'I wish I were in Queen Anne Street East. And there's an end on't.' Malone was not about to let the flame go out, so that Boswell may have felt harassed by his collaborator: 'Your kind attention to my Book is wonderful', but 'let us ... *now* resolve not to look any more on the Book with a nice critical eye, but let the press work away. Yet the improvements are such we cannot regret the *curious* attention that has been bestowed.' Malone also supervised the table of contents,[41] plates, index, and other physical features of the book. 'You have certainly

---

[38] *B–M Corr.*, p. 266.   [39] *Hebrides*, 1st edn., pp. 16–17; Hill-Powell, V, pp. 25–26.
[40] 5, 13, 15 and 19 October, *B–M Corr.*, pp. 200–1, 208, 226, 227–28.
[41] Malone had definite ideas on how the *Tour* should be arranged (to Boswell, 5 November, *B–M Corr.*, p. 267).

the art of Bookmaking and Bookdressing in the utmost perfection', Boswell acknowledged. Boswell left Edinburgh on 12 November, bringing his materials for the *Life* with him, as Malone had suggested. From his point of view, he could not leave too soon.[42]

He stayed in London only for a month, but it was enough for them to bring the second edition to the verge of publication. And with the Macdonald quarrel behind him, Boswell was able to return to his old relaxed self in Malone's company. He was with him every day until he left on 22 December. On his last day, he wrote in his journal: 'I called once more on my amiable Malone, and he and I paid a visit to Sir Joshua.' That affectionate 'my' says much. Further evidence of their intimacy and trust lies in the final codicil to his will added on the 22nd: 'Having entire confidence in the discretion honour and talents of my friend Edmund [*sic*] Malone Esqr. I, in case of my death leave to him the care of all my Collection of Papers and Letters and Memorandums for writing the Life of Dr. Johnson...'[43] He left his papers behind in London, but instead of removing them to Queen Anne Street East, he left Malone the keys to a bureau and trunk containing the papers in the homes of Dilly and General Paoli, his Corsican friend whose political cause he had championed years earlier. It was sensible of him to leave his papers in London. Malone had told him more than once that he could never write the *Life of Johnson* anywhere else.

The second edition received, again, mixed reviews. One anonymous attack in the December issue of the *Gentleman's Magazine* censured Boswell for his vanity, nationality, and general absurdity, and claimed that Johnson had told Boswell the journal was not fit for publication.[44] Malone was incensed. It was 'very provoking that such a quantity of nonsense should be talked and written about Johnson. I have not time to answer half of it but I positively will do something. Facit indignatio.' Boswell was delighted his friend planned to 'knock this foe and two or three more against one another.'[45] Malone sprang to Boswell's defence in a 5,000-word article in the January issue of the *Gentleman's Magazine*.[46] He signed the article 'Anti Stiletto', which translated was 'Anti-Steevens', whom Malone suspected was the author of the December article. 'I suppose you have got the Gent. Magazine today', he wrote to Boswell on 1 February; 'I have, you see, worked hard for you.'[47]

[42] 30 October, 8, 2, and 11 November, *B–M Corr.*, pp. 262, 275–76, 266, 277.
[43] See Pottle, *Pride and Negligence: The History of the Boswell Papers* (New York, 1982), p. 9. On 28 May, Boswell added a codicil designating him one of the three executors of his manuscripts and letters.   [44] *Gentleman's Magazine*, LV (December, 1785), 959.
[45] 3 January 1786, *B–M Corr.*, p. 283; and p. 284.
[46] *Gentleman's Magazine*, LXVI, 17–23.
[47] *B–M Corr.*, p. 294. A third edition came out later in the year. See Malone to Boswell, 13 January 1786 (*B–M Corr.*, p. 289).

4

If Malone gave Boswell confidence, discipline, and stability, Boswell gave
Malone cheer. When he was not morbidly depressed, Boswell was a sociable
and adventurous companion. With Courtenay and Reynolds frequently
joining in, The Gang could brighten anyone's day. Throughout the 1785
summer of their intense collaboration, Boswell organized excursions and
encouraged Malone into female company. On 2 July he breakfasted with
him before a boating party to Richmond. Bad weather forced them to
cancel, but in the evening they walked to Westminster and 'fixed' a boat
for the next day. They were too late for the boat in the morning, so with
Malone's sisters, who with their brother and sister-in-law had stopped in
London on the way to the Continent, they set off for the gardens of
Richmond Old Park 'in a coach ... Courtney and Wyndham to follow.' In
Richmond they met Margaret Stuart, Margaret Boswell's old friend, who
'suggested King Henry's Mount *for our party*, and sent desert [*sic*]. Quite
pleasant. Tea at Castle Inn.' It was a lovely English summer day spent in
lovely gardens, the sort of outing to which Malone almost never treated
himself.[48]

Boswell organized another rural outing on 7 July with Malone, the
'ladies' – presumably again Malone's sisters and sister-in-law – and
Courtenay, this time to Twickenham to see Hampton Court, Strawberry
Hill, and Pope's famous, but by then pillaged, grotto. As a gesture of
friendship towards Malone, Walpole waived his rule that only four visitors
were allowed into Strawberry Hill at one time and admitted all six of them.
They then dined in Bushy Park, the royal park adjacent to Hampton Court,
'in the air.' Boswell and the same ladies were dinner guests several times at
Malone's house or at Malone's brother's, where one evening the happy
news awaited them that Richard Malone had officially been created Baron
Sunderlin of Lake Sunderlin in May, and that at last he had received his
patent and could now use his title. At Lord Sunderlin's on 10 July, Boswell
gallantly 'on *knee* did obeisance to *my Lady*.'[49]

The festive dinners continued throughout the summer and autumn.
Boswell writes of a dinner at Courtenay's on 29 July with 'choice company'
that included himself, Reynolds, Malone, Burke, and Windham: 'We had
admirable Burgundy and Claret', he notes, 'and excellent conversation.
We saw no Ladies, but had coffee and tea in the drawing room.'[50] Perhaps
it was Boswell who placed a note in the *Public Advertiser* on 4 August,
contrasting the sparkling conversation on one such occasion with the dull
society of noblemen and politicians too frequently publicized in the papers:

---

[48] 2 and 3 July 1785, *Malahide*, XVI, p. 104.
[49] 7 and 10 July 1785, *Malahide*, XVI, pp. 106–7.
[50] 29 July 1785, *Malahide*, XVI, p. 115.

'Many a dull dinner is announced in the newspapers given *to divers of the nobility* by temporary statesmen. How much superior was "the feast of reason and the flow of soul" at Mr. Courtenay's table last week? There sat Mr. Courtenay himself – Mr. Windham – Mr. Malone – Colonel [John] Erskine – Mr. [George] Dempster [MP] – Mr. Boswell – Mr. Burke!'[51] It was during this period that Malone began to see a great deal more of Burke. They were both dinner guests at Windham's the following evening, for example, with Lord Sunderlin, Courtenay, Reynolds, and Boswell, where they sat until eleven and then, in Boswell's words, 'walked out, sauntered a while, and then eat [*sic*] cold meat and drank negus [port with lemon juice] at the Prince of Wales's Coffeehouse, Conduit Street.' 'We have had many pleasant days together', Reynolds remarked at summer's end.[52]

In short, Boswell widened Malone's circle of friends for him. Courtenay's *Ode: To Edmund Malone, Esq*, the first draft of which Malone modestly helped revise in January 1786, celebrates the life that balances work, love, friendship, and joy – a mixture that characterized this, perhaps happiest, period of Malone's life:

> Whilst you illumine Shakspeare's page,
> And dare the future critick's rage,
>   Or on the past refine,
> Here many an eve I pensive sit,
> No Burke pours out a stream of wit.
>   No Boswell joys o'er wine.
>   ...
> Whilst through this pathless waste we stray,
> Are there no flowers to cheer the way?
>   And must we still repine?
> No; – Heaven, in pity to our woes,
> The gently-soothing balm bestows
>   Of Musick, Love, and Wine.
>   ...
> Enjoy the present fleeting day,
> And leave to Heaven the rest.[53]

For ten more years Malone and Boswell would remain the most intimate of friends, and for seven of those years the *Life of Johnson* would be their great common cause.

[51] *Public Advertiser*, 4 August 1785.   [52] *Boswell 1782–85*, p. 341.
[53] Malone added two stanzas (see Malone to Boswell, 3 January 1786, *B–M Corr.*, p. 282). It was printed in the *Gentleman's Magazine* in January, 1786, LVI, 66–67.

7

Deep in Shakespeare

1

It was well known that Malone was pushing himself hard all this time to bring out his portable edition of Shakespeare quickly after Reed's edition, which was certain to appear before the end of 1785. But his sights were already set on the large octavo edition that would include an extensive, but as yet undetermined, editorial apparatus. With this edition he planned to redefine Shakespearean study. And with Capell gone, Steevens calling himself a 'dowager editor', and Farmer in semi-retirement as the reclusive Master of Emmanuel College, Cambridge, the edition could earn him pre-eminence in Shakespearean scholarship.

The hundreds of hours he gave Boswell over the *Tour* and then the *Life of Johnson* slowed him down, but he simply pushed himself harder. 'My Shakspeare', he wrote to Warton on 23 November 1785, 'hardly leaves me time for eating, or sleeping';[1] and to Charlemont he wrote optimistically on 17 December, 'My edition of Shakespeare takes up all my time at present. I have printed about half my work, but it will be a full year before it will be completed.'[2] His strategy of beginning with the printing of the edition when he had completed about half of it doubled the burden of his task once his printer caught up with him, since he had to correct printed sheets even as he prepared new material for the press. The printer frequently stood still, waiting for new copy, while Malone struggled to keep him occupied. 'I am still very busily employed on that work', he told Percy in September 1786, 'the printing [of] it being a much more tedious business than I at first conceived ... However, I am now getting on apace. I am at present printing the sixth and seventh volumes, and the whole is to be comprized [*sic*] in ten, small octavo.' He flattered himself, he said, that he could finish in early May 1787, but he was having second thoughts: 'I have been so often deceived in my calculations that I dare not be too confident.'[3]

Under such pressure, he declined to travel to France with his family in the spring of 1786. His brother, sister-in-law, and two sisters passed through

---

[1] BL Add. MS. 42561, fol. 165. [2] *HMC*, XIII, 8, p. 31.
[3] 28 September 1786, *P–M Letters*, p. 34.

London in April or early May hoping to entice him. Catherine, who always kept in touch more than anyone else in the family, wrote to him on 9 June from Nice, 'an absolute Paradice [*sic*]' with its innumerable walks amid 'a mist of Orange trees', its sweet shrubs, sea, and breezes. Alluring images, surely; but the burdens of editing left him little time for regret.[4]

2

A well-informed contributor to the *Morning Post* in October 1785, after singling out Malone's forthcoming Shakespeare edition for anticipatory praise, waggishly asked whether the commentary in both Reed's announced edition and the one that rumour had it Ritson was preparing might not better appear 'without the text of the plays, in a volume or two by themselves.'[5] Malone in no way disapproved of Reed's project. The geniality of the man discouraged contentiousness and Malone had only respect for his edition of Robert Dodsley's *Old Plays* and his very useful *Biographia Dramatica* (1782; a revision of David Erskine Baker's *Companion to the Playhouse*, 1764). The two men remained the best of friends, dining frequently at each other's homes. Reed even called on Malone for help with his revisions of the *Johnson–Steevens* edition, which Malone was happy to give. He corrected old notes and supplied new ones. As for the text, Reed was not doing any fresh collating, but was simply reprinting the 1778 text. Malone helped him make it more correct in places where it had been demonstrably wrong, and looked forward to its appearance in December, not least, one may suppose, because about one-third of the new notes were his.[6]

If Malone had contentious rivals, they were Ritson and Steevens. One of the virtues of Reed's revised edition was that his contributions enabled him to even the score with Ritson quickly. Ritson at the time was on peaceful terms with Reed, but Malone and Reed must have agreed that this was the occasion to put Ritson in his place. Malone took his innings in several signed notes that are still extant in his hand in Reed's corrected copy of the 1778 *Johnson–Steevens* edition in the British Library. Others signed 'Editor' were equally critical. Ritson thought these were by Steevens until Reed told him he had written them: 'I must ... entreat you ... to consider me and me only as the author of every line signed Editor ... no person whatever interfered ... directly or indirectly but myself... '[7] On hearing that, Ritson transferred his allegiance from Reed to Steevens. To Reed he wrote on 22 February 1788, 'You adopted a mode of conduct which it would have been

[4] Arthur O'Neill Collection, 46B; OFB.   [5] *Morning Post*, 19 October 1785, p. 36.
[6] See J. Gilmer, *Isaac Reed*, p. 84. Reed deleted only three of Malone's thirty-three notes from the 1778 edition and 1780 *Supplement*. His edition was published on 15 December 1785.
[7] 22 February 1788. See *The Reed Diaries*, ed. Claude E. Jones (1946), pp. 277–78; also Arthur Sherbo, *Isaac Reed, Editorial Factotum* (1988).

perfectly natural for me to expect from Mr. Warton or Mr. Malone, but certainly not from you.'[8] Two years after Reed's edition came out and about one year after Malone's portable edition had forestalled Ritson's own plans for such a work, Ritson broke into print again with another stinging pamphlet, *The Quip Modest*, pillorying Reed but this time also setting his sights squarely on Malone.

Ritson's resentment, which is apparent throughout *The Quip Modest*, is understandable. One reason for it was that a review of his *Remarks* back in the August 1783 issue of the *Critical Review* had accused him of purloining notes from Malone's *Supplement*; he was now determined to defend himself. He calls Malone Reed's 'skulking friend' because often he corrected him anonymously.[9] More specifically, he picks apart his past work for its misleading glosses, linguistic ignorance, and obsessive distrust of the Second Folio. For the most part, his corrections are reasonable, but he spoils his effect with his language: 'I should be glad to know if it be possible for any person who has read but two lines of Shakspeare, and has but two grains of common sense, to betray stronger symptoms of a very imperfect acquaintance with his sense, language, metre, or any thing else.'[10] He even attributes Malone's inability to understand Shakespeare's English to his Irishness.

It must have amazed Malone and Reed that Ritson was polite to Steevens in *The Quip Modest*. Castigating the 'literary hangmen', the reviewers who had laughed at and scorned his *Remarks*, he finds in Steevens a brilliant exception: 'I wish to declare, that the candour, liberality, and politeness which distinguish Mr. STEEVENS, utterly exclude HIM from every imputation of this nature.'[11] These two assuredly were strange bedfellows. Steevens must have thought so, too, but did he relish seeing someone else trim Malone's sails?

Malone continued to have serious reservations about Steevens' work. These surfaced again in a strongly worded letter to Lord Charlemont in June 1787. His provocation was yet another Shakespeare project. Alderman John Boydell, publisher of engravings and proprietor of the ambitious and idolatrous 'Shakespeare Gallery' in the late 1780s – a failed exhibition of commissioned paintings of scenes from Shakespeare's plays – had undertaken a lavish folio (not published until 1803) that would include a text plus numerous engravings illustrating the several plays. It was to sell for eighteen guineas and six hundred people had subscribed even before the proposals were made public. There would be little in the way of editorial

[8] Cited from H. A. Burd, *Joseph Ritson: A Critical Biography* (1916), p. 75. See also Bronson, *Joseph Ritson*, pp. 488–93.   [9] Ritson, *The Quip Modest*, p. 19.
[10] Ibid., pp. 18, 16. In his copy of *The Quip Modest*, Malone made a number of X marks in pencil, but only one note; it reads: 'When blockheads set up for reformers they shd be accurate' (Bodleian, Malone 150).   [11] Ritson, *The Quip Modest*, p. vii.

commentary. Boydell asked Malone for help with it, but the pressures of his own work made him decline, though he offered plenty of encouragement.[12] Steevens, on the other hand, according to Malone, quickly pushed his way to the 'head' of the scheme and became its editor. In the letter to Charlemont, Malone praised Steevens for his editorial skills, but lamented that he still adhered to the text of the last *Johnson–Steevens* edition, which 'by collation, revision, etc., I have restored and corrected ... in not less than a thousand places.' Quite a claim. These were not 'fanciful changes', but substantial restorations of 'the reading of the original and authentic copies, and of the true order of the words, which has been disturbed and tossed about most capriciously by various of our predecessors.' He added that he never departs from the old quartos and First Folio 'without fear and trembling.'[13]

In Reed's variorum, Malone irritated Steevens by criticizing his editorial methods.[14] Since Steevens fancied himself to be retiring as the acknowledged monarch of Shakespearean editors, it infuriated him to see his authority being gradually eroded, especially in a new version of the very edition which had made his reputation. After the Reed edition came out in the middle of December, Steevens tried to convince Malone to agree to retain in his forthcoming edition those notes of his that Malone had corrected, but with his rebuttals. He wanted, in effect, the last word.[15] Malone would have none of this. *He* would decide which notes would or would not appear in his edition. But he offered a compromise: in those instances where he chose to keep a Steevens note that he had corrected, either further altered or not, Steevens would have the chance to add a rebuttal before the pages went to the press. Steevens grudgingly accepted relegation to the 'tail of the Play', as he put it, provided the reader is told 'where we are to be looked for.'[16] To which Malone forcibly replied that his method has been to rush 'at once to the midst of things [i.e. the heart of the matter]', providing what he believed to be 'the true interpretation, (be it whose it may) without mentioning the various glosses that had preceded.' He added that he had been no more 'merciful' to himself than to the others.[17] Steevens' appeal moved him, for the record, to add this passage to his preface: 'I have examined the notes of all the editors, and my own former remarks, with equal rigour; and have endeavoured as much as possible to avoid all controversy, having constantly had in view a

---

[12] See Malone to Boydell, 5 December (Folger), about his embarrassment over being praised and Boydell censured in the *Morning Herald*.   [13] *HMC*, XIII, 8, pp. 51–52.

[14] See W. C. Woodson, 'The Printer's Copy for the 1785 Variorum Shakespeare', *Studies in Bibliography*, 31 (1978), 208–10; and Arthur Sherbo's reply, 'George Steevens' 1785 Variorum Shakespeare', *Studies in Bibliography*, 32 (1979), 241–46.

[15] See Malone's accommodating letter to Steevens, 19 January 1786 ([Donald and] Mary Hyde Collection).   [16] Steevens to Malone, 'Sunday night', June 1786 Folger, Y.c. 1434 (32).

[17] N.d., 'Tuesday morning', Folger, uncatalogued.

philanthropick observation made by the editor above mentioned [Dr Johnson]: "I know not ... why our editors should, with such implacable anger, persecute their predecessors." ' 'I believe', he adds, 'that not a single valuable explication of any obscure passage in these plays has ever appeared, which will not be found in the following volumes.'[18] 'Philanthropick' is not a word that immediately comes to mind to describe Malone's editorial treatment of Capell and Ritson, or even of Steevens, but he felt he was opening up a new era of Shakespearean scholarship and being as generous and fair as his editorial judgment allowed. The point is, of course, that it fell to him to decide what is 'valuable explication.'[19]

Malone's objective was to go beyond a laboured recapitulation of who had said what about this or that passage in the past century. Except for Capell, successive editors had loaded the text with pedantries that were becoming laughable. In 1785, for example, a comical satire, *The Etymologist*, mocked Steevens – the 'Commentator of Commentators, the conjectural, inventive, and collatitious' – but also more broadly parodied 'the august and learned body of reviewers' and 'all the Commentators who ever wrote, are writing, or will write on Shakespeare.'

As his own edition would not exactly be lean on commentary, Malone anticipated criticism. In his preface, therefore, he deplored the 'idle notion' that Shakespeare had been '*buried under his commentators*' and that notes were '*necessary* evils.' What he *was* against, and others should be, too, was the commentary of past 'innovators' – that is, editors like Pope, Theobald, and (especially) Warburton[20] – who had altered passages simply because they felt they were incorrect, infelicitous, or unworthy of the great poet. That was the era of 'conjectural criticism and capricious innovation', when 'notes were indeed evils' and 'ingenious sophistry' reigned in support of 'idle conjecture.' That age had now 'happily past away' and 'rational explanation' had replaced 'conjecture and emendation.' He shared Johnson's wish that 'we all conjectured less, and explained more.' Following Capell's example (though without giving Capell enough credit for it), he saw himself establishing new standards based on exacting research:

When our poet's entire library shall have been discovered, and the fables of all his plays traced to their original source, when every temporary allusion shall have been pointed out, and every obscurity elucidated, then, and not till then, let the accumulation of notes be complained of. I scarcely remember ever to have looked into a book of the Age of Queen Elizabeth, in which I did not find somewhat that tended to throw a light on these plays.

[18] *PP (1790)*, I:i, p. liv.
[19] Steevens appeared to resent Reed's friendship with Malone (to Malone, undated letter, 'Wednesday night', probably late 1786 or early 1787, Folger Y.c. 1434 (31)).
[20] On Warburton, see Malone.to Percy, 28 September 1786 (*P–M Letters*, p.34).

Therefore, he concluded, it is about time we heard 'no more of this barbarous jargon concerning Shakspeare's having been *elucidated* into *obscurity*, and buried under the load of his commentators.'[21]

3

In his early work on the new edition, Malone still had, as Ritson snidely put it, his 'mushroom assistants.'[22] Steevens hated the idea of being one of them, but he was, along with Farmer, Tyrwhitt, Warton, Burney, Nichols, Reed, and Walpole.[23] Burney's help was limited to musical history and terms. He and Malone had been meeting regularly at The Club, but their friendship warmed when Malone turned to him for help. One of the most genial of men, he eagerly responded; he liked especially to discuss ideas with Malone '*viva voce*', as he put it in his first known letter to him on 17 October 1785. Unable to see him that day because he was ill, he 'scribbled in bed' a letter explaining Shakespeare's use of the musical phrase, 'out of time', in *Twelfth Night*. 'Shakespeare is very fond of alluding to musical terms & in general does it with great accuracy', he told Malone, although 'no notice has been taken of this by any commentator that I have met with.'[24] Thus began an uninterrupted friendship of twenty-seven years.

As for Thomas Warton, he was as reliable and tirelessly helpful as ever. There are many letters between the two about Shakespeare between 1785 and 1790, one of which is especially evocative for a reader who, in the 1990s as in the 1780s, finds himself with icy fingertips and toes on a winter's day in the Bodleian. He could not bring himself to look up something just yet that Malone has enquired about, Warton complained, because 'the weather has been too severe for writing in the Bodleian Library, where no fire is allowed.'[25] Warton was vital to Malone's research on the history of the stage and on the order of Shakespeare's plays. His research for an edition of Milton's poems in 1785 had made him an expert on the seventeenth century, including John Aubrey who knew so many eminent people in the second half of the century. One letter of Malone's on 25 April brims with questions sufficient to keep Warton busy for hours. 'Any information on the above points', Malone concluded, 'may be of use in setting the chronology of Shakspeare's Plays, of which I enclose you my Arrangement, as I have now revised and corrected it.'

[21] *PP (1790)*, I:i, pp. lvi–lvii.

[22] See Arthur Sherbo, *The Birth of Shakespeare Studies: Commentators from Rowe (1709) to Boswell–Malone (1821)* (1986), pp. 125–139.

[23] On Walpole's help, see W. S. Lewis, 'Edmond Malone, Horace Walpole, and Shakespeare', in *Evidence in Literary Scholarship: Essays in Memory of James M. Osborn*, eds. Rene Wellek and Alvaro Ribeiro (1979), pp. 353–62.

[24] The letter is lost, but see Catalogue 326, item 98, of Myers & Co.

[25] 21 February; Edinburgh University Library, Laing Mss., II, 614.

On a more personal note, Malone added: 'Some of your friends here have spoken of you for the Laureat [sic], and wish you to think of it for yourself. [William] Whitehead [Poet Laureate from 1757 to 1785] redeem'd the fame of the place, and the crown may now be worn with honour.'[26] He felt they needed a detached Laureate, like Whitehead, who could see the limitations and absurdities, as well as honours, of the place. Warton was offered and did accept the Laureateship in 1785 and held it until his death in 1790.

In late August 1786, Malone suddenly lost one of his assistants and good friends, Thomas Tyrwhitt. Tyrwhitt was a kindred spirit, partly because he had criticized the *Johnson–Steevens* edition on the grounds that it neglected the early quartos. 'Learning has suffered an irreparable loss in the death of poor Mr Tyrwhitt', Malone told Boswell on 4 September; he was 'if not the best, one of the best scholars in England, and a man of most amiable manners. I believe you saw him here one day.'[27] Tyrwhitt would be especially missed at the British Museum, he told Percy, because since becoming Curator he had put the Museum into 'much better order than he found it in.' 'I particularly feel his loss', he added, 'because besides the intercourse with so ingenious and amiable a man, I was sure of always obtaining from him the most accurate information on any point...'[28]

It is surprising to see him also telling Steevens that without Tyrwhitt around to applaud, his sense of achievement in his new edition would not be so sweet. Steevens could be forgiven for not shedding too many tears over this:

I had promised myself some pleasure from presenting Shakspeare to him, and from receiving the approbation of so excellent a critick, for what little I have been able to do to our author; – but how delusive are all such speculations! Perhaps the hand that is now writing may be as cold as poor Tyrwhitt's, before Shakspeare is ready to issue from the press.[29]

Alas, poor Yorick! Still, the last remark does show dismay at how much he has left to do. The huge amounts of material he was collecting began to depress him. He kept having to adjust his publication schedule backwards. His letters are sprinkled with hopeful predictions that by the spring the printer would have all the sheets, or that by the summer he would be finished with proofs, or that by the following Christmas he hoped to send Charlemont the published volumes. These self-imposed deadlines came and went, and still he found there was more to do.

Though he lost Tyrwhitt's encouragement, the next year Malone gained Dr Farmer's, whose *Essay on the Learning of Shakespeare* back in 1767 had

---

[26] 25 April; BL Add. Ms. 42561, fol. 157.   [27] *B–M Corr.*, p. 326.
[28] 28 September, *P–M Letters*, pp. 33–34.
[29] Undated letter, but c. August–September 1786, Folger, uncatalogued.

demonstrated his brilliance as a Shakespearean critic. In the words of one of the ablest appraisers of eighteenth-century Shakespearean scholarship, Farmer 'lived unostentatiously in his college, dispensing hospitality, collecting his library, and with no solicitude about his fame. He is the author of only one little book; but it is packed with matter of the first value, and its publication may be taken to mark roughly the next [research] stage in Shakespearian scholarship.'[30]

Malone trusted Farmer's readings of Shakespeare more than perhaps those of anyone living.[31] Farmer had not published anything since his *Essay* and, sequestered at Emmanuel College, had assumed something of a reputation for indolence, but in September 1786, Malone decided to 'run down to Cambridge for a few days', as he put it to Percy, 'to press him into the service' of his current work on the authorship of the three parts of *Henry VI*. One of Farmer's greatest contributions to Shakespearean study had been his commentary on *Henry VI*; Malone hoped to obtain from him any unpublished information that the older man might have on the subject. 'I shall be a little mortified if he should not give me some support', he remarked to Percy, 'but he is so lazy that I doubt whether he will do anything, though he has half promised me.'[32]

He failed to get to Cambridge this time. Perhaps Farmer neglected to invite him; or perhaps he was put off because Steevens happened to be staying with Farmer. A year passed, during which Malone completed his important *Dissertation on the Three Parts of Henry VI*. It was only after he received a copy of this that Farmer, perhaps galvanized by the realization that he had missed the chance to contribute to an important work, wrote back with apologies and regrets, adding,

As I remember, you have *some* of my Arguments but not *all*. I suppose the plays originally *Marlow's*, & alter'd after his Death by *Shakspeare*. This I argued from *style* and *manner*; with many quotations from passages contradictory to others in Shakspeare's genuine plays, and others *clashing* in the *Henrys* themselves, which show different hands... In the last Edit. [Reed's] many things taken from *conversations* or a *pencil'd margin* by *Reed* or *Steevens*, when they were with me, are... blunder'd, & sometimes sheer Nonsense.[33]

Farmer was too late to help, but in October Malone was desperate to escape London for a change of scene; Farmer also might still prove useful.[34] This time he was successful. 'I made an excursion to Cambridge to see my friend Dr. Farmer, and am but lately returned from thence', he announced to Lord Charlemont on 24 October. 'For near three years I had not been

[30] Smith, *Shakespeare in the Eighteenth Century*, p. 52.
[31] Malone wanted Farmer's portrait; see letter to Ozias Humphry, n.d., OFB 25.104.
[32] 28 September 1786, *P–M Letters*, p. 35.
[33] 9 August 1786 (BL Add. Ms. 30262, fol. 24v).
[34] See *Boswell 1785–89*, p. 146 (*Malahide*, XVII, p. 46).

out of London for more than two days, so that Shakspeare has no great reason to complain of me.'[35] Reed was also there and recorded in his diary that Malone was warmly welcomed. On 1 October, Reed 'Walked with ... Mr. Malone [and others] ... to Jesus College, the Castle, and St John's College where we saw the Pictures in the Lodge.' On 4 October: 'Breakfasted ... with the Master [Farmer] & Mr. Malone. Went with them to the Publick Library ... ' The next day they visited the Trinity College Library, where they read several of Isaac Newton's letters, and they even took in the anatomy schools a few days later. There were also dinners with several other masters of colleges. All in all, a gratifying fortnight. He returned with Reed in the London coach on 13 October.

4

Malone's *Dissertation* merits some separate attention, not only because it influenced critical opinion about the authorship of the three parts of *Henry VI* but also because of what it suggests, explicitly and implicitly, about Shakespeare's earliest experience as a playwright. Malone's conclusions about these plays and the poet's apprenticeship as a dramatist were to remain uncontested for over a century and a quarter.

In its fifty closely printed pages, Malone spares himself no pains. He disagrees strongly with Capell's and Dr Johnson's assertions that the *Henry VI* plays are all the work of Shakespeare. Examining every scene of each play, he compares the texts printed in the First Folio with the patently inferior quarto texts printed in 1594 and 1595 under the titles, *The First Part of the Contention* and *The True Tragedy of Richard Duke of York*, and sets out the bold argument that Shakespeare was not their original author. On the contrary, the three parts of *Henry VI*, as printed in the First Folio and as we know them today, are Shakespeare's revisions of the earlier plays of uncertain authorship. They were written, he says, by more than one person – he suspects Robert Greene and George Peele – and the first play was not written by the same hand or hands that wrote the second and third. Much in them is Shakespeare's, he shows, but there is much also that is not. Among other flaws in the plays, their historical inaccuracies prove that other dramatists originally wrote them.[36] He is careful to cite Farmer's authority to back up his argument that at the beginning of his career Shakespeare revised other people's plays.[37]

[35] *HMC*, XIII, 8, pp. 59–60.
[36] De Grazia describes Malone as controlling 'the activity of the text' by expecting the plays to include verifiable facts and thereby vindicating his own epistemology (*Shakespeare Verbatim*, pp. 128–29).
[37] See *PP* (*1790*), I: i, p. 283. Malone asked friends to keep his essay confidential before publication (*HMC*, XIII, 8, p. 60).

This problem of authorship launched Malone directly into more recalcitrant questions as to how, when, and with what preparation Shakespeare began writing for the stage. He had to have answers to these questions because his essay on the chronology of the plays compelled him to, and also because he had begun to collect material towards a *Life* of the poet. He believed that biography, criticism, textual editing, and literary history all had to keep pace with each other. Without his knack for synthesis, it has been said, 'the bulk of nineteenth-century [Shakespeare] criticism would have no backbone at all.'[38]

Tyrwhitt's work, in spite of its thesis that Shakespeare was the original author of the *Henry VI* plays, encouraged Malone to argue that Shakespeare was *not* the author. In his *Observations and Conjectures* (1766), Tyrwhitt offered biographical evidence that he believed proved him right. The evidence was a passage in Robert Greene's *A Groatsworth of Wit* (1592) which remains today the earliest known mention of Shakespeare as a dramatist:

there is an upstart Crow, beautified with our feathers, that with his *Tygers hart wrapt in a Players hyde*, supposes he is as well able to bombast out a blanke verse as the best of you: and beeing an absolute *Iohannes fac totum*, is in his owne conceit the onely Shake-scene in a countrey.

Tyrwhitt argued that the 'upstart Crow' was the young, ambitious, presumptuous, plagiarizing Shakespeare who was making a name for himself in the late 1580s or early 1590s as both player and playwright. He read the phrase, 'Tygers hart wrapt in a Players hyde', as a specific allusion to a line in *3 Henry VI*: 'O tiger's heart wrapt in a woman's hide!'[39] Moreover, he thought there would be little point to the allusion if Greene was not specifically suggesting that Shakespeare wrote the line. It was one more piece of evidence in his general brief that Shakespeare wrote the whole play, as well as the other two parts of *Henry VI*.

In his first effort in 1778 to list Shakespeare's plays chronologically, Malone had used this discovery to support the same view. With a push from Farmer, however, and after editing most of the other plays, from which he acquired a more sensitive understanding of Shakespeare's wit, versification, and intellect, he changed his mind in favour of the thesis, first put forward by Theobald, that Shakespeare was the reviser. Certain passages were surely too bad to be the poet's, or bad in a way that Shakespeare never was. Confidently, he took up Greene's 'upstart crow' passage again as objective evidence. But he interprets it this time as 'the chief hinge' of his argument: Greene had sneered at Shakespeare as one 'beautified with our feathers'

---

[38] Peter Alexander, *Shakespeare's 'Henry VI' and 'Richard III'* (1929), p. 119.
[39] *3 Henry VI*, I, iv, line 137.

because the latter had taken – 'stolen' would be closer to Greene's meaning – and revised one or two of the *Henry VI* plays which he and his friends had written. Malone proves to his own and his contemporaries' satisfaction (the matter continues to be argued today) that at the beginning of his career Shakespeare revised other people's plays, 'in the workshop.'[40]

Malone insists that the 1594 quarto and 1595 Folio editions of the *Contention* and *True Tragedy* were texts of the plays Shakespeare revised. They were not 'memorial reconstructions', or so-called 'bad' quartos, put together by 'auditors' after attending performances of Shakespeare's own *Henry VI* plays. In fact, none of the fifteen plays by Shakespeare extant in quartos, he maintains, is a memorial reconstruction. Except for two, the extant quartos were all published from manuscripts 'stolen from the playhouse and printed without the consent of the authour.' That, he says, made them more authoritative than the First Folio texts of these plays, for the Folio editors ('to save labour, or from some other motive') had used the less reliable quartos, not actual manuscripts, in arriving at those texts. Anyone familiar with the methods of the printing house, he observes, knows that in successive printings from one edition to another all sorts of errors inevitably creep in. The Folio texts do contain valuable corrections of corrupt passages in the quartos, but the quarto texts (the first editions) were closer to the manuscripts and therefore more authentic and reliable.[41]

Richard Porson, Professor of Greek at Cambridge University after 1792, thought the *Dissertation* one of the most convincing pieces of criticism he had ever met with,[42] but modern scholarship has disagreed with him. W. W. Greg argued that from 'this original misconception of Malone's sprang a whole jungle of critical and biographical error' from which Shakespeare scholarship did not escape until the work of Peter Alexander and Madeleine Doran in the late 1920s.[43] The consensus now is that *Part I* is the work of several hands, including Shakespeare's, and that the copy for the First Folio was a transcript of the authors' manuscript, altered somewhat by a reviser or bookkeeper of some sort. As for *Parts I* and *II*, they are both credited to Shakespeare; *The Contention* and *The True Tragedy* are seen by most critics as 'bad' quartos, memorially reported versions derived essentially from the same text as that printed in the more authoritative First Folio. Skilled

---

[40] On Malone's nineteenth-century reputation, see F. P. Wilson, 'Shakespeare and the "New Bibliography"', in *Studies in Retrospect* (1945), p. 115. For early twentieth-century criticism of Malone on Shakespeare's start as a dramatist, see P. Alexander, *Shakespeare's 'Henry VI' and 'Richard III'*, p. 119, and *TLS*, 9 October and 13 November 1924; W. W. Greg, *The Editorial Problem in Shakespeare*, 1942; and (defending Malone) J. Dover Wilson, 'Malone and the Upstart Crow', and his introduction to *2 Henry VI* (1952), section II (a), 'Back to Malone'.

[41] *PP (1790)*, I: i, pp. xii–xviii.

[42] Boswell Junior quoted Porson's comment in *PP (1821)*, XVIII, p. 597.

[43] W. W. Greg, *The Editorial Problem in Shakespeare*, pp. 50–52. For a critical point of view supporting Malone, see J. Dover Wilson, *2 Henry VI*, pp. xiv–xix, 13; and, 'Malone and the Upstart Crow', p. 56.

bibliographers also were quick to point out that Malone possessed neither the bibliographical nor biographical information needed to make such assertions. There was, in fact, no objective evidence whatever that most of the quartos were published from Shakespeare's manuscripts and that most of their texts were therefore more reliable than the texts of those same plays in the First Folio. Nevertheless, the equation 'early' = authority held powerful sway for some twentieth-century textual critics, including Greg. It is ironic that one of Malone's earliest and most influential textual, biographical, and critical theories has also been one of the most contested.

5

During the five years leading up to the publication of his 1790 edition, Malone hunted tirelessly for information about Shakespeare. In the end he discovered more facts about his life than were known before or have been discovered since. He also disproved as merely legendary a few favourite stories about him, several of which had been perpetuated by Rowe, who wrote the only substantial biographical account (1709) before Malone and became the chief source for others. Most of Rowe's biographical account is comprised of stories passed on to him by Betterton, who picked up 'what Remains he could' in Stratford from conversation with local people. Rowe's *Life* was therefore of little use to Malone, for whom authenticity came from archival records, almost never from local gossip.[44] 'Rowe was, I believe, no great hunter of Mss.', Malone told Warton.[45] His research, in fact, would have been easier if Rowe had never written a word, for he had not only to present the facts he discovered, with some reasoned conjecture, but also to demonstrate the spuriousness of popular anecdotes. He did this by printing Rowe's *Life* with liberal annotations, correcting him whenever his own research showed him to be wrong. Many of the pages contain as few as five lines of Rowe, with the rest taken up by Malone's notes in fine print.

Malone understood perfectly the genealogy of traditional treatments of Shakespeare's life, from the poet's death to his own period. He understood their contexts and the points about Shakespeare they were trying to make. But it did not matter to him what they were saying about Shakespeare if they were false and generations had taken them as truth. If a story is false, who could trust the reasons for including it in a *Life* anyway? If, as de Grazia will have it, the point of many of Rowe's stories was to dramatize occasions or 'a critical juncture' of Shakespeare's life, rather than relate historical events, Malone would have argued that they, as well as the

---

[44] See de Grazia, *Shakespeare Verbatim* (chap. 2) for a new theory that Malone's documentary authentication of Shakespearean biography severed Shakespeare from the so-called traditional biographical context.   [45] September 1789, BL Add. Ms. 42561, fol. 212.

spurious stories, were not worth the paper they were written on.[46] If a biographer is not accountable to the facts, he may as well be writing fiction. That was exactly what he thought Rowe had written.

Sadly, the pressures to publish his edition, which kept mounting as he continued to delay it, prevented him from writing a *Life* in narrative form. His discoveries were so plentiful and diverse, and made over so long a period, that he was unable to organize them with the necessary speed. It would not have been difficult to form a new *Life*, he wrote, 'less meagre and imperfect' than Rowe's had he had enough time. The work on the *Life* had proved to be more exciting for him than anything else in his career. The thrill of his discoveries and the expectation of turning up more spurred him on. His 'inquiries' had been 'carried on almost to the very moment of publication.'[47] He had long-term plans of weaving 'the whole into one uniform and connected narrative', but his main obstacle, which obviously he could not admit in his preface, was that he shrank somewhat from the demands of writing a narrative. With so much material already collected, he knew a complete *Life* would be a formidable task.

As Shakespeare's biographer, he faced other obstacles. Although Shakespeare did enjoy the status of a celebrated dramatist in the seventeenth century, he was not widely 'read, admired, studied, and imitated' until the eighteenth century. Nor was there a disposition to see in him one of the great poets of all time. Moreover, there was a comparative lack of interest in biography, a new genre, and in history itself apart from the ancients:

the enthusiasm of some one or other of his admirers in the last age would have induced him to make some inquiries concerning the history of his theatrical career, and the anecdotes of his private life. But no such person was found; no anxiety in the publick sought out any particulars concerning him after the Restoration, (if we except the few which were collected by Mr. Aubrey,) though at that time the history of his life must have been known to many...

Among those, he continues, who could easily have supplied detailed information about Shakespeare's life in that age ('as deficient in literary curiosity as in taste') were the poet's sister Joan Shakespeare Hart who did not die until 1646; her son William who became an actor and died in 1639; Shakespeare's favourite daughter, Susanna, who married Dr John Hall and lived until 1649; his second daughter, Judith, who was still in Stratford in 1662; and the younger Thomas Combe, to whom the poet bequeathed his sword and who did not die until 1657.[48] It is curious that Malone appears not to have known of Joan Hart's grandson, George Hart, who had seven children and whose descendants are still living today.

---

[46] See de Grazia, *Shakespeare Verbatim*, pp. 106–7.   [47] *PP (1790)*, I:i, p. lxiii.
[48] Preface, *PP (1790)*, I:i, pp. lxxii–lxxiii.

If Malone had known of George Hart, he would have moved heaven and earth to track down his family. The fact is that he himself showed signs of having been seduced by the romance of such potential material. He rejected most of Rowe's *Life*, but he was willing to accept biographical material that was just as likely to be 'legendary' and incompatible with his quest for authenticity as the stories Rowe told. The information would have been as subjective and arbitrary as the accounts of Shakespeare that circulated, in one form or another, between his death and Malone's period. But Malone was ready to credit family lore more highly, depending on the source, until his research should prove the family wrong.

For almost all of his research on the *Life* and the *Account of the English Stage*, Malone turned to the early printed books and documentary archives in Chancery, the Stamp Office, the diocese of Worcester, the Tower of London,[49] the Remembrancer's Office in the Exchequer, and the office of the Lord Chamberlain. Some assistance he had, but it still required of him a great deal of leg work.[50] At times he complained of exhaustion and tired eyes. As he was not the first to discover, much study is a weariness of the flesh; he further aggravated the problem, as almost everyone in his time did, by reading with insufficient light. Writing to Warton on 4 December 1789 about Milton's blindness, he remarked, 'I write almost in the dark, have this moment observed that I have taken the wrong side of the paper ... '[51] To William Gifford, the editor of Ben Jonson, Malone recalled on 25 March 1803 that his eyesight was 'injured irreparably about fifteen years ago by poring nightly for some weeks with a small wax-candle, held over the Stratford Register, in order to discover all the baptisms &c. of Shakspeare's family. If you have ever had occasion to examine a parish-register of great bulk, where every word must be read to discover a few names, you will easily conceive how troublesome a task that was.'[52] His sister Harriet implored him to be careful: 'Your last letter so far from being a dull one was the pleasantest I have had [in] a long time because you said your Eyes were better; persevere my Dearest Edmond in not reading or working by Candle light.' He did not, could not, follow her advice – not if he was to publish without many more delays. 'I grudge you no labour except that of sight', Jephson wrote in the same collaborative letter; 'but to be able to *finish* in time is the great object to us all, & there is always so much to do at winding up the bottom of a publication.'[53]

His spirits, if not his eyes, received a boost when, in June 1789, he struck it rich twice. Hunting for records on the history of the theatres in

[49] See Malone to [Thomas Astle], 18 November 1789, OFB 25.86.
[50] See Malone's preface, *PP* (*1790*), I:i, p. lxxviii.   [51] BL Add. Ms. 42561, fol. 214.
[52] Bodleian, Ms. Montagu, d.8, fol. 229.
[53] 9–11 September 1789 (Arthur O'Neill Collection). Malone's letter to Harriet about his eyes is dated 29 August 1789.

Shakespeare's day, he discovered the Office-book of Sir Henry Herbert, Master of the Revels during the reigns of James I and Charles I, covering the years from 1622 to 1642. Since the responsibilities of the Master of the Revels included licensing all plays acted by the several companies as well as supervising court performances, and for these viewing rehearsals, supplying props and costumes, and paying the actors, Herbert's records are primary source material for the theatre historian. Malone could not believe his luck in stumbling over this treasure, which rather romantically he found 'in a very mouldering condition' in an old chest that had remained unopened for one hundred and thirty years. But his eyes were scarcely up to the discovery, as he told Warton in August: 'My eyes have nearly been destroyed by deciphering some parts of it, where either the ink has faded or part of the paper mouldered away.' He added, 'this discovery is so much beyond all calculation or expectation, that, I will not despair of finding Shakspeare's pocketbook some time or other.'[54] It was fortunate that he promptly made a transcript of the Office-book because the manuscript has since disappeared.[55] Warton replied to the news by hoping that 'Shakespeare's Pocket-book will follow.'[56]

The other even more important discovery was waiting for him at Dulwich College. Several years earlier he had discovered there Edward Alleyn's diary and found its contents disappointing. But now – 'Just as this work [his edition] was issuing from the press' – he learned that 'a large folio volume of accounts kept by Mr. Philip Henslowe, who appears to have been proprietor of the ROSE Theatre near the Bankside in Southwark', had been found at Dulwich by the Librarian. The Librarian, who from past correspondence knew of Malone's work, gave him the news immediately. It remains the most important Elizabethan source of early theatrical history that has ever been found. Henslowe, a tight-fisted theatrical tycoon, kept his diary from 1592 to 1603, recording the props and scenery of his and other companies, as well as details of costumes, attendance, admission prices, and profits. He also recorded the plays he purchased, for which he drove hard bargains, and the names of actors who owed him money. 'A still more curious part of this Ms.', Malone noted, 'is a register of all the plays performed by the servants of Lord Strange, and the Lord Admiral, and by other companies, between the 19th of February 1591–2 and November 5, 1597.' He had to append large extracts from Henslowe at the end of his *Account* because, like Herbert's Office-book, he found them too late. He told Boswell in July that the discovery 'will throw me back a fortnight' but that

---

[54] 17 August 1789, BL Add. Ms. 42561, fol. 208v.

[55] Malone's transcript, with some later additions by George Chalmers in 1797 and 1798, is the only record of the document. See John Quincy Adams's reconstruction, *Dramatic Records of Sir Henry Herbert* (1917).

[56] 20 August 1789 (courtesy of A. C. Lee, Hatch Thoke, Compton, Winchester).

luckily he had received the diary 'on the very day when I had ordered my last sheet of the *Hist. of the Stage* for press. I immediately stopp'd it, and shall be able to include several curious matters in a couple of sheets.'[57] Such valuable materials, he said in his preface, caused his early short *Essay* on the stage to swell 'to such a size ... that it is become almost a new work.'[58]

The Henslowe papers, the first archival manuscripts he was allowed to borrow, reveal his habit of not returning such papers promptly or at all, even after being asked for them. Because he was able to persuade institutions to lend him manuscripts, he put temptation in his way. It was not uncommon for eighteenth- and nineteenth-century scholars to ask such favours, but one could go too far. When, for example, Percy was collecting old British ballads for his *Reliques* in 1762, he matter-of-factly asked Warton to send him a few manuscripts from the Bodleian, a request Warton found extraordinary: 'how the Duce [*sic*] came you to imagine, that such *valuable* M.S.S. as you speak of, could be got out of our University Library? I dare not own that I send any of the *printed* Books out of Town, which now & then brings me into ridiculous circumstances.'[59]

So far as we know Malone never presumed to ask Warton for manuscripts from the Bodleian or Ashmolean, but he did feel – and those whom he asked generally agreed – that the exalted subject of his research warranted special privileges. Once he had useful papers, he was reluctant to part with them in case he needed them again, and since his publications were always delayed, he tended to keep them too long. He was allowed to keep the Henslowe materials for so long because he paid for the privilege.[60] Eventually, he returned them, but borrowed them again on 26 March 1806, in a trunk and basket.[61] It seems that this time he never returned them. Most portions did find their way back to Dulwich between 1818 and 1821 via his literary executor James Boswell Junior, who discovered the Dulwich material among Malone's papers after his death and published much of it in the last volume of the Boswell–Malone edition of Shakespeare (1821).[62] Other portions have been lost and exist, like Herbert's Office-book, only in Malone's printed transcriptions.

Malone's carelessness in returning the Dulwich manuscripts is not so alarming, however, as his apparent readiness to cut out portions of them for his own permanent use. Recent research on Henslowe's diary provides

[57] 8 July 1790, *B–M Corr.*, p. 374.
[58] 'Historical Account of the English Stage' *PP (1821)*, III, pp. 288–89; and the preface, p. lxi. Extracts from Henslowe's diary run from pp. 288–331, with extensive notes.
[59] Northamptonshire Record Office, Sotheby Ecton Collection, Box X 1079, folder E(S) 1206, fol. 31 (cited in Davis, *Thomas Percy*, p. 92).
[60] John Bowles informed Chalmers on 5 September 1797 that Malone never returned the books he borrowed from Dulwich College (Add. Mss. 22900, fol. 351).
[61] See Malone's memo regarding his receipt of 'a trunk and basket' from Dulwich containing the Alleyn and Henslowe manuscripts (Folger, uncatalogued).
[62] *PP (1821)*, XXI, pp. 389–420.

incontrovertible evidence that he snipped out fragments he knew he would
need for his exposure of the Ireland Shakespeare forgeries in the mid-1790s
and for his next Shakespeare edition – especially the expanded history of
the English stage and a section on Elizabethan 'manners' he wished to
write as part of his *Life of Shakespeare*. At least a dozen excisions from the
diary can be traced to him. About half of these have been recovered in the
form of slips pasted to the flyleaves of books now in the Bodleian. The rest
are fragments, three of which made up an entire leaf. As a critic who has
gone into the matter has recently observed with memorable under-
statement: 'the instincts of the collector and antiquary perhaps overcame
the discipline of the scholar and lawyer on occasion, and it seems to the
point that he especially prized autographs.'[63]

The Herbert Office-book and the Henslowe diary helped Malone clarify
much about Shakespeare's life. The almost forty letters he wrote to The
Revd. James Davenport of Stratford, shortly before and after publication of
his edition, were even more productive. In his first letter in April 1788, he
commissioned him to look into the Stratford parish register for information
about the birth and death of Shakespeare, his family, and certain Stratford
neighbours such as the Combes and Quineys. Receiving no reply, he wrote
again almost two weeks later, apologizing for his forwardness and
describing his edition as a 'publick service' – a project from which he was
not obtaining any personal profit: 'I am sensible that an entire stranger has
no right to intrude on the leisure of another; nor should I have ventured to
do it on this occasion, if the information sought had not been for a publick
work, and of such a nature as not to be readily obtained by any other
mode.'[64] Then he repeated his questions and added a few.

Davenport thrilled Malone on the 15 April with a twenty-page letter
crammed with important details, especially about Shakespeare's father,
answering Malone's queries point by point. In subsequent letters, he
saturated Davenport with a multitude of questions. 'It seems strange to
me', he declared, 'that in the period of about 170 years, whole generations
should be swept away, and have become entirely extinct. I beg to know
whether I am mistaken in this respect, and whether any of the families of
Greene, Nashe, Harte, or Hathaway, yet survive.'[65] New Place intrigued
him most because it and its successive owners might lead him to
Shakespeare papers. It even inspired him to write a poem about its garden.
'In giving an account of [the present owner] Mr. Hunt's garden', he wrote
to Davenport, 'I could not help breaking out into a poetical rhap-
sody ... "*con amore*".'[66] He wisely decided not to publish it.

---

[63] Remington T. Patterson, 'Edmond Malone and "some curious Manuscripts" relative to the
      stage', a forthcoming study.   [64] 2 April 1788, *M–D*, pp. 1–3.
[65] 26 April 1788, ibid., pp. 14–20.
[66] Malone thought of publishing the poem (to Davenport, 6 May 1788, ibid., p. 26).

At the end of April, Malone invited Davenport to Queen Anne Street East. It would have made more sense to visit him in Stratford, where he could have seen a few of these documents for himself, visited the sacred sites, and interviewed certain people like Hunt, but the demands of the printing house kept him close to home. Davenport felt, it seems, that if he could not bring Mohammed to the mountain, he would bring the mountain to Mohammed. He arranged for the Stratford Parish Register to be lent to Malone – a remarkable favour, even in those days. 'I will examine the register as expeditiously as possible', Malone replied, 'and will transmit it again in a very few days... ' At his suggestion, the valuable Register was sent by the Birmingham coach; his servant would meet the coach so that 'the parcel may go through as few hands as possible.' A mix-up caused some momentary anxiety, but the parcel arrived on his doorstep at eight on the evening of 5 May. He sat down to read this treasure-trove immediately, forcing his eyes to decipher sometimes excruciatingly small handwriting: 'I sat up till two o'clock, and almost blinded myself by poring over the books which you have so obligingly furnished me with', he wrote the next day.

Immediately, he discovered that Shakespeare's son was named Hamnet, not Samuel. 'This discovery', he announced to Davenport, 'knocks a fine-spun theory of mine about the date of the play of *Hamlet*, in the head; but I am not at all concerned about that.' Malone was, however, frustrated to find no record of Shakespeare's marriage, which he thought might mean that the poet married Anne Hathaway in London. 'This is not a matter of mere idle curiosity', he reassured Davenport, 'for should his marriage be ascertained to have taken place in London, it would fix the period of his coming to the metropolis, which still remains unsettled.'[67] He never found the answer; nor has anyone else.

The Register also put him on the scent of the Hart family. William Hart, a hatter, had married Shakespeare's only sister, Joan, but virtually nothing was known of their marriage or their descendants. 'My predecessors, I find', he told Davenport, 'were not near so diligent as they might have been; for ... Shakspeare Hart [Joan's great-granddaughter], who was born in 1666, could have learned many anecdotes about Shakespeare from her father, George Hart, who was born in 1636, and who had undoubtedly conversed with Shakespeare's daughter, Judith Queeny [i.e. Quiney].'[68] He discovered, however, that the only surviving member of the Hart family was in dire financial straits, living in Shakespeare's birthplace.

Thomas Hart's economic plight aroused Malone's pity and dismay that 'a remote descendant of our great poet's sister was in such distressed circumstances.' It was a national disgrace. He therefore resolved to call upon 'admirers of Shakspeare' to raise a little subscription to help him. He

[67] 6 May 1788, ibid., p. 25.   [68] 19 May 1788, ibid., pp. 33–34.

would start with members of The Club, on whom he thought Hart 'has certainly a claim.'[69] Later, he thought better of this appeal. 'I am but a very bad solicitor', he confessed to Davenport on 25 June, 'for I could not prevail upon myself to start the subject of Mr. Thomas Hart at the Literary Club a few days ago, and consequently I have been able to procure but a very small sum for him, the greater part of which I have received from my own family.' He sent ten pounds with the hope that it would be 'of some use to the poor man.'[70]

Finished with the Register, this time he returned it promptly, first having it bound in 'Russia backs' by a bookbinder.[71] At last he had enough new material to complete his notes for the *Life*. He could not delay publication any longer. Everyone expected his edition sometime in 1789, at the latest. Boswell had begun to think that Malone would not publish his edition much before his own *Life of Johnson* appeared. He attributed the delay partly to the presence of Malone's family in Cobham, Surrey, where they had rented a house for six months the preceding year, during which, Boswell said, 'his labour was much intermitted.'[72] He might have added that Malone was also giving him countless hours of help with the *Life of Johnson*. The edition did not appear in 1789, nor on 23 April 1790, Shakespeare's birthday, as Malone had hoped.[73]

Partly responsible was another Stratford personality named John Jordan, an eccentric repository of Shakespeareana from Stratford, who in March 1790 sent Malone his collection of spurious information, *Memoirs and Historical Accounts of the Families, of Shakespeare (alias Shakespere) and Hart*. These accounts and genealogies had almost as little documentary basis as the ones Betterton gave to Rowe. Jordan, whose idolatry of Shakespeare knew no bounds, was a wheelwright fallen on hard times whom the locals nicknamed the Stratford Poet. Around 1780 he had written his *Original Collections on Shakspeare and Stratford-on-Avon*, followed about a decade later by the collection he sent Malone. Neither was publishable. A decent and inoffensive man who looked every inch the local sage, he concocted his genealogies for Shakespeare from references to documents he found in the *Johnson–Steevens Shakespeare*, oral traditions, and a little forgery.[74]

Malone quickly saw he could trust virtually nothing Jordan sent or told him. 'Jordan being often inaccurate in small matters', he observed to Davenport on 12 March, 'I cannot implicitly confide in his account.'[75] But for a while Malone held out hope. He also felt sorry for Jordan, who on 29 March 1790 wrote to him plaintively, reciting the business misfortunes that

[69] 29 May 1788, ibid., p. 38.   [70] 20 June 1788, ibid., p. 39.
[71] 25 June 1788, ibid., p. 41.
[72] See Malone to Jordan, 31 March 1790, *Malone–Jordan*, p. 14.
[73] 23 April 1790, *M–D*, pp. 48–49.
[74] Schoenbaum, *Shakespeare's Lives* (rev. edn., 1991), pp. 131–32.
[75] 12 March 1790, *M–D*, p. 48.

had befallen him and his family at the hands of an unscrupulous brother.[76] 'The poor man has sent me a very sad tale indeed and I wish to do him some service'; but first he asked Davenport to verify his story. In the meantime, Davenport was to tell the headmistress of the local school that Malone would pay the small fees for Jordan's children.[77] As everything Jordan said about himself, unlike what he said about Shakespeare, was found to be true, Malone tried to find him employment. Raising another subscription, he set Jordan up as a carpenter, sending two guineas immediately for 'absolute necessaries' and then the considerable sum of forty pounds, 'of which above a fourth part' came again from his family.[78] The carpentry idea failed, but he forwarded more subscription money that he had 'succeeded beyond my expectations' in raising.[79]

After a few weeks, Malone realized that Jordan had little useful information to give him, apart from a drawing of New Place (that Malone published) from a vanished drawing of 1599 and a copy of Shakespeare's father's will.[80] It is therefore surprising that Jordan had Malone's ear and that Malone went to such lengths to help him. Why did he not dismiss him out of hand as another contributor to the Shakespeare-Mythos and harshly denounce him as another forger? Was not Jordan potentially a harmful deceiver? At his feet, in fact, could be laid the blame for planting the seeds of deception in the young mind of William Henry Ireland, the most sensational forger ever of Shakespeareana. A few years later, Malone would expose and humiliate Ireland; why not Jordan in 1790? The answer to this question reveals much about Malone's temperament. Except for his clumsy and harmless forgeries, Jordan was an honest character, genuinely intoxicated by the Shakespearean iconography all around him. He was like those over-enthusiastic tour guides one sometimes encounters in country houses and literary museums who have a proprietary feeling for their subject. Literary deception, trickery, and misrepresentation are what made Malone's temper flare, but Jordan's motive was not to deceive or exploit. Moreover, he enjoyed a reputation for embellishing minutiae about Shakespeare; he was himself part of the Shakespeare 'industry' in Stratford that had begun to flourish and fascinate after Garrick's Jubilee. And he was poor, a figure worthy of charity. A charitable man, Malone was drawn by all of this to be tolerant and kind towards him.

In the last year or so before publication, Malone became curious about the relatively neglected manuscripts of John Aubrey, the seventeenth-century Oxford antiquarian and biographer. They consisted of anecdotes

---

[76] 29 March 1790, *Malone–Jordan*, p. 14.   [77] 1 May 1790, *M–D*, p. 50.

[78] 15 June 1790, *Malone–Jordan*, p. 23.

[79] 3 July 1790, *Malone–Jordan*, p. 28; 5 June and 9 July 1790, *M–D*, pp. 52–53, 55.

[80] Malone was unaware that a sketch (1737) existed of New Place by George Vertue (Schoenbaum, *Shakespeare's Lives*, pp. 179–80); see Frank Simpson, 'New Place: The Only Representation of Shakespeare's House, from an Unpublished Manuscript', *Shakespeare Survey*, 5 (1952), 55–57.

and biographical vignettes that Aubrey had collected and written over many years, many composed with information obtained first-hand from people who were Shakespeare's contemporaries. Malone knew of the manuscripts through transcriptions by Aubrey's Oxford contemporary Anthony à Wood in his book, *Athenae Oxonienses* (1691–92), and he knew that Farmer had sceptically read some of them for his *Essay on the Learning of Shakspeare*. It occurred to him in the autumn of 1789 that they deserved a closer look.

His curiosity was awakened by a rereading of Warton's *The Life and Literary Remains of Ralph Bathurst* (1761), in which Warton took from the Aubrey manuscripts a four-line epitaph for a wealthy Stratford citizen named John Combe that Aubrey claimed Shakespeare wrote. Since Rowe had also quoted the lines to insinuate bad taste or even malice on Shakespeare's part,[81] Malone asked Warton, in September 1789, to ascertain whether Rowe was accurate in his use of Aubrey or had even seen the manuscripts. If Rowe had never consulted Aubrey, that fact would raise further doubts about the authority of Rowe's *Life*. 'I should be also glad to know', he asked Warton, 'in whose hands Aubrey's MSS were in the year 1709 [the year Rowe published his *Life*], and when they first were lodged in the [Ashmolean] Museum.'[82]

Warton transcribed the passage and sent it to Malone, who saw that Rowe had got it wrong. Aubrey had quoted the lines not as an example of bad taste but rather of Shakespeare's good-natured humour. Malone was, therefore, confident that Rowe had never read the Aubrey manuscripts. His mind raced ahead. What else might Aubrey reveal? During the next few months he discovered that Aubrey's friends included Hobbes, Milton, Dryden, Ashmole, and Sir William Dugdale – but 'I wish to increase my list', he told Warton on Christmas Day, 1789.[83] He later learned that Aubrey had kept notes on Shakespeare, Jonson, Milton, Hobbes, Sir John Evelyn, and Sir John Denham, among others.

All very promising, but was Aubrey reliable? Malone knew that Anthony à Wood had quarrelled with Aubrey, very likely abused his notes by pillaging them without giving credit, and spoke of him disparagingly. Taking his cue from Wood, Farmer had judged Aubrey a disorganized and an undependable eccentric – a 'pretender to Antiquities, roving, magotie-headed, and sometimes little better than crased'.[84] If his use of Aubrey's notes was to be credible, he would have to rehabilitate him in a separate

[81] On Rowe's version, see Schoenbaum: *William Shakespeare: A Compact Documentary Life* (1977), pp. 242–44; see also *Shakespeare's Lives*, p. 181.   [82] BL Add. Ms. 42561, fol. 212.
[83] BL Add. Ms. 42561, fol. 216. Warton replied on 7 January 1790 (Houghton Library, Harvard University, 'Autograph File') that much of the material he is giving Malone is quoted from memory and from a 'Pocket book 30 years old'.
[84] Farmer, *An Essay on the Learning of Shakespeare*, ed. D. Nichol Smith, *Eighteenth Century Essays on Shakespeare*, p. 194.

essay at the end of his *Historical Account* of the stage, arguing for his reliability.[85]

Though Malone's rehabilitation of Aubrey is self-serving in that he had much to gain from it, his defence is sound.[86] After quoting at length Aubrey's anecdotes on Jonson, which he shows to be grounded on facts unnoticed by seventeenth-century biographers, Malone gives all of Aubrey-on-Shakespeare verbatim. No one had ever done this before. He examines Aubrey's accounts point by point, considering first his assertion that Shakespeare's father was a butcher and then moving on to anecdotes about the date of the poet's removal to London and his first occupations when he got there. He considers Aubrey's remarks on Shakespeare's personality and what he looked like, a legacy he left for a relative, his tenure as a teacher in the country, and his excellence (unlike Jonson) as an actor. Everything Aubrey wrote about Shakespeare Malone evaluates in terms of Shakespeare's will, published testimonies of contemporaries, meanings of crucial seventeenth-century words, similarities between related professions, Shakespeare's learning, and the plays themselves. He notes that when Aubrey makes an obvious mistake, it is mere carelessness and does not damage the credibility of the anecdote itself. Not all Aubrey's accounts of English writers ought to be adopted, he cautions, but 'it seems to me much more reasonable to question such parts of them as seem objectionable, than to reject them altogether, because he may sometimes have been mistaken'.[87] Malone had opened up the possibility of a new project for himself: a complete edition of Aubrey's *Lives*.

6

Malone finally published his edition on 29 November 1790. With his *Account of the English Stage*, the extracts taken from Aubrey's manuscripts, Henslowe's diary, Herbert's Office-book, and the revised essay on the order of the plays, the work possessed an unprecedented originality and authority. Malone's scholarly reputation soared. 'In the following work, the labour of eight years', he writes in his preface, 'I have endeavoured with unceasing solicitude, to give a faithful and correct edition of the plays and poems of Shakspeare.' Though he admits he has many limitations as a Shakespearean, he insists that want of zeal is not one of them. One modern critic has called the edition, with some justice, 'the most sustained work of literary scholarship to have appeared in England' by that date.[88]

Malone's commentary on Shakespeare's life includes new information on

---

[85] See Oliver Lawson Dick's assessment of Aubrey in the introduction to his edition of *Brief Lives* (1949; rev. edn. 1958).   [86] *PP (1790)*, I:ii, pp. 166–71.

[87] *PP (1790)*, I:ii, pp. 168, 170–71, 173–83.

[88] James M. Osborn, 'Edmond Malone and Oxford', in *Eighteenth-Century Studies in Honor of Donald F. Hyde*, ed. W. H. Bond (1970), p. 325.

the poet's father, the Ardens (his mother's family), and their descendants.
He takes up the story handed down by Aubrey that Sir William Davenant
was Shakespeare's godson. He gives an extensive history of New Place, with
a detailed account of the famous mulberry tree which the poet was
supposed to have planted at the back of the house in 1609. He explodes the
old story that he poached deer from Sir Thomas Lucy's Charlecote Park,
three miles outside Stratford, and that he penned some satiric verses at Sir
Thomas' expense. He considers what he did after he left school in Stratford,
arriving at the theory that he spent time as a country lawyer's clerk and
perhaps also as a type of law-teacher for three years in London. There is a
sketch of his relationship with Jonson, an account of his finances and
properties, a look at the illness that caused his death, and an assessment of
the bust perched on the wall overlooking his grave in the chancel of Holy
Trinity Church in Stratford, which he took the trouble to compare with
genuine prints then extant to ascertain whether it was modelled after any
of them.[89] This last piece of commentary later was to land him in a good
deal of trouble. He also published for the first time several wills (including
the first accurate text of Shakespeare's will[90]); many deeds, including a
mortgage deed he obtained (with Walpole's and Hannah More's help)
from Garrick's widow;[91] parish register extracts; and a range of documents
having to do with the poet's life.

   De Grazia's study of Malone's influence on Shakespearean studies
argues that his unprecedented commitment to authenticity 'insulated'
Shakespeare in a uniquely distorting late eighteenth-century apparatus,
'shoved him back into the remote world of documents and records', and
made him into a 'relativized enclave', prescribing or dictating the terms
according to which he is accepted and read.[92] Malone's own view was
simpler, widely comprehensible in his own period, and has remained so
ever since among mainstream scholars. He hoped simply to uncover as
much truth as he could. From now on, he was insisting, nothing old or new
could be trusted without documentary support.

   The account of Shakespeare's life shared pride of place in the first of the
edition's ten volumes with the *Historical Account of the English Stage*, a 331-
page treatise chronicling the 'internal economy and usages of the English
theatres in the time of Shakspeare.' Following a forty-page survey of
medieval and pre-Shakespearean drama, pieced out with long quotations
from Warton's *History of English Poetry*, Malone describes the evolution of
playhouses in London in the last quarter of the sixteenth century. He

---

[89] See *Shakespeare's Lives*, pp. 177–83, for a more complete account of Malone's discoveries.
[90] See ibid., *Shakespeare's Lives*, appendix.
[91] Walpole wrote to Hannah More, 4 February 1788, asking her to obtain for Malone, 'a man of
   honour', the precious deed from Mrs Garrick (*Walpole Corr.*, XXXI, pp. 259–60). The deed is
   now in BL, Egerton Ms. 1787.   [92] De Grazia, *Shakespeare Verbatim*, pp. 10–11.

concentrates on the Globe, his account of which was the first to be published, and Blackfriars because it was in these houses that Shakespeare's plays were performed. He takes a special interest in the types of stage sets used, showing correctly – against Steevens' opinion – that scenery generally was minimal. 'In the early part, at least', he states, 'of our author's acquaintance with the theatre, the want of scenery seems to have been supplied by the simple expedient of writing the names of the different places where the scene was laid in the progress of the play, which were disposed in such a manner as to be visible to the audience.'[93] He also notes, less reliably, that Shakespeare's plays received very little assistance from elaborate costuming.

Malone then considers the management of the theatres, the companies of players, and the names of the players themselves, supplying over sixty pages of biographical vignettes, fifteen of these on Shakespeare himself consisting of material he had acquired too late to include in his *Account*. Even in a historical treatise like this, he could not absent himself long from biography. Finally, having dealt with the periods of dramatic history up to and including Shakespeare's, he completes his study with 'a transient view' of the fortunes of the poet's plays on the stage from his death to 1741,[94] the year David Garrick made his reputation at Goodman's Fields in the role of *Richard III*.

All in all, it was by far the fullest account of the poet's life, his work, and the context of both that had so far appeared and, despite its shortcomings, remains a milestone in Shakespeare studies.

7

Malone did not linger in London basking in the afterglow of publication. Having put off for several years a visit to his family in Ireland,[95] he tied up a few loose ends – mostly concerning Boswell's *Life of Johnson* which was also moving into its final stages – and left for Dublin hastily on 19 November, content to share his moments of glory with his relatives and close Irish friends.[96]

A little of his anticipated pleasure at publication was gone, not only with the earlier death of Tyrwhitt, but also, in May of 1790, with the death of Warton. There was nobody whose applause he would have valued more. Members of The Club, however, were enthusiastic. Boswell reported on 4 December that while the appearance of the edition was not greeted with any 'external noise', 'no publication seized more speedily and surely on the

---

[93] *PP (1790)*, I:ii, p. 89.
[94] On Shakespeare's reputation in the seventeenth and early eighteenth centuries, see Taylor, *Reinventing Shakespeare*, chaps. 1–2.   [95] Malone to Boswell, 8 July, *B–M Corr.*, p. 374.
[96] The *St. James's Chronicle* thought Malone's departure significant enough to take note of it in its issue for 23–25 November 1790, no. 4618, 4.

attention of those for whose critical taste it was chiefly intended.' 'Sir
Joshua is pleased', he wrote, 'though he would gladly have seen more
disquisition (you understand me).'[97] Only Windham 'found fault with you
for not taking the profits of so laborious a work.' Daines Barrington's only
regret was that there should be a 'dryness' between Malone and Steevens,
'as you have treated him with great respect.' 'I understand that in a short
time, there will not be one of your books to be had for love or money', he
was glad to say.[98]

All that was welcome, but most gratifying of all was Burke's approval.
Burke, who had become Malone's good friend despite the awkwardness
over the passage on his wit in Boswell's *Tour to the Hebrides*, was so impressed
by the *Historical Account of the English Stage* that on the very day of
publication, after reading almost all of it, he promptly wrote to Malone in
Ireland praising its contribution to human nature: 'It is of all things the
most instructive, to see, not only the reflection of manners and Characters
at several periods, but the modes of making this reflection, and disposition
of mankind.' Elaborating on the value of literature to the cultural health of
an entire nation, Burke draws a powerful analogy with political overtones,
implying that Malone was doing his part on behalf of humanity,
civilization, and English culture: 'The stage indeed may be considered as
the Republick of active Literature; and its History as the History of that
state. The great events of political History when not combined with the
same helps towards the Study of the manners and Characters of men, must
be a study of an imperious nation.' He then implores Malone to proceed
with more of this public-spirited type of labour – after, that is, some well-
earned rest:

You have taken infinite pains, and pursued your Enquiries with great Sagacity, not
only in this respect, but in such of your Notes as hitherto I have been able to peruse.
You have earned your repose by publick Spirited Labour: But I cannot help
hoping, that when you have given yourself the relaxation which you will find
necessary to your health, if you are not called to exert your great Talents, and
employ your great acquisitions, in the transitory service to your Country which is
done in active Life, you will continue to do it that permanent Service which it
receives from the Labours of those who know how to make the Silence of their
Closets more beneficial to the world than all the noise & Bustle of Courts Senates
and Camps.[99]

Boswell had told Malone that at The Club on 30 November Burke, though
full of 'anti french Revolution rage', found time to praise 'the clearness and
accuracy of your dramatick History.'[100] This appears to imply that in

[97] See *B–M Corr.*, p. 378, note 21.
[98] Boswell sent reviews on 4 and 16 December, although Malone chides him (23 January) for
    sending so few (*B–M Corr.*, pp. 391–92).   [99] *Burke Corr.*, VI, pp. 181–82.
[100] *B–M Corr.*, pp. 377–78.

Burke's mind anti-revolutionary sentiment and Malone's 'dramatick History' – or, more comprehensively, all of Malone's Shakespeare work as embodied in the 1790 edition – shared common intellectual–political ground. They were both efforts to reassert the sanctity and inviolability of the past. Just as Burke found in the patrician and stable order of English history since the Glorious Revolution an argument against the radicalism of the future, against especially the social and political chaos of the French Revolution and its threat to England, Malone retrieved and brought to the public's attention the historical facts that made Shakespeare and English drama what they were. He not only recovered England's dramatic history – which Burke believed was an important service to English society, more beneficial to the public than 'all the noise & Bustle of Courts Senates and Camps' – but thereby also made a case against new (factually unfounded) interpretations of Shakespeare, spurious additions to the canon, and aberrations such as forgeries. Burke apparently made the same connection between his political philosophy and Malone's Shakespearean research when in return for Malone's gift of the 1790 edition he sent him his recently published *Reflections on the Revolution in France*. Their common antipathy towards French drama (governed as it was by formal rules) as well as French politics, also played a part in Burke's response to Malone's edition.

Gary Taylor, however, in *Reinventing Shakespeare*, takes the political theme to the point of suggesting that Malone's work was an element in a political equation, fashioning Shakespeare into 'an ad hoc native model, scornful of a priori principles, adopting and adapting accepted national practice, endorsed by subsequent generations.'[101] There is no denying Malone's anti-revolutionary fervour, and if Burke patriotically wanted to equate his history of the stage with the history of the state, that was fine with Malone. But Malone was a scholar and literary historian, not a polemicist. He was not 'reinventing' Shakespeare; he was de-mythologizing him. Facts, not politics, drove his research.

De Grazia has also argued that Malone's historicism impelled him in his notes to 'correct' Shakespeare's history plays where they differed from historical fact. This historicism served 'to protect Malone's present as well as Shakespeare's past'; he used it to reconcile the differences between the customary in Shakespeare's age and the Enlightenment values of his own time. It was another way of 'reinventing' Shakespeare with a 'relativizing apology.' If Malone demonstrated that linguistic and cultural practices in Shakespeare's time were 'antiquated and obsolete', and if he used these facts to explain the plays, what he was doing was using them as a

---

[101] See Taylor, *Reinventing Shakespeare*, pp. 132–33. For the politics of Malone's and Burke's views of Shakespeare, see also Bate, *Shakespeare Constitutions*, pp. 138–39; and de Grazia, *Shakespeare Verbatim*, pp. 6–8. On Burke's relationship with Malone, see D. C. Bryant, *Edmund Burke and His Literary Friends* (1939), pp. 233–55.

'convenient and commodious cache for what could not conform to [his own] standards.' Neither did Malone take into account, this reasoning goes, Shakespeare's adaptation of history, Roman and English, towards artistic ends. If the poet violated chronology or was guilty of other historical anachronisms in the history plays, Malone had to 'blame' him for it, otherwise implictly he would be condoning the disregard for facts that was anathema to him as a scholar: 'Malone expected the plays, no less than the biographical anecdotes, to evince the facts.'[102]

This thesis that Malone created Shakespeare in the image of his own and his age's critical standards, however, while an interesting theory, pre-supposes an astonishing naivety on Malone's part. Apart from the lack of evidence that Malone was protecting 'Enlightenment' ideals with his use of documented facts, it is curious to suppose that he was unresponsive to Shakespeare's artistic and thematic use of history, that he was chiefly interested in whether the poet was accurate or not. His commentary is full of insight on Shakespeare's treatment of language and history. He does often point out that Shakespeare's history was wrong, but not to blame him for it, in spite of at times using a tone not unlike what he used in exploding spurious stories about his life. His research, in fact, on Shakespeare's departure from historical truth amounts often to source study, as well as presents data for the study of the dramaturgy involved. Nobody had properly performed this useful task before.

In 1790, a literary–political cast of mind is not overt in Malone's writing. Later, under the influence of the threatening course of events in France and his own developing friendship with Burke, it would colour his criticism of authors other than Shakespeare, especially Reynolds and Dryden, not because they encouraged it but because he happened to be working on them in the decade following the Revolution. For the present, Burke's support delighted him: 'I have had such a letter from Burke as you would reposite among your most precious muniments', he wrote proudly to Boswell, 'and indeed I value it very much. It would be idle to pretend not to be proud of the praise of such a man.'[103] Burke did not stop there, for on 6 January he praised him again to Boswell: 'I have read his history of the stage, which is a very capital piece of criticism and antiquarianism. I shall now read all Shakspeare through in a very different manner from what I have yet done – when I have such a Commentator.' 'Will not *this* do for you my friend?', Boswell asked.[104]

With such praise ringing in his ears, the mixture of petulance and praise in Steevens' response probably rankled less. By the time Malone's edition came out, Steevens was well into a fourth *Johnson–Steevens* edition, designed to win back some of the limelight that had passed to Malone, as well as to

[102] De Grazia, *Shakespeare Verbatim*, pp. 125–29.   [103] *B–M Corr.*, pp. 377–78.
[104] Ibid., p. 387.

Reed. According to another letter from Boswell, at The Club on 14 December Steevens graciously acknowledged that Malone's 'labour on Shakspeare exceeded that of the whole Phalanx' of other editors, but 'he made no secret of his intending in his next edition of *Johnson and Steevens's Shakspeare* (for of that title he boasts) to assume all your Prolegomena and all your notes which he likes, and that he will put yours *last* where *others* have preceded you. Also that he will exalt Monck Mason, and give due praise to Ritson.'[105]

Ritson feigned surprise at being discredited and pillaged in Malone's edition, and wrote disingenuously to Joseph Cooper Walker – later a friend of Malone's – in Dublin:

I have just dipped far enough into Mr. Malones [*sic*] edition of Shakespeare to find he has not been sparing of epithets whenever he has occasion to introduce me to the notice of his readers. In fact, I believe I originally gave him some little provocation. But I thought your countrymen had been remarkable rather for the suddenness of their anger than the duration of malignity. Have the morals of this worthy editor been corrupted by his long residence amongst us?[106]

Although Steevens had a higher regard for Ritson's notes on Shakespeare than Malone did, his strategy was to use Ritson as a stick with which to beat Malone. Courtenay, who told Malone that the sale of the edition was rapid and that 'elegance, correctness, and accuracy of research are universally allowed to be characteristic of the work', had his own version of Steevens' motives: he made 'some objections to the manner of your arranging your notes, by which ... you had given yourself precedence to former Commentators; this he proposes to amend in his work; – but professed his disinclination to any critical controversy; – and said He w[oul]d still call his Edition – "Johnson's & Stephens".' But Courtenay, making the political connection again, reassured his friend, 'Your Work, like Burke [and] Church, is *first*, & *middle* & *last* in the minds of your friends.'[107]

8

For the most part, Malone was pleased with his public reception. Most of the reviews praised him highly, especially for his astonishing labours and 'classical elegance of manner.' The *Gentleman's Magazine* for December carried a review praising mostly his 'principal aim ... to ascertain the *genuine text* of Shakspeare, from the earliest editions.' The reviewer was impressed by Malone's scientific methods of collation, by which he had 'detected every variation in every copy' and made hundreds of emendations – 'a genuine text has been formed.'[108] The reviewer also hoped that Malone would soon make separate books out of his *Life of Shakespeare* and

---

[105] 16 December 1790, *B–M Corr.*, pp. 381–82.   [106] 14 December 1790, OFB 33.6.
[107] 15 December 1790, Beinecke, Ms. Vault Shelves Courtenay.
[108] *Gentleman's Magazine*, LX (December 1790), 1124–25.

his account of the English stage. But Malone could be easily irritated. He complained to Boswell of this reviewer's 'fobbing me off' without quoting from the edition, in spite of the wealth of new material – a conspicuous slight as far as he was concerned, a 'brief and lame account.'[109] In other reviews, there were complaints about the small typeface[110] and some carping by reviewers growing tired of mushrooming Bardolatry and excessive annotation. The *Public Advertiser* grumbled wearily on 2 December: 'If plenty of *editions* can confer immortality, Shakespeare bids fair to reach the latter days of the world. Two new editions have appeared within the last six weeks – and three more are in the press...'[111] A late and very sharp review in the *Critical Review* for December 1791, protested, 'We have little hesitation in saying, that these minute enquiries *have* been carried too far.'[112]

This last review, the most critical Malone received for his edition, deserves a closer look. What irritated some of Malone's contemporaries was the note he struck of extreme self-confidence, both in himself and his methods. The *Critical Review*, after citing his remark that in choosing commentators' notes he had 'in general given the true explication of a passage, by whomever made', complained that 'an editor less confident of his own abilities would have said, "given *what appears to me to be the* true explication".' The reviewer gives no example, but he might have used Malone's note to the phrase, 'to grunt & Sweat', in *Hamlet* (III.i.76). Johnson had substituted 'groans and sweats', for although he admitted that all the 'old copies' had 'grunt and sweat', it is a reading that 'can scarcely be borne by modern ears.'[113] Steevens had agreed with him. Malone disagreed with them both in a fairly imperious manner: 'I apprehend that it is the duty of an editor to exhibit what his author wrote, and not to substitute what may appear to the present age preferable: and Dr. Johnson was of the same opinion... To the ears of our ancestors it probably conveyed no unpleasing sound.'[114] The reviewer went on to claim that Malone's prolegomena was about the same as in the last *Johnson–Steevens* edition and that therefore there was nothing new worth quoting from it. It also took up Malone's claim that 'if even every line of his plays were accompanied with a comment, every intelligent reader would be indebted to the industry of him who produced it', replying that every reader 'of common sense' could understand nearly all of Shakespeare that is 'worth understanding' without assistance from an editor who has the annotating sickness.[115]

---

[109] *B–M Corr.*, p. 409.

[110] Malone regretted the small typeface, to Joseph Warton, 12 September 1791 (BL Add. Ms. 42561, fol. 232).   [111] *Public Advertiser* (2 December 1790), 3.

[112] *Critical Review*, 2nd ser., III, 362.   [113] *J–S* (1st edn. 1773), X, p. 236.

[114] *PP* (*1790*), IX, p. 290.   [115] *Critical Review* (December 1791), 363–65, 369.

These were outrageous criticisms, Malone thought, if not written by Steevens almost certainly directed by him. An anonymous 'Letter' in the *Gentleman's Magazine* sprang to his defence, signed 'Philalethes', though its indignant tone, which he adopted whenever he encountered distortion of fact, suggests he may have written it himself.[116] The 'Letter' did not address Malone's allegedly superior air, but it alerted the reader to the rich harvest of new material in the edition and defended Shakespeare and his commentators over the past thirty years – and, by implication, the scholarship that produced Malone's extensive editorial apparatus. If Shakespeare is teeming with 'absurdities' and 'vapid nonsense',

then Dr. Johnson, Mr. Steevens, and Mr. Malone, have most egregiously mis-spent their time these thirty years past; and it is highly incumbent on the relations of the two latter gentlemen to put them into some place of confinement, appropriated [*sic*] to those unfortunate persons whose minds are deranged.[117]

On a more personal note, Malone was embarrassed by a review that appeared in the *Public Advertiser* for 11 December 1790.[118] He was certain it was written by his old schoolfellow, Viscount Mountmorres (Hervey Redmond Morres), who a few years later shot himself in a fit of madness. The reviewer wrote about Malone's youthful interest in acting, as if it mysteriously explains his greatness as an editor. Malone's response to this 'silly account' has biographical interest. He disliked the suggestion that he spent his youth loitering around Dublin theatres. Someone ought to have the 'charity' to correct this nonsense, he told Boswell on 23 January:

Anyone would imagine from it that from my early youth I had been a dangler upon theatres, and were ... well acquainted with the birth parentage education of all the dramatick tribe ... My having performed a trifling part in a school-play, when quite a child, has no more relation to my publishing the works of Shakspeare, than any other fact in the world: yet according to this writer, it gave a colour to all my future life. – The truth is, I never thought of commenting on Shakspeare till about fifteen years ago, and am so far from a frequenter of theatres, that I do not go there a dozen times in a winter. If a man pretends to be a biographer, he should mention the father of his hero; he should tell where he was bred; in what college he was educated, with what degree of reputation he passed through it, etc. etc. – In short Lord M. had much better confine himself to french translation or Irish Politicks, and leave his school fellows to the care of wiser heads.[119]

As he told Josiah Boydell a few years later, the danger of such a review is that he might be suspected of having written it: 'The exaggerated

---

[116] Pottle suggested Boswell as author, *Literary Career of James Boswell, Esq...* (1929), p. 233. I believe internal evidence more plausibly suggests Malone.
[117] *Gentleman's Magazine*, LXII (January 1792), 41–42. Thomas Pearne impartially compared Malone's edition with Steevens' 1793 edition (*Monthly Review*, September 1793 and March 1794, XII, 57–61; XIII, pp. 241–68). Malone thought it was 'prudently written' (Beinecke, Malone 150).   [118] *Public Advertiser*, 11 December 1790, 1.
[119] *B–M Corr.*, pp. 392–93.

commendations of friends are sometimes as hurtful as the malevolence of enemies; especially in this age of newspaper artifice, when the vain and the mercenary, instead of leaving their works to the candid judgments of the publick, daily condescend to be the secret heralds of their own fame.'[120] One might add, incidentally, that Malone was not guiltless in supporting his own publications with arranged reviews. He did not write them himself, but from time to time he did ask Boswell or some other friend to write a positive review for him.

Malone was now one of the most highly esteemed literary scholars of his day. But where would he go from here? What other scholarly publication could compete with a complete edition of Shakespeare? It was not long, however, before he thought of a new Shakespeare project with a different twist, one that would earn him some money and solve the problem of the small typeface in his edition. He told Joseph Warton in September 1791, 'I am going very soon to undertake a handsome quarto edition of our great poet, with the notes in the same page and in a good legibile [sic] character, which I reckon will employ five years at least: but it will only be an amusement, all the laborious work being now over.'[121] One wonders why he expected it to take five years if most of the labour was behind him. Perhaps he thought the Aubrey edition had priority; or possibly he thought it would take him that long to complete a *Life of Shakespeare*. It seemed like a good idea, and he even published 'Proposals' for it, but otherwise he did not have a clear idea of where he was heading from here.

At least he knew what he did *not* publish. He was extremely annoyed over the publication in 1793 of a complete seven-volume duodecimo edition of Shakespeare described on the title page as 'Accurately printed from the Text of Mr. Malone's Edition, with select explanatory Notes.' The booksellers brought out this cheaper edition independently to capitalize on Malone's edition, but he felt they had given the impression that he had authorized, or even been responsible, for it. He objected most to the misconception that he had selected which notes from his edition would be included. He angrily denied his involvement in the *Gentleman's Magazine* for March 1794, threatening reprisals. 'In order ... to prevent ... misinterpretation, and abuse of his name, by which a work is ascribed to him for not one line or word of which he is answerable', he wrote in legalistic language, he warned:

if *hereafter*, in any sale-catalogue, private or public, or at any auction of books or shares of copies, the said edition of Shakspeare's plays ... shall be described, set up, or sold, as his work, or if it shall be exhibited in any bookseller's shop with his name affixed thereto, as soon as he shall have been made acquainted with the fact, he will immediately publish the name of such bookseller or proprietor of copies as one, not

---

[120] N.d., OFB.   [121] BL Add. Ms. 42561, fol. 232.

only guilty of injurious imposition in this respect, but as a person likely to act in his other dealings with the publick with as little good faith as he must appear to do in this instance ...

John Nicols, editor of the magazine, evidently felt the issue was less clear cut than Malone made out. He therefore published, following Malone's statement, the reply of the booksellers, who insisted the edition was printed 'literally' from Malone's text 'for the same proprietors, by the same printer, with precisely the same types', with the long notes 'curtailed' and the dissertations 'wholly omitted.' They added this was done with Malone's 'acquiescence', who 'was previously consulted ... and knew the progress of the volumes as they passed through the press.' To illustrate this, they even quoted from Malone's letter to Farmer, which the latter may have supplied them, that he was not entitled to the edition's merits, 'whatever they may be, nor answerable for any of its defects. It is, I make no doubt, carefully executed.' Nicols could not resist adding his own comment that the edition is 'a very good one, and such as would not disgrace the name of an Editor, however high his rank in Shakesperian or any other lore.'[122]

  While there is no evidence that Malone intimidated the booksellers or made them stop advertising the edition, the episode does suggest that at this point he may have been uncertain of how to wear his newly won fame as the leading Shakespearean who had raised editing and scholarship to a new level. At first, he liked the idea of some more publicity and influence; then he appears to have had second thoughts about how his name was being used. In addition, he had his own quarto edition in mind. What is beyond doubt is that now he was under close public scrutiny. He would have to watch his step.

[122] *Gentleman's Magazine*, LXIV:I (January–June 1794), 447–48.

8

Boswell's *Life of Johnson*

1

Apart from his Shakespeare edition, Malone's greatest commitment in the late 1780s was to act as midwife to Boswell's *Life of Johnson*. After seeing Boswell's *Tour to the Hebrides* through to a third edition in 1786, he began to urge Boswell to move ahead with the *Life*. Boswell's progress, however, was hampered by family demands, stretches of time spent at Auchinleck, and his legal career. Malone kept telling him he would not be able to write it anywhere except in London, but how could he afford to live there for the long period required, especially if he brought his family?

While he was travelling the Northern circuit in March 1786, Boswell heard from Malone of a new publication that galvanized his plans to write Johnson's biography. Hester Lynch Thrale Piozzi had just published her *Anecdotes of the Late Samuel Johnson*. Aware of the resentment felt by many towards her because of her marriage to her children's music teacher, Gabriel Piozzi, and her neglect of Johnson in his old age, she was under no illusions about how she would be treated when she published anything on Johnson.[1]

Johnson's demands and occasional gruffness had often been a trial to her in her busy life of caring for a husband, children, and a house, but she had loved him and only months before their separation had called him 'Friend, Father, Guardian, Confidant.' She was the most important person to him during the last twenty years of his life. Defensive and guilty, however, she had talked herself into resenting him at the time she announced she was marrying Piozzi and moving out of her house in Streatham where he had been made to feel at home for eighteen years. She told herself he had been a burden and that he was ungrateful for all her care. She nurtured this sense

---

[1] See Malone's journal, 9 August 1791, describing Fanny Burney's rift with Mrs Thrale (Prior, 'Maloniana', p. 413). On Mrs Piozzi's *Anecdotes*, see Richard Wendorf, *The Elements of Life: Biography and Portrait-Painting in Stuart and Georgian England* (1990), pp. 191–206; William McCarthy, *Hester Thrale Piozzi: Portrait of a Literary Woman* (1985), chap. 4; and W. J. Bate, *Samuel Johnson*, pp. 556–60, 566–77, 588–90.

of injury for years, somewhat in spite of herself, and soon after his death it surfaced in her book.

Drawing on her stock of Thraliana, she wrote the *Anecdotes* entertainingly but with a sharpness that often denigrates him. Horace Walpole judged that her 'panegyric is loud in praise of her hero – and almost every fact she relates disgraces him.'[2] One modern critic has even remarked that her book evinces a 'savage neurosis.'[3] Still, as Johnson's most recent biographer has judged, her book could easily have been more caustic and defensive than it was; it was, in fact, often generous: 'It is to Mrs. Thrale's credit that some of her generous feelings about Johnson ultimately returned – enough at least to allow her to print, without too much defensiveness, the anecdotes and accounts of him that she had been writing over the years.'[4] Malone's judgment of the book was colder and more hostile: it was marred by anecdotes drawn from an imperfect memory and motivated by greed.

Malone had read only half of Mrs Piozzi's book when he wrote to Boswell about it on 25 March, the day it appeared: it would be a 'high Treat' for him, for it is 'very entertaining', but 'the stories are *strung* too thick on each other – and she does not *dramatise* sufficiently. She has got many of your unpublished stories and some of them not so well as you have them.'[5] Two days later, after he had gone through the book twice, he was outraged. Her anecdotes are flawed, he told Boswell, with 'evident weakness, and flimzy [*sic*] statement.' She does not 'write about Johnson *cordato animo*' and 'would have the reader think that the eighteen years intercourse with J. was a *bondage*, which she endured *to please Mr Thrale*, but when he was dead it became insupportable; – and so she was forced to fly to Bath: – when in truth she was flying not *from* Dr. J. but *to* a new husband; who does not appear upon the canvass [*sic*].'[6] Nonetheless, as Malone admitted in a private memo, inaccurate and 'artful' as they were, Mrs Piozzi's anecdotes had 'caught something', and on the whole 'the publick is indebted to her for her lively ... account of Dr. Johnson.'[7] He was grateful to Mrs Piozzi for preserving so many colourful moments in Johnson's conversation, though extremely critical of her misrepresentation. Boswell agreed she had 'a great deal of valuable Memorabilia, which prove themselves genuine', but, not putting too fine a point on it, called her 'a little artful impudent malignant Devil' who 'seems to have no *affection* for our great friend.'[8]

As usual, Malone wanted to act, to retaliate, but thought perhaps he

[2] Letter to Sir Horace Mann, 28 March 1786, *Walpole Corr.*, XXV, p. 636.
[3] W. K. Wimsatt, 'Images of Samuel Johnson', *Journal of English Literary History*, 41 (1974), 367.
[4] *Samuel Johnson*, pp. 567–68. Wendorf has shed some light on the psychology behind Mrs Piozzi's *Anecdotes* by describing the parallel between conversation and writing in her literary 'method' (*Elements of Life*, p. 194).   [5] *B–M Corr.*, pp. 308–9.
[6] 27 March 1786, *B–M Corr.*, p. 311.   [7] Prior, 'Maloniana', p. 364.
[8] 31 March 1786, *B–M Corr.*, pp. 314–17. See Mary Hyde, *The Impossible Friendship: Boswell and Mrs. Thrale* (1972), pp. 68–171.

should leave it to Boswell to 'trim' her. He was certain, at least, they should publish their reply within the month and not leave it to a note in the third edition of the *Tour to the Hebrides*, as Boswell had tentatively suggested. On 7 April he advised Boswell, who was soon to return to London, that although Courtenay and he agreed Mrs Piozzi had to be answered immediately, 'great *address* will be necessary in constructing the answer, – which we will sit down to, when you return to town.' 'I have some thought of sending some strictures on her book to the G. M. for this month', he added.[9]

Soon after Boswell returned to London from the circuit on 10 April, he, Courtenay, and Malone 'concerted my Answer to Mrs Piozzi'.[10] In the meantime, to relieve some of his anger, Malone had been busy writing some of his own notes on the *Anecdotes* towards some intended public statement. He gave them to Boswell, who later inserted a few into his *Life of Johnson*. In one, which he wanted Boswell to identify vaguely as by an 'eminent critick', he attributed Mrs Piozzi's biased portrait of Johnson's character to the compression of twenty years' conversation into 'a small volume.' As a result, though some 'severe things' were 'doubtless' said by Johnson during that time, 'they who read the book in *two hours*, naturally enough suppose that his whole conversation was of this complexion.' The fact is, he added, 'I have been often in his company, and never *once* heard him say a severe thing to any one... When he did say a severe thing, if was generally extorted by ignorance pretending to knowledge, or by extreme vanity or affectation.'

While Malone's motive in such a note was to set the record straight, not to whitewash Johnson, his main intention, one he would have stuck to if he had been writing Johnson's biography himself, was to present him in the best light possible. This is also evident in another of his notes that Boswell used. Addressing himself to Mrs Piozzi's account of a dinner at Reynolds' where Johnson told Hannah More she was praising him too much and had better 'consider what her flattery was worth, before she choaked [*sic*] *him* with it', Malone chided Mrs Piozzi for concealing certain facts in order to portray Johnson as a harsh and unkind man. 'Now let the genuine anecdote be contrasted with this', he wrote in his best legal manner. At Sir Joshua's one evening, Hannah More met Dr Johnson: 'She very soon began to pay her court to him in the most fulsome strain. "Spare me, I beseech you, dear Madam", was his reply. She still *laid it on*. "Pray, Madam, let us have no more of this"; he rejoined. Not paying any attention to these warnings, she continued still her eulogy. At length, provoked by this indelicate and *vain* obtrusion of compliment, he exclaimed,

[9] *B–M Corr.*, pp. 321–22.
[10] 15 April 1786, *Boswell 1785–89*, p. 59 (*Malahide*, XVI, pp. 184–85).

"Dearest lady, consider with yourself what your flattery is worth, before you bestow it so freely."' 'How different does this story appear', Malone noted, 'when accompanied with all these circumstances which really belong to it, but which Mrs. Thrale either did not know, or has suppressed.'[11]

After Boswell published the *Life of Johnson*, in which he illustrated Mrs Piozzi's inaccuracies, Malone continued to write marginal comments in his own copy of the *Anecdotes*, perhaps for publication, highlighting errors that Boswell did not expose and which he wished to appear in print. These marginalia exude anger. He was not inclined to be forgiving, even if he allowed that she had some grounds for her irritation. About her claim that over the years Johnson had tried her patience – 'the patience of a woman', as she put it – he scoffed, 'This single sentence is a sufficient proof of the falseness and hollowness of the writer since for eighteen years she never hinted to any mortal that Johnson wearied her patience, but on the contrary was very proud of her guest and delighted with his company.' Her patience ran out only when he remonstrated against her marrying a music master. Fortunately, he confined this piece of *ad hominem* criticism to his private notes. The same is true of his note on Mrs Piozzi's account of Johnson's chaotic household: 'This writer can never represent anything correctly and justly; – all is to be overcharged and wrought up so as to make a high finished picture. From these words one might suppose Johnson had 20 in family.' Malone was incredulous about her charge that Johnson characteristically spoke roughly to people: 'Another gross misrepresentation. All the rough things that he said in 20 years she had carefully & maliciously treasured in this book.'[12] Trifling errors, one might argue, but to Malone they epitomized her flawed and unreliable account. He eventually accepted Boswell's rebuttals as sufficient, for he never published anything of his own against her. Indeed, it seems clear that another of Malone's motivations in castigating Mrs Piozzi was his alliance with Boswell: he wanted her to be bad because he wished to help clear the way for his friend. To some extent, the same was true of his attitude towards Sir John Hawkins.

Hawkins was Boswell's other major rival in Johnsoniana, whose biography of Johnson appeared in March 1787, generally provoking more derision than hostility. Although in some respects he was well placed to write Johnson's biography, having known Johnson ever since he first came to London, Hawkins was handicapped by his inability to write clear English. The newspapers delighted in burlesques such as that his work

[11] Hill-Powell, IV, pp. 341–42.
[12] Malone's notes on the Piozzi *Anecdotes* are unpublished. They have survived only in a copy now in the Sterling Library, Yale; see pp. 5, 16.

would have to be translated into English, and so on.[13] Hearing from Malone that Boswell had resolved to give up wine, Courtenay had earlier written to Boswell in a fright, 'Dont [sic] think of quitting the Joys of wine – as you threaten in your last; if you do – Your life of Johnston [sic] will resemble – Sir J. Hawkins.'[14] But Malone, not mincing words, took an almost obsessive dislike towards Hawkins' *Life*: 'this stupid biographer, and the more flippant and malicious Mrs. Piozzi, have miscoloured and misrepresented almost every anecdote that they have pretended to tell of Dr. Johnson.'[15]

Malone's bad opinion of Hawkins' *Life* again often strayed into *argumentum ad hominem*. Bishop Percy, he wrote, 'concurred with every other person I have heard speak of Hawkins, in saying that he was a most detestable fellow. He was the son of a carpenter, and set out in life in the very lowest line of the law.' Or, as Malone put it in his journal, Hawkins 'never lived in any real intimacy with Dr. Johnson, who never opened his heart to him, or had in fact any accurate knowledge of his character.'[16] He felt this last fact was one of the reasons Hawkins was unkind to Johnson in his biography.[17] According to Boswell, Malone suggested to Club members that they draw up 'a solemn Protest ... to go down to Posterity, declaring that Hawkins' was a false and injurious Account.' The more level-headed Reynolds did not go along with this, though Boswell agreed, resolving that the protest 'should not sleep.' With Malone's help he pursued Hawkins relentlessly.[18]

Malone briefed Boswell about how to denigrate Hawkins in his biography. He prepared a list of comments and annotations, keyed to page numbers in Hawkins' biography, under the following prolific headings: 'His inaccuracy', 'His bad taste and misrepresentation of Johnson and his writings', 'His own bad style', 'His illiberal and unconstitutional notions', 'Rigamarole', and 'Absurdity.' Under 'misrepresentation', he attacked Hawkins' contention that Johnson edited Shakespeare reluctantly and that therefore the edition could not possibly add to his reputation; Hawkins was a blockhead 'who knows nothing of what he has done for Sh[akespeare].' Johnson frequently admitted that '*every* work that he ever engaged in was so executed. And that ... is the truth.'[19] 'Blockhead' had become one of Malone's favourite terms of abuse when he attacked authors of 'slip slop',

---

[13] On Hawkins' *Life* and its reception, see Bertram H. Davis, *Johnson Before Boswell: A Study of John Hawkins' Life of Samuel Johnson* (1960; reprinted 1973). References below to this work are taken from the Greenwood Press edition.   [14] 29 September 1788, *B–M Corr.*, p. 356.
[15] Prior, 'Maloniana', p. 393.
[16] Prior, 'Maloniana', pp. 425–27. Boswell made the same point in the opening pages of the *Life*, Hill-Powell, I, p. 28.   [17] Davis defends Hawkins, *Johnson Before Boswell*, chaps. 6 and 8.
[18] 27 November 1787, *Boswell 1785–89*, p. 156 (*Malahide*, XVII, p. 57).
[19] Davis, *Johnson Before Boswell*, pp. 188–94. This manuscript list is in the William Salt Library, Stafford.

as he once described Mrs Piozzi's *Anecdotes*, though the word reflects as much his own quick temper. In this instance, he saw Hawkins endangering Johnson's reputation and usurping Boswell's place as his only qualified and sufficiently talented biographer.

2

Neither Piozzi's nor Hawkins' early instalments in the race to cash in on Johnson's life and career upset Boswell as much as Malone. He knew he had far more anecdotes, recorded conversations, letters – more were coming in all the time – insight, and sensitivity than his rivals. He also was backed by most of The Club. What worried him most was whether he would finish soon enough to capitalize on the popular interest in Johnson before it waned. An even more serious worry may have been, ought to have been, whether he would finish at all. Since his writing was second to his desire for a reliable income in London, and since self-discipline was not one of his strong points, almost certainly he never would have finished his biography before he died in 1795 had it not been for Malone's unstinting support and help.

Boswell began to write the *Life of Johnson* in July 1786, while he was in London attempting to establish himself at the Bar. Malone was there encouraging him from the beginning. Boswell records in his journal over one hundred working sessions with Malone over the next three years. 'He raised my spirits to a manly pitch', Boswell wrote on 3 June. They breakfasted together on the first of every month, dined together – 'I cannot dine with you forever. I had better board with you', Boswell joked – took tea together, and joined in happy excursions as 'classical travelling companions' to Oxford (in May) and out into the countryside near Kensington, Dulwich, Richmond, Twickenham, and elsewhere. On one excursion to Dulwich in mid-July, they dined under a tree, sharing the shade with a colony of ants. 'I furnished cold roast beef,' Boswell wrote, 'some slices of ham, a loaf, two bottles of port, a bottle of Cyder, salt, tablecloth, plates, glass, knives and forks', while Courtenay brought along two bottles of Madeira and Malone a couple of roasted chickens.

It was not all work and no play, but Malone urged Boswell on constantly, though not oppressively. He told him to avoid women and wine, rebuked him for his overly ambitious ideas about promotion and patronage and his obsession with the figure he could cut in the world, and recommended that he buckle down to make his way in his profession if he really wanted to establish himself in London. On 11 July, Boswell entered in his journal this typical record of Malone's influence:

Fortunately Malone called on me Tuesday, and with his judicious and elegant spirit roused me from despair. He urged that I must act rationally; that I must not appear so ridiculous as to fly off from Westminster Hall before there was time for its being well known that I was in it; that I must fulfil what I had proposed, and must certainly be at least one winter at the bar ... that I might then go to Scotland and bring up my wife and two eldest daughters for the winter and live upon a very moderate scale; and that all my notions about *inferiority* were *pride*, which ought to be repressed. He thus saved me from acting in a way of which I must have repented grievously.[20]

It was good advice, though not long remembered.

When he finally got down to writing, Boswell was not sure how to organize his materials. Malone's early advice was to 'make a skeleton with references to the materials, in order of time.' On 13 July, he went to Malone's and 'with his assistance traced Dr. Johnson's publications chronologically through the *Gentleman's Magazine*, and wrote their titles down under each year.' (Malone used this method himself a few years later when he began his own biographical research into Pope, Dryden, and Shakespeare.) When he began to write, he wrote fast, regularly taking his script to Queen Anne Street East and receiving generous praise for it. 'His conversation never fails to console and cheer me', he wrote on 7 November; 'he encourages me to go on with Johnson's *Life*. One morning we revised a part of it, which he thought well of, and dispelled my vaporish diffidence; and he surprised me another day with a page of it on two different types, that we might settle how it was to be printed.' That was a clever stratagem, for Malone understood better than most how an author's morale can be boosted by seeing his prose in print.[21]

The progress was far from smooth, however. Malone did his best to keep Boswell on a well-balanced regimen of work and recreation, but there were temptations all around, many of them of Malone's own making as he tried to keep his friend's spirits up with entertainment of one kind or another, sharing perhaps Courtenay's fear that if Boswell gave up wine, he would wind up writing like Hawkins. On 8 March 1788, Boswell 'yielded to an invitation to dine at Malone's next day, after some objecting, he [Malone] having said that I now did everything proper but nothing pleasant.'[22] If anything, however, there were too many dinners with The Gang, Burke, Kemble, Windham, and many others; too many late nights and early mornings at Malone's, Reynolds', and Courtenay's, or at his own lodgings playing whist and talking of literature and life's prospects;[23] too much wine; and too many women. Malone began to think so, for on 1 May Boswell wrote ruefully: 'He lectured me upon my intemperance and on my

[20] *Boswell 1785–89*, p. 82 (*Malahide*, XVI, p. 189).

[21] *Boswell 1785–89*, pp. 83, 96–97 (*Malahide*, XVI, pp. 192, 205–6; XVII, p. 7).

[22] *Boswell 1785–89*, p. 195 (*Malahide*, XVII, p. 75).

[23] For a typical night, see 26 April 1788, *Boswell 1785–89*, pp. 218–19 (*Malahide*, XVII, pp. 98–99).

delaying Johnson's *Life*, on which I was to rest my fame.'[24] Malone was able to turn his work on and off at will, but Boswell was not.

As the months passed, Boswell's family, profession, and estate demanded that he leave London for long periods, and once he left, it was impossible for him to get any writing done. 'You will be very angry when I confess to you', he wrote guiltily to Malone on 12 July 1788, that he had not written 'a single page' of the *Life* in six weeks at Auchinleck because of indolence and an aversion to 'sedentary exertion.' 'Now do not scold me', he pleaded, 'for, I promise to set apart so much time for the Life, that the rough draught shall be all done, and brought with me to town early in October; and you know that till the rough draught be finished we cannot proceed in the Metropolis.' Malone then upbraided him for his 'too tedious delay', but it did little good. Two months later, chiefly because of his preparations to run for Parliament in the next General Election, still he had done 'literally nothing': 'It will require an exercise both of your philosophy and indulgent friendship to make allowance for me... I see that *the Whole* will be of London manufacture.' He planned to return to London by mid-October and would then 'set myself *doggedly* to my task' – an uncomfortable allusion to Johnson's remark that no moments of composition were 'happier' than others and that 'a man may write at any time, if he will set himself *doggedly* to it.'[25] 'I beg of you to comfort me', Boswell appeals, 'instead of scolding me.' 'I have always found you a mild Confessor.'[26]

3

During the summer of 1788, Malone desperately needed rest. Shakespeare and Boswell had worn him out. As Boswell was out of town and they could not work on the *Life of Johnson* together anyway, and in spite of the considerable pressures of his Shakespeare edition, he convinced his sisters and sister-in-law, who did not need much convincing, to spend some time with him while his brother attended to business in Scotland.

'My ladies', as Malone called them, were warmly welcomed into his friends' homes, especially Reynolds', Burney's, and Windham's. They joined in the round of dinners, teas, plays, and excursions that he arranged for them. One June day they dined with Windham in Richmond Park.[27] On another morning Malone was lucky 'to light on Burke', whom he invited for dinner that evening to meet his family. 'He came to us, & was in great spirits – various, talkative, and delightful', Malone told Boswell on 12 August; 'he was a great treat to my sisters, who had never seen him

[24] *Boswell 1785–89*, p. 221 (*Malahide*, XVII, pp. 105–6).
[25] Boswell cites Johnson's remark in the *Life*, Hill-Powell, V, p. 40.
[26] *B–M Corr.*, pp. 343–44; 18 September 1788, *B–M Corr.* pp. 352–53.
[27] *Windham Diary*, 13 June 1788, p. 140.

before, and who were much flattered by his notice. Having sat between
them, and got after into some metaphysical or rather moral disquisition
with them, they sustained the argument so well that when they went from
table, he exclaimed to me, "Who are those two very extraordinary
women?"'[28]

'And what becomes of Shakespeare amidst all this hurry of... parties
with Ladies, and rural felicities?' Boswell asked. He felt less guilty about his
own halting progress: 'Pray Sir may I be allowed to ask Are not you the
Commentator upon Shakspeare? I need never be ashamed while you stand
between me and publication – while Mr. Malone's coach stops the way.'[29]

After several days of this, the ladies, alarmed by the pain Malone's eyes
were giving him, decided their brother needed some countrifying and
complete rest. But with the printer hungry for Shakespeare copy, he did not
want to stray too far from the city. He had in mind Sarah Loveday's
furnished house in Camberwell, which her family had left, or Dulwich,
where (he told Boswell) 'if you should be able to return to *your work*, I hope
we shall be able to give you a bed, – without *ants* to disturb you.'[30]
Dulwich, though, was not rural enough for the ladies, and Camberwell
may have reminded him too much of his unhappy courtship of Sarah
Loveday, so eventually they settled on a house in Cobham, Surrey, twenty
miles from London.

When it came time for their holiday at Cobham Park, Malone's
normally placid home was turned upside down. In addition to getting
ready for a long absence, he had to prepare his house for redecoration,
probably at the instigation of his sisters. More than a decade of bachelor
living amid the paraphernalia of scholarship had to be shifted. 'I have a
great deal of arrangement to make in my house', he wrote in some despair
to Boswell two days before leaving, 'and am presently to engage in an
arduous business – the taking down all my books and putting them into my
drawing room, preparatory to my house being painted, inside and out: a
most disagreeable business, that I have deferred from year to year till it can
be deferred no longer.'[31] It was hard work, but Boswell felt that the 'clean
freshness' would do very well; 'you will *live pleasanter*.'[32]

Malone loved their interlude in rural Surrey, a 'summer in a fine country
and a very pleasant retirement, though within 20 miles of London.'[33]
Courtenay and Robert Jephson visited him there, as did Boswell after he
returned to London in early November, though he quickly became

---

[28] *B–M Corr.*, p. 349. One of the 'entertainments' to which Malone took his sister was the Hastings
impeachment trial (see *B–M Corr.*, pp. 336–37, 342). On Malone's praise of the 'richness of
imagery' in Burke's speeches, see 11 April 1788, *Boswell 1785–89*, p. 209 (*Malahide*, XVII, p. 92).

[29] *B–M Corr.*, p. 346. See also 12 August 1788, *B–M Corr.*, p. 351.   [30] Ibid., p. 339.

[31] 12 August 1788, ibid., p. 348.   [32] 18 September 1788, ibid., p. 354.

[33] To Charlemont (no date); not in *HMC*, but see photostat letter (OFB).

'wearied of the country' and retreated to London after a couple of nights to resume work on the *Life of Johnson*.[34] Shakespeare came to a standstill. He told Boswell, 'I have been two or three times in London to see how they were going on at my house; and must spend two days there the beginning of next week to put my library in order, and to leave the front room (which is now entirely covered with books and lumber) free for the painters.'[35] In late November, his family returned home – he would see them in Ireland a year later – and he moved back to his freshly decorated house to resume the life of the bachelor scholar.

4

Boswell had been in London for two weeks, working assiduously and keeping away from 'fermented liquor', when on 17 November he announced to Malone that day and night he had 'laboured at the *Life*, and what I wonder at, have done very well.' He had only a year and a half of the first draft left to write.[36] Thus far Malone had been his advisor and encourager, not his collaborator. The new year would change that.

When Boswell arrived in London without his wife, who was seriously ill at home and could not travel, he moved his lodging to a small house at 38, Queen Anne Street West, Cavendish Square, so that he could be closer to Malone, although the house was far too small to accommodate his whole family.[37] They agreed to revise the first draft together. On 10 January 1789 he explained optimistically to a friend that after he finished the first draft he and Malone would 'prepare one half perfectly', with 'nice correction', and then send it to the press by February 'so as to be out by the end of May.'[38] He would miss his target by about two years.

Boswell feared that once Malone published his Shakespeare edition he would leave for a holiday in Ireland; there could be no more collaboration after that. When news came from home in the spring of 1789, therefore, that his wife was dying, he agonized whether he ought to tear himself away from Malone and speed to her. Malone urged him to go, but he hesitated. When he finally arrived home, he found her dead. In his grief, he pleaded from Scotland for Malone to delay his departure for Ireland: 'If I can have the benefit of your revision of my *Life of Johnson* for any reasonable time were it but three weeks ... I would settle matters so before setting out from hence ... When I am once more in London, I shall not slacken till my *Magnum Opus* is launched.' 'What a satisfaction is it to me, My Dear Malone', he added, 'that I have such a friend as you.'[39] Malone himself

---

[34] Letter from Boswell to his wife, 29 November 1788, *Boswell 1785–89*, p. 253. See Boswell to Malone, 17 November, *B–M Corr.*, p. 359. [35] 29 September 1788, *B–M Corr.*, p. 357.

[36] Ibid., p. 360. [37] 10 January 1789, *Boswell 1785–89*, p. 265 (*Malahide*, XVIII, p. 10).

[38] Boswell to Temple, 13–14 October 1789, Ms. Pierpont Morgan.

[39] 8 July 1789, *B–M Corr.*, pp. 364–65.

was making 'no great progress' and was not on the verge of leaving London soon, but he urged Boswell, the 'sooner you come to us the better it will be for us all.'[40]

So Boswell, to his delight, found Malone still in London when he returned in October. The revision work 'by so acute and knowing a critick as Mr. Malone is of most essential consequence', he wrote on 30 November 1789, 'especially as he is *Johnsonianissimus*, and as he is to hasten to Ireland as soon as his Shakspeare is fairly published, I must avail myself of him *now*.'[41] He pushed himself hard. Many entries in his journal over the next several months register his impatience and resentment when he and Malone were interrupted. The journals for 1789 and 1790 abound with phrases like 'Dined quiet with Malone, and revised so much of Johnson'; 'at Malone's evening revising *Magnum Opus*'; 'With Malone in the evening; revised and grew better'; 'Dined quietly at home in order to be at Malone's to revise, having refused invitations from Lord Lonsdale, Penn, and General Paoli.' On one possibly embarrassing Sunday evening, they were interrupted because Malone 'had a Dulcinea with him' – Boswell's polite term for a prostitute. There are some twenty-eight separate journal references in the next ten months to his revising with Malone. On 12 December 1789, he renewed the lease on his little house for another six months – 'I thought this might do well to keep near Malone.'[42]

Their method of revising was the reverse of their system for the *Tour of the Hebrides*. Instead of Malone reading the draft to Boswell and then writing the corrections in the margins or on papers apart, Boswell read to Malone and wrote the corrections on the manuscript himself.[43] There are fewer revisions, therefore, in Malone's hand and it is difficult to tell from the manuscript which suggestions were his. The few notes and queries Malone did write on the proofs and revised sheets suggest he preferred more elegant Latinate words and less colourful periodic sentences – 'transcribe', for example, instead of 'write' and 'performances' instead of 'literary labours' (which Boswell replaced with 'works').[44]

By the end of 1789 they had revised a third of the draft and hoped to publish by May. Boswell's plan was to begin sending sheets to the press once they had revised half of the manuscript, so in January they discussed the form in which the work should be published. With his knowledge of printing, Malone was indispensable. 'I had talked of printing my *Life of Johnson* in folio, rather than in two volumes', Boswell noted in his journal

[40] 19 August 1789, ibid., p. 367.
[41] 30 November 1789, *Letters of James Boswell*, collected and ed. by Chauncey Brewster Tinker (1924), II, pp. 381–82.
[42] 17 November, 2 December, 23 November, 11 December 1789, *Boswell 1789–95*, pp. 16, 20, 17, 22 (*Malahide*, XVIII, pp. 5–7, 10); 12 and 13 December 1789, *Boswell 1789–95*, pp. 22–23.
[43] On Malone's revisions of proof sheets of the *Life of Johnson*, see *B–M Corr.*, pp. 178–79.
[44] *B–M Corr.*, pp. 178ff. See Boswell's Advertisement, Hill-Powell, I, p. 7).

for 13 January; 'Malone said I might as well throw it into the Thames, for a folio would not now be read.' Malone's idea, which they adopted, was to print a thousand copies in quarto with another thousand in reserve in octavo.[45]

They worked into the summer, but in June, just as they were in full stride, Boswell left for Carlisle in vain pursuit of political patronage at the hands of Lord Lonsdale. Only one-third of the *Life* had been printed and 350 pages still remained to be revised.[46] Boswell felt wretched. 'You have had distress of mind', he wrote to Malone, but 'your active spirit never failed within you. I have heard you say that you never sat listless by the fire.' But he had been sitting by the fire in misery day after day. All his old worries had returned to 'vex' him, especially the frustration that 'I lose those hours which you could now have given me for revising my M.S. and that perhaps you may be gone before I get back to town. Even the fear of not being in London when at last your Shakspeare comes out is shocking. My dear Freind [*sic*]! for GOD's sake if you possibly can let me have some consolation.' Malone replied firmly:

I will not say that your present situation is not an unpleasant one; but surely you have greatly magnified all the evils which you have described. The first and great consideration is, that the whole is but *temporary*, and that as soon as you return to town and have got completely rid of the *aristocrate* [an allusion to Lord Lonsdale], you will be just as well as ever. Where misfortunes happen that are likely to give a colour to a man's whole life, there is reason enough for being cast down, if not for complaining: but this is not your case. The being well or not being well with – [Lonsdale] has nothing to do with your changing Scotland for London, with the embarrassments of your fortune, with the difficulty of educating your children, and twenty other circumstances, that you have enumerated by way of aggravating the account.

With a glance at his own past misfortunes that '*cling about the heart*', he cited Bacon, '"wise men have enough to do with things present and to come: therefore they do but trifle with themselves that labour in past matters".'[47]

Malone continued to revise the manuscript even in Boswell's absence, refining the prose, banishing Scotticisms, altering the tone, and, most important of all, deleting or altering passages in which he thought Boswell compromised himself too much and offended Johnson's friends, living or dead. From one offensive passage in which Boswell quoted Johnson's use of the word 'Thyrasis', which means an infestation of lice, to describe John Wilkes' rebellious supporters, he removed a couple of lines and asked, 'Why raise up against him a host of enemies, by telling a thing that need not be told, and in which perhaps your information may have been inaccurate? I

[45] *Boswell 1789–95*, pp. 32–33 (*Malahide*, XVIII, pp. 19–21).
[46] Boswell to Sir William Forbes, 2 July 1790, Fettercairn, Box 87, no. 1346.
[47] 30 June and 8 July 1790, ibid., pp. 368–70, 371–72.

do sincerely believe that my friend Lord Charlemont, if he had read that passage in your book, would have thrown it into the fire.'[48] When Boswell returned, they kept at it together, though his energy often flagged. He was in awe of Malone 'I merely attend to the progress of my *Life*', he wrote in his journal on 10 September 1790, 'and that by no means with great assiduity, such as that which Malone employs on Shakspeare.'[49]

Suddenly, in late November, a few days before his *Shakspeare* was published, Malone left for Ireland and Boswell continued on his own. From Ireland, from which he did not plan to return until May, Malone could offer only general advice. His last known suggestion came on 23 December: 'Pray take care of colloquialisms and vulgarisms of all sorts. Condense as much as possible, always preserving perspecuity and do not imagine the *only* defect of stile, is repetition of words.'[50]

Anxieties crowded in on Boswell. 'Your absence is a woeful want in all respects', he wrote to Malone on 18 January 1791. His spirits were down and he feared that the part of the *Life* he was revising on his own would be inferior to the rest. On 29 January, he craved Malone's 'vigour of mind, and warmth of heart [that] make your friendship of such consequence that it is drawn upon like a Bank.' Steevens made matters worse by 'kindly' telling him at The Club that he had 'overprinted, and that the curiosity about Johnson is *now* only in our own circle.' Steevens, he has been 'certainly informed', had been 'depreciating' his biography, 'so that I fear the sale of it may be very dubious.' Plagued by money problems, he wondered whether he should accept the bookseller George Robinson's offer of one thousand pounds for the copyright, or hold on to the rights, as he preferred to do, and hope that sales would be brisk? 'Pray decide for me', he implored Malone, 'and if as I suppose you are for my taking the offer inform me with whom I am to treat. In my present state of spirits, I am all timidity. Your absence has been a severe stroke to me.'[51]

He also asked Malone for a loan of one thousand pounds. 'I *will* not sell, till I have your answer as to this', he wrote. But Malone could not spare the money. Poor investments, an increasing appetite to buy books,[52] and the depressed money market caused by the threat of a French invasion had depleted his bank account: 'I am sure when you consider that my little fortune is but just sufficient to live even on my contracted scale and that it will by no means bear any further diminution, you will think that I have abundant reason for this determination.' He suggested instead that the

---

[48] 8 July 1790, ibid., pp. 373–74.   [49] *Boswell 1789–95*, p. 108 (*Malahide*, XVIII, p. 94).
[50] *B–M Corr.*, p. 387.
[51] *B–M Corr.*, p. 390; to Malone, 29 January 1791, pp. 394–95; to Malone, 25 February 1791, p. 405; 29 January 1791, p. 395.
[52] For Malone's expenditures on books in the 1780s, see Ms. Malone 34, fol. 177. See also James M. Osborn, 'Edmond Malone: Scholar–Collector', 11–37.

printer Henry Baldwin or the bookseller Charles Dilly might give him an
advance, saving him from surrendering the copyright. Courtenay could see
that Boswell was almost 'melancholy mad' and that nobody except
Malone was likely to be able to help him. So in a letter in early March,
Malone tried again to rouse his friend, this time invoking the power of
religion to overcome intemperance and self-condemnation:

> Your account of yourself for some time past is very deplorable, but is not your
> depression entirely owing to yourself, I mean to your own almost uniform
> intemperance in wine? Without being a very strict moralist, one may say that it is
> surely *unwise* to indulge in such excesses *habitually*, and that the sure consequence of
> wild and intemperate riot for one half the year, must be the lowest depression
> during the other. Besides, to talk more seriously; what do the name and all the
> forms and ceremonies of religion signify, if they have not some relation to our
> *actions* ...

But it was lack of money, not excess of wine, that tormented Boswell. Both
Dilly and Baldwin eventually came through with two hundred-pound
advances each, which with some unexpected credit in Scotland enabled
Boswell to keep the rights to his book. In light of the several editions of the
Life of Johnson which followed each other fairly quickly, in all of which
Malone played a crucial part, it would have been a colossal error for
Boswell to part with the copyright. 'I am quite resolved now to keep the
property of my MAGNUM OPUS', he told Malone, 'and I flatter myself I shall
not repent it.'[53]

As Malone stayed longer in Ireland than he expected, he was powerless
in the last few weeks before publication to do anything but advise Boswell
again to be extremely careful not to offend people in his quoting of
Johnson's conversation. Sensing danger, Percy, Reynolds, Burke, and
Burney also appealed to Malone to keep Boswell on a tight rein. Percy,
especially, who more than the others was concerned with his reputation,
urged Boswell on 24 March 1791, 'before it be too late, to take a retrospect
thro' your book, and cancel any accidental Escapes ... where Dr. J. has
thrown out Severe Censures on the personal Characters of Individ-
uals ... Such effusions he never did nor could seriously mean.'[54] Boswell
assured Malone, 'I would wish to avoid all cause of quarrel or even ill
will.'[55] Malone remained apprehensive, but he congratulated Boswell on
'drawing so near a conclusion'; he regretted he would 'not be in London
either at the publication of your work or my own, after all the time that we

[53] 10 February 1791, *B–M Corr.*, p.399; 24 February, p. 401; 5 March, pp. 408–09; Courtenay to
Malone, 22 February, OFB. Dilly advised accepting a thousand pounds (20 February, *Boswell
1789–95*, p. 126 (*Malahide*, XVIII, p. 107).

[54] *The Correspondence and Other Papers of James Boswell Relating to the Making of the Life of Johnson*, ed.
with introduction and notes by Marshall Waingrow (1969), p. 398.

[55] 9 March and 12 April 1791, *B–M.Corr.*, pp. 413, 415.

have passed together while both were going on.' Still, if publication were to be delayed until the second week of May, 'I may yet be present at the launch, for I hope to see you by that time.'[56]

He made it back in time, for the *Life of Johnson* did not appear until 16 April, the twenty-eighth anniversary of Boswell's first meeting with Johnson. When he opened the covers of a work he had nurtured and coaxed along for over five years, he read with pleasure Boswell's praise of him in the Advertisement. While 'it is but fair to him to mention that upon many occasions I differed from him, and followed my own judgement', Boswell wrote:

I regret exceedingly that I was deprived of the benefit of his revision, when not more than one half of the book had passed through the press; but after having completed his very laborious and admirable edition of SHAKSPEARE, for which he generously would accept of no other reward but that fame which he has so deservedly obtained, he fulfilled his promise of a long-wished-for visit to his relations in Ireland; from whence his safe return *finibus Atticis* is desired by his friends here, with all the classical ardour of *Sic te Diva potens Cypri*; for there is no man in whom more elegant and worthy qualities are united; and whose society, therefore, is more valued by those who know him.[57]

But there was no time for complacency. Steevens had been proved wrong; interest in Johnson had not waned. The biography was hugely successful, with about half the copies printed sold within a month. Another edition was called for right away.[58] Malone, already deep in new historical research, supervised revisions towards a second edition and helped Boswell round up more of Johnson's correspondence. At Malone's home on 10 November 1792, Boswell marvelled at his apparently inexhaustible energy: 'Paid a visit to Malone. Found him, as I always have done, engaged in literature, so as to have no weariness ... '; 'Malone's conversation ... always animates me in some degree', he noted on 26 November. Whenever he called on him, he found him 'fully occupied in historical and biographical researches, on which he was intent, while I had absolutely no pursuit whatever.'[59]

As publication of the second edition drew near, something came up which incensed Malone against Boswell as never before. For the new Advertisement, which would be published with the first, Boswell patted himself on the back by quoting from an interview he had had with the King in the early days of his work on the biography. Among other things, Boswell wrote, the King said to him, 'There will be many lives of Dr. Johnson; do you give the best.' He flattered himself that he had 'obeyed my SOVEREIGN'S

[56] 14 April 1791, *B–M Corr.*, pp. 417–19; Malone to Percy, 26 April (*P–M Letters*, p. 54).
[57] Hill-Powell, I, pp. 7–8.
[58] On the earnings from the *Life*, see 9 December 1795 (*DF*, II, p. 366).
[59] 10 November, 26 November, 17 December 1792, *Boswell 1789–95*, pp. 196, 201, 207–8 (*Malahide*, XVIII, pp. 175–76, 181, 188).

commands.'[60] Accidentally discovering this 'wild Rhodomantade', as he called it, at the printer's a couple of months before publication, Malone could scarcely believe Boswell's lapse of good taste. 'You have an undoubted right over your own reputation, and to expose yourself in any way you think proper', he shot at him on 13 May 1793, but if Boswell persevered with 'the wild Rhodomantade', he must ask 'not as a favour, but a *right*, that you would cancel whatever relates to me in the former Advertisement.' Boswell could not degrade himself 'without injuring at the same time the characters of those whom you mention as your friends. Poor Sir Joshua is in his grave [he died on 28 February 1792], and *nothing can touch him further*; otherwise he could not but blush, that his name should appear at the head of a dedication, followed by such an Advertisement...' He signed the letter, 'Yours always very sincerely in *private*, but by no means wishing to be *pilloried* with you in *publick*.'[61]

Boswell attributed Malone's irritation to the rough treatment Steevens gave him in his new edition of Shakespeare, just published, especially in the Advertisement: 'I knew that Steevy's stabs had hurt you; but I did not apprehend to that degree of irritation which your *hyper*critical letter indicated.'[62] Ritson, who had picked up a rumour about their quarrel, pitied Boswell, 'a sort of parasite to Malone', at the hands of that 'mercurial commentator.'[63] Never doubting Malone's 'real friendship', Boswell insisted that 'every man is at liberty to put himself forward in the style he likes best and his praise of his friends in a very different style must not be confounded with his own personal Rhodomantade.'[64] Nonetheless, after discussing the matter with Courtenay and the Bishop of Salisbury, he rewrote the passage under Malone's direction, though later, again without Malone knowing it, he substituted another version, prefacing it with an allusion to Malone's quieter manner of wearing success and fame: 'There are some men, I believe, who have, or think they have, a very small share of vanity. Such may speak of their literary fame in a decorous style of diffidence. But I confess, that... to restrain the effusion of delight, on having obtained such fame, to me would be truly painful. Why then should I suppress it?'[65] Malone's comment on this disagreement, years after Boswell's death, is poignant: 'I expressed myself so strongly, that for the only time I think in the whole course of our acquaintance, he lost his good humour. Of course I gave the matter up.'[66]

[60] Cited in Pottle, *The Literary Career of James Boswell*, p. 158.   [61] *B–M Corr.*, p. 423.
[62] Ibid., p. 424.   [63] 9 September 1793, OFB.   [64] *B–M Corr.*, p. 424.
[65] Hill-Powell, I, p. 12.
[66] Malone to Forbes, 5 July 1798, Fettercairn, Box 87 (unnumbered).

5

After his second edition came out, Boswell's spirits sank, no longer sustained by work. He suffered acutely from post-*magnum opus* let down. He wanted political preferment, but could not get it. To ward off depression, he proposed, in Joseph Farington's words, 'a small society for the winter to meet at each others [*sic*] Houses, not to exceed 8 persons. Boswell, [Ozias] Humphrey [*sic*], myself, George Dance, Malone, & [Lord] Petre were mentioned to begin with.'[67] Nothing came of the idea, so he clung to Malone instead. 'Went to Malone's at five', he wrote in his journal for 18 January 1794, 'and waited till he came home, and was made welcome to a share of his dinner.' Malone saw that he needed to relax and 'pressed a second bottle, the greatest part of which I could not resist drinking. However, we had good talk.' There was time for advice as well as wine: 'I dined *tête-à-tête* with Malone very cordially', he wrote on 13 February. 'He talked like a practical philosopher against my being discontented with my lot in life.'[68] From Auchinleck in November, aching to be back in London to do he knew not what, he recorded his debt to his dearest friend with a touching mixture of tenderness and despair: 'How have you been? enviable man! What a number of events have happened since I left you, that would have agitated me, had I been in London. Pray write to me ... I can see no prospect in life but a thick fog... My Dear Malone, in whatever state I am I never forget your kindness to me, and the innumerable moments of happiness which I owe to you...'[69]

On the evening of 14 April 1795, at a Club dinner which Malone attended, Boswell suddenly was taken seriously ill and had to be carried home. As Farington put it, he 'went out no more'[70] and died on 19 May. Malone had noticed, as he told Forbes on 25 April 1796, that when Boswell returned from Scotland, 'he seemed to think himself entitled to more than usual indulgence, in which he went on so rapidly that I had no longer as formerly any kind of influence over him.' He blamed himself, together with Windham and Courtenay, for not trying harder, 'for he was ductility itself and had high opinion of us all, and would I am sure have entered into any engagement with respect to temperance that we should have proposed to him.'[71] Two days after Boswell died, Malone told Windham what his loss meant to him: 'I shall miss him more and more every day. He was in the constant habit of calling upon me almost daily, and I used to grumble sometimes at his turbulence; but now miss and regret his noise and his hilarity and his perpetual good humour, which had no bounds. Poor fellow,

---

[67] *DF*, I, p. 91.   [68] *Boswell 1789–95*, pp. 277, 287 (*Malahide*, XVIII, pp. 252, 265).
[69] 18 November 1794, *B-M Corr.*, pp. 429–30.   [70] *DF*, II, p. 346.
[71] Malone to Forbes, 25 April 1796, Fettercairn, Box 87 (unnumbered).

he has somehow stolen away from us without any notice, and without my being at all prepared for it.'[72]

Boswell was gone, but Malone's services in his memory and on behalf of his children continued. There would be more editions of the *Life of Johnson* to see through the press – the third in 1799 – but more immediately, he served as guardian in London for Boswell's children, Veronica, Euphemia, and James. 'We shall never forget Mr. Malones [*sic*] kindness to us', Euphemia wrote to Forbes on 3 July; 'he has given us much good advice and that in the most pleasing manner.' Tragically, Veronica died in September, just four months after her father, leaving Euphemia vulnerable and on her own. In later years, she would become an embarrassment to her father's distinguished friends, but in those late months of 1795 Malone helped sort out her financial affairs, arranged (from Oxford) the funeral of her sister, and determined where she would live.[73] Alone among the Boswell children, however, it was James Junior with whom he developed an affectionate, fatherly relationship that lasted to the end of his life. During the Christmas holidays, when Boswell's brother showed himself reluctant to take the boy in from Westminster School, he welcomed him into his home.[74] A likeable and intelligent young man with literary tastes, Malone recognized in him a kindred spirit, a capacity some day to publish portions of the mass of manuscripts that Boswell left behind in his London house and at Auchinleck. The irony was that James Junior would honour Malone, not his father, in this way.

Malone's most lasting service to Boswell's family in the months following his death, one that placed great strain on his eyes, was as literary executor.[75] In 1785, we recall, Boswell had named Malone, Forbes, and Temple his literary trustees having discretionary power over his manuscripts and letters. They would decide what, if anything, to publish, and when. All three took their charge seriously, though Boswell chose only Malone for literary judgment.[76]

It was a daunting task. The volume of manuscripts at both Auchinleck and in London would require months of sifting and organizing before anyone could decide anything about publication. Temple died fifteen months after Boswell without having had a chance to do more than consult with the other two, on whose shoulders the bulk of this complicated work

---

[72] 21 May 1795, *The Windham Papers*, ed. Lewis Melville (1913), I, pp. 297- 98. See also *DF*, II, p. 465.

[73] See Euphemia Boswell to Forbes, 18 July 1795, Fettercairn, Box 88, F2, no. 203.

[74] See James Boswell Junior to Forbes, 2 January [1796], Fettercairn, Box 88/F1, no. 200; and Euphemia Boswell to Forbes, 6 January [1796], Fettercairn, Box 88/F2, no. 220. See *DF*, II, 463, 465.

[75] On Malone's conduct as Boswell's literary trustee, see Pottle, *Pride and Negligence*, pp. 11–27; and David Buchanan, *The Treasure of Auchinleck: The Story of the Boswell Papers* (London, 1975).

[76] See *DF*, II, p. 346.

therefore fell. To us two centuries later, what ensued is fascinating since scarcely any of Boswell's manuscripts were published by Malone and most of them disappeared and were thought to have been either destroyed or sequestered at Auchinleck until the early twentieth century, when they were discovered in one of the most sensational literary discoveries in the history of English literature.

Malone cannot be blamed either for their disappearance or fragmentation. He was more anxious about the safety of the manuscripts in London (which included most of the journals) than Forbes was in Edinburgh over the literary manuscripts brought to him from Auchinleck by Boswell's nineteen-year-old son, Alexander. Forbes' plan was to review the manuscripts at Auchinleck while Malone examined the ones Boswell left in his house in Great Portland Street in London. Then they would exchange them by post.[77] After combing through the London manuscripts – which apparently did not include Johnson's letters to Boswell[78] – Malone told Forbes on 25 April 1796 he thought Boswell's journals extremely 'curious' and publishable in a decade or so by James Junior, 'a promising young man', who would have to edit them, for Boswell had written them 'in the freedom of his heart.' 'As these Journals are the only Mss. of any value that he has left and their loss would be irretrievable', he preferred to hand them over in person in London. He was not yet ready to part with the journals anyway because they were too full of memories for him and he found himself 'so mixed with melancholy at reviewing scenes in many of which I was myself engaged' that he could not proceed as quickly as he wished.[79]

Because Forbes thought he was too cautious, Malone relented and sent Forbes the entire London collection probably sometime in 1797; all Boswell's manuscripts, therefore, were in Forbes' possession in Scotland between then and 1806. Not until after 1806, when Forbes died, did Malone play a part again in the fate of these manuscripts. He arranged for 'a large parcel' of them to be sent to James Junior in London for his 'inspection and consideration', and he assumed that by 4 May 1809, when he wrote to Euphemia who hoped to make some money from them, all of these had been returned to Scotland: 'They are now deposited at Auchinleck; in which repository, I trust, they will be suffered to remain in peace.'[80] He was wrong. Either James kept many of them or later retrieved

---

[77] See Forbes to Malone, 14 August 1795, *Malahide, I*, p. 5; and 30 June 1796 (Scottish Record Office, Adam Collection, III, pp. 98–100).

[78] On Malone's search for the Boswell–Johnson correspondence, see Buchanan, *The Treasure at Auchinleck*, pp. 320–21.

[79] On Malone's affection for James Boswell Junior, see his letter to Forbes, 2 November 1796, Fettercairn, Box 87 (unnumbered). Malone recommended Brasenose to Boswell.

[80] Malone to Euphemia Boswell, 4 May 1809 (listed and cited in Pocock Sale Catalogue, 10 May 1875, Lot 143).

them from the Auchinleck archives, for when he died suddenly in 1822 they were sold along with his own papers and library. This first known fragmentation of the archives would have dismayed Malone since as one of Boswell's literary trustees he had taken very seriously the charge to keep them all together and safe.[81]

6

In his double capacity as Boswell's literary executor and former editorial collaborator, Malone in 1798 decided it was time to bring out the third edition of the *Life of Johnson* that Boswell had been preparing just before his death. It took time away from his other work, but there was no one else in a position to do it; he also felt the edition could earn some money for the Boswell children. It was another of several literary memorials, in the forms of editions, memoirs, and monuments, that over the last twenty years of his life he arranged and produced for friends.

He added to the edition all of Boswell's revised notes, as well as several hundred of his own – those not signed, he tells the reader, are his. He also expanded the index.[82] Commanding most of his attention was the editorial policy. How liberally should Boswell's friends and acquaintances be allowed to alter the text in deference to injured feelings and reputations? Boswell himself had resisted such revisions, but now that he was gone would it not be better for all concerned, and for posterity, to temper or delete a few of the more offensive passages?

Forbes strongly favoured such emendations. He implored Malone on 22 May 1798 to cut out of the *Life* whatever could prove 'injurious to the reputation of any person dead, or that could hurt the feelings of any one living' – especially Bishop Percy, who after the first edition could scarcely bear to speak to Boswell or attend The Club if he knew he would be present.[83] Malone would have none of this. In his reply on 5 July, he said he could not compromise one of his tenets of scholarly editorship, 'I am most clearly of opinion, that the work of an author is sacred; and that we have no right to make any alteration whatsoever in his *Life of Johnson*, unless where a *matter of facts*, as a date, &c. may be corrected by documents which he has himself left for the third edition.' 'I had much talk with him on that subject', he added, 'and some things were changed or omitted on my advice: but to make any change of that sort, now, would surely not be warrantable: it would be *no longer Mr Boswell's work*, but that of the editor.' As for Percy, a passage in the first edition certainly gave him 'great offence, & he was, rather unreasonably, offended with *me* for not preventing its appearance, as if I were responsible for any part of my friend's work!'.

[81] See Pottle, *Pride and Negligence*, pp. 28–29.
[82] See Malone's Advertisement to the edition, Hill-Powell, I, pp. 14–15.
[83] Forbes to Malone, 22 May 1798, Fettercairn, Box 87, no. 331.

Boswell had, however, agreed to alterations for the second edition and 'the Bishop & he were afterwards good friends, and we all often met at the Literary Club, so near the time of our poor friends [*sic*] death.'[84] Given the pressure from Forbes, Burney, and others, this was a difficult tightrope for Malone to walk. Forbes initially resisted Malone's argument,[85] but eventually, grudgingly, came around.

The question of editorial policy did not surface again as Malone shepherded subsequent editions of the *Life of Johnson* through the press. He had helped to protect the text and now it was established. For the 1804 edition, he encouraged Forbes to search through Boswell's manuscripts for Johnson's letters, which nobody could find. Boswell 'kept all Dr. Johnson's letters to himself in one bundle and arranged in the order of time', he explained on 2 May 1804, 'and this bundle must be either in your possession or at Auchinleck.'[86] Where were Johnson's letters to the poet and historian James Macpherson and Lord Chesterfield, among others, which in his *Life* Boswell said he was depositing in the British Museum, for posterity?[87] Forbes had such little success finding items that Malone began to believe Boswell's papers were in a bigger mess than he thought. 'I had conceived', he wrote to Forbes, 'that Mr. Boswell had kept Dr. Johnson's Letters addressed to himself in a distinct parcel' but if not, all the papers required arranging in chronological order 'to be preserved as an honourable testimony to the Author, in the Library at Auchinlecke [*sic*]? As Johnson's handwriting is so remarkable, I should hope it would not be attended with much trouble.'[88] Less than a handful of Johnson's letters to Boswell have ever been found.

Malone would have been wise to visit Fettercairn and go through the manuscripts himself, but there was no time because the fourth edition (1804) was already being printed.[89] Also, as usual, he was tied to London. He needed to accelerate his work on Shakespeare, which had slowed to a crawl. He would produce two more editions of the *Life* in 1807 and 1811, helped by James Junior, who had contributed notes to both the third and fourth editions and whom Malone asked to keep an eye out for missing letters as late as 1808.[90] This small collaboration was for Malone a happy postscript to his cherished friendship with the young man's father. It would bear other fruit years later when it was James Junior's turn to assume responsibility for Malone's papers and the task of publishing his *magnum opus*.

[84] Fettercairn, Box 87 (unnumbered).
[85] See Forbes to Malone, 20 July 1798, Fettercairn, Box 87, no. 332.
[86] Waingrow, p. 603.   [87] 3 March 1804, Waingrow, p. 602.
[88] Waingrow, pp. 604–5.
[89] On Malone's fourth edition of the *Life of Johnson*, see *DF*, VII, p. 2507.
[90] See Malone to Boswell Junior, 28 September 1808, Waingrow, pp. 606–7.

1 *Samuel Johnson*. Oil, unknown artist, c. 1784.

2 *George Steevens*. Engraving by George Cooke from an oil painting by E. Haytley, 1812.

3 *Isaac Reed*. Engraving by C. Knight after painting by Silvester Harding for Harding's
Shakspeare Illustrata, 1791.

4 *Joseph Ritson*. Engraving by James Sayer after drawing by James Sayer. 22 March 1803.

5 *Thomas Warton*. Oil by Sir Joshua Reynolds, 1784.

6 *Thomas Percy.* Mezzotint by William Dickinson, 1775, after oil by Sir Joshua Reynolds, 1773.

7 Sir Joshua Reynolds. Oil, self-portrait, c. 1780.

Le
Camille Des Moulins. anglice
Joe Miller. Orateur vif & sans Culotte

8 *John Courtenay.* Drawing by James Sayers, n.d.

9 *A Literary Party*. Engraving by W. Walker after oil by J. E. Doyle. Shows from left to right: Boswell, Johnson, Reynolds, Garrick, Burke, Paoli, Burney, Thomas Warton, and Goldsmith, n.d.

10 *David Garrick*. Oil by Sir Joshua Reynolds, 1776.

11 *William Windham*. Oil by Sir Thomas Lawrence, c. 1803.

12 *James Boswell*. Oil by Sir Joshua Reynolds, 1785. Malone described this as 'a perfect and very characteristic likeness'.

13 *Edmund Burke*. Oil by Sir Joshua Reynolds, 1774.

14 *Mrs Hester Thrale* (afterwards Piozzi). Oil by Robert Edge Pine, 1781.

15 *Thou art a Retailer of Phrases*. English School, 1800. Dr Johnson appears as a ghost to Boswell at his desk.

16 *Revising for the Second Edition.* 15 June 1786.

17 *The Biographers*. 1786. Shows Hester Thrale Piozzi, Courtenay, and Boswell. The bust of Dr Johnson looks down on them, displeased. Johnson also appears as a bear in Boswell's *Journal of the Tour*, in which Boswell is writing.

18 *Titianus Redivivus; – or – The Seven Wise Men consulting the new Venetian Oracle, a Scene in ye Academic Grove*. No. 1. 1797. Shows three critics in the foreground; the one in the middle, holding a volume of Shakespeare, is Malone.

19 *Joseph Farington*. Drawing by George Dance, RA, 1793.

20 *Dr Charles Burney*. Drawing by George Dance, RA, 1794.

21 *Fanny Burney*. Drawing by her cousin E. F. Burney.

9

Interruptions and disappointments

1

When Malone returned from Ireland in 1791 and began to help Boswell with a second edition of the *Life of Johnson*, he brimmed with optimism and energy. He had left London before his edition was published, one of a number of respected editors and scholars; he returned as the leading Shakespearean and perhaps the most respected scholar in England. His scholarship had put before him an open door and he was eager to walk through it to even greater fame. There were several paths he could take. He briefly considered producing an edition of Beaumont and Fletcher or an edition of John Aubrey's *Lives*. He had not given up the idea of an edition of Pope with biographical material; and as he had promised in the preface to his 1790 edition, he intended to publish a handsome quarto edition of Shakespeare that would include more information about the poet's life. He saw this lavish edition, to be printed in fifteen volumes and 'ornamented with engravings', as a contribution to national pride, 'a *desideratum* in English literature.'[1] After a few years of research, he extended the plan to twenty volumes and then was forced by the economic climate to drop the idea entirely. He continued his Shakespearean research, though by then he had also dropped the idea of Beaumont and Fletcher, and Aubrey editions. The 1790s, in fact, were filled with interruptions, both personal and literary, to his Shakespeare work. A few of these interruptions were productive, such as his study of Dryden; others were distracting or destructive.

Johnson had attempted to dissuade Malone from embarking on an edition of Pope, but he had remained interested. In 1791, he again sought advice, this time from Lord Hailes (Sir David Dalrymple), whose judgment on contemporary literary matters was well respected. 'I have it in contemplation, at some future period, (when Shakspeare shall be quite exhausted)', he wrote on 17 October, 'to derive some amusement from

---

[1] *Letter to the Rev. Richard Farmer, D.D.* (1792), p. 10n. See Malone's contract for the edition (November 1791) with the bookseller George Robinson (Ms. Malone 1046–1057); and to Charlemont, 15 November 1793 (*HMC*, XIII, 8, p. 222).

giving an edition both of Pope and Dryden.' He continued by indulging in
a pastime of his, some bashing of Bishop Warburton whose edition of Pope's
works appeared in 1751. In his Pope edition Warburton 'has done every
thing he ought not to have done, and omitted to do what he ought to have
done.' Not only that, he 'wearies his readers with a dull commentary in
which he finds out schemes and meanings that the poet never thought of;
and is entirely silent about the personal allusions and anecdotes of the day,
about which, as he lived so near the time, he might easily have obtained
much information.'[2] Hailes did not agree about Warburton: 'Let me be
allowed to say this for my old friend Bishop Warburton, that he avows that
he *left undone* what he thought it unfit for him *to have done.*'[3]

Malone had already done a good bit of groundwork on Pope. In the
Bodleian Library there are two booklets crammed with notes, mostly on
Pope, which he began in the early 1780s and added to perhaps between
1791 and 1794. Most of his notes are about the poet's canon and cite
anecdotes either from people who knew Pope (like Joseph Spence and Lord
Marchmont) or from people who knew Pope's friends and could illuminate
aspects of the poet's career that Warburton had ignored.[4]

While Malone was doing this research, Joseph Warton, whose work on
Pope he did not respect,[5] put him on to the scent of Spence's *Anecdotes*, a
mine of information about Pope, as well as about Dryden. Spence is the
richest biographical source on Pope from the early eighteenth century,
apart from the poet's letters, that is known to exist. On 6 January 1792,
Malone recalled a conversation with Warton 'respecting Spence, author of
the *Anecdotes*, whom he maintained Dr. Johnson had under-rated … They
are, Dr. Warton says very entertaining, and full of curious information.'[6]
According to Warton, Spence at one point had an agreement with the
publisher Robert Dodsley for the publication of his *Anecdotes*, but both he
and Dodsley died before they could bring it out, and later the *Anecdotes* were
suppressed by Spence's executors because of (in Malone's words) 'so many
personal strokes affecting persons then living.' The Duke of Newcastle, who
then owned the manuscripts, was still honouring the executors' ban on
publication, but to a literary 'bird-dog' like Malone, as one critic has called
him, that was not necessarily the last word.

Almost two years elapsed before he was able to read the *Anecdotes*. Then

---

[2] National Library of Scotland. On Pope's plans for a Pope edition, see J. M. Osborn, 'Dr.
Johnson on the Sanctity of an Author's Text', 928–29.

[3] 20 October 1791, Bodleian, Ms. Eng. Letters C.15, fol. 72 (Prior, p. 254).

[4] The booklets are in Ms. Malone 30.

[5] See Malone's annotations of Warton's two-volume *Essay* on Pope (South Kensington Museum
Library, no. 10436).

[6] Prior, pp. 184–85. On Malone's use of the *Anecdotes*, see James M. Osborn (ed.), *Joseph Spence:
Observations, Anecdotes, and Characters of Books and Men* (1966), I, pp. xciv–xcvi. Hereafter cited as
Anecdotes.

the Duke of Newcastle proved even more generous than expected, allowing Malone to transcribe as many of them as he wished for his own use. Although by this time he had decided to work on Dryden before Pope, he wrote on 7 November 1794 in some excitement to Charlemont about this 'invaluable treasure' from which he expected to draw much for a life of Dryden, 'not in competition with Johnson's admirable account of him and his works, but as a supplement to it. He had these anecdotes, but he did not take half so much out of them as he might have done.' Eventually, the anecdotes would also 'furnish several elucidations for an edition of Pope, which I meditate some time or other.'[7] That month he copied out the more interesting extracts, which came to almost three hundred pages in transcript, most of them on Pope. He also added a number of notes to the anecdotes, which are still useful today. Malone also imposed his own order on Spence's rather chaotic arrangement, grouping all material relating to Pope in the first section under 'Popiana'; all material on Shakespeare, Dryden, and other English poets in a second section; and miscellaneous items in a third.[8] Although he never published the transcript, he used it in all his subsequent work, mostly for the Dryden edition. It was published in 1820 by John Murray, Lord Byron's publisher, who used it, and its arrangement of the anecdotes, for an octavo edition of Spence.[9]

2

While Malone was deciding what scholarly project to take on next, Ritson attacked him again. Early in 1792, Ritson published an abusive pamphlet that even bore Malone's name in the title, *Cursory Criticisms on the Edition of Shakspeare published by Edmond Malone*. Ritson's biographer has acknowledged that the pamphlet, the fruit of ten years of animosity and frustration, 'passes in scurrility anything else which he ever published.'[10] The pamphlet interests us not because of what it suggests about Ritson or even about Malone's scholarship, but because of how Malone responded to it.

Ritson begins briskly in his preface:

Mr. Malone will take this [criticism] exceedingly ill, for Mr. Malone has a very high opinion of himself, and a very mean one of everybody else. But I confess I do

[7] *HMC*, XIII, 8, p. 254.
[8] The two-volume transcript is in the Folger, with the note that he wrote it out in November 1794. See *Anecdotes*, I, pp. xcv–xcvi.
[9] See the Advertisement of Murray's edition (possibly by James Boswell Junior) crediting Malone with improving the organization of the anecdotes (*Observations, Anecdotes, and Characters of Books and Men Arranged with Notes by the Late Edmund [sic] Malone Esq.*, pp. iii–iv). See Osborn's edition, I, pp. xcvi–xcvii.
[10] Bronson, *Joseph Ritson*, pp. 494–95. On Ritson's attack on Malone, see Bronson, pp. 494–542; and Osborn's rebuttal, 'Ritson, Scholar At Odds', pp. 427–29.

not seek to please Mr. Malone: I wish to rescue the language and sense of an admirable author from the barbarism and corruption they have acquired in passing through the hands of this incompetent and unworthy editor. In a word, I mean to convict and not to convince him.[11]

Ritson's desire to convict emanated from two causes. One was his irritation (which he shared with a number of others) over Malone's scholarly ego. One critic in the *St. James's Chronicle* for 2 June 1792 called Malone a 'Dictator perpetuo' seeking to monopolize the editorship of Shakespeare. Others in years to come would say the same thing. Another cause of Ritson's anger was the way Malone slights his contributions to Shakespearean scholarship in the 1790 edition. Ritson borrows a line from *Macbeth* (which he put on his title page) to compare Malone to a 'faulcon, tow'ring in her pride of place.' Clearly, Malone denigrates Ritson and fails to give him credit for many ideas and facts that he uses. His anger and indignation over being abused in Ritson's *Remarks* was behind this. He adopts a strategy of neglect. When he quotes from Ritson's *Remarks*, he identifies his source as 'ANONYMOUS' or 'an anonymous writer.' He does this in spite of having said in his preface that he would not omit 'a single valuable explication of any obscure passage' that had ever appeared.[12] It is only when Malone disagrees with Ritson that he identifies him, frequently with a disparaging epithet or a sneer such as that his wit is 'too thick to shine, and too heavy to mount.'[13]

But Ritson's erudition was considerable. His biographer sees six broad criticisms that he made of Malone: errors in collation, ignorance, lack of candour, bad taste, a deficient ear for metre, and his complete rejection of the Second Folio – the last being his most sustained target.[14] He caught Malone on errors of judgment in thirty-six notes, although most of them are minor.

That much, at least, ought to be said to explain the background to, if not to justify, *Cursory Criticisms*. But Ritson's invective spoils much of the scholarly effect of his criticism. He indulges in words and phrases such as 'asinine', 'ridiculous EDITOR', 'blundering foreigner', 'Paddy from Corke [*sic*]', and 'superannuated jack-ass.' His parting shot is at what he sees as Malone's 'too exalted... opinion of his peculiar merits, and too sovereign ... contempt for those who dare call them in question.'[15]

Ritson's pamphlet disturbed Malone's serenity. His copy of the pamphlet, now at the Bodleian Library, abounds with evidence of personal animus, with insults underlined or marked and defiant marginal comments

---

[11] Ritson, *Cursory Criticisms*, p. ix (mispaginated as vii).

[12] *PP (1790)*, I:i, liv–lv. Malone resolutely neglected Ritson's fifteen notes on *King Lear*.

[13] *PP (1790)*, VIII, p. 64.

[14] On Malone's debt to Ritson, see Bronson, *Joseph Ritson*, pp. 495–96.

[15] Ritson, *Cursory Criticisms*, p. 104.

ornamenting almost every page.[16] As we have seen, it was his practice to
mark up a publication like this if he thought he might publish a response to
it. In this case, he used his marginalia to write a lengthy reply published in
April 1792. In order to endow his pamphlet with added authority, he writes
it in the form of a letter to one of the great living Shakespeareans, entitling
it, *A Letter to the Rev. Richard Farmer, D.D.* He told Joseph Warton on 2 May
that he wrote it because he had to 'rectify some facts which by those who
are not very deep in the subject might be misunderstood.' Hoping not to
'elevate' Ritson, he added, he had not even mentioned the title of Ritson's
pamphlet.[17] The pamphlet seethes with anger, but he rarely lets himself, in
the words of Ritson's biographer, 'mount visibly beyond the limits of the
drawing-room tone which he affects.'[18] It is not known how Farmer, who
had no taste for this sort of squabble, responded to his name being linked
with Ritson's in this way, but Malone opens by addressing him directly:
'Though you have long left the *primrose path* of poetry and criticism ... you
will, I am confident, very cheerfully spend an hour with me in traversing
the old Shakspearian field, where we have so often expatiated on the "ever-
fruitful subject" of our great dramatick poet and his Commentators.'

Addressing first Ritson's sweeping accusations that he was incompetent,
Malone allies himself with the worthy and famous against this interloper.
His scholarship is endorsed, he says, by the likes of Farmer, Reynolds,
Warton, and, not least, Burke, 'whose mind is of such a grasp as to embrace
at once the greatest and the minutest objects, and who, in the midst of his
numerous and important avocations, has always found time for the calmer
pursuits of philosophy and polite literature ... '.[19] He then accuses Ritson of
'hyper-criticism ... duly furnished with unblushing cavil, false argument,
and false quotation'; and with

> captious art,
> And snip-snap short, and interruption smart,
> And demonstration thin, and theses thick,
> And major, minor, and conclusion quick.
>
> (Pope, *Dunciad*, II, 239–42)

He says he is unable to sustain such 'a heap of rubbish as has been raked up'
by Ritson – worthy only of 'neglected trash' in the bookseller's warehouse
– in order to fill enough pages to make a respectable pamphlet, so instead
he will concentrate on the crucial matter of his editorial principles.

Ritson had accused him of both textual hypocrisy and inaccuracy, of
going back on his statement in the 1778 *Supplement* that the text of
Shakespeare's plays after Steevens' work 'seems finally settled.' Was all
Malone's collating then necessary? Did he not do it merely to justify a new

---

[16] Ms. Malone 150.   [17] 2 May 1792, Folger, uncatalogued.
[18] Bronson, *Joseph Ritson*, p. 519.   [19] *Letter to the Rev. Richard Farmer*, p. 3.

edition and set himself up as 'the Critic'? This charge embarrassed Malone because it suggested he had flattered Steevens merely to get ahead. So he reminds the reader what he had actually said: 'Having a very high opinion of the diligence, acuteness, and learning of Mr. Steevens... I in common with the rest of the publick considered myself as much indebted to his labours; and therefore did not hesitate to say that the text of the author on which he had been above years employed, *seemed* to be finally settled... I said only what I strictly and sincerely thought.' Soon Malone realized that Steevens had not consulted all the early quartos and that 'a task equally new and arduous' lay ahead of him if he was to establish a more authoritative text, a text that would achieve 'the restoration of the poet's words.' He ended up making 1,654 emendations, he adds, and yet Ritson could find only eight textual errors in over 100,000 lines. It would therefore seem, he adds facetiously, that he 'might have corrected them [the plays] in *one thousand six hundred and sixty-two.*' He promises to make good these eight in the royal quarto edition which he says, recklessly, 'I am now about to put to press.'[20]

As for Ritson's charge that he had no ear for poetry and should have emended many of Shakespeare's lines by altering the number of syllables in many words, Malone replies that it was Shakespeare's method, in common with several of his contemporaries, to stretch out words for the sake of the rhythm by adding syllables. In most of these cases, he states vigorously, no editor has a right to emend the lines unless there is authority for the emendation in the earliest editions – earlier, that is, than the Second Folio. After defending again his rejection of the text of the Second Folio, except where it corrected obvious printing house errors in the First Folio, he scoffs at Ritson's protest that he should have included more notes by critics and declares that 'occasional critics' or 'critics by profession' – by which he means poorly informed literary hacks as distinct from scholars – are 'absolutely below serious notice.'[21] There was nothing conciliatory in any of this.

Malone hoped this unpleasant skirmish would now disappear from the public view, but he had stirred up a hornet's nest that for months the papers tried to keep buzzing. He had both supporters and detractors. One anonymous writer in the *St. James's Chronicle*, calling himself 'Criticaster', commends Malone as a good man as well as critic: 'To those who know Mr. Malone personally, his manners and conduct proclaim him *A Gentleman* – Those who read his work cannot entertain a different opinion of him; particularly if they have perused the virulent attacks which have been made on him, and the mild manner in which he generally, if not universally,

---

[20] Ibid., pp. 3–4, 8–9.
[21] Ibid., pp. 30–35, 38. On Malone's *Letter*, see Bronson, *Joseph Ritson*, pp. 519–22.

repels them.'[22] In May, on the other hand, the *St. James's Chronicle* carried a rebuttal of Criticaster by someone calling himself 'Retrospectus' (conceivably Ritson himself or even Steevens) who repeats Ritson's claim that Malone lacked an ear for poetry and thus could not be counted on for sound textual readings. In this, he observes, Malone 'resembled the Psalmist's adder, by *stopping his ears* against the enchanting sounds of sense and metre, sound they *never so* smoothly or *wisely*.'[23]

In the next few years, Ritson mellowed and even recommended Malone's writings to friends. In a letter to John Nichols after the publication of Malone's *Inquiry* into the Shakespeare forgeries of 1796, he wrote, 'You will do Mr. Malone great injustice if you suppose him to be in all respects what I may have endeavoured to represent him in some', and he recommended a few of the essays in his 'prolegomena.'[24] For Malone, however, Ritson always remained the literary arch villain, an enemy he had in common with Warton and Percy.[25] In the last decade of his life, Ritson's behaviour became increasingly eccentric; he resorted to an extreme form of vegetarianism and eventually went insane. On 9 December 1802, a few months before Ritson died, Malone said unforgivingly in a letter to Percy, 'Viper Ritson has published a 5s. book on the immorality of eating animal food. He lives it seems on milk and puddings. I should have thought he lived on vinegar and horse flesh.'[26] But Malone had another, more subtle, antagonist in Steevens, who throughout all this turmoil in the papers, which he thoroughly enjoyed, was busy preparing his fourth edition of Shakespeare that he hoped would restore him as the leading Shakespearean.

Steevens' edition, published in the spring of 1793, deeply embittered Malone in a way that Ritson's writings never did. Even before Malone published his edition in 1790, it was well known that Steevens meant to publish his new edition chiefly to revenge himself against Malone for demonstrating the inadequacy of the *Johnson–Steevens* text. In spite of Percy's comment to Steevens on 1 April 1793 that he was 'persuaded [the new edition] leaves *nil desiderandum* with regard to their favourite author',[27] Malone believed that Steevens committed three sins in his edition: he tacitly accepts Malone's laboriously collated text of the plays without giving him any credit for it or acknowledging its value; he argues throughout against Malone's editorial methods, taking Ritson's side in championing the Second Folio; and he insults Malone by using one hundred and fifty of Ritson's notes from his *Remarks* (1783) (stripped of

[22] 29 March 1792, no. 4832, p. 4, column 1.   [23] 8–10 May 1792.
[24] *The Letters of Joseph Ritson, Esq.*, II, pp. 122–23.
[25] Malone wrote copious marginalia in his copy of Ritson's *Bibliographia Poetica* (1802), calling him (among other things) 'self-sufficient and shallow', 'ignorant', and a 'scoundrel' (BL, c.60.g.12, p. 295).   [26] *P–M Letters*, pp. 128–29.   [27] 1 April 1793, Folger, C.a. 10, no. 136.

their combative language) and about three hundred entirely new Ritson notes never before published, thereby setting Ritson up as one of the chief commentators in the edition and of the age.[28]

Malone was furious. 'All that we have been contending for these twenty years', he complained to Percy on 14 October, 'is endeavoured to be overturned in Mr Steevens's late edition: the heart is once more changed to the *right* side; a new system set up; and the most capricious alterations, omissions and interpolations adopted, under pretence of rectifying the *metre*. According to the new code, Sr T. Hanmer's ought to be considered as a standard edition.' Although 'his book [text] was actually printed from mine', he continued, 'the *metre* is *now* what the publick attention is to be drawn to, and every one is to mend it just as he pleases.'[29]

Steevens' edition amounted to a declaration of war for Malone. He decided to use his projected fifteen-volume quarto edition to retaliate. 'I mean to trim him as well as I can', he assured Charlemont. He would 'throw down the gauntlet, not by the hints and hesitations of oblique depreciation, as he has on all occasions served me in his late book, but by a fair and direct attack. He shall find me what he has not spirit enough to be himself, an open and, I trust, an honourable adversary.' Whatever Steevens' motives, Malone could not bring himself to see any value in Steevens' use of Ritson's notes. By 'taking up such a despicable fellow as Ritson by way of co-adjutor', Steevens had forfeited respect as a textual scholar. 'I am resolved to give him no quarter.'[30] Charlemont's reply was predictable: 'You know I always disliked the man.'[31]

Ritson's biographer has gone even further in assessing Malone's resentment towards Steevens and unforgiving animosity towards Ritson by suggesting that Malone was the most likely person 'to have consigned to oblivion' three manuscript volumes of Ritson's notes on Shakespeare. The volumes were purchased by the booksellers Longman and Rees in December 1803, and then disappeared. Malone resolved, so the argument goes, to buy these volumes and destroy them. In his correspondence with Percy, he had kept up a diatribe against 'maniac' Ritson, denigrating out of hand his recent publications on animal food and metrical romances; gleefully recommending in, May 1803, a cartoon by James Sayer of Ritson 'grazing'; and complaining that the publishers probably intended to publish Ritson's notes in order 'to weigh against my edition, when it shall appear.'[32] In other words, he was angry enough to commit such a literary crime.[33] It is true that Ritson brought out the worst in him. Apart from the

[28] Bronson, *Joseph Ritson*, p. 527. For opposing accounts of Steevens' endorsement of Ritson, see Bronson, pp. 527–41; and Osborn, 'Ritson, Scholar at Odds', p. 422.

[29] *P–M Letters*, p. 65.   [30] 28 October 1793, *HMC*, XIII, 8, p. 219.

[31] 15 November 1793, *HMC*, XIII, 8, p. 222. Malone did not outgrow his resentment; see to Percy, 5 June 1802, *P–M Letters*, pp. 93–95.   [32] *P–M Letters*, pp. 147, 158, 161.

[33] Bronson, *Joseph Ritson*, p. 542.

complete lack of evidence backing up this allegation, however, Malone's character argues against it. He may have been astonishingly careless about returning manuscripts he borrowed, and we know he damaged several of the Dulwich manuscripts to further his scholarship; but the purchase of manuscripts for the sole purpose of destroying them would have violated what he stood for as a scholar and historian of English literature.[34]

3

It is surprising that Malone never read manuscripts at Oxford before 1792–93, although he visited there twice in the 1780s, once to see the Picture Gallery and once with Boswell to visit Thomas Warton.[35] Not until he decided to explore Aubrey's and Anthony à Wood's papers at the Ashmolean and Bodleian Libraries did he make a research trip to Oxford in the summer of 1792. 'Having long wished to devote some time to a rummage of MSS at Oxford', he informed Charlemont in July, 'I accompanied my brother and family there on their way to Ireland and stayed a fortnight there after they left it, and employed my time so much to my satisfaction that I mean to make another visit there [in September].'[36] Charlemont envied him: 'after having seen the whole world Oxford was the most worthy of a traveller's attention.'[37] Malone returned to Oxford on 16 September, staying this time for about six weeks, determined to 'attack the Aubrey papers, and make a fair transcript of them', as he told John Price, for forty-five years the Bodleian's Librarian, 'whose kindness and attention during my late visit to Oxford' Malone had much appreciated.[38] With a view to publishing them, he transcribed 174 of Aubrey's *Lives*.[39] He was never happier than when 'rummaging' with manuscripts, in spite of the strain on his eyes.

After about three weeks Windham joined him in Oxford. Windham introduced him to several university dignitaries, and together they dined, drank tea at coffee-houses, and searched and read in the Bodleian. Windham's diary shows he enjoyed particularly their reading sessions in the Bodleian. At times the cold October days made study there 'inconvenient', but on 7 October they sat in the library 'reading letters of Hobbes, [Esmond] Halley, Sir I. Newton, [Robert] Hook, [John] Lock[e], and

---

[34] See Osborn's defence of Malone, 'Ritson, Scholar at Odds', pp. 425–26.
[35] Regarding Malone's several trips to Oxford, for research and other reasons, see Osborn, 'Edmond Malone and Oxford', pp. 323–38.
[36] 10–16 July 1792, *HMC*, XIII, 8, p. 196.   [37] 20 August 1792, *HMC*, XIII, 8, p. 198.
[38] Malone to Dr John Price, 23 July 1792 (Hyde Collection). See Malone's letter to Charlemont, 7 August 1792, *HMC*, XIII, 8, pp. 196–97.
[39] See Ms. Aubrey 7 (Ashmolean). The two volumes of transcriptions ended up in the Bodleian (Ms. Eng. Misc. d. 26–7), after being pillaged by scholars over the years. See A. Clark's edition of Aubrey's *Lives of Eminent Men* (1898), I, p. 22; and Richard Wendorf, *The Elements of Life*, pp. 108–23.

others, of no consequence in themselves, but affording at least specimens of their handwriting: they were written upon various occasions to Aubrey, whose life and history Malone is now employed about.'[40]

They were in Oxford together again the following July, but not chiefly for scholarly reasons. They attended the installation of the third Duke of Portland, former Prime Minister, as the new Chancellor of the University. Malone found the event memorable because on the last day, probably at Windham's instigation, he was awarded an honorary doctorate (DCL).[41] Here in this university town so important to his research, as part of a political event, he was awarded an honorary degree acknowledging his Shakespeare work. The French Revolution, the increasing threat of rebellions at home and in Ireland, and worries about Jacobinism provided a political background. Burke, Windham, Percy, and the Duke of Portland, who became a good friend, were all there. Percy even delivered the opening sermon against the excesses of the French Revolution. None of this was coincidental. By then, Malone had been drawn into a small band of Burke's most ardent defenders. The political complexion of this Oxford visit, and the reassurance he doubtless gained from it, began for him a period of unusually active, hypersensitive political thinking that surfaced at least three times in the 1790s in his biographical and critical writing.

Malone had grown fond of Burke, but he was ambivalent about his conversational manner, which he said 'were it not for the great superiority of his talents and knowledge would be disagreeable.' He told Farington that 'his eloquence and habitual exertions in company' kept his guests 'too much under'; he also told him that Reynolds and Windham 'thought better of his talents than most others did.'[42] When it came to the substance of Burke's talk and writing, however, Malone was a true believer. When Thomas Paine attacked Burke in *The Rights of Man* (1792), Malone called him 'despicable and nonsensical.'[43] He later scribbled the epigram, 'Age of Reason = Age of Treason, fits Tom to a "T".'[44] He had little use for Charles James Fox. Telling Charlemont, in February 1794, of public fears that France could invade England with ten to twenty thousand men, he bitterly reported that Fox called people with such views 'alarmists', 'for names, you know, on all such occasions, serve among the mob instead of long arguments.' Burke's reply to Fox, he went on, was that 'alarmists' was what 'thieves who mean to plunder a house exclaim against the watch-dogs, who make such a tremendous noise that honest folks cannot get their

[40] See Mrs Henry Baring (ed.), *The Diary of the Right Hon. William Windham 1784–1810* (1866), pp. 261, 263.

[41] Seventeen others were awarded the DCL on this occasion (*Jackson's Oxford Journal*, no. 2097, Saturday, 6 July 1793); see Osborn, 'Edmond Malone and Oxford', pp. 326–31.

[42] *DF*, III, p. 478; IV, p. 1262; III, p. 806.

[43] Letter to Charlemont, 3 December 1792, *HMC*, XIII, 8, p. 204.

[44] Malone's copy of Richard Graves's *The Festoon*, OFB pc 73.

livelihood.' 'Fox and his little phalanx' were ranged against the 'whole nation', he told Charlemont in May, following a fairly sharp exchange at The Club; it was so distracting that 'we in general keep clear of politics if we can.'[45] Outside The Club, Malone was not inclined to stay clear of politics. 'The question is not now whether we shall have this administration or the other', he wrote in December 1792, 'this king is a good or a bad one, but whether we shall have any king in this country, or a protestant parliament in Ireland ... ' How could any Englishmen countenance the 'specie of which we are now possessed at Paris ... the plunder of all the churches, the sale of all the noblemen's houses, effects and estates, and the immense multitudes of rich persons whom they have put to death only on account of their riches'? If this were to continue two or three more years, he complained two years later, 'there probably will not be a single person living in the country who ever saw the old court, or had the education of a gentleman.'[46]

Greater even than his horror over the atrocities in France was his fear that Jacobins in Parliament and in the country, not to mention Jacobin editors of journals like the *Analytical Review*, would ignite an English revolution.[47] The prospect so worried him that he was easily alarmed by pro-revolutionary and 'egalitarian' speeches by Fox and Sheridan and, more sensationally, by the reformers John Horne Tooke and John Thelwall – especially if it seemed to him that parliamentarians like Windham were allowing such people too much play. To him, as to Burke, these voices were threatening the fabric of the British constitution. It frustrated him he was not in Parliament and therefore had no public voice on such issues. In the 1790s, it sometimes seemed to him that he would have been better placed as a 'publick man' in Parliament than as a scholar in a quiet study in Queen Anne Street East.

Burke was doing his best in the House of Commons, but Malone did not always think Windham was. As Secretary for War in Pitt's government, as well as a close personal friend, Windham was the logical person for him to urge to act and speak more vigorously against the forces of sedition. He wrote firm, even strident, letters to him. 'I would not only part with my coat', he announced on 30 October 1793, 'but strip myself to my skin' to carry on the war against France. With 'words that burn' the nation must be told about the atrocities across the Channel and, especially, how the barbarous French had killed their Queen. On 16 November 1795, he went to hear Windham speak in a debate on the Treasonable Practices Bill.

[45] 20 February and 28 May, *HMC*, XIII, 8, pp. 230, 239.
[46] To Charlemont, 14 December 1792 and 28 May 1794, *HMC*, XIII, 8, pp. 207, 240.
[47] On the impact of the French Revolution on eighteenth-century British society, see *The French Revolution and British Culture*, eds. Ceri Crossley and Ian Small (1989), especially essays by Clive Emsley and Brian Rigby, pp. 31–62, 63–83.

More frustration. He was past bearing silently the 'cold' speeches he was hearing from 'your side of the House', speeches 'too much on the *defensive.*' Windham must 'carry the War into the Enemies' Quarters; and to mark them out plainly and directly as men, who, if they do not conspire and intend to overturn the Constitution, *act* as if such were their intentions ... '. He was furious over the 'baseness and malignity' of Fox, who maintained that seditious writing and 'harrangues' could never overthrow a constitution. Did he not know history? What did he think the Puritans were up to for ten years before 1644, when the Bishops were abolished? Could he not see in the present crisis obvious parallels to events leading to the Civil War and execution of Charles I? As for the 'idle babble' of Sheridan, whom in a later letter he called 'a black and determined conspirator', he could only quote Henry V's dismissal speech to Falstaff, 'Reply not to me with a fool-born jest.'[48]

Windham read these effusions sympathetically, and may even have worked into his speeches a few of Malone's ideas, supported as they were with historical precedents, quotations, and other documentary apparatus. But Malone's main hope for Britain's salvation was Burke. He knew Burke wanted to retire from politics, but he saw no reason why he should stop writing. Something more than the *Reflections* was needed, though: 'Burke is perfectly well', he informed Charlemont in August 1792, 'and the youngest man of his age I know, though he is always representing himself "emeritus" and unfit for service. I wish he would devote the remainder of his years to literature.'[49] To Burke himself he wrote in December: 'You will do the most essential service if from any notes you may have by you, you can make out the principal parts of your speeches [in the Commons] on this subject, and publish them speedily.'[50] But Burke, whom Malone once described as writing only 'on the spur of some particular occasion'[51], joined in the anti-Jacobin attacks only once more, and then not until 1796–97, with his *Letters on a Regicide Peace.* In fact, in his scholarly writing Malone struck at the 'pretended philosophers of France' more than Burke did.

4

In spite of his declining interest in Aubrey, in 1793 Malone secured an agreement with Charles Lloyd, Keeper of the Ashmolean Library, that prevented anyone else from even looking at the Aubrey manuscripts until he was able to publish them. This earned him some bad publicity. Three or four years later, James Caulfield, a bookseller who had been denied access to the papers, scolded him for his arrogation of the material in his stinging

---

[48] 30 October 1793, 18 and 29 November 1795, BL Add. Ms. 37854, fols. 127–29v, 134–41 (*Windham Papers*, I, pp. 162–64, 314–22).   [49] 10 August 1792, *HMC*, XIII, 8, p. 197.
[50] 16 December 1792, *Burke Corr.*, VII, p. 323.   [51] *DF*, II, p. 366.

pamphlet, *An Enquiry into the Conduct of Edmond Malone, Esq. Concerning the Manuscript Papers of John Aubrey, F. R. S. in the Ashmolean Museum, Oxford* (1797). Caulfield claims that he first transcribed portions of the manuscripts in 1788, four years before Malone first examined them, but that when he heard of Malone's work with them in 1792, he called on him to find out what he planned to do with them. Caulfield writes: 'he then informed me he intended to put them forth to the world on the same scale as his last edition of Shakespeare, and without the embellishment of plates, on which I told him our ideas were widely different, as I intended to publish my edition in one splendid volume, with the portraits engraved from the original pictures in the same repository as the Mss...'. To this, Malone expressed 'great surprise' and suggested that Caulfield was out of his depth embarking on such a project since he lacked the necessary competence.[52] Malone later used 'his interest at Oxford to stop my pursuit', for on his next visit to the Ashmolean, Caulfield says he found a paper cover placed over the manuscripts on which Malone had written, 'These fragments collected and arranged by E. M. 1792.' He was told that '"in consequence of a letter from Mr. Malone to the keeper, Charles Lloyd, Esq," the Manuscripts were no longer to be consulted, particularly, however, excluding me.' They were then locked up. Caulfield is also amazed that Malone, 'who had every advantage authority could give him', was even allowed 'the almost unknown indulgence of having the Manuscripts and Pictures removed to his house from the Museum, for his greater convenience in copying and transcribing...'.[53] He complains of Malone's 'big bloated pride' in habitually asserting 'an exclusive privilege of making use of these Papers from his first application to transcribe them.'[54]

Caulfield's pamphlet illustrates that the public persona Malone had acquired as the leading scholar of his age was not without its annoyances. He had become a good target for editors, commentators, and antiquarians who, like Caulfield and Ritson, were shut out of the influential and authoritative Johnsonian world of letters and were reduced to ineffectual pamphleteering.

Malone never published his transcriptions of Aubrey's *Brief Lives*, though as late as 1802 he still planned to do so.[55] Instead, he decided to push ahead with a biography of Shakespeare when George Robinson, worried about sales of Steevens' new edition, shocked him in May 1793, by cancelling his contract for the quarto edition.[56] This placed his plans in 'a very quiescent state', he told Charlemont, but it also threw him into a different gear. In order to interest the booksellers in a new edition, he realized he had to write

[52] Caulfield, *Enquiry into the Conduct of Edmond Malone*, pp. 8–9.   [53] Ibid., pp. 12–17.
[54] Ibid., pp. 17–19.
[55] See Malone's letter to John Price, 19 November 1802, BL Add. Ms. 26133.
[56] 6 September 1793, *Boswell 1789–95*, p. 231 (*Malahide*, XVIII, p. 206).

a complete biography, as well as prepare other background material, as soon as possible. His history of the stage and all his dissertations on Shakespeare, together with a new and complete *Life* of the poet, in two volumes, would serve 'as a specimen of a new projected edition without any plates.' Still smarting from criticism of the small type in the 1790 edition, he was determined to have the new edition appear in quarto.[57]

He launched himself into the research for a new biography with extraordinary energy, examining thousands of documents at the Rolls Office and the Record Office in the Tower. But even as he did so, he began to fear the task of turning his mounting collection of material into a readable narrative. 'From all these different sources', he declared to Charlemont, 'if I can but manage the various information I have procured tolerably well, I hope to make at least a very curious life.'[58]

Malone had other problems besides writer's block. For one thing, he had too much on his plate. Shakespeare, Beaumont and Fletcher, Aubrey, Pope, and Dryden – all these projects created the impression of energetic scholarship, industry, and ambitiousness. Boswell, we recall, was awed by Malone's drive, though Ritson, Steevens, and other rivals interpreted it more as an unprecedented manifestation of scholarly egocentrism. Ritson, always keen to broadcast news of Malone's scholarly problems, heard that all was not well. 'I do not find that Malone's famous 4to "is going on with spirit"', he wrote to Joseph Cooper Walker on 9 September 1793, 'or that it is going on at all.' Alluding to rumours that Malone was going to publish the lives and works of Dryden or Milton, or both, or whatever, he added smugly that he was 'in the supposed condition of St Paul & that much reading (learning, I can not say) "hath made him mad."'[59]

It was not madness but his eyes that troubled Malone's work. He insisted on doing all his own reading, but the strain on his eyes was often too much. 'Don't go on poking into small crabbed manuscripts, or you will be as blind as Tiresias', Robert Jephson warned him. 'Can't you get some young lusty Epidaurian-eyed drudge to make out the text for you, and so save your own peepers?'[60] Charlemont, too, was worried: 'All I dread is that your sight, with which mine has a sad fellow-feeling, will never hold out to the end of your pursuit, and the bare idea of your having examined *three thousand antiquated papers* [from Worcestershire], the greater part of which were consequently legible with the utmost difficulty, makes, I confess, my poor eyes ache ...'[61]

Malone also consistently underestimated the amount of research and time he would need for the *Life of Shakespeare*. Details began to pile up as he unearthed facts and exploded traditional stories about Shakespeare. He

[57] To Charlemont, 27 May 1794, *HMC*, XIII, 8, p. 238.
[58] To Charlemont, 15 November 1793, *HMC*, XIII, 8, p. 221.   [59] OFB 33.11.
[60] 16 May 1793, Prior, p. 200.   [61] 22 November 1793, *HMC*, XIII, 8, p. 224.

was wildly optimistic when he told Percy on 3 June 1794: 'Tho' my new edition of Shakspeare sleeps at present, I hope soon to rouse the old Bard again. I have got thro' about half his *Life* and hope to finish it this summer; and mean to prefix it to all my Dissertations &c. which I intend to reprint in two volumes Quarto ... But this will take up near two years.'[62] It would take a good deal longer than that.

5

Once he decided on a complete *Life of Shakespeare*, Malone was quick to reopen correspondence with the The Revd. Davenport in Stratford. 'Will you allow me, after a long interval', he asked on 10 April 1793, 'once again to resume our Shakspearian disquisition.' As in the past, he was reluctant to leave his comforts in London. He was now over fifty and finding fairly onerous the prospect of travels to distant archives, where more often than not he would have to work in cold and poorly lit rooms. Perhaps he recalled his father's and Boswell's acute dislike of travels in the legal circuits. It was infinitely preferable, if possible, to have others do his research for him, under his direction. His eyes would also be grateful for that.

In his letter to Davenport, he was off and running with questions about fires in Stratford during Shakespeare's life; the story that Charles I's Queen, Henrietta Maria, spent three weeks in Stratford in 1643; Shakespeare's property and current prices during his lifetime; and some late seventeenth-century anecdotes about the poet's having been a papist when he died and the alleged poaching excursion at Charlecote Park that he had read at Corpus Christi College, Oxford, the preceding summer. Much of this information could be checked, he said, in the Stratford Corporation books.[63] Davenport, probably appalled at how much work was involved, and probably at Malone's instigation, replied that again he had obtained permission from the Mayor and Corporation to send the books themselves to Malone, with the understanding that they would be returned as soon as conveniently possible.[64] The books arrived at Queen Anne Street East on 15 April and in no time Malone thought he found the name of the poet's schoolmaster.[65] But the books, even at home in acceptable light, punished his eyes. As he told Charlemont, the records 'were written in so old a hand that I was some weeks employed merely in reading them.'[66]

Even after Davenport sent him the remaining Corporation books before 1650, Malone knew he could not escape another visit to the Stratford area to 'rummage' through manuscripts for himself. As he explained to Charlemont, 'When I had advanced some way in the life, my brother and

[62] *P–M Letters*, p. 70. See Malone to Charlemont, 15 November 1793 (*HMC*, XIII, 8, p. 222).
[63] 12 April 1793, *M–D*, pp. 61–62.   [64] Shakespeare's Birthplace Ms. 122, fols. 51–52.
[65] Malone to Davenport, 15 April 1793, *M–D*, pp. 62, 66–75.
[66] 15 November 1793, *HMC*, XIII, 8, pp. 220–21.

his family came to Harrowgate [*sic*], in Yorkshire, where I went ... to see them, and, after their return to Ireland, I resolved to devote a fortnight to a thorough examination of everything that either Worcester or Stratford could furnish.' In late August 1793, hoping, even expecting, to come up with a sensational discovery, he left for two weeks in Worcester and Stratford.[67]

Malone was the first Shakespearean scholar ever to search systematically through the Stratford records for facts about Shakespeare's life. After a week of digging with 'ardour and perseverance', he wrote to Boswell of a sudden thrill of discovery followed by deep disappointment:

Here have I been up to my elbows every day this week past in old papers and parchments, and by the favour of the Corporation have picked up several little particulars for my life of Shakspeare. I worked every day from ten till it was nearly dark, which prevented me from writing to you before this time. In such a cause you will not wonder at my ardour and perseverance. I met with one letter to Shakspeare, but after the most diligent search I could not find his answer, which would have been an *eureka* indeed; nor with a single scrap of his handwriting. I think however that through a channel which these papers have opened to me, I shall be able to get at it.[68]

Sadly, he failed to find it. Shakespeare's reply 'would have been a great curiosity', he lamented, 'and what is provoking is, it ought to have been in the bundle where this was found (a parcel of letters to and from a Mr [Richard] Quiney whose son afterwards married the poet's daughter) and this *should* have been among the papers of Shakspeare's granddaughter, wherever they are.' At least he found the signatures of almost all Shakespeare's family and friends, though not Shakespeare's itself.[69] He returned to London, lugging with him several thousand documents. With his earlier study at home of the Stratford documents and his work in several London archives, this Stratford visit carried him much further into the unexplored world of Shakespeare's life than anyone had ever travelled before.

Malone returned home from Stratford with more than manuscripts and documents. With Davenport's permission, he brought back a mould he took from Shakespeare's bust in Holy Trinity Church. The bust, according to legend, was commissioned and put in its place by Shakespeare's son-in-law, Dr John Hall. 'I mean to bring the great bard to town with me in the Chaise', he informed Boswell from Stratford, 'I mean the best part of him, his head; of which I have got an admirable mould.'[70] In London, he then engaged the sculptor Joseph Nollekens – who was to carve the Johnson monument – to make a mask and then a model. According to Malone –

---

[67] Malone to Charlemont, 15 November 1793, *HMC*, XIII, 8, p. 221.
[68] 1 September 1793, *B–M Corr.*, p. 427.   [69] 21 September 1793, *P–M Letters*, p. 60.
[70] 1 September 1793, *B–M Corr.*, p.427.

and he was correct – the problem with the original was (and remains) that by 'being placed at least three feet too high, it is never seen rightly', but with his model, 'we shall now be able to judge whether this representative is entitled to any credit as a resemblance.' Since he, unlike Steevens, believed in the authenticity of the Droeshout and Chandos portraits, he concluded that a resemblance between them and the bust argued that the bust was made from a death mask of the poet.[71]

The bust also tempted him to perform a 'public service' that several of his contemporaries and subsequent generations of Shakespeareans have mocked as an egocentric blunder. Believing that 'some strolling players' about forty years earlier had painted the bust in colours, he obtained permission to restore it to what he thought was its original stone colour.[72] The truth is that in 1748 another John Hall, as part of a restoration of the bust, had merely renewed the colours. James Boaden, for whom Malone could do no wrong, judged generously that he painted the bust white 'to gratify a perhaps purer taste' and that the new colour 'better suited to the sacred edifice which contains it.'[73] Others disagreed. An unflattering epigram in the *Gentleman's Magazine* in 1815 read,

> Stranger, to whom this monument is shewn,
> Invoke the poet's Curse upon Malone;
> Whose meddling zeal his barbarous taste betrays,
> And daubs his tombstone, as he mars his plays.[74]

And George Hardinge, in a burlesque of Malone in 1801, entitled *Another Essence of Malone*, would not let the public forget what he saw as Malone's stupid whitewashing of the bust. Malone's initiative did more to harm his reputation than anything else he ever did. His authority was such, however, that it was not until 1861 that the colours were restored.

If the mayor and other Stratford authorities were grateful to Malone for his painting of the bust, they appear not to have shown it. About one month after he returned from Stratford, Davenport told him that the new mayor of Stratford was unhappy he still had the Corporation books. The mayor was nervous because the original receipt of delivery, which had been sent to the former mayor responsible for the loan, was lost.[75] That receipt, Malone replied, was supposed to have 'armed him sufficiently against any cavil or objection that might be made', but he enclosed another to mollify the new mayor: 'You know my great object is to illustrate the life of Shakspeare', he reminded Davenport, 'which so far as these papers are

[71] 15 November 1793, *HMC*, XIII, 8, pp. 221–22.
[72] See Malone to Boswell and Charlemont, 1 September (*B–M Corr.*, p. 427) and 15 November 1793 (*HMC*, XIII, 8, p. 221).   [73] Boaden, *Inquiry*, pp. 30, 35.
[74] *Gentleman's Magazine*, LXXV (1815), 390. Boaden derided such 'pointless epigrams', which are inspired by 'personal hostility' (*Inquiry*, pp. 36–37).
[75] 12 October 1793, *M–D*, pp. 77–78.

concerned cannot be done without at the same time doing honour to
Stratford; and this, I hope, the late mayor will have the goodness to
represent to the corporation.' Moreover, he had done a 'yeoman's service'
for the Corporation by sorting and arranging these papers, 'a rude mass of
confused lumber', under various headings such as 'Fires at Stratford',
'Contributions during the Rebellion', and so on; and when he did return
them he would 'take care that all the papers relating to the same matter
shall be kept together and properly indorsed.'[76] He knew that if he returned
the records, the only way he could finish the *Life* would be either to borrow
them again, which the Corporation was not likely to allow, or make several
more trips to Stratford, which he did not want to do. In any case, without
the records as a convenient reference tool, he feared he would lose his
momentum, though he was beginning to lose that anyway because of
interruptions and his straying into other projects.

In May 1794, he told Charlemont again that he had finished the first half
of the *Life*, which he felt was the most difficult part, and that he would have
finished it all by now if, as he brought Shakespeare 'to the threshold of the
London stage', he had not decided to take a 'short view of the prevailing
manners, customs, etc. at that time, and of the state of poetry and poets just
when he came to the metropolis.' This project was a labour of love, and
already he had read twenty to thirty tracts written in Shakespeare's time
that were 'very entertaining', but this excursion into 'all the little modes of
life' meant that he had to stop writing the *Life*.[77] Such interruptions in the
next few years were among the major miscalculations in Malone's career.

No other literary scholar had ever made such extensive use of archival
documents. The Stratford authorities, however, were less interested in the
refinements of his project than in recovering their records, but they could
not pry them away from him. They gave in two or three times and then
more or less forgot about them.[78] One day more than a decade later, a new
generation of Stratford town clerks woke up to the fact that he still had
them. In December 1805, they bluntly told him they thought twelve years
was long enough for any scholar to keep books on loan: 'Mr. Hunt [town
clerk] has himself, and several others have called upon you repeatedly for
these papers, and you have as repeatedly promised they should be carefully
returned, and the Corporation do conceive they are by no means well
treated.' They needed the books dating from 1563 to 1650 immediately, so
'we must inform you that in case they are not ... delivered, that we shall be
under the necessity of applying to the Court of King's Bench in order to get

---

[76] 12 October 1793, *M–D*, p. 81.
[77] To Charlemont, 27 May 1794, *HMC*, XIII, 8, p. 238.
[78] Jordan spent most of 27 June 1799 at Malone's house on the (especially for him) awkward
errand to retrieve the Stratford Corporation's documents; Malone kept the papers (*Malone–
Jordan*, pp. 49–50).

them restored.'[79] This time he had no choice but to return almost everything he had borrowed. He felt as if someone had removed his lifeline.

6

There were other interruptions, two literary and one personal. For several months in the spring and summer of 1794 his time was 'almost entirely taken up' with passing Robert Jephson's poem, *Roman Portraits*, through the press.[80] Work on the *Life* came to a standstill. In a letter to Charlemont in May, he also mentioned his newest project, a *Life of Dryden* to prefix to an edition of the poet's prose works. 'So here is work', he sighed, 'and consequently amusement, enough cut out. But the great work of all yet remains, and, what is worse, I have not the smallest prospect towards it.' This 'great work' was not Shakespeare but another attempt to get married. The *Life of Shakespeare* seemed to him, at this point, far more achievable than marriage.

Most of his friends did not expect him, aged fifty-three and after having had his marital hopes dashed twice, to embark on a courtship again. Still, he had been keeping his eyes open.[81] Boswell remarked in September 1790, that William Temple's daughter was much admired 'even by the critick Malone.'[82] Boswell appears to have been more surprised by that than by the Sunday evening they were interrupted by Malone's 'Dulcinea'.[83] Late in 1793, before Malone left London on a Shakespeare errand, Windham (who would love to have been a successful matchmaker) encouraged him to visit the family of John Crewe, MP, at Crewe Hall in Nantwich, Cheshire. Knowing that a pleasant unmarried lady, Maria Bover, only a few years younger than Malone, lived in the neighbourhood, Windham wrote to Mrs Crewe to encourage her to invite Malone to make the visit.[84] She did and he accepted. Not long after arriving at Crewe Hall in late November or early December, he was swept off his feet by the accomplished Miss Bover; he stayed for ten days.[85]

---

[79] A photostat of this letter survives in the Boswell Papers, Yale.

[80] 27 May 1794, *HMC*, XIII, 8, p. 238. *Roman Portraits*, dedicated to Malone, was published in 1794. Malone's help was purely editorial.

[81] According to Sir Gilbert Eliot, Malone was interested in courting Mary Palmer ('the fair Palmeria'), Sir Joshua's niece. See Eliot's letter to his wife, 5 April 1792 (*The Life and Letters of Sir Gilbert Eliot*, ed. the Countess of Minto (1874), I, p. 6); and Boswell to Malone, 12 July 1788, *B–M Corr.*, p. 345. But Malone could never seriously have expected to marry her, whose aspirations had always been set much higher, as he knew. She married the Marquess of Thomond.

[82] Boswell to Temple, 15 September 1790, Tinker, *Letters of James Boswell*, II, p. 401.

[83] 13 December 1789, *Boswell 1789–95*, p. 23 (*Malahide*, XVIII, p. 10).

[84] See *The Windham Papers* (1913), I, p. 159; and *Miscellanies of the Polybiblon Society*, 'The Crewe Papers', IX, p. 29.

[85] Boswell noted in his journal for 3 January 1794 that Malone stayed ten days and 'was courting Maria Bover', *Boswell 1789–95*, p. 274 (*Malahide*, XVIII, p. 249).

She was attracted to him initially, but he courted her too intensely, as he had Sarah Loveday, and she cooled. By mid-December, he was writing despairingly to his brother about the 'derangement' of his mind and the impossibility of concentrating on his books. His brother entreated him on 18 February 'to exert your self with all your might to overcome this sad disappointment, or it will embitter all your little moments. I own it is very hard, but I know great endeavours will effect great things.' He urged him to write to Miss Bover again.[86] He persevered and, with encouragement from the Crewes, spent the New Year with them. Miss Bover, though gracious and kind, was not encouraging. In February, he told Charlemont circumspectly of his disappointment, leaving him to read between the lines: 'these two months past I have been entirely engaged by a business in which I was very deeply interested, and the result of which I should have communicated to you among the very first of my friends, if, as I had every reason to hope, it had been a happy one, but ... it has unfortunately ended only in vexation and disappointment ... '.[87] But he did not give up. In the spring, he missed several Club meetings, neglected his *Life of Shakespeare*, and continued to torment himself. Windham recorded in his diary for 18 May 1794 that he accompanied Miss Bover to Mrs Crewe's for dinner and found Malone there, too.[88] But all of Windham's efforts were coming to naught. Boswell thought he knew why, telling Farington that 'Malone is respectable and gentlemanlike rather than shining.'[89]

Charlemont hoped to comfort him by reproaching Maria Bover, but Malone would hear nothing against her: 'she is the only woman from whom I ever had one kind word. Nothing could be more unfortunate; she was everything that could be wished, suitable in years to such an old fellow as myself (and to be that, and still very desirable, is a rare union), cheerful, sensible, companionable and engaging.' One obstacle was Miss Bover's engagement some years before to a man who had since 'not acted in such a manner as to secure her esteem' but from whom she could not now disentangle herself. Jephson commiserated succinctly: 'Nothing but your evil genius, who seems to have discovered with cruel sagacity where you are most vulnerable, could have dashed so fair a prospect.'[90]

As the months passed, Malone struggled to keep his hopes alive: 'I think between this and Christmas the matter must be determined, one way or the other, and much of the comfort of my little remnant of life (for comfort is all I look for now) will depend upon that determination.'[91] On Christmas Day 1794, in the highest suspense, he wrote to Charlemont, 'My

[86] Bodley Ms. Malone 39, fol. 235.   [87] 20 February 1794, *HMC*, XIII, 8, p. 228.
[88] Windham, *Diary*, p. 310.   [89] *DF*, I, p. 174.
[90] 21 November 1794, Prior, pp. 213–14. See also Charlemont to Malone, 27 May and 4 June 1794 (*HMC*, XIII, 8, pp. 238–39, 241).
[91] Malone to Charlemont, 7 November 1794, *HMC*, XIII, 8, p. 253.

matrimonial hopes are not quite extinct, but hang on the strangest thread imaginable.' The new year came and still Maria Bover could not decide, though Boswell's information was that Malone's hopes were extinct. He told Farington in January that Malone had 'offered himself' to her but 'is not accepted', and that though 'obliging in his manner, He has never been a favorite [sic] of the Ladies, He is too soft in his manners.'[92] Boswell was right, even if Malone, against all odds, dreamed of success. Charlemont, who thought it was over before it actually was, was devastated: 'She has been able strongly to attach you, and must therefore be a woman of excellent sense ... Yet one thing I am sure she wants – namely, prudence. Since of all the men I ever knew, you are the best adapted to make happy the woman of your choice in the state of wedlock.' Only Malone's 'literary turn' would rescue him from despondency: 'Shakspeare may, perhaps, now be more profitable to you than ever he has yet been.'[93] In the last known reference in 1804 to his failure to marry, Farington wrote poignantly of Malone's remark (at the age of sixty-three) that 'the happiness of his life arose from his having a small indepeandance [sic] ... a bit of study which occupied his mind', but that contrary to appearances he 'had lived a life of much anxiety from being disappointed in hopes & wishes which related to domestic Union (Marriage) that must now no longer be looked for.'[94]

On 6 October 1797, Malone's brother was awarded a new patent as Baron Sunderlin of Baronston. The patent provided that in the case of Sunderlin's not having any children, when he died 'the Rights Privileges ... Immunities and Advantages to the said Dignity of a Baron' would devolve on the younger brother. This made Malone feel his failure with Maria Bover even more acutely, for as Sunderlin was not likely to have any children, his own lack of a family meant, as he told Catherine, that 'the new peerage will be quite thrown away.' For the sake of the peerage, he might try again, but now it was probably too late and, in any event, he was getting too fussy. In an undated letter to Catherine from Philip Metcalfe's house in Brighton, a resort he preferred to either Bath or Cheltenham and where on this visit he dined with the Duke of Beaufort and the Prince of Wales, he saw no ladies (partly because of his eyesight) who pleased him as potential wives:

I was two or three times at the rooms, but I can scarcely see anything in large lighted apartments. It is surprising how little beauty or attraction there is in the world, at least to a prepossessed mind. I dined with three or four private families, friends of Metcalfe, where there were ladies... And yet among all these various groups I did not see a single woman, gentle or simple, but Lady Worcester, that

[92] *DF*, 23 January 1795, II, p. 295.
[93] Charlemont to Malone, 7 November 1794, *HMC*, XIII, 8, p. 253.
[94] *DF*, 29 January 1804, VI, p. 2228.

appeared to me to have the smallest attraction. How therefore should I ever get a
wife? Or what ground have I to expect after all that has happened that any but a
mere dowdy will accept my hand? Yet I still keep on hoping that something may
happen – and unless it does, the new peerage will be quite thrown away.[95]

The sadness of this climax to Malone's relations with women cannot be
overstated. Sometime after he failed to win Maria Bover, he scribbled a few
sad verses of resignation. All fame was mere vanity if not shared with a
loving wife:

> Vain – wealth and fame and fortune's fostering care,
> If no fond breast the splendid blessings share;
> And each day's bustling pageantry once past,
> There – only there our bliss is found at last.[96]

7

Added to this disappointment, which must have taken its toll on his work,
writer's block was plaguing him. He 'shrunk from the labour of digesting'
his materials for the essay on Elizabethan manners and poetry 'and putting
them into form.'[97] As for the *Life of Shakespeare*, 'after all, I have written but
half of it, though the materials are collected for the whole.' He could write
about the anxieties of 'grappling' with composition only to Charlemont,
his 'confessor.' All he had been able to do with the 'account of the manners
of the time', which had 'delayed me much', was 'but collect and make
abstracts from various quarters.' He had 'always found the pursuit
pleasanter than being "in at the death"'; 'in collecting materials to any
particular point, one's ardour and researches are daily rewarded by some
new discovery; but the arranging and putting them into proper form is, if
not a dull, at least an anxious and laborious business.'[98] He knew there
were plenty of envious and hostile readers out there waiting for him to take
a false step. As for the history of manners, he never even began to write it
out.

Malone, however, could continue his research, even if he could not write.
The next summer, in July, after a two-month holiday with his family in
Cheltenham, he returned to Worcester for four days, 'immersed in musty
wills of above two hundred years date, many of which had not been opened
in all that period.' He was in his element, though he caught a 'disorder'
there that he told Charlemont 'might have proved dangerous had I not
from going thence to Oxford and finding myself much out of order, taken
James's powder, which I happened to have with me.' Eleven weeks in

---

[95] The undated letter is quoted in Prior, pp. 239–40.
[96] Prior, p. 213. Prior does not mention his source for these verses.
[97] To Charlemont, 27 May 1794, *HMC*, XIII, 8, p. 238.
[98] 7 November 1794, *HMC*, XIII, 8, pp. 251–52.

Oxford followed during which each day 'from the hour of breakfast till it was dark, that is, near six hours every day' he wearied his hands and eyes not over Shakespeare but in transcribing Aubrey's manuscripts.

Back in London, he determined to give his eyes, 'which were a good deal affected', some badly needed rest.[99] But he was immediately caught up in the furore over the audacious and controversial Shakespeare forgeries. After that, he did very little work on Shakespeare until after the new century had dawned. The forgeries, a brief flirtation with a biography of Spenser,[100] a memoir and edition of Reynolds, friendship with Burke and insurrection in Ireland, and a *Life* and edition of Dryden all conspired to delay his *magnum opus*. He was well into his sixties when he returned to it.

[99] To Charlemont, 29 December 1795, *HMC*, XIII, 8, pp. 266–67.
[100] See J. C. Walker to Malone, 12 October 1796 (Add. 77); Blakeway to Malone, 11 January 1801 (Arthur O'Neill Collection); and Malone to Percy, 5 June 1802, (*P–M Letters*), p. 98.

10

The Club of Hercules: exposing
Shakespeare forgeries

1

No one appeared to know in advance of publication the details of an essay that Malone quietly added to his 1790 edition entitled, 'Shakspeare, Ford, and Jonson.'[1] It was his first exposure of a literary forgery since Chatterton, though a minor one, by Charles Macklin, who when Malone wrote his essay was already ninety-one. The essay served notice again about how uncompromising Malone could be when he was convinced of a literary fraud. But Macklin was a relatively unimportant prelude to his comprehensive exposure of the most sensational forgeries in the eighteenth century by William Henry Ireland. Macklin was in his nineties and Ireland was only a teenager, yet it did not matter to Malone what a forger's age was. Both these forgeries concerned Shakespeare; to him that made them especially serious offences. He pounced on them with documentary evidence, 'using those rules of evidence which regulate trials of greater importance.'[2] He was out to convict.

There was an irony to the Macklin detection that was not lost on Malone since it was Macklin who had helped the boys direct and produce plays at Dr Ford's school in Dublin in the late 1740s. Macklin was also well liked and many felt that, at his age, he ought to have been allowed to live the rest of his life without being accused of a forgery he was supposed to have committed in 1748. This also occurred to Malone, of course, and in his essay he was careful to be civil and courteous in his treatment of Macklin personally; but he would not pull back once on the scent of a forgery.

Malone accused Macklin of forging the pamphlet, *Old Ben's Light Heart Made Heavy by Young John's Melancholy Lover*. In his 'Letter' (containing the pamphlet) that appeared in the 23 April 1748 issue of *The General Advertiser*,[3] Macklin had said the pamphlet was written in the reign of Charles I. The author of the pamphlet, allegedly a contemporary of Jonson's, strongly

---

[1] *PP (1790)*, I:i, pp. 387–414. See also *PP (1821)*, I, pp. 402–35. My citations below are from the 1821 edition. On Macklin's pamphlet, see Schoenbaum, *Shakespeare's Lives*, pp. 184–86; and de Grazia, *Shakespeare Verbatim*, pp. 108–9. [2] *PP (1790)*, I:i, p. 388.
[3] The paper was later called the *Public Advertiser*.

rebuked Jonson for his ingratitude to Shakespeare, 'who first introduced him to the *theatre and fame.*' He also claimed that Jonson's jealousy even extended to Ford, for 'Ford was at the head of the partisans who supported *Shakespeare's fame* against *Ben Jonson's invectives.*' Malone, who in this vein Boswell once called 'the careful reasoner', argued that in the pamphlet Macklin was merely exploiting the traditional stories of a rivalry between Jonson and Shakespeare in order to obtain some good advertising for the benefit night of a revival of Ford's *The Lover's Melancholy* – a revival in which his wife was acting.

In deference to Macklin's age and stage reputation, Malone says he had sought out the old man for the facts and assured him then that 'no kind of disgrace could attend his owning that this letter was a mere *jeu d'esprit,* written for an occasional harmless purpose.' Macklin, however, pleaded he could not remember much about the letter and that the pamphlet itself had been lost at sea in 1760. So Malone decided to press his point, confident he would be able 'to produce such testimony as shall convict our veteran comedian of having, sportively, ingeniously, and falsely, (though with no malice afore-thought,) invented and fabricated the narrative ... contrary to the Statute of Biography, and other wholesome laws of the Parnassian Code ... in this case made and provided, for the ... certainty and authenticity of dramatick history.'[4]

In accusing Macklin, Malone uses evidence from manuscripts, registers, and printed sources. He presents 'facts of the greater part of which no writer of the time, conversant with dramatick history, could have been ignorant.'[5] Macklin was relatively unimportant to him. Documented facts are all. Moreover, the facts took him beyond the issue of forgery into biographical research on Jonson. With the help of the documents his research turned up, he composed a more correct biographical sketch of Jonson than had ever before been available, contradicting several spurious stories about him. Since Jonson was Poet Laureate, Malone also wrote a long section on the history of that title based on official documents, the first such account. Other facts about Shakespeare's and Jonson's contemporaries also surfaced. He could have gone on much longer exploring the ripples emanating from Macklin's forgery, demonstrating to his contemporaries the sort of documentary research that literary history now demanded, but, fortunately for him, deadlines intervened and he had to stop.

Steevens, who had accepted *Old Ben's Light Heart* as authentic and published it in his 1778 edition, rejected Malone's argument, comparing him 'to one who brings a sledge hammer for the demolition of a house of cards.'[6] A number of Malone's friends also did not like the idea of the essay; Reed and Charlemont, for example, although admiring his scholarship,

---

[4] *PP* (*1790*), I:i, p. 390.   [5] *PP* (*1790*), I:i, p. 397.   [6] See *J–S* (*1778*), I, pp. 219ff.

could not accept that Macklin was capable of forgery and were embarrassed by Malone's extraordinarily detailed attack. Boswell, when Malone asked him from Ireland to 'draw it into notice, *quietly*' in the papers, declined to do so. He could not help dissenting 'as to my old friend Macklin's having been the inventor of the statement which you have refuted with complete nay almost superflous success, I mean with a superfluity of proof and argument.' Boswell told him that other members of The Club felt the same way. He could not, therefore, write a piece for the paper 'lest I should either oppose you, or seem to agree in the charge of falshood against poor Charles, who unquestionably could not *himself* be the Author of the statement.' He did acknowledge, however, the brilliance of Malone's case, 'as it shews what a lawyer and judge you might be if you would.'[7]

Malone felt no compunction to apologize for what Steevens called his sledge-hammer approach. Instead, he warned all would-be forgers 'to deter from invading the rights or property of others by any kind of fiction', at least because of the '*inefficacy* and *folly* of it; for the most plausible and best fabricated tale, if properly examined, will crumble to pieces.' William Henry Ireland, an eighteen-year-old attorney's clerk, must not have read this, for five years later he served up his own Shakespearean 'fiction.' If Steevens was right that the Macklin essay evinced how well Malone could wield a sledge-hammer, then these forgeries would incite Malone to drop something like a literary nuclear bomb on their perpetrator.

2

> Four forgers in one prolific age
> Much critical acumen did engage
> ...
> Fraud, now exhausted, only could dispense
> To her fourth son, their threefold impudence.
>
> (William Mason, 1797)

Soon after Boswell died in May 1795, Malone joined his brother and family in Cheltenham for a few weeks. These reunions were becoming more important for him and more frequent. There was nothing particularly pressing for him to get done in London, and the rest to his eyes was welcome. After about six weeks there, where he partook of 'the usual "operose" employments of a water-drinking place', the party headed for Malvern for one week before breaking up. After that, it was to Oxford, where he hoped to arrive by 15 September and meet Windham.[8] Windham never came, but Malone remained for eleven long weeks, leisurely

---

[7] 23 December 1790, 18 January 1791, *B–M Corr.*, pp. 386, 388.
[8] See Malone's letter to Windham on 31 August 1795, BL Add. Ms. 37854, fol. 132 (printed in the *Windham Papers*, I, pp. 302–3).

transcribing a few of Aubrey's *Lives* and other manuscripts. He returned to London around 8 December, after about a five-month absence, ready to push on with his *Life of Shakespeare*, only to find that the town was buzzing with excitement over the 'discovery' of some Shakespearean papers.

Malone told Forbes, in April 1796, that soon after he returned 'a work made its appearance, which was particularly interesting to me, of which you have probably seen many accounts in the Newspapers; I mean, some pretended manuscripts of Shakspeare, of the forgery of which I was fully convinced before their publication, from various circumstances that had come to my knowledge.'[9] This pamphlet, written by Samuel Ireland, the forger's father, appeared on 24 December 1795 with the impressive title, *Miscellaneous Papers and Legal Instruments under the Hand and Seal of William Shakspeare: including the Tragedy of King Lear and a Small Fragment of Hamlet, from the Original MSS. in the Possession of Samuel Ireland, of Norfolk Street*. It climaxed the rumours in London that had been building ever since the father took his son's first forgeries to the Herald's Office in mid-December 1794 and had them pronounced authentic.

The forgeries, at least those published in the *Miscellaneous Papers*,[10] included letters from the Queen and the Earl of Southampton to Shakespeare; the poet's verses to 'Anna Hatherrewaye'; his letters to her, Southampton, and Richard Cowley; his Profession of Faith; agreements between Shakespeare and fellow actors Heminges, Condell, and John Lowin; new versions of *King Lear* and *Hamlet*; a Deed of Gift from Shakespeare to an ancestor of Ireland's (also named William Henry) that conveniently explained how all these papers came to end up in a single chest in an unidentified nobleman's country house; and sundry documents complete with Shakespeare's marginalia from his own library. Ireland also wrote two plays he tried to pass off as Shakespeare's entitled *Vortigern and Rowena* and *Henry II* (both printed in 1799).

Malone was convinced at least as far back as February 1795, that the manuscripts were forgeries. Initially, he was suspicious over the way the Irelands displayed them to the public in February at their home in Norfolk Street, inviting some people and excluding others. Boswell was allowed in and kneeled as if before a shrine to kiss the parchments. He died three months later apparently still believing he had witnessed the greatest literary discovery in history.[11] Dr Parr and Joseph Warton saw them, too, and became believers. Ritson saw them, but he was not fooled. Neither Steevens nor Dr Farmer even applied to see them, but the younger Ireland's anxiety was such that it is doubtful they would have been allowed

---

[9] 25 April 1796, Fettercairn, Box 87 (unnumbered).

[10] Not all the forgeries appear in the publication. See Schoenbaum, *Shakespeare's Lives*, p. 219.

[11] See Malone to Forbes, 25 April 1796, about Boswell's 'bravado' subscription to Ireland's proposed publication of the Shakespeare papers.

to.[12] Malone anticipated that the Irelands' doors would be closed to him; in any case, he wanted to see the papers but not at Norfolk Street. The leading authority of Shakespearean biography has reasoned that as the greatest living authority on Elizabethan literature Malone would have run a risk by going.[13] He would have been closely watched. If in the crush of visitors he had been unable to examine the manuscripts well enough to make a careful judgment, people might have interpreted his silence as an admission of their authenticity. If later he changed his mind, he would be mocked in the papers for inconsistency. That is what happened to James Boaden, then the editor of the *Oracle* newspaper, who changed his mind, published his new views in *A Letter to George Steevens*, and then was attacked for them.[14] Malone's plan was to see the manuscripts without the Irelands knowing it. This is where his old friend John Byng came in.[15]

Joseph Farington talked to Malone at length about the subject the day after the forgeries were published and in his diary recorded Malone's account of his secret efforts to see them.[16] Malone told Byng, who was a friend of Samuel Ireland's and 'an ignorant man in such matters... and violently prejudiced in favor of their authenticity', that if he could persuade Ireland to bring the manuscripts of Lord Southampton's correspondence and articles of agreement between Shakespeare and Hemminges and Condell to his (Byng's) house, 'I will produce a fac simile [*sic*] of Lord Southampton's hand writing which will at once ascertain the matter.' He begged Byng not to mention his name, 'let it be only a *gentleman*.' Byng proved, indeed, to be 'an ignorant man in such matters.' He failed to see the need for secrecy and actually showed Malone's note to Samuel Ireland, who copied it and proceeded to pass it around 'to many persons as a proof that Malone desired to obtain a sight of the manuscripts in a clandestine manner.' Needless to say, the manuscripts never arrived at Byng's house, though Malone arrived at the appointed hour to see them. Ireland's own version of what happened may well have been true. According to him, Malone thought the papers had been taken to Thomas Caldecott's house – a 'believer', friend of Ireland's, and ineffectual Shakespearean enthusiast who envied Malone's success – so he quickly dispatched Ozias Humphry there for permission to inspect them. Ireland later wrote the following note on the episode, which is worth quoting because it captures the flavour of this farce:

On Sunday Feb:1: 1795 Mr. Humphrey [*sic*], the painter called at Mr Caldecott's chambers & left Mr. Malone's card – requesting permission for him to call at Mr

[12] In his *Confessions* (not published until 1874), William Ireland wrote how he was terrified by Ritson's examination of the forgeries. On Ritson's letter to a friend describing his visit, see Schoenbaum, *Shakespeare's Lives*, p. 220.   [13] Ibid., pp. 193–235.

[14] J. Wyatt, *A Comparative Review of the Opinions of Mr. James Boaden* (1796).

[15] On Byng's involvement, see Schoenbaum, *Shakespeare's Lives*, pp. 201–2.

[16] 1 January 1795, *DF*, II, pp. 463–64.

C's – to view the Shakspere papers – to which Mr C. replied that they were not, nor ever had been in his possession, but that they were in the hands of Mr Ireland of Norfolk St: where they had been ever since their discovery & from whence Mr. C. observed – he believed they would not be removed into the house of any person whatever, unless he Mr. I. should be requested to wait on his Majesty with them – which he should certainly as his duty required comply with – At the same time Mr Caldecott informed Mr Humphry that he believed it was Mr Irelands intention not to shew them to any Commentator or Shakspere monger whatever – This answer it would be imagined should have satisfied any such person as Mr M. or at least have prevented his application to any other person, or through any other channel than that of Mr Ireland himself – instead of which Mr Malone in a very unbecoming and ungentlemanlike manner – applied to my friend Mr Byng in a letter ... [17]

Ireland's story sounds plausible, given Malone's keenness to see the forgeries. Malone was very annoyed over Byng's blunder.[18] Now he had no choice but to wait ten months until they were published.

After he read them, he no longer wanted to see them. On 29 December 1795, he announced to Charlemont that the *Miscellaneous Papers* 'confirmed what I always thought, that they are direct and palpable forgeries.' He had gone through the work, taken notes, and decided he must compose a prompt reply dedicated to Charlemont: 'I trust in your usual goodness and kindness to me that you will not be displeased at the thought of our thus going down to posterity together.' He needed to hurry, for he was 'afraid of being anticipated by others, and shall hurry on the publication with all possible speed. I hope to have finished the manuscript by Thursday night (I am now writing on Tuesday), to get to press on Friday, and to publish my letter on the 8th of January.' The perpetrators were 'a broken Spitalfields weaver' and a conveyancer's clerk, but he would avoid mentioning their names so as not to be pelted by them in the newspapers. He was already smarting from an attack in that morning's *True Briton*.[19]

The *True Briton* taunted Malone on 29 December for his eagerness to expose the forgeries: 'such *impetuosity of criticism* hardly promises the *elaborate* and *patient* research which the subject demands. It would be unfair to arraign Mr. MALONE of want of candour, before we know what his work may contain; but we wish, for his own sake, that he had not displayed so much *eagerness* to commence the *attack.*' As for Charlemont, who was also chided, the writer remarked, 'How the Earl of CHARLEMONT should have the dedicatory honours of Mr. MALONE's threatened Pamphlet ... many people are at a loss to guess – We presume it is because he is *Generalissimo* of the *Irish Volunteers.*'[20]

[17] Ireland's transcript is in the BL Add Ms. 30346, fols. 69–70.
[18] See Byng to Malone, 8 March 1796, Ms. Malone 38, fol. 64; and fol. 63.
[19] *HMC*, XIII, 8, pp. 267–68; and Charlemont's reply, 7 January 1796, p. 270.
[20] *True Briton*, no. 3 (29 December 1795).

Malone got into print sooner than he thought, in the 1 January issue of the *Gentleman's Magazine*, but his article did not prove forgery; it was merely a quick way of getting a hearing ahead of others. 'It must be regarded as a singular phenomenon', he begins, 'th[a]t not any of Shakspeare's veteran commentators appear upon the list' of subscribers to Samuel Ireland's publication. As for the forgeries themselves, he observes that the nearest resemblance he has found to the spelling in these manuscripts is in the Rowley poems and that this had immediately raised his suspicions: 'The Shakspeare of Mr. Ireland, like the Rowley of Chatterton, has also many verbal anachronisms.'[21] But whereas Chatterton's were clever, Ireland's showed a total ignorance of Elizabethan orthography, as is hilariously evident to anyone who has read the little love poem that Shakespeare is supposed to have enclosed in his letter to Anne Hathaway:

> Is there inne heavenne aught more rare
> Thanne thou sweete Nymphe of Avon fayre
> Is there onne Earthe a Manne more trewe
> Thanne Willy Shakspeare is toe you.

He imagines republican sentiments in the forgers' statements that, in the context of atrocities and carnage in revolutionary France, make the forgeries even more repulsive to him. He stresses that this is an opening volley and that he plans further detective work, a thoroughly scholarly and detailed analysis of the forgeries. This will give him a chance to display his knowledge of Elizabethan literature and manners and be a good advertisement for his forthcoming edition.

The public expected his attack – his *Inquiry* as he called it – at any time, but Malone refused to be hurried. An anonymous note in the *Morning Chronicle* for 16 February, mischievously suggesting that he would publish before the end of the month, elicited his angry reply in the *Gentleman's Magazine* for 24 February that he was 'too fond of a retired and private life, ever to introduce his name unnecessarily into a newspaper.' Whatever the motivation behind the Advertisement in the *Morning Chronicle*, it would not induce him 'to publish his Detection of this Forgery sooner than suits his own convenience, or before he has rendered it as perfect as he is capable of making it, which ... may probably be about the 8th or 10th of March.' If he had been content merely to detect 'the most inartificial and bungling forgery ever attempted', he scoffed, his task would have been easier and finished long ago. At stake, however, is 'the reputation and character and history of his great MASTER.' A 'wider range' is required, a 'survey [of] the manners of the time as well as the state of the stage.' He hopes also to come up with 'something of entertainment as well as instruction.'[22]

Malone nettled a few friends as well as enemies with his lofty tone in this

---

[21] *Gentleman's Magazine*, LXVI (January 1796), 7–8.   [22] Ibid., (24 February 1796), 92.

article. Boaden disliked his fretfulness: 'Mr. Malone talks rather peevishly of the "*meretricious* and *undesirable* celebrity of a newspaper" ... We trust no writer will henceforward offend this fastidious gentleman with anything so irksome to his feeling as *diurnal praise*.'[23] Samuel Ireland himself recklessly taunts Malone in the *Morning Herald* for 'after having so long threatened to knock the *Shakespearian trunk* to atoms', claiming 'that all his tools are not ready for this curious operation.' On behalf of the 'Irelandites', he challenges Malone 'to the drawing, and not only deny his power to knock out the *artificial bottom*, but even his ability to discompose a single hair of their favourite *old trunk*!'.[24] Others chimed in, but Malone worked on confidently.

He silenced his critics permanently and put an end to the war between the believers and disbelievers by publishing on 31 March a book of over four hundred pages imposingly titled, *An Inquiry into the Authenticity of Certain Miscellaneous Papers and Legal Instruments, Published Dec. 24, MDCCXCV. and Attributed to Shakspeare, Queen Elizabeth, and Henry, Earl of Southampton*. As he told Forbes in April, the book had 'employed my whole time for three months, and considering that it was both written and printed in that time, it does not appear to me that I was an idle workman.' The work succeeded commercially 'beyond my warmest expectations, five hundred copies having been sold in the first two days after publication.' Most agreed it was an extraordinary achievement to write a book of this length in less than three months. In a large paper copy of the *Inquiry* now at the Folger Shakespeare Library, he wrote (with some pride, one imagines): 'Begun Jany 10. Began printing Jan. 18. Finished at the press March 28, 1796.'[25]

This is not the place to record the younger Ireland's desperate twists and turns throughout 1795 to please and deceive his disapproving and unloving father.[26] Chatterton's forgeries had inspired him, but while Chatterton's forgeries were brilliant, Ireland's were audacious, impudent, and blundering.[27] Both he and his father were in disgrace after Malone's *Inquiry*; and in different ways one feels pity for them both. But Malone did not attack them personally. He certainly had no idea of the extenuating father–son relationship that induced the young man to embark on such a foolhardy scheme, or of their obsession with antiquarianism. As he said more than once, his concern was with Shakespeare and truth, not personality.

On the other hand, the *Inquiry*'s exposure of the forgery's 'wild flutter of fiction' is often an angry piece of work. A number of people thought he had been too harsh, and something of a backlash did occur that pilloried him for heaping arrogant and lofty scorn on an adolescent. Others mocked him,

[23] *The Oracle* (9 March 1796).   [24] See 29 February 1796 entry, *DF*, II, p. 501.
[25] Folger 79.2 M29.1. See *DF*, II, p. 477.
[26] For such a summary, see Schoenbaum, *Shakespeare's Lives*, pp. 193–220.
[27] For a portrayal of young Ireland, see 1 January 1796, *DF*, II, p. 464.

again, for his sledge-hammer methods. Even in modern times, a critic has occasionally rebuked him for excessive fervour. John Mair, for example, in his journalistic book *The Fourth Forger* (1938), called it 'four hundred vituperative pages', a 'brutal analysis', and a 'brilliant conjunction of scholarship and spite.'[28]

The *Inquiry* is a prosecution of a literary felony. Malone leaves no stone unturned. His first step is to question William's provenance for the papers. He draws an analogy with the law, pointing out that if a will or some form of testamentary writing were to be proved in court, the court would need to know where it was found, how long it had been in a person's possession, and to whom he had previously mentioned it. Regarding the Shakespeare papers, Malone concludes (no fewer than ninety pages later), the 'ground of such questions is obvious', for Ireland has not provided a shred of this kind of evidence except that a country gentleman has allowed him and only him to reveal the contents of his priceless chest. He then proceeds to an extremely detailed and systematic analysis of the orthography, phraseology, dates, handwriting, and historical facts in Samuel Ireland's book.

Malone brings to bear on his argument a great deal of scholarship, including information he had just culled from the Dulwich College manuscripts still in his possession. Eleven of fourteen entries from Henslowe's diary appear in the *Inquiry* for the first time, in addition to three autographs, one or more of which he may have cut out from the manuscript.[29] He publishes facsimiles of Ireland's attempts at Shakespeare's, Heminge's, and Southampton's signatures alongside facsimiles of authentic signatures he had acquired with Farington's and Thomas Astle's help, and thus is able to show graphically how inept the forger has been. He scrutinizes the poet's letter to Anne Hathaway for its spelling, terms of address, and sentiments, finding faults with them all that anyone even slightly familiar with Elizabethan manners and Shakespeare could easily have avoided. 'The sentiments are not suited to Shakspeare's character', he judges. Malone finds a host of anachronisms in the poet's Deed of Gift to his mythical contemporary William Henry Ireland, such as that Shakespeare's company were not in possession of Blackfriars until 1613, that the existence of Ireland's ancestor is never proved, that *King Lear* (the manuscript of which was purportedly given to William's ancestor) had not yet been written by the date of the Deed, that the other plays Shakespeare 'gave' to Ireland had already been sold to his company, that *Henry VII* does not exist, and that the Deed's legal phraseology abounds with inaccuracies. To the manuscript of *King Lear*, Malone applied his knowledge of Elizabethan printing: Shakespeare 'could not have written with his own hand any play

---

[28] *The Fourth Forger: William Ireland and the Shakespeare Papers*, pp. 166, 167, 170.

[29] Remington P. Patterson, 'Edmond Malone and "some curious Manuscripts relative to the stage"'. See also *Inquiry*, pp. 215–16.

in which metrical speeches are written unmetrically, and the most ridiculous blunders occur in every page... The lines are throughout numbered in the margin, a practice unexampled in our author's time: the sheets are written only on one side, contrary to the universal custom.'

In his summation, Malone rounds on the 'artificer or artificers of this clumsy and daring fraud', who know nothing 'of the history of Shakspeare, nothing of the history of the stage, or the history of the English language.' The dates and 'almost all the facts mentioned, are repugnant to truth, and are refuted by indisputable documents.' 'If any additional proof of forgery is wanting', he concludes, 'I confess I am at a loss to conceive of what nature it should be.'[30] There must have been despair in young Ireland's heart the day he read these words and realized how thoroughly and inescapably he had been exposed. Malone had shown that no forgery could stand up to 'indisputable documents.'

The *Inquiry* is at times facetious and droll, but it would have been more readable and entertaining if Malone had been able to see the more farcical side of the forgeries. Others laughed a good deal more over their absurdity, such as the writer for *The Telegraph* on 14 January, who concocted this letter from Shakespeare to Jonson:

Tooo MISSTEERREE BEENJAAMMIINNEE JOOHNNSSONN.

DEEREE SIRREE,

Wille you doee meee theee favvourree too dinnee wythee meee onn Fridaye nextte, attt twoo off theee clockee, too eattee sommee muttonne choppes andd somme poottaattoooeesse.

I amm, deerree Sirree,
Yourre goodde friendde,
Williamme Shaekspere.[31]

Malone does try a little burlesque towards the end of his book. He imagines himself 'pleading the cause of our great dramatick poet before the ever-blooming God of melody and sun' and transported to Mount Parnassus 'where Apollo and his nine female assessors were trying this question, and were pleased to call on me to deliver my sentiments, as Counsel for Shakspeare.' Amid bay trees, ivy, aromatic shrubs, and other natural emblems of poetic inspiration, he spotted Shakespeare, whom he recognized by his resemblance to 'the only authentick portrait of him, which belonged to the late Duke of Chandos, and of which I have three copies by eminent masters.' He was playing bowls at the top of the hill with Spenser, Suckling, Davenant, and Garrick, 'wholly inattentive' to the Court proceedings, although Apollo was only a few paces away. His 'old and surly antagonist', Ben Jonson, was there, too, seated on an empty cask and not joining in the game because of the 'great corpulency and unwieldiness of his frame.'

---

[30] *Inquiry*, pp. 352–54.   [31] *The Telegraph*, 14 January 1796.

Suddenly, the judgment comes down from the Court. Apollo orders 'a *hue* and *cry* after the delinquents, and for consigning the MSS. to Dr. Farmer, Mr. Steevens, Mr. Tyrwhitt, and Mr. Malone to be burned', but the hand of justice falls most harshly not on the forgers but on the believers:

With respect to the multitude of persons of each sex and of all ages and denominations, who had flocked during the preceding year to see these spurious papers, and expressed the highest admiration of them, (they were so brown and so yellow, so vastly old, and so vastly curious!) the Ringleaders, who were then in custody, should be dismissed with only a gentle reproof, and an admonition never again to pronounce judgment on matters with which they were not conversant.

Not so fortunate were those who appeared in print, declaring 'relentlessly' that the papers were authentic, people like Caldecott and George Chalmers. To them more severe judgment would be meted out.[32]

Walpole, among others, did not like the conclusion. He told Farington, 'Malone's criticism was convincing, but the latter end of the volume, where he attempts humour, had better have been omitted.'[33] This sort of humour is not the antiquarian's right weapon; it is out of character with the rest of the work and belongs in the papers with other ephemera of its kind, not in a serious publication. Walpole, we recall, had said much the same thing about his exposure of Chatterton. Farington recorded Malone's own estimation of his *Inquiry*. Comparing his analytical powers with Johnson's, Malone judged that had Johnson written on the forgeries, 'He would have preceded the investigation by a general review of forgeries and their effects; and in the course of his examination disputations would have risen on passages, which would have elucidated and strengthened them. I ... think only of facts, and confine my mind to them.'[34]

Among the efforts of the Irelands to put a brave face on things after the *Inquiry*, there was one that turned into a fiasco and made things worse for them. Samuel Ireland persuaded Sheridan, Manager of Drury Lane, to stage *Vortigern*, William's full-length forged play, on 2 April. Malone attended the performance. He sat in a private box where as the *persona non grata* of the evening he was less visible. Farington, who was also there, colourfully described what happened.[35] To retaliate against Malone and his 'malevolence' in the *Inquiry*, Ireland drew up a handbill attacking him and had it distributed to the audience before the performance. This infuriated Malone, who could not take any criticism easily, much less this scurrilous sort. But he had no choice but to wait for the play to begin. The audience was disposed to give the play a fair hearing, but its patience quickly grew thin and the evening ended in a riot of laughs and groans. Malone's response to this theatrical travesty and the 'scurrilous advertise-

---

[32] *Inquiry*, pp. 355–66.   [33] *Walpole Corr.*, XV, p. 335.   [34] *DF*, II, p. 466.
[35] 2 April 1796, *DF*, II, pp. 517–18.

ments & hand bills published by Ireland' was only to suggest 'that somebody should publish an acct. of Irelands [*sic*] progress through life that his character may be fully known.'[36] He found little in the evening to smile about.

The reviewers on the whole applauded the *Inquiry*. The *Gentleman's Magazine* for June was particularly impressed. One could almost forgive the forgers, it noted, 'for this single reason, that they have drawn forth a detection from this able master' whose 'intimate acquaintance with every thing relative to his great Master, as he styles him, gives him a decided preference in the list of his champions.'[37] The reviewer in the *Analytical Review*, like most of the public, cheered that 'Mr. Malone again comes forward, to perform the meritorious office of detecting frauds, and chastising audacity', and he suggested that the forgers could now assume 'a niche in the *honourable* gallery of Nodots and Corradinis, Psalmanazars, Lauders, and Chattertons.'

The one criticism the *Analytical* reviewer made, Malone had heard before. It is a good thing the author earned some money from the book, wrote the reviewer, at two guineas per volume, otherwise 'we might be disposed to regret, that so much ingenuity and diligence have been bestowed upon so unworthy a subject: for who would lift the club of Hercules against a dwarf?'.[38] Even among Malone's friends, the feeling lingered that he had squandered his time when he should instead have been pushing on with the *Life of Shakespeare*.[39] He felt that way himself. As late as 29 July, when he returned from a few days with Burke at Taplow, Mary Palmer's estate after she married the Earl of Inchiquin, he still had not returned to his most urgent work. 'I have twenty things on the anvil', he confided to Charlemont, 'and know not which to sit down to first, but I think it will be the life of Shakspeare, which I wish to finish, lest by any fatality I should be prevented from completing it ... I am now in town, I think, for the summer, and shall not stir from my library except for health-sake.'[40]

There were, however, more serious criticisms in the papers than the one about his overkill. Malone was roasted for his political bias in the *Inquiry*, as he knew he would be, especially for his vicious attack on the French Revolution. Pouncing on a comment, for example, that Ireland attributed to Shakespeare in a forged letter – about there being a 'Gyldedde bawble

---

[36] 3 April 1796, *DF*, II, p. 518. See 12 January, *DF*, II, p. 469.

[37] *Gentleman's Magazine*, LXVI, 492. In April, *Gentleman's Magazine* published a score-card of the believers and disbelievers of the forgeries, including Banks, Courtney, Lord Orford, Percy, Farmer, Steevens, Malone, Reed, and Ritson (vol. 66, p. 267).

[38] *Analytical Review* (April 1796), XXIII, 386.

[39] See William Temple's diary, 20 May, *Diaries of William Johnston Temple, 1780–1796*, ed. Lewis Butany (1929), p. 177; and Michael Kearney to Malone, 9 December 1797, Ms. Malone 39, fol. 21.   [40] 29 July 1796, *HMC*, XIII, 8, p. 277.

thatte envyrounes the heade of Majestie' – he accuses the forger of supporting 'those modern republican zealots who have for some time past employed their feeble, but unwearied, endeavours to diminish that love and veneration which every true Briton feels ... for ROYALTY ... '. He went on to speak of the 'detestable doctrines of French Philosophy and the imaginary Rights of Man.'[41] He sent Burke a copy of the *Inquiry*, which he modestly called 'poor linsey woolsey stuff', scenting trouble: 'As for my political principles, which I have more than once introduced, I expect to be attacked for them by those who are in the pay of the French Regicides ... but why should you have that honour all to yourself? Your friends surely have a title to some little share of it.'[42] One reviewer highlighted what he saw as the bathos in Malone's vendetta against the Revolution by accounting for it with David Hartley's philosophical principle of the association of ideas: 'He was employing his mind on *antiquated* and *musty* manuscripts; this recalled to his recollection, by the law of resemblance, his own *antiquated* and *musty* prejudices.'[43]

Burke, now living in retirement and mourning the recent death of his only son, replied with comfort and praise. He had reached the seventy-third page of the *Inquiry* at a first reading, he reported, before falling asleep, the former 'not greatly' contributing to the latter. In the same spirit that he praised the 1790 edition, he celebrated the *Inquiry* as honouring the nation and its ideals – exaggerated praise, to be sure, but reflecting the pressure of the revolution felt by all cultural discourse in the 1790s and especially his sense of the importance of Malone's work to the continuity of British tradition and values. Burke, like Malone, linked literary forgery with the 'false pretence and imposture' of radical philosophies that would either turn their backs on or fraudulently distort the past. The 'Criticism' that detects deception, just like political writing that censures social anarchy, has 'grown very rare in this Century', he writes; 'you have revived it with great advantage.' Even Malone's elegant writing illustrates the growth of orderly cultural consensus: 'you have in the most natural, happy, and pleasing manner ... given us a very interesting History [of] our Language during that important period, in which after being refined by Chaucer it fell into the rudeness of civil confusion and ... continued in a pretty even progress, to the state of correctness, streng[th] and elegance, in which we see it in your writings.' If Malone's stridency and peremptory documentation and defence of the past brings the wrath of anarchists down upon him, at least he is in good company: 'Johnson used to say, he loved a good hater. Your admiration of Shakspeare would be ill rooted indeed, if your Taste (to talk of nothing else) did not lead you to a perfect abhorrence

---

[41] *Inquiry*, pp. 148, 151.
[42] 1 April 1796, Sheffield City Libraries Archives, Wentworth Woodhouse Muniments Burke Papers 1/3209.   [43] *Public Advertiser*, XX, 234.

of the French Revolution, and all its works.' The literary scholar cannot, or should not, remain isolated from the large events of the age. He thanks Malone for the 'great entertainment' he has given not only as a critic, but also 'as an Antiquary, as a Philologist, and as a Politician.'[44]

But Burke also felt that Malone should not go down that particular track again. It was time to perform an even larger service for the world of letters. A year later, he was delighted that his friend was engaged in writing a memoir of Reynolds: 'I am very glad that after you have detected imposture and exposed dullness, you are going to do justice to real merit and genuine genius. Nobody can pay this debt of friendship [to Reynolds] better than yourself.'[45]

3

'It is not supposed that any reply to Mr. Malone is in the press', Steevens told Isaac Reed on 23 May, 'not withstanding the bluster that has been made about it.'[46] Four replies, however, materialized over the next two years. Samuel Ireland was the first to retaliate, but not until eight months after the *Inquiry*, with his eighteen-penny pamphlet, *Mr. Ireland's Vindication of His Conduct*. Malone had implied that he was an impostor, so he tries to salvage some of his reputation by protesting his innocence and describing his loss of money and time. He even compromises his son by quoting a letter from him proving that he, Samuel, did not forge any of the manuscripts. Ireland also hints he was working on an analysis of Malone's character and methods as a scholar. This came out the following year, with Caldecott's help, under the title, *An Investigation of Mr. Malone's Claim to the Character of Scholar, or Critick, being an Examination of his Inquiry into the Authenticity of the Shakspeare MSS*. A flimsy and sad effort from a defeated man still maintaining the authenticity of the manuscripts, the work nonetheless catches Malone out on a few careless mistakes, but there was precious little in it to engage Malone's or anyone else's serious attention.

More substantial attacks came from George Chalmers. First there was his lengthy (over six hundred pages) *An Apology for the Believers in the Shakspeare-Papers* (1797), where with new material he argues against Malone's methodology and, to a lesser extent, for the authenticity of the papers. He hoped it would spur Malone to answer, and it almost did. Malone's copy of the book is full of marginalia suggesting a plan to fire back. Ritson, for once not quarrelling with Malone, reported to Joseph Cooper Walker in Dublin that 'Malone is every day expected to return the blow. It is a game of push-pin in ill-blood.'[47] Steevens was astonished by this 'most virulent invective against Mr. Malone', especially since all the

---

[44] 5 April 1796, Beinecke, C698; *Burke Corr.*, VIII, pp. 455–56.
[45] *Burke Corr.*, VIII, pp. 455–56.   [46] OFB, Box 75, no. 89.
[47] Folger, PR 2950 C5 (Cage).

surviving editors of Shakespeare were 'censured in the lump.' 'Can your Smock-Alley, my Lord', he asked Percy, 'or our St Giles's, produce any thing more low and vulgar than this is?' 'The backs of all our Cats are consequently up', he added; 'Malone, however, may have ample reprisals ... Chalmers has certainly batter'd down some of Malone's cornice, but his citadel is as firm as ever.'[48] But Charlemont advised Malone firmly against retaliating, for 'I take it for granted that he is scarcely worth your answer, which may probably counteract your purpose by raising him into notice.'[49]

Malone agreed, though Chalmers contributed to Shakespeare scholarship in this work and Malone came to fear his resourcefulness in finding important documents and publishing them. He settled instead for an irrelevant sentence on Chalmers (whom he did not mention by name) that he forced into his narrative memoir of Reynolds in 1797. The Ireland forgeries, he writes, have recently 'found a puny, but perfectly homogeneous, champion, whose mortified vanity has prompted him to abet and countenance a silly fiction, by confident and groundless assertions, false quotations, and arguments still more flimsy and absurd than the imposture itself.'[50] Farington, who with others of Malone's friends closed ranks against Chalmers, remarked, 'He is very angry at Malone and calls him the *Public Accuser*. [Daniel] Lysons says Chalmers is a heavy man & the Book is ill written ... Stevens [*sic*], said of Chalmers, that He has flogged himself with his tail till He has become enraged.'[51] Chalmers flogged himself for two more years and then published another six hundred-page work that few people read, registering in the title his frustration that Malone had not replied to his earlier book. He titled it, *A Supplemental Apology ... Being a Reply to Mr. Malone's Answer, Which Was Early Announced, but Never Published* (1799).[52] By then the controversy was dead. W. L. Mansel, Vice-Chancellor of Cambridge University, told Malone what he did not need to be told: 'you have a rare Antagonist & Foil. Never surely was malignant Dullness so pitted against Genius & Intellect.'[53]

That Malone did not reply to either of Chalmers' vindictive attacks was a good sign. There were several large projects piling up on his plate, and it would have been madness to waste any more time on matters related to the forgeries. And yet for a time he fully intended to publish a second edition of the *Inquiry*, where he would retaliate against his critics. In his copy of the *Inquiry*, he wrote copious revisions in the margins of every page and on interleaved sheets. He even pasted in cuttings from articles in the press to

---

[48] Steevens to Percy, 30 January 1797, Beinecke.
[49] 9 October 1797, *HMC*, XIII, 8, p. 310.
[50] Reynolds, *Works* (corrected 2nd edn., 1798), I, p. xxxiii.
[51] 13 January 1797, *DF*, II, p. 746.   [52] See Schoenbaum, *Shakespeare's Lives*, pp. 234–35.
[53] 23 April 1800, BL Add. Ms. 27, fols. 161–62. Ritson responded negatively to Chalmers' latest work in a letter to J. C. Walker, 5 August 1799, OFB 33.31.

which he scribbled replies. On the flyleaf, he wrote, 'For a second edition.'[54] It looks as if he completed these extensive revisions, which must have cost him hours of hard labour. But he did not publish a second edition, no doubt because he realized there was no market, not because he was battle-weary. He hated to let his critics walk away unchastened.

As it was, he had trouble concentrating on the work he knew he should be doing. There were interruptions, he was deeply dispirited by events in France and Ireland, his eyes made reading difficult, and he was more perplexed than ever by attacks of writer's block – although it seems hard to credit this in view of his celerity in writing the *Inquiry*. Farington, to whom Malone confided his strongest feelings, diagnosed the problem this way in August 1799: 'Malone has great pleasure in collecting materials, and in all the research necessary to prepare for publication, and in considering evidence: but shrinks from the exertion of pleading – or forming for publication the matter which He has collected.'[55]

[54] Malone's annotated copy is in the BL, c.45.e.23.
[55] *DF*, 4 August 1799, IV, pp. 1262–63.

11

Art and politics: homage to Reynolds and Burke

1

Malone knew art well, especially historical and portrait painting. In his journal, he touches frequently on the interrelation of literature and painting, as when he describes his two excursions with Reynolds in July 1789 to Edmund Waller's house, Hall Barn, to examine the paintings, notably the portraits of Waller.[1] He was well known for his knowledge of portraits and their whereabouts. We have already noted that his was the best private collection of engraved literary 'Heads' in England, especially after he acquired many items from Steevens' collection; and that he was the first to give Shakespeare portraiture the scholarly attention it needed. His expertise on English literary-historical painting reflected his commitment to the use of documents in order to authenticate the past. Indeed, it was central to his biographical interests. In Malone's eyes, a painting, drawing, engraving, or sculpture qualified as an authenticating document as much as an early edition or a manuscript. Such iconography was crucial to what he called his 'antiquarian researches.' It is not surprising, therefore, that he was the close friend of several eminent painters, including Reynolds and Farington, and a valued member of the Royal Academy of Arts.

Another artist who respected Malone's knowledge of art was John Singleton Copley, who in 1785 asked his advice on a painting he had under way of *Charles I Demanding in the House of Commons the Five Impeached Members*. A portraitist, Copley had won his fame in the colonies before the War of Independence by painting George Washington and other American patriots. The painting was overtly political, for the King's confrontation with Parliament was supposed by many to have created civil disorders that did not end until the Glorious Revolution. There was, to be sure, a political impulse behind Malone's interest in this painting, one that he shared with Copley. In his reply to the painter, he stressed that Charles I's conduct in this incident was a breach of parliamentary privilege, from which 'all the

---

[1] See Prior, pp. 155, 161–63. At Hall Barn, Malone wrote in his journal: 'I weighed at Hall Barn (Mr. Waller's) Oct. 4th, 1791, eleven stones two pounds. Height five feet six inches and a half' (Prior, 'Maloniana', p. 319).

ensuing disorder and civil wars' emanated. Not until the accession of William and Mary to the throne in 1688 was 'the liberty of freedom' inherent in the British constitution ensured.

Politics aside, however, Copley was one of the late eighteenth-century school of 'artist–antiquarians' who believed a historical painting had to be historically accurate.[2] In this respect, he and Malone were like-minded in their approach to art. Emphasizing the importance of scrupulous historical accuracy, Malone advised Copley to read about his subject, especially the first volume of Hume's *History of Great Britain* (1754), to get his facts straight. He also insisted that all fifty-eight figures in the painting must be as authentic likenesses as possible: Copley would need to devote 'a month or two in the summer to visiting the seats of the nobility, where pictures might be found of some of whom portraits have not been discovered.' To help him on his way, he gave him a list of eighty-five portraits and told him where many of them could be found, which were the most accurate, and what features the painter ought to borrow from each of them.[3]

Entries in his journal for 1789 also suggest Malone's absorption in buying drawings, tracking down engravings, identifying paintings, and recording anecdotes about artists.[4] On 1 June, for example, he bought from Francis Parsons, the 'ingenious picture cleaner and painter', eight drawings by the elder Jonathan Richardson, including two each of Pope, Milton, and Shakespeare, all of which date from the 1730s. On his next visit to Malone's house a few weeks later, Reynolds volunteered his opinion on Richardson's drawings, one that Malone, because of the opportunity the drawings afforded him to link art and literature, recorded: 'on looking over the elder Richardson's drawings, [he] said he understood his art very well scientifically; but that his manner was cold and hard. [Richardson] was Sir Joshua's pictorial grandfather... He was always drawing either himself or

---

[2] On the 'artist–antiquarian' school of painting and Copley's painting, see Roy Strong, '*And When Did You Last See Your Father?*': *The Victorian Painter and British History* (1978), pp. 24–29, 137–38. On Copley's painting, see Julius David Prown, *John Singleton Copley in England 1774–1815* (1966).

[3] Strong discusses Malone's letter to Copley in *The Victorian Painter*, p. 28, as does Julius David Prown in *John Singleton Copley*, pp. 337–40. The entire letter is reprinted in Martha Babcock Amory, *The Domestic and Artistic Life of John Singleton Copley, R.A.* (1882), pp. 450–53.

   De Grazia has argued that Malone, 'rather than drawing the event [of Copley's painting] into the grand sweep of English history' succeeded in locking it 'into a frame singularly its own', cutting it off from the tradition by which historical painting represented the past 'through a stock vocabulary of columns, drapes, generalized antique architecture, and constuming'. Malone therefore participated in 'a disruption of a homogeneous past' by establishing the 'period' or uniqueness of the historical moment in Copley's painting, just as he caused a similar disruption by 'creating' factually a uniqueness in Shakespeare and his time (*Shakespeare Verbatim*, pp. 95–97). Malone's reply to this argument would have been simply that it was precisely against stock generalizations and traditions that he was arguing; that by helping Copley base his painting on unique, documentable facts he was protecting the event it depicts from misappropriation in the past, present, and future.

[4] See Prior, 'Maloniana', pp. 397–406.

Pope, whom he scarcely ever visited without taking some sketch of his face.'[5]

At such moments as those at Hall Barn and when he advised Copley, Malone was exploring the historical sense that he felt underlay, or should underlie, most art, endowing it with important ideas. He was not merely compiling information or establishing the provenance of this or that portrait, but rather seeking to elucidate literature, history, and art in terms of each other. This pastime in a small way accounts for the delays of several of his publications: there was always a drawing, a sketch, or a hitherto unknown painting to consult or have copied or engraved which would shed light on his subject. He could not consider writing biographies of Dryden and Shakespeare without unearthing as much of the pictorial iconography connected with them as he could find: images of themselves and their houses, landscapes, and families. 'It would be very satisfactory', he states with conviction and some frustration in his journal in 1788, 'if contemporaries would hand down to posterity their opinion concerning the likenesses of portraits of celebrated men of their own time.'[6] 'Don't you like to know', he asked Charlemont after having read in manuscript Aubrey's descriptions of Waller, that the poet was 'somewhat above the middle stature, thin body, not at all robust; fine, thin skin, his face somewhat of an olivaster, his hair frized [sic], of a brownish colour; full eye, popping out and working; oval faced; his forehead high and full of wrinkles; his head but small; brain very hot and apt to be choleric'.[7]

Malone practised what he preached, for in addition to writing twenty-five (and editing the rest of several hundred) brief 'Lives' of eminent 'ancient' and contemporary figures from various fields for three quarto volumes entitled, *The Biographical Mirrour* (1795–98), he helped the editor Silvester Harding acquire engravings of 'Heads' of all those featured. For the rest of his life, he remained interested in the project, scouring the countryside in search of even more 'Heads' for another volume that was, unfortunately, never published. In March 1805, he told Percy he wanted to include an engraving of him for the last volume: 'It will contain in the whole 150 engraved heads, many never before engraved, and some, (of which there [are] already prints) engraved from new and different pictures: with short memoirs of 3 or 4 pages, allotted to each engraving ... I assisted him [Harding] with a few of the Lives; and would take care that nothing but what is fitting should be annexed to this print.' He even planned, in his capacity as the unofficial chronicler of The Club, a 'splendid volume containing the engraved portraits of those who have ever been members'. By then, there were sixty-six in all, for twenty of whom there were no prints, although he assured Percy he knew how to obtain small Indian-ink drawings of them.[8] By August 1807, he was 'in a fair way of completing my Collection of the heads of the Literary Club. I have got near 60, and there have been but 69 persons of it from the beginning: so I shall make a splendid book of it, that will make a figure a hundred years hence. Let Posterity, therefore, look to it.' Posterity never had a chance, though, because he never published his collection; nor has Malone's collection survived.[9]

2

After Reynolds' death on 28 February 1792, Malone noted in his journal that he had lived 'in the greatest intimacy' with the artist ever since 1779, when Reynolds first painted his portrait.[10] Johnson's death deepened their friendship because it drew them together in the common cause of preserving his memory. Their friendship was also nourished by Reynolds' considerable literary knowledge and his reputation as a literary critic, as well as by Malone's artistic interests. In printing Reynolds' note on the Fool in *King Lear* for his 1790 edition, Malone dissented from his opinion but praised him as one 'whose observations on all subjects of criticism and taste are so ingenious and just, that posterity may be at a loss to determine, whether his consummate skill and execution in his own art, or his judgment on that and other kindred arts, were superior.'[11]

On a more personal level, it was Sir Joshua's happiness and geniality that appealed to him, a happiness which sprang, Malone wrote, 'from virtuous employment, pursued with ardour, and regulated by our own choice.'[12] To Farington, Malone once remarked that Sir Joshua was 'a rare instance of a man relishing pleasure, yet suffering little from disappointments, or what others would have thought mortifications. He certainly had not very strong feelings.'[13] In his *Account* of Reynolds' life, Malone describes him as entirely without pretentiousness, a quality which 'if I do not greatly deceive and flatter myself... principally operated in attaching him to the person to whose province it has fallen to pay this slight tribute to his memory.'[14]

Since Shakespeare kept Malone in London almost all the time in the late 1780s, there were plenty of opportunities for him and Reynolds to see each other. In the winters, he dined with Reynolds about twice per week, 'and

[8] 28 March 1805, *P–M Letters*, pp. 174–75. See also pp. 185, 196, 198–99.
[9] To Andrew Caldwell, 18 August 1807, Folger, uncatalogued. See Appendix A regarding an undated catalogue (at the Bodleian Library) in Malone's hand of his collection of poets' 'Heads'.   [10] Prior, p. 190. See also Prior, 'Maloniana', p. 434.
[11] *PP (1790)*, VIII, p. 527. James Northcote quoted Malone's remarks on Reynolds in his *Memoirs of Sir Joshua Reynolds* (1813), pp. 83–84.
[12] *Account of the Life and Writings of the Author*, Reynolds, *Works* (2nd corrected edn., 3 vols., 1798), I, pp. l–li. Below I cite from the second edition. The memoir is cited as *Account*.
[13] *DF*, 21 January 1796, II, p. 478.   [14] Reynolds, *Works*, I, pp. l–li.

in the evenings [I] dropped in whenever I was disengaged.'[15] For these
dinners in the 'Reynoldsian style' (Boswell's phrase), they would often
have the company of Burke, Courtenay, Boswell (if he was in town), and a
galaxy of other personalities. Malone recalls sitting down one evening at Sir
Joshua's table 'with fifteen persons, eleven or twelve of whom had made a
distinguished figure in the world.'[16] Virtually none of Malone's friends
could match Reynolds' hospitality. Malone told Farington, 'how difficult
it would be to establish a Plan for collecting select Society in the way Sir
Joshua Reynolds carried his on.' He could think of only three others who
could attempt it, Banks, Burke, and Windham, but each 'is unfit in many
respects.' Reynolds 'on the contrary relished all the varieties of Character
& knowledge and assuming little himself, each person was encouraged to
conversation.'[17] There was a magic to his dinner-evenings, which in his
Account Malone describes:

The marked character of his table, I think, was, that though there was always an
abundant supply of those elegancies which the season afforded, the variety of the
courses, the excellence of the dishes, or the flavour of the burgundy, made the least
of the conversation; though the appetite was gratified by the usual delicacies, and
the glass imperceptibly and without solicitation was cheerfully circulated, every
thing of this kind was secondary and subordinate; and there seemed to be a general,
though tacit, agreement among the guests, that *mind* should predominate over *body*;
that the honours of the turtle and the haunch should give place to the feast of wit,
and that for a redundant flow of wine the flow of soul should be substituted.[18]

Reynolds valued Malone's company in London enormously. When Malone
was away in Ireland for six months in 1790–91, he could scarcely bear it. He
wrote to him on 8 March 1791 that while he did not wish to appear like a
'Toad-eater', he would nevertheless 'venture to say this much, that you are
every day found wanting and wished for back, and by nobody more than
your very sincere friend...'.[19] Mary Palmer, ('fair Palmeria'), Reynolds'
niece, whom for a brief period Malone had vaguely hoped to marry but
who eventually married brilliantly to become the Marchioness of
Thomond, said many years later of her uncle's affection for Malone: 'Sir
Joshua Had a great regard for *Mr. Malone* in whom He saw what he
approved.'[20] When one of Sir Joshua's eyes developed a cataract – he lost
the use of the eye entirely in 1789 – Malone wrote anxiously to Boswell, 'If
any thing should happen to him, the chain of our society at least, would be
sadly broken: – but let us hope the best.'[21]

[15] Letter to Charlemont, 7 November 1794, *HMC*, XIII, 8, p. 253.
[16] Malone to Boswell, 13 January 1786 (*B–M Corr.*, p. 288). In his *Memoir* of Malone, James Boswell Junior wrote: 'Though he had little relish for noisy convivial merriment, his habits were social, and his cheerfulness uniform and unclouded' (*PP (1821)*, I, p. lxx).
[17] 21 January 1796, *DF*, II, p. 478.   [18] Reynolds, *Works*, pp. ci–cii.
[19] Ms. Malone 26, fol. 147 (*Letters of Sir Joshua Reynolds*, ed. F. W. Hilles (1929), pp. 210–11).
[20] 28 September 1806, *DF*, VIII, p. 2865.   [21] 19 August 1789, *B–M Corr.*, p. 366.

Reynolds loved the city and avoided the countryside. Malone writes in his *Account* that he showed 'very little relish for a country life and was always glad to return to London, to which he was not less attached than Dr Johnson: with him justly considering that metropolis as the head-quarters of intellectual society.' Both men, however, enjoyed the occasional visit to friends in the country. They took one excursion together, probably their last, to Burke's estate, Gregories, near Beaconsfield, in September 1791, five months before Reynolds died. Worried he would lose the sight in his other eye and fearful that he might have a stroke,[22] Reynolds had by then begun to give his friends very great concern about his health. Malone found it all the more remarkable, therefore, that on the way home from Beaconsfield Reynolds 'left his carriage at the inn at Hayes, and walked five miles on the road, in a warm day, without his complaining of any fatigue'.[23] One should add that it was almost as remarkable that Malone, who joined him, also felt robust enough to walk those five miles, for he generally found it unpleasant to walk merely from library to library on hot London summer days.[24]

Malone's worst fears were well founded, for Sir Joshua died the following February. No death of any of his great London friends ever saddened him as much. He wrote about this loss in his journal, his last entry for three years, as he explains when he takes up the journal again in 1795: 'The loss of that most valuable and amiable man I have felt almost every day since; and being unwilling again to recur to the subject, I for three years wholly discontinued my former practice of recording such anecdotes as I could collect from those friends with whom I conversed.' It would have shown 'great want of taste and sensibility', he adds, 'not to have loved and admired such a uniformly cheerful man.'[25] Reynolds' death even moved him to write an elegy that he never published:

> Farewell, dear friend! In vain I try
> To think of thee without a sigh.
>
> ...
>
> The loss is not to art alone
> Which plac'd thee on Apollo's throne,
> Society has lost still more,
> Which both the good & wise deplore:
> Thy friends dispers'd, of joy bereft,
> No stand, no central point have left;
>
> ...
>
> To these, the nation's light & pride,
> Of wit the source, of taste the guide,
> From all the heart most precious deems
> Thy loss an amputation seems.[26]

[22] See Malone to Boswell 19 August 1789 (*B–M Corr.*, p. 366).
[23] Reynolds, *Works*, I, pp. xxxix–xl, lxiv. See Prior, pp. 190–91.
[24] See Malone to Boswell, 4 September 1786 (*B–M Letters*, p. 326).
[25] Prior, p. 190, and 'Maloniana', pp. 433, 435–36.
[26] Ms. Malone 30, fols. 113–14.

Charlemont understood how he felt: 'I... ought, perhaps, still more to grieve for you, my dearest Edmond, who have lost the society of a friend so justly dear, of a companion so truly valuable.'[27] In his grief, Malone was moved by a legacy of two hundred that Reynolds left him so that he could purchase, as Boswell put it, 'one of his pictures to keep in remembrance of him.'[28] Which painting he chose is unknown.

Reynolds appointed Malone, Burke, and Metcalfe co-executors of his estate. Malone ended up doing most of the practical work settling the estate over the following years, especially regarding Reynolds' manuscripts, paintings, and drawings, but to begin with, Burke and he together saw to the funeral arrangements, newspaper notices, and an appropriate inscription on a tablet for his tomb in St Paul's.[29]

After the funeral, one of Malone's first tasks was to act on his friend's request that he publish a complete edition of the *Discourses*.[30] He did not come to this project unprepared because he had worked with the *Discourses* before. From as early as 1786 to shortly before his death, Reynolds had benefited from Malone's editorial and critical assistance in preparing four of his *Discourses* (nos. 12–15) for the press. 'I wish you would just run your eye over my Discourse [the thirteenth]', he wrote on 15 December 1786, 'if you are not too much busied in what you have made your own employment. I wish that you would do more than merely look at it, – that you would examine it with a critical eye, in regard to grammatical correctness, the propriety of expression, and the truth of the observations.' In December 1788, he asked Malone to add 'a little elegance' to the style of the fourteenth *Discourse*.[31]

Malone, therefore, knew the kind of help Reynolds frequently asked for with the *Discourses* – since 1769 Reynolds had made it his practice to show the drafts of his *Discourses* to Johnson and Burke for revisions and suggestions,[32] – and was in a good position to defend him against a damaging rumour after his death that Johnson and Burke had written large portions of them. In his *Account*, he denounces the rumours with plenty of

---

[27] 1 March 1792, *HMC*, XIII, 8, p. 187.
[28] Boswell to Alexander Boswell, 23 February 1792, *Malahide*, XVIII, p. 293. See also Reynolds, *Works*, I, p. lxvi.
[29] See Burke to Malone, 18 March 1792 (*Burke Corr.*, VII, pp. 335–37). Malone described the funeral in several papers and the *Annual Register* (1792), 66–69. Malone also proposed that Reynolds' picture or bust be set up in The Club's meeting room (to Charlemont, 13 March 1792, *HMC*, XIII, 8, pp. 188–89).
[30] See Malone to Charlemont, 13 March 1792 (*HMC*, XIII, 8, pp. 188–89). Regarding Malone's work on the Reynolds edition, see Hilles, *The Literary Career of Sir Joshua Reynolds*, pp. 193–98.
[31] New York Public Library. See Hilles, *The Literary Career of Sir Joshua Reynolds*, pp. 184–85, on what Reynolds may have sent Malone.
[32] Lipking considers Reynolds as a painter–philosopher in *Ordering of the Arts*, chap. 7.

evidence. They merit only silent contempt, he writes, but he cannot resist his 'duty to refute the injurious calumny, lest posterity should be deceived and misled by the minuteness of uncontradicted representation'. He says that in sifting through Reynolds' papers he has not found any of the *Discourses* in Burke's or anyone else's handwriting and is as convinced that 'the whole body of those admirable works was composed by Sir Joshua Reynolds; as I am certain that at the moment I am employing my pen in vindication of his fame.' As for the help he himself gave Reynolds, he assures readers it was limited to four of the later *Discourses*. These, 'in his own handwriting, and warm from the brain, the author did me the honour to submit to my perusal; and with great freedom I suggested to him some verbal alterations, and some new arrangements, in each of them which he very readily adopted.' Thinking back possibly to that five-mile walk from Burke's house, he recollects, 'Of one I remember well he gave me the outline in conversation, as we returned together from an excursion to the country, and before it was yet committed to paper. He soon afterwards composed the *Discourse* conformably to the plan which he had crayoned out, and sent it to me for such remarks on the language of it as should occur to me.' Malone concludes facetiously: 'Such was the mighty aid that our author received from those whom he honoured with his confidence and esteem.'[33]

But Malone did not let the matter rest there. In his second edition, he added a passage that tried to discredit lingering 'insinuations' that may entertain 'the envious and malignant' but merit only 'silent contempt' from 'the judicious and ingenuous part of mankind.'[34] In July 1798, he was still agitated about the rumours, in a letter to Forbes referring to his defence of Reynolds against 'a calumny or rather a vile misrepresentation which has been propagated, that he was not the author of his admirable *Discourses*. I trust I have done it so satisfactorily, that we shall never hear another word upon that subject.'[35] That was optimistic. Reynolds would not be cleared and Malone's case vindicated until the mid-1930s.[36]

Malone's work on the Reynolds edition traces again the pattern of delays that characterized all his major scholarly work. He began to bring together Reynolds' works very soon after he died, and from a letter to Charlemont in August 1792, it appears that he had already given some copy to the printer by then.[37] Then the project began to swell. After Reynolds' funeral, on 13 March, Malone informed Charlemont he had decided to add three of his *Idler* essays on painting, which simply required reprinting.[38] He did

[33] Reynolds, *Works*, I, pp. lxxxi–lxxxii.   [34] Reynolds, *Works*, 2nd edn. I, pp. xlii–xliii.
[35] 5 July 1798, Fettercairn, Box 87 (unnumbered).
[36] See Hilles, *Literary Career of Sir Joshua Reynolds*, introduction, pp. xviii–xix, and the chapter, 'The Making of the *Discourses*', pp. 128–43.   [37] 10 August 1792, *HMC*, XIII, 8, p. 197.
[38] *HMC*, XIII, 8, p. 189.

not then mention the *Journey to Flanders and Holland*, which at some point in the next three years he also included. It had never been published before, but since Reynolds had already revised it Malone had little to do with it. Much more demanding was William Mason's translation (first published in 1783) of Charles Alphonse Du Fresnoy's influential poem, *De Arte graphica* (*Art of Painting*), which Reynolds apparently had wanted the edition to include (with his own notes) as the chief authority on the rules of painting, adapted for British taste. Mason intended to revise his translation himself, but eventually the unenviable job fell to Malone.[39] 'I am at present on Mason's translation of Du Fresnoy, and long to get through it', he complained to Charlemont in November 1794: 'the Latin of the original is so crabbed and unclassical that it is painful to look at it, and to sound it would, I am sure, break one's teeth.' The edition was 'going on very slowly', though he had 'printed all the "Discourses"' and hoped 'to be able to have them ready for publication by the first of the new year. I think you will be pleased with it, though in many places it is little more than a "catalogue raisonnee", but always sensible, natural, and judicious.'[40] Several months later, in April, Boswell mentioned that the edition 'is now in the press, under the care of that accurate critic, my friend Mr. Malone.'[41] And many months after that, Malone remarked to Charlemont that 'dear sir Joshua's works shall certainly appear before Christmas' – Christmas 1796, that is.[42] Finally, by 1 December 1796, according to Reynolds' sister, Frances, whom Malone had just asked for last-minute information, the edition 'was ready for the press'.[43] But that did not include the *Account*, the proofs of which were not in Malone's hands until late March 1797; he dated its completion 25 March.[44] The complete edition was finally published at the end of the month, five years after he began it.

3

By far his biggest task was to write the *Account*, which ran to one hundred pages in the first edition. Malone planned merely a memoir, not a definitive *Life*, although a few of his friends encouraged him to take on the latter. Although he knew that anything less than a detailed *Life* would very likely be superseded quickly, he did not have time for the extensive research a full biography required. His memoir was, in fact, superseded when James Northcote, portrait painter and member of the Academy at the same time as Malone, published his *Life of Reynolds* in 1813. In his preface, Northcote

[39] See Mason to Malone on 26 May 1792, *HMC*, IX, 2, p. 485.
[40] 7 November 1794, *HMC*, XIII, 8, pp. 253–54.
[41] Tinker, *Letters of James Boswell*, II, p. 455.
[42] To Charlemont, *HMC*, XIII, 8, pp. 253, 277.
[43] Frances Reynolds to her sister Elizabeth Johnson (Hilles Collection).
[44] See 22 March 1797, *DF*, III, p. 804.

dismisses Malone's contribution by announcing that he is writing a proper *Life*, 'a task which Burke declined and Malone has not performed.' With Malone in mind, he implies he is far more qualified to write it because he is a painter: in the past 'the labour of writing the Lives of Painters has been left to depend solely on the skill and ingenuity of those who knew but little concerning the subject they had undertaken, in consequence of which their work is rendered useless and insipid.' Northcote fails to acknowledge that the value of Malone's *Account* is that he wrote it from his own knowledge and love of Reynolds, with personal anecdotes, and with the use of several of the painter's fragmented manuscripts to which he had access. Northcote relied on it for a good deal of his information, much of it unobtainable anywhere else.[45]

When Malone decided to write the *Account* in the spring of 1795, the first person he asked for help was Burke. He may even have been thinking of some kind of collaboration on a brief narrative of personal recollections. Burke, however, who had already written a brief sketch of Reynolds for the papers, doubted the wisdom of a memoir. The problem, as he explained to Malone on 22 May, was that Reynolds' life rarely touched on 'great publick Events'; nor did his life contain enough dramatic 'private adventure' – 'indeed any adventure at all' – to sustain a fuller treatment:

What you are to say of the Character, merely as the Character, of a man, must, to have any effect, consist rather of a few light marking touches than of a long discussion, unless it relates to some of those various & perplexed Characters, which require a long investigation to unfold ... I do not know whether you have the sketch I drew. It has marks of the Haste & the emotion under which it was done. But I believe you will find that a great deal more cannot be said.[46]

It is not likely that his Shakespeare research ever allowed Malone to consider seriously a full-dress biography, but Burke's conviction that Reynolds' life was too uneventful for such a work would have struck him as short-sighted and misguided. Had Burke forgotten Johnson's observation almost half a century earlier, 'It is frequently objected to relations of particular lives, that they are not distinguished by any striking or wonderful vicissitudes ... But this notion arises from false measures of excellence and dignity, and must be eradicated by considering, that in the esteem of uncorrupted reason, what is of most use is of most value.'[47] Moreover, Johnson had defined useful biography as that which brings us closer to the 'real character.' Had not Boswell demonstrated that principle triumphantly? Nonetheless, Burke admitted 'something better could be done by our combination than singly', and he began to write out his own

[45] For Northcote's patronizing attitude towards Malone, see his *Life of Reynolds*, p. 283; cited in Hill-Powell, V, p. 129, n.1.   [46] *Burke Corr.*, VIII, pp. 251–52.

[47] *Rambler*, no. 60 (13 October 1750), *The Yale Edition of the Works of Samuel Johnson*, ed. W. J. Bate and A. B. Strauss (1969), III, pp. 320–21.

recollections of Reynolds. Illness stopped him before he could put down
more than a couple of hundred words. Malone did not discover what he
had written until January 1798, far too late for the first edition and barely
in time for the second.[48]

When Malone finally got down to writing the *Account*, it took him just one
month to finish it. He sent it to the press immediately. There was no time
to send it to Burke, who was too ill to read it anyway; it would have to 'take
its fate in the world without the benefits of many hints which I am sure you
could have suggested on the subject.'[49] He wrote it 'con amore', he told
Frances Reynolds, although 'it lacks those brilliant colours which I was
very desirous Mr Burke should have given, yet I trust it will be considered
as a faithful portrait, which is indeed all the merit it can claim.'[50]

When the *Account* appeared in the handsome quarto edition of the
Works,[51] it was warmly received. The *Annual Register* called it an 'elegant'
edition and praised the *Account* for having been 'drawn up in plain and
unassuming language', although it judged eccentrically that the *Discourses*
so thoroughly presented a 'history' of Reynolds' mind, 'as far as his art is
concerned, that nothing is left to his biographer's ingenuity and penetration
on the subject.'[52] On a more personal level, Reynolds' niece thanked
Malone charmingly with an invitation: 'May I hope to prevail on you to
come and take a family dinner with us to morrow at five & receive my
thanks for the masterly, beautiful, and true character you have given of my
Dear Uncle.' The *Account* touched her deeply; she could not express what
she felt when she read it – 'No one but Mr Malone (who knew him so well)
could have drawn it with equal justice, and I may venture to say, none with
such Elegance and judgment. I thank you with all my heart, and pray come
to morrow ...'[53] As for Burke, whom Malone praised extravagantly in the
Account, he acknowledged Malone had succeeded: 'Your Life of him is
worthy of the subject, which is to say a great deal.' 'I cannot finish this part
of my letter', he added feelingly, 'without thanking you for the very kind
manner in which you are pleased to speak of me – far, indeed, beyond
anything which I can have a claim to, except from your extraordinary good
nature.'[54]

Others were less enthusiastic. Before publication, Reynolds' quarrelsome
sister, Frances, remarked cynically to her sister that Malone, 'the greatest
friend and admirer of Sir Joshua that he ever had perhaps', would write

[48] Burke's manuscript, with Malone's notes, is in the Forster Collection, Victoria and Albert
Museum, Ms. 48 DZ; printed in the *Life* of Reynolds by C. R. Leslie and T. Taylor (1865), II,
pp. 637–38; see also *Burke Corr.*, IX, p. 329.

[49] 14 April 1797, *Burke Corr.*, IX, pp. 308–10.   [50] 3 May 1797, OFB 25.124.

[51] 1797 edition, pp. 494, 497. Malone came out with a three-volume second edition in 1798, and
third and fourth editions in 1801 and 1809.

[52] The edition was advertised in the *London Chronicle* on 28 April.

[53] 3 May 1797, Add. 83–84.   [54] 4 May 1797, *Burke Corr.*, IX, pp. 326–27.

'such an immaculate character as ... will be held up no doubt for humanity to copy after.'[55] She was right. Malone's *Account* is an unbalanced panegyric that uses Johnson as a key to Reynolds' brilliance. Reynolds is frequently glorified simply because he is one of Johnson's most intimate friends. But Johnson, who keeps appearing as an oracle pronouncing on this or that subject, is often irrelevant.[56] It gradually dawns on the reader that Malone is constantly looking for an opening to introduce him.

There are other irrelevancies. He writes a characteristically long note, for example, about a method of colouring that has been discovered recently in some old manuscripts. By association, the mention of old manuscripts makes him think of how sceptical the public has been of archival discoveries since the Ireland Shakespeare forgeries. This in turn enables him to remind his readers of the forgeries and write a scathing attack not only on the Irelands but also George Chalmers, who was currently attacking him. Little of this is about Reynolds.[57]

As in his exposure of the Irelands, Malone also slips in some anti-Jacobinism calculated to please Burke as well as the King, to whom he planned to present a copy of his edition. 'I have introduced a long tirade against our *parliamentary Jacobins*', he told Burke, 'that I hope you will be pleased with.'[58] He cannot resist a digression on the dangers in England of internal threats and 'seditious declamations', the 'pestilential contagion suspended in our atmosphere.'[59] Having referred belligerently to France as that 'OPPROBIOUS DEN OF SHAME, which it is to be hoped no polished Englishman will ever visit', he offers this emotional critique of Burke and his *Reflections on the Revolution in France*:

he well knew how eagerly all the wild and erroneous principles of government attempted to be established by the pretended philosophers of France, would be cherished and enforced by those turbulent and unruly spirits among us ... and long before that book was written, frequently avowed his contempt of those 'Adam-wits,' who set at nought the accumulated wisdom of the ages, and on all occasions are desirous of beginning the world anew.

'If at last we must fall', he adds, 'let us fall beneath the ruins of that fabrick which has been erected by the wisdom and treasure of our ancestors, and which they generously cemented with their blood.'[60]

When Burke read these lines, he had already been living in retirement at Gregories for three years. He was ill and had far from a sanguine view of the world. In his resigned, somewhat self-absorbed letter to Malone on 4 May 1797, he was certain that Malone saw events abroad and at home just as gloomily as he did: 'I see nothing but what tends to make my retreat even

[55] Hilles Collection.
[56] Reynolds, *Works*, 2nd edn., I, pp. xvii–xxv.
[57] Ibid., I, pp. xxxii–xxxiii.
[58] 14 April 1797, *Burke Corr.*, IX, pp. 309–10.
[59] Reynolds, *Works*, I, pp. lviii–lix.
[60] Ibid., I, pp. xlii, lvi–lvii.

into the feeling of my own illness a sort of consolation ... Every thing menacing from abroad, every thing convulsed within, – the violent convulsion of feeble nerves.' As to the unrest in Ireland, which deeply disturbed Malone and broke into violence the following year, he continued: 'I expect nothing else from what has been done in that country ... we must concur in sorrow concerning the melancholly [sic] fact of the situation of that country.' He wished Malone every success with his Shakespeare and similar 'virtuous and liberal pursuits, as long as the state of the World will permit you to continue them.'[61] The Duke of Portland, who accompanied Malone when he presented the edition to the King, very likely thought that his attack on the French Revolution was one of the chief virtues of the memoir of Reynolds. Portland wrote to him on 10 May that there could be no person 'but yourself who can suppose you can have occasion for any introduction any where, but more particularly to a Prince whose Love of Learning and Learned Men is no less conspicuous than his Constancy and Zeal in support of the Liberties of Europe & the Cause of Religion and Good Order.'[62]

The *Account* records several facts about Reynolds' paintings and personal appearance that otherwise may have been lost. In addition to listing his history paintings, Malone (with his appetite for this kind of detail) also mentions their purchasers and the prices paid for them. He runs through all the known self-portraits and where they were, lists all the known engravings of Reynolds, and devotes two pages to his appearance.

More usefully, his biography contributes a good deal to what is known about Reynolds' life because he depends heavily on what Reynolds told him about his life. For many of the facts, therefore, we have only Malone's word to go on. He claims, for example, that Reynolds told him he wasted three years (from the age of nineteen to twenty-two) at his Devonshire home after having spent two years studying under the portrait painter, Thomas Hudson: it was 'as so much time thrown away ... as related to a knowledge of the world and of mankind', and 'he ever afterwards lamented the loss.' Reynolds' biographers in the early nineteenth century were reluctant to believe this, but Henry Beechey in 1846 was inclined to give Malone the benefit of the doubt because he was a first-hand witness and because Malone was Malone: 'we shall probably be inclined to attach more credit to the assertion of Mr. Malone, than on a first view of the subject appears to be consistent with fact ... for his veracity cannot be doubted.' Malone's personal recollections are especially valuable when they touch on Johnson and The Club.[63] Writing of Reynolds' first meeting with Johnson, he observes that Reynolds was 'lucky enough',

[61] *Burke Corr.*, IX, pp. 328–29.
[62] Ms. Malone 26, fol. 151. See Malone to F. Reynolds, 3 May 1797 (OFB 25.124).
[63] Reynolds, *Works*, I, pp. xlv–xlvii, xlix.

to make a remark...which was so much above the common-place style of conversation, that Johnson at once perceived that Reynolds was in the habit of thinking for himself. The ladies were regretting the death of a friend, to whom they owed great obligations; upon which Reynolds observed, 'You have, however, the comfort of being relieved from the burthen of gratitude.' They were shocked a little at this alleviating suggestion, as too selfish; but Johnson defended it in his clear and forcible manner, and was much pleased with the *mind*, the fair view of human nature, which it exhibited, like some of the reflections of Rochefaucault. The consequence was, that he went home with Reynolds, and supped with him.

It is in this vein, for which Malone drew heavily from his journal, that the *Account* moves leisurely along.[64]

There is a modest amount of art criticism in the narrative as well, although most of it is limited to Reynolds' abilities as a history painter. Trying to come to terms with the expression of feelings in Reynolds' pictures, Malone observes that painters before him had been unable to endow their paintings with 'a historic air', the very quality he had helped Copley achieve in his painting of Charles I entering Parliament. Reynolds, however, showed 'how much animation might be obtained by deviating from the insipid manner of his immediate predecessors.' It was 'in the historical department [that] he took a wider range; and by his successful exertions in that higher branch of his art, he has not only enriched various cabinets at home, but extended the fame of the English School to foreign countries.' As he himself had been painted by Reynolds, he writes that instead of 'confining himself to mere likeness... he dived, as it were, into the mind, and habits, and manners, of those who sat to him.'[65] While this is thoughtful and suggestive, and reiterates his notion that historical painting is the 'higher branch' of the art, Malone knew little about the technicalities of portrait painting and, wisely, is reluctant to write about them.

He is also reluctant to identify the formative influences on Reynolds' work, although he finds 'a few slight hints' from the artist's papers about how he attained excellence in his profession – passages which he was 'unwilling to suppress'.[66] While that is about as far as he is willing to go as an art critic, William Blake thought even that was too far. In his copy of Malone's edition (now in the British Library), Blake impatiently scribbled several combative comments next to Malone's occasional attempts at art criticism. For example, when Malone remarks that Reynolds excelled as a colourist but did not produce 'so brilliant an effect of colour' as the Venetians did, Blake carped, 'Why are we told that Reynolds is a great Colourist and yet inferior to the Venetians'? Or when Malone remarks that Reynolds 'laboured as hard with his pencil, as any mechanick working at

[64] Reynolds, *Works*, 2nd edn., I, pp. xxvi–xxvii; *Literary Works of Sir Joshua Reynolds*, ed. Beechey, pp. 46–48.   [65] Reynolds, *Works*, 2nd edn., pp. lxi–lxii, xxiii–xxiv.
[66] Ibid., I, p. lvii.

his trade for bread', Blake sneered, 'The Man who does not Labour more
than the hireling must be a poor Devil.'[67]

Blake initiated the literary depreciation of Reynolds' art, and it is more
instructive to read his comments in that light than as a frontal assault on
Malone's incompetence as an art critic. But his resentment over Reynolds'
authority and the neo-classical principles he represented was fanned by the
authority of Malone's edition – 'The Book' that a recent critic has
described as authoritative in its way as Malone's Shakespeare.[68] For most
readers, Malone's edition comprised, as he himself puts it, 'the whole
science and practice of painting.' Even Henry Fuseli advised his audience
at the Royal Academy to consult Malone's edition: 'His volumes can never
be consulted without profit, and should never be quitted by the student's
hand...'[69]

Probably the most valuable feature of Malone's *Account* is his use of
autobiographical manuscripts that he was lucky to find among Reynolds'
papers. 'I have found some detached and unconnected thoughts', he
announces, 'written occasionally, as hints for a Discourse, on a new and
singular plan, which he appears, at a late period of his life, to have had in
contemplation to compose, and deliver to the Academy; and which he
seems to have intended as a history of his mind, so far as concerned his art,
and of his progress, studies, and practice...'[70] As many of these were
unpolished and unquotable, Malone had to revise them in order to include
them.[71] The problem is that since Malone did not tell the reader where he
altered Reynolds' prose, many of the extracts have been reproduced into
our own times as entirely Reynolds.'

Malone's publisher, Cadell, paid Malone three hundred pounds for the
copyright to the first quarto edition, but Malone did not pocket a shilling
of it. From the beginning of the project, he intended to waive his right to
some or all of the money in favour of a proposed fund to raise a monument
for Reynolds opposite Johnson's in St Paul's. Burke believed that was what
Malone should do. If he thought of the edition as entirely his own work,
Burke told him, then 'in common justice the money is your property'; but
Burke felt that as an executor the right thing for him to do was hold the
proceeds 'in trust' for the monument. He asked Malone to suggest the idea
tactfully to Lady Inchiquin: 'You remember that after his death it was
talked of in his Club, and in a manner resolved upon that a monument

---

[67] On Blake's marginalia, see Lipking, *The Ordering of the Arts*, pp. 164–69. Blake's marginalia have
been published in *The Complete Writings of William Blake*, ed. G. L. Keynes, 1957.
[68] Lipking, *The Ordering of the Arts*, p. 165.
[69] Fuseli, *Lectures on Painting, delivered at the Royal Academy* (1820), p. 446.
[70] Reynolds, *Works*, 2nd edn., I, pp. xii–xiii.
[71] On Malone's revisions, see Reynolds, *Works*, 2nd edn., I, pp. xiv–xx. See Hilles, *The Literary
Career of Sir Joshua Reynolds*, p. 196, for a comparison of one of Reynolds's manuscript passages
and Malone's published revision of it.

should be erected for him, the basis of which should be laid in the subscriptions of the Club.' To get things going, Burke said he was ready to subscribe a hundred pounds. Lady Inchiquin had received the lion's share of Reynolds' estate and in 1795–96 realized an additional fifteen thousand pounds from the sale of his collection of masters and his own works,[72] but she insisted that the monument should be raised from public subscription, not huge private donations. Like Burke, she offered a hundred pounds, and with the three hundred pounds from Cadell this took them one-third of the way toward the cost of the monument.[73]

Years later, in 1805, Malone told Percy he had put Cadell's three hundred pounds 'into the Stocks; to gather and make a fund to come in aid of this Monument, whenever it could be effected. – Without this, the Subscription of the Club would go but a little way.'[74] In fact, the subscription had gone nowhere for eight years. The Club, not for the first time, was unsuccessful in raising money, and Malone himself seemed to forget about the project. In June 1803, Lady Inchiquin (now Lady Thomond) complained to Farington of Malone 'delaying to forward the business' of the monument.[75] She was right, Malone had lost interest, but this was because getting people to reach into their pockets for donations had never appealed to him. Also, his work on Dryden had intervened from 1797 to 1800, and the urgency he was beginning to feel about his Shakespearean research made him even less inclined to spend time raising money.

Finally, in 1805, Lady Thomond nudged him into action. When Nollekens declined to sculpt the monument, she arranged for John Flaxman to do it for £1,100. Then she pushed Farington to ask Malone (as executor) to have the Royal Academy obtain from the Dean and Chapter of St Paul's permission to use 'the 4th Place under the Dome for a Monument to Sir Joshua.' Farington recorded Malone's remark in January 1805, that he 'had not found an opportunity to move the Literary Club on the subject, but had spoke to several of them separately.'[76] After some more lobbying at The Club and an advertisement in the St James's Chronicle, the money began to trickle in while Flaxman worked on the model.[77] 'I think it promises well', Malone wrote to Percy; Flaxman was 'immediately to proceed on the work itself; but I imagine it will take near two years to execute.'[78] Two years later, in March 1807, the completed sculpture was approved by Malone,

[72] See DF, II, 299, 361, 432–33, 493–94; and Malone to Threadway Russell Nash, 6 July 1796 (Worcester College library, Oxford).
[73] To Malone, 4 May 1797, Burke Corr., IX, p. 328.
[74] 19 March 1805, P–M Letters, p. 168. See also 11 June 1805, DF, VII, p. 2573.
[75] 28 June 1803, DF, VI, p. 2066–67.   [76] DF, 31 January 1805, VII, p. 2507.
[77] 7 July 1806, P–M Letters, pp. 208.
[78] Malone to Percy, 6 May 1807, P–M Letters, pp. 221–22. See Flaxman's account book, 1 September 1808 (Walpole Society, 42 (1940), 92).

Metcalfe, and Lady Thomond, and it was exhibited to the public at Somerset House that year. Flaxman may have finished it in two years, but the monument was not erected until 1813, sadly the year after Malone's death.

Malone's 'homage' to Reynolds, then, continued in one way or another until the end of his life. For no other friend in the Johnson circle did he continue his 'service' for so long and with such affection. It was another way of keeping alive those personal memories that in the new century appeared to him as a vanished 'golden age.'

4

Except for the publication of Reynolds' *Works*, the year 1797 was generally gloomy for Malone. There were rebellions in Ireland, which disturbed and frustrated him deeply, and Burke, Walpole, and Farmer all died that year. He could not remember a more dispiriting year. 'I begin to think I shall see every one I ever loved drop into the grave', he complained to Windham.[79] As he was not an executor of Burke's estate, he could do little more than attend his funeral, for which Burke's wife invited him to be a pallbearer. Burney asked Malone to accompany him in his carriage, noting his regret 'that the bones of our illustrious friend should not honour Westminster Abbey.' They travelled together, first to the Duke of Portland's home at Bulstrode, then to Beaconsfield for the funeral, and then back to Bulstrode where they dined with Windham, Portland, and the Duke of Devonshire.[80] They all felt, as Malone told Farington, that Pitt 'should have moved for a Monument to Burke.' As he did not, and as it was beyond Malone's resources to organize another subscription, Burke, unlike Johnson and Reynolds, would never have such a memorial.[81]

But even if Malone had tried to raise interest in a monument for Burke, he probably would have failed. Even many of his friends did not share his wholehearted devotion to Burke and his political ideas. Charlemont, for one, judged Burke more objectively than Malone: 'His heart was excellent. His abilities were supernatural; and a deficiency in prudence and political wisdom alone could have kept him within the rank of mortals!' Charlemont could also see that Malone's political ideas, like Burke's, were 'too gloomy, and, as everyone must in times like these be somewhat prejudiced, your criterion is by no means a certain one.' Malone thought 'too much and too deeply of politics', which could not help but be 'extremely unwholesome to a man who, like you, loves his country and loves mankind.'[82] His hostility

[79] 12 June 1798, BL Add. Ms. 37854, fol. 144 (*Windham Papers*, II, p. 73). See Malone's letter to Charlemont on 29 July 1796, *HMC*, XIII, 8, p. 277.
[80] Burney's letter is at Brigham Young University.   [81] 19 July 1797, *DF*, III, p. 874.
[82] 21 March 1796, 19 August, 9 October 1797, *HMC*, XIII, 8, pp. 271, 281, 308.

towards insurrection was so intense, Charlemont thought, that he could not tell the difference between constructive and destructive causes. For years, the two men had disagreed over how to deal with the Irish rebellions. In 1794–95, radicalism in Ireland had begun to evolve from a constitutional to an underground movement, with radicals looking increasingly to France for help. Malone was for putting down rebellions wherever they raised their spectral heads, whereas Charlemont, who lived in Ireland, felt that the best way to defuse the tension was to address the causes and experiment by making concessions – something Pitt's government was set against. 'Your ministers, or rather minister, seems neither to care for, think of, nor indeed to know Ireland', he wrote impatiently in October 1794. They are 'teazing [*sic*] us into a fever.'[83] What was needed was new measures, new concessions, and (above all) new ministers. By October 1797, Ireland had almost reached the boiling point, but Charlemont realized he and his old friend had to agree to disagree: 'But no more of politics. I do not much like writing to you on a subject where, though in the main I am sure we think alike, we do not entirely agree.'[84]

Malone remained intransigent. One letter he wrote to Windham in June 1798, urging him to be less moderate in denouncing the radicals, is remarkable for its dislike of the Irish Catholic peasantry, whom he insists cannot be likened to the English peasantry. The 'lower Irish' could not be 'managed' the way the 'lower English' are; if attempted, the policy would end in 'delusion and ruin', for they are 'a cunning, false, perjured, ferocious and sanguinary people', and have been such for centuries. The only thing to do was 'bind them up' and maintain those old laws which have kept the peace and which the government in the past twenty years have been repealing by way of appeasement. Windham replied in exasperation, 'Suppose I admit that they are what you describe, what can be done? You would not have us kill them all.'[85] One thing Malone did, of which Windham doubtless approved since it was a literary effort, was to revise and help publish Charles Jackson's *A Narrative of the Sufferings and Escape of Charles Jackson* (1798). Malone saw this as a way to vindicate his opinions on the Irish peasantry, for in his work Jackson publicized the rebels' massacre of ninety-five people on the bridge at Wexford in June 1798, and exposed the consequences in Ireland of 'wild, irrational French notions of liberty and equality' – a phrase such as Malone might have written himself. Malone even recommended a second edition and provided notes for it.[86]

---

[83] Charlemont to Malone, 29 October 1794, *HMC*, XIII, 8, p. 251.
[84] Charlemont to Malone, 9 October 1797, *HMC*, XIII, 8, p. 281.
[85] 12 June 1798, *Windham Papers*, p. 73.
[86] See *DF*, III, p. 1050. Letters to Malone from Ireland during the 1798 rebellion are in Ms. Malone 39.

After the fighting capacity of the insurgents was brutally destroyed by the middle of July 1798, the government at Westminster resolved to incorporate Ireland fully into Great Britain. But Malone, in a minority among his English friends, was against Union: 'Malone disapproves the Idea', Farington wrote in his diary for 19 August, 'as derogatory from the dignity of Ireland, and, in his opinion, not likely to produce [benefits] which by some are supposed.'[87] After heated debate, especially in Ireland, in the closing months of 1798 and over most of 1799, the Act of Union was passed in 1801. Malone, like most its opponents, was quickly reconciled to it.

Thus ended a decade of revolution and rebellion. By midsummer, 1798, Malone's sense of achievement over his 1790 *Shakespeare* had faded and increasingly seemed irrecoverable. He had been diverted from his variorum edition by political events, seemingly endless biographical research on Shakespeare, work on the Aubrey manuscripts, the preparation of a new edition of Boswell's *Life of Johnson*, forgeries, and services on behalf of Reynolds. Now was the time to take up the Shakespeare edition and bring it out forthwith.

[87] See *DF*, III, pp. 1045, 1047–51.

12

John Dryden and the closing of the century

1

Back in October 1796, Malone reassured Charlemont that he was going to abandon every other project and concentrate on his biography of Shakespeare, 'lest by any fatality I should be prevented from completing it', and that after that he would devote himself to 'Dryden's prose, with a few curious original letters of his.'[1] The Dryden project was in his mind at least by June 1793, when he mentioned it in a *Gentleman's Magazine* advertisement.[2] By 1798, Dryden had priority over Shakespeare. The magnitude of the Shakespeare biography and the variorum edition daunted him and publication in the near future seemed highly unlikely. It was better to get into print more quickly with Dryden, even though, as his remark to Charlemont about a 'fatality' suggests, he knew it was risky to use his declining energy and tired eyes on Dryden instead of Shakespeare. Still, his desire to publish some original research as soon as possible prevailed, and by August 1798, he was pulling out all the stops in the cause of Dryden.

Malone decided in favour of Dryden at this juncture because Joseph Warton was already preparing a complete edition of Pope's works eventually published in 1797 – at just about the time Malone began to concentrate on Dryden. He made the decision even though he was convinced that Warton was an incompetent scholar who was bound to produce an inferior edition, and his work was, indeed, poorly received. All Burney could find to say about it when Warton died in 1800 was that 'his bitterness against one of the founders of the Club, Dr. Johnson, is disgraceful. Indeed there is little new in his notes, but his endeavours to depreciate and invalidate every opinion of that literary & moral giant.'[3] William Lisle Bowles, a clergyman, produced a ten-volume edition of Pope in 1806, but Malone liked it no more than Warton's. To Percy he wrote: 'instead of applying himself to discover the numerous allusions, and the characters and names of the persons referred to, in the Moral Essays and

---

[1] 29 July 1796, *HMC*, XIII, 8, p. 277.   [2] *Gentleman's Magazine*, LXII (June 1793), 536.
[3] To J. C. Walker, 2 February 1801 (Bernard Quaritch Catalogue no. 429).

Imitations of Horace more particularly, [Bowles] wearies the reader with endless conjectures about the poet and L[ad]y Mary W. Montagu, and Martha and Teresa Blount.' Instead of 'ascertaining *facts*, and tracing exactly when each piece appeared, and what variations the author made', he has served up a collection of 'fanciful hypotheses.' He has managed to come up with some new Pope letters, but the whole collection is 'most miserably arranged', 'those written in 1738 or 1740 being very frequently *followed* by others written in 1715 or earlier.' For Malone, the only rational method of printing letters was chronological, 'without the least relation to the persons by whom they are written, or to whom they are addressed. They thus become a kind of History.'[4] The tasks of the editor and biographer ought to be complementary, with those of the former leading naturally to those of the latter.

By October 1797, Malone was well into editing Dryden's prose works. Ritson heard about his work, as well as about Warton's plans for an edition of Dryden's poetry,[5] and could not resist quipping to Joseph Cooper Walker, 'It is say'd, indeed, that Dr. Warton is about to edit the poetical works of Dryden; & that Mr. Malone, who does not understand poetry, is to superintend his prefaces & prose. *Par nobile patrum!* [a noble pair of elders!]'.[6] Charlemont was more encouraging: 'I long to see your edition of Dryden's prose works, as I know of no compositions in our language which better deserve such an editor.'[7]

From October 1797 to publication, Malone relied heavily on his old friend James Bindley, Senior Commissioner of Stamp Duties, for research help. Bindley not only had access to many records at the Stamp Office but also owned a fine library of rare books, which included the huge annotated collection of Dryden's contemporary Narcissus Luttrell. Bindley used it frequently to extract this or that detail for Malone, at times also transcribing lengthy passages for him. He served, in effect, as Malone's research assistant, saving him a huge amount of library work.[8]

Once he started writing, he fed the printer with copy throughout the autumn of 1797 and into the next year at the same time as he searched for Dryden letters to help him annotate the prose works. By late summer 1798, he had found enough letters to make a prominent feature of them in the

[4] 11 August 1807, *P–M Letters*, pp. 230–31. Bowles had asked Malone for help with his edition in 1803 (Ms. Malone 38, fol. 122).
[5] See Warton's letter to Davies, 26 September 1797 (Bodleian, Ms. Eng. Lit. d. 74, fols. 142–43).
[6] Ritson to Walker, 13 October 1798, OFB 33.27.
[7] 9 October 1797, *HMC*, XIII, 8, p. 310.
[8] In the Advertisement to his edition, Malone praised Bindley's 'urbanity, classical taste, and various knowledge, [which] are only exceeded by his great liberality in the communication of the very curious materials for literary history, and the illustration of temporary allusions, which his valuable library contains' (*The Critical and Miscellaneous Prose Works of John Dryden ... and An Account of the Life and Writings of the Author*, ed. Edmond Malone (1800), I, p. v). Malone–Bindley correspondence on Dryden is in Ms.Malone 38.

edition. 'I mean to prefix to the collection of Dryden's prose-works', he informed Burney in August, 'as many of his letters as I can find. I have collected about a dozen either in print or MS., beside a considerable parcel of those which passed between him and old [Jacob] Tonson, his bookseller, with which I have been favoured by Mr. [William] Baker, member for Hertfordshire, who is Tonson's heir.'[9] Baker's Dryden–Tonson letters were a windfall. There were seventeen, none of which had ever been published before; they comprised the largest single collection of the poet's letters he would ever find. He also received a batch from John Nichols.[10] These encouraged him to revive his idea of writing biographically about Dryden, though (always wary of competing with Johnson) he had in mind only a few brief 'authentick & new Notices', as he told Burney, because 'after Dr. Johnson's admirable Recount, it would be great presumption to think of writing a new regular Life of him.'[11]

In October 1798, attacks of rheumatism stopped Malone in his tracks and he was compelled to seek relief at Cheltenham for six weeks. Cheltenham, however, was dull and ineffectual. Bindley commiserated and wished him back home in London: 'As I did not hear from you I concluded that Cheltenham afforded nothing to tell, & thinking your proposed stay there, nearly elapsed, almost expected to see you walk in some Evening to your Bohea, in the usual manner, & find me with my legs crost, & purring to myself like a cat in the chimney corner.'[12] Bindley's convivial bohea and conversation would have appealed to him, but he decided first to try four weeks of the healing waters of Bath, where he must have recalled with sadness his mother's desperate and unsuccessful effort to recover her health more than forty years earlier. Michael Kearney wrote to him there on 29 November: 'I shall be happy in hearing that you are free'd from those gouty symptoms you complain'd of, and can give your time to Dryden without such disagreeable interruption.' He recommended 'the use of fleecy hosiery for your rheumatic complaint... Do try it on the part affected. It is to be got at No. 99 Holborn.'[13]

Whether it was the hosiery, the waters, or a change in scene or attitude, he was back in London on 4 January 1799, relieved of his rheumatism, announcing to Nichols, 'Dryden['s] Prose is all printed, and the publication only waits for some account of him.'[14] 'Some account' was Malone's cautious way of describing any improvement on Johnson, which as he told Bishop John Douglas 'is extremely hazardous; nor should I attempt it, but that I am enabled, by the aid of authentic documents, to verify several

---

[9] See *DPW*, I:i, pp. iii–iv; Malone to Baker, 26 April 1800 (Beinecke, Ij. D848).
[10] Nichols to Malone, 13 February 1798, Ms. Malone 39, fol. 144.
[11] 21 August 1798, Folger, uncatalogued.   [12] Ms. Malone 38, fols. 33–34.
[13] Ms. Malone 39, fols. 23–24.
[14] 4 January 1799, Folger, uncatalogued; printed in Nichols, *Illustrations*, V, p. 465.

mistakes which have been transmitted from book to book relative to him.'
He promised that in every point he was striving 'to procure the best
intelligence that the nature of the subject would admit ... '[15] Over the next
four months he worked diligently, gathering further material, organizing it,
and (the most difficult part for him) writing it. He was determined not to
let the biography delay publication of the edition indefinitely, as his
biographical work on Shakespeare was doing to his variorum edition. His
friends, too, were looking for early publication. In March, Bindley again
tempted him with bohea, 'whenever it suits you to look in upon me, & shall
be glad to hear you say you have finished your work.'[16] He hoped to
publish by the end of May.[17]

Two letters from Lady Elizabeth Dryden on 20 and 30 April, however,
upset his schedule.[18] Dryden's great-great niece, Lady Elizabeth, lived at
Canons Ashby, the Dryden family estate in Northamptonshire; she was
also an acquaintance of Malone's sister-in-law. As a last-minute thought, he
had written to her on 12 April, explaining he was on the verge of publishing
a *Life* of her famous ancestor and asking if there were any old family papers,
including letters, relating to him at Canons Ashby that she might let him
see. 'It gives me the highest satisfaction', she responded on 20 April, 'to
find that such an able pen as yours is employed upon a subject very worthy
of it, that of the life of a great master of poetry and an exalted genius', but
she had bad news: there was nothing she knew of at Canons Ashby that
bore 'the least trace of having been in Mr. J. Dryden's family.' However,
she explained what she knew about her family, the poet's son who briefly
inherited Canons Ashby and the family title, and the poet's own farm at
nearby Blakesley, and assured him she would look through some of the
steward's books from the beginning of the century as soon as she got over
her cold, for 'they are locked up with other writings in a cold place.'
Nothing turned up, though on 30 April she was more optimistic: 'I have
heard that several pictures, letters, and manuscripts of the poet's were at
Chesterton in Huntingdonshire, the seat of Sir Robert Douglas' brother
[Robert Pigott], with whom the poet was on very friendly terms.'[19]

He followed up this lead immediately. He asked an acquaintance in
Shrewsbury, The Revd. John Brickdale Blakeway, who at the time was also
contributing notes to the third edition of Boswell's *Life of Johnson* that
Malone had under way, to enquire after the Pigotts, descendants of the

[15] BL, Egerton 2186, fols. 104–5.   [16] Ms. Malone 38, fol. 85. This letter is undated.
[17] See his letter to William Forbes, 17 April 1799, in an extra-illustrated volume, *The Life and Correspondence of David Garrick*, V, p. xxi, TS 937.3, Harvard Theatre Collection, Harvard College Library.
[18] On Malone's correspondence with descendants of the Dryden family in 1799, see James M. Osborn, *John Dryden: Some Biographical Facts and Problems* (1940), pp. 46–49.
[19] *The Collection of Autograph Letters and Historical Documents formed by Alfred Morrison* (2nd ser., 1896), privately printed, III, pp. 156–59.

Dryden family. Blakeway, whose family had worked as servants to the Pigotts at Chesterton in the early part of the century, discovered that a sister of the last Pigott to own Chesterton, Miss Honour Pigott of Bath, was said 'to have several papers relative to their great relations.'[20] Malone dashed off a letter to her and then waited for three painfully long weeks before he had a reply, in the meantime looking into other sources of Dryden letters and asking people to inspect the records at Westminster School and Trinity College, Cambridge,[21] for traces of the poet's years there. Not for the first time, he was torn between two impulses: on the one hand, the pressure to write and publish, so that he could return to Shakespeare; on the other, the desire to hunt for still more scraps of information. Mrs Pigott's reply, when it arrived on 31 May, disappointed him: too much family gossip and too few facts. But as an afterthought she slipped in the information that a Mrs Gwillim in Whitechurch, Herefordshire, owned several of Dryden's letters, or so at least she thought; and that a painting of the poet by Sir Godfrey Kneller had been in the possession of her elder sister, but owing to a quarrel when the family sold the Chesterton estates in 1777 her eldest brother 'moved the Picture & we have not been able since to know where it is which we most Anxiously wish to do.'[22] She remembered as a young girl gazing at it often with pleasure and that it was 'a Half length and large wig, with a wreath of Bay In His Hand.'[23]

The prospect of finding a cache of Dryden's letters was enticing enough to justify delaying publication for at least a few more weeks. In the meantime, growing bolder, he pushed ahead with an extended biography, busily fed the printer, and read proofs. When Boswell's son, Alexander, saw him on 5 June, he told Forbes he was 'very busy with a Book which he hopes to get out in about three weeks.' 'I made my stay short', he added, 'as the Devil was at his door with a proof sheet.' To Sir William Musgrave, just retired as Curator of the British Museum, Malone confessed on the same day that he has been 'so busily employed by the Life of Dryden which is now printing, that I have not for some time had a moment to spare.' On 11 June, Bindley, chiding him for not writing his name in valuable books from his library that he lent out, fretted that he had not seen his friend for some time: 'I presume you have determined not to see me again, till you can say "Iamque opus exegi" [I have now completed the work] &c. I hope illness had not prevented you, & then all is right.' Malone managed to attend the Club dinners fairly regularly, but few caught sight of him at other times

[20] To Malone, 8 May 1799, Ms. Malone 27, fols. 41–43.
[21] William Lort Mansel, Vice-Chancellor of Cambridge University, informed Malone of Dryden entries in the Trinity College records for 1652 and 1655 (Ms. Malone 27, fols. 165–66); see also Ms. Malone 27, fols. 167–68.   [22] 31 May 1799, Ms. Malone 27, fols. 144–46.
[23] 15 June 1799, Ms. Malone 27, fols. 147–50.

during these weeks.[24] For the first time in a decade, he was working briskly and fluently on a major project.

Mrs Pigott kept saying she would arrange for him to see Miss Gwillim's Dryden letters, but he could not wait for her. He sought out Mrs Ann Ord, her relative and one of the original 'Blue Stockings', who as it happened lived near to him in Queen Anne Street East.[25] On 13 May, Mrs Ord informed him that only one box of letters had survived, the rest at Chesterton having been destroyed when the family 'removed from the Old Mansion.'[26] Eventually, after several agonizing months of waiting, on 10 October he received from Miss Gwillim (via Mrs Ord) a box containing 'all the Letters from the Poet Dryden now to be found among his family papers.' He also received from her, again passed on by Mrs Ord, particulars of the family that he quickly (and awkwardly) slipped into his biography. Mrs Ord thought too much fuss had been made over the sixteen letters, that they would not be 'so interesting as might have been expected',[27] but one critic has judged that 'they reveal a side of Dryden's personality to be observed nowhere else. If Malone had not run them to earth, it is quite possible that they would have been dispersed before ever reaching the hands of an editor.'[28]

Flushed with this success, Malone turned to Knole Castle next. He believed he would find among the Dorset Papers at Knole Dryden's letters to the poet Charles Sackville, the sixth Earl of Dorset, patron of poets and a favourite of Charles II. Dryden praised Sackville's poetry in 'Of Dramatick Poesy' and dedicated several poems to him. Malone was convinced that Dryden's letters to him, if he could find any of them, would provide a rich harvest. 'I had a notion that something valuable might be found in that repository; (particularly concerning Dryden)', he told Percy in 1802, 'and about three years ago, got a friend to apply to the Duchess on the subject, (the Duke being then in a state of dotage) ... '[29] The Duchess initially gave him permission to search through the Knole archives, but when he followed up the invitation and contacted William Wraxall, later created a baronet but then acting as a resident literary advisor or secretary for Her Grace, the door was slammed in his face. Wraxall maintained that the Duchess planned to publish the Dorset papers herself and did not fancy sacrificing the collection, or any Dryden letters that may be in it, 'in order to enrich another Work.' Dryden letters, 'if such should be found, (for hitherto only three have appeared)', would be published along with those of Suckling, Prior, Shadwell, and 'many other eminent Persons of the last

[24] 5 June 1799, Fettercairn, Box 87, no. 65; Ms. Malone 27, fols. 88–89; Ms. Malone 38, fol. 37.
[25] Malone helped Burney publish 'Memoirs and Character of the late Mrs. Ord', *Gentleman's Magazine*, LXXVII (July 1808), 581–83.   [26] Ms. Malone 27, fol. 175v.
[27] Ms. Malone 27, fol. 177. Malone's correspondence with Mrs Ord is in Ms. Malone 27, fols. 104, 175, 192.   [28] Osborn, *F&P*, p. 48.   [29] 28 October 1802, *P–M Letters*, p. 107.

Century.' That was blunt enough, but Malone smelled a rat. When he insisted he had the Duchess' permission, Wraxall replied coolly, 'I put your Letters to me, & my Reply, into the Duchess's hands, before they were sent. I forward this Letter, from *Knole*, which, I dare say, will be a satisfactory Proof to you of the Duchess's Participation in, & Approbation of my present Answer.'[30] Malone, who did not think it was satisfactory proof at all, suspected that Wraxall wanted to publish the papers himself and was denying him access to the collection on his own initiative. He was right. Wraxall's days at Knole were numbered. He was soon dismissed and control of the papers devolved on Lord Whitworth, who had married the Countess. Whitworth, however, was no more helpful. He told Malone he had recovered the papers from 'the plagiaristick hands of Mr. Wraxall' and was keeping them to himself until he could publish them. In any case, he doubted there were 'any letters of Shakspeare, or any materials interesting to Mr. Malone, with a view to the work he has in hand.'[31] Malone never saw the manuscripts; nor did anyone else publish any portion of them in his lifetime. If he had, he would have found much material to shine light on Dryden's period. It fell to later scholars to find it.

He wrote to several other great country houses where he hoped that Dryden letters in tidy bundles might be lying undiscovered or forgotten in trunks, chests, or cabinets. His failures, which far outnumbered his successes, were galling because while no one besides Lord Whitworth, Wraxall and William Bromley actually refused him permission to see archival documents, several owners of collections did not even bother to reply.[32] His frustration is evident in the list of 'Persons in whose Cabinets letters written by Dryden may probably be found' that he appended to his biography of Dryden. 'If they would but search their family papers', he moaned, he was sure much more could be discovered and preserved about the poet for future biographers.[33] 'It is wonderful how careless some of our most ancient families have been in these matters', he told Percy.[34]

One good cache of Dryden letters eluded him for the first edition, but after publication he went after it again with Percy's help. It belonged to William Bromley, whose name he included in his appended list. He knew Bromley had at least three or four letters from Dryden to William Walsh, the critic and poet and friend of Pope, but he could not persuade Bromley to let him see them. His inclusion of Bromley's name in the list, however, caught Percy's eye, who knew Bromley well and immediately offered to intervene.[35] Malone told Percy that he knew, not merely suspected, that

---

[30] Ms. Malone 27, fols. 171–72.
[31] Arthur O'Neill Collection, NLS; see Prior, pp. 271–72.
[32] See Ms. Malone 27 for a collection of such letters.
[33] *DPW*, I:i, Appendix V, pp. iv, 567–69.   [34] *P–M Letters*, p. 124.
[35] 8 September 1800, *P–M Letters*, p. 77.

Bromley owned three or four letters, that he had applied to him through a friend, and that he had been turned down. Another attempt by Percy would be splendid, only it must be done subtly: 'I believe the best way will be, not to state any thing of a former application having been made to him, but to take up the matter *de novo*, and by way of inquiry, &c.' The problem was that Bromley 'has got a strange notion that publishing Letters of this kind is a kind of invasion of the rights of the dead: so, to overcome that prejudice will be the great point to be laboured.' This could be done by letting him see that Dryden's letters to Walsh 'would appear in good company' and that others, even descendants of the poet, felt no such reluctance. Even Dr William Vyse, the Archdeacon of Coventry, for example, had recently given him a few letters from Dr Johnson to his mother for his next edition of Boswell's *Life of Johnson* (1804). And while he was on the subject of Johnson, there was no better authority on the matter: 'Johnson himself, I am sure, would have had no doubt on such a question; for he always maintained that the instruction of the *living* was not to be sacrificed to refinements of this kind.'[36] 'I hope your Lordship may find the *mollia tempora fandi* [an opportune time for speaking]', he added, 'for these letters would be a valuable accession to my book, if I should live to give another edition of it.'[37]

Thanks to Percy, Bromley turned out to be so accommodating and amiable that Malone could not understand why 'he had not given them *at first*' so that they could have been included in the first edition. Bromley owned more letters than Malone thought. Five he sent right away, followed by five more a few days later that Malone 'with great difficulty dug' out of two old commonplace books, the handwriting of which was so miserable that 'the sagacity of an Oedipus is requisite to decypher every second word.'[38] The effort cost his eyes, but it was a valuable accession, Malone's last great discovery of Drydeniana.

2

Slowed down by the mass of biographical material that his enquiries and the correspondence produced, Malone's publication date receded. 'The Life of Dryden creeps slowly on', he reported to Burney on 15 August 1799; 'it will make with the assistance of his Letters, a small Volume.'[39] Three months later, he was still no nearer publication. By this time, people were looking forward to the biography more than to the prose works. Distressed that Malone had spent the entire summer in London working when he should have 'invigorated' his health by 'amusing excursions' in the countryside, John Kearney admitted on 19 November that even after

---

[36] Hill-Powell, II, p. 60.   [37] 13 September 1800, *P–M Letters*, pp. 81–82.
[38] 2 June 1802, *P–M Letters*, pp. 95–96.   [39] 15 August 1799, Folger, uncatalogued.

Johnson's *Life* he had 'always desired a more full account' of Dryden. 'Your work will form a more strictly biographical view' than Johnson's, he added.[40] Bishop Douglas wrote to him on 10 November that he hoped to meet him in St James's Street after Christmas, 'by which time your Life of Dryden will, probably, be ready for the Amusement of the Public.'[41] It was not.

In January, he was still trying to accommodate new information he was receiving from, among others, Mansell about Dryden's Cambridge days and Burney about musical matter.[42] By 6 February, he felt hopeful enough to allow, 'I have almost finish'd my task; but have still 70 or 80 pages of *Letters* to print. They are extremely curious.'[43] Three more months passed. On the first day of May, the edition at last appeared, priced at two guineas for the four volumes.[44] Sending Burney word on 28 April that an advance copy awaited his commands, he exulted, 'I feel very light and airy at present, and intend to be an idle *Bond Street* gentleman for this month to come.'[45]

In his Advertisement to the edition, Malone sums up his sense of achievement as a biographer:

by inquiries and researches in every quarter where information was likely to be obtained, I have procured more materials than my most sanguine expectations had promised; which if they do not exhibit so many particulars concerning this great poet as could be desired, have yet furnished us with some curious and interesting notices, and cleared away much confusion and errour [*sic*]; and enabled me to ascertain several circumstances of his life and fortunes, which were either unknown, or for almost a century the subject of uncertain speculation and conjectures.

Two of his chief objectives are apparent in this passage. One was his intention to expose the errors in many of the accepted stories about Dryden, several of which, unlike those about Shakespeare he discredited, were conceived and circulated to malign Dryden. In a manner reminiscent of his attacks in 1790 on spurious stories about Shakespeare, he writes, 'Unfortunately, all of the accounts of Dryden and his works were one continued tissue of inaccuracy, errour [*sic*], and falsehood. Very little had been handed down, and of that little the greater part was untrue.'[46] The other objective was his determination to publish anything he turned up that had any bearing on the poet's life and work.

These two objectives account for two other features of the edition: its attacks on the perpetrators of the falsehoods, whenever he can identify them, argued with his usual common sense and a parade of virtually

[40] Ms. Malone 39, fols. 33–34.   [41] Ms. Malone 27, fol. 153.
[42] See Malone to Burney, 21 August and 30 December 1799 (Folger).
[43] Malone to Dr Burney, 6 February 1800, Folger, C.a.2 (6).
[44] Advertised in *St. James's Chronicle*, 29 April (6601), and published 1 May.
[45] 28 April 1800, Folger, c.a.2 (7).   [46] *DPW*, I:i, pp. vi, 2.

unassailable facts; and a distracting surfeit of detail that at its best provides historical perspectives of a kind scarcely ever before linked to critical discussions of literary figures, and at its worst needlessly interrupts the narrative and wearies the reader. The tone of both the *Life* and the notes to the prose works becomes alternatively indignant and erudite, aggressive and scholarly, digressive and urgent, boring and dramatic, reflecting the conflicting personality traits of Malone as gentleman, lawyer, meticulous scholar, exposer of frauds, and angry denunciator and political polemicist.

The *Life of Dryden* is the most thoroughly researched literary biography written up to that time. Malone's sources, extensive and diverse, included the Ballard, Rawlinson, and Aubrey manuscripts at Oxford – with which his old friend The Revd. John Price, the Bodleian Librarian, was enormously helpful; the Royal, Harleian, Sloane, Birch, and Rymer manuscripts at the British Museum – a short walk from home; and the writings and reminiscences of Dryden contemporaries such as Anthony à Wood, Francis Lockier, Bishop Thomas Burnet, Thomas Birch, Gerard Langbaine, William Oldys, Matthew Prior, John Oldmixon, Charles Gildon, Peter Motteux, Luke Milbourne, John Ward, Arthur Maynwaring, Giles Jacob, Colley Cibber, John Dennis, and dozens of others. All of the information about Dryden he found in these sources he had to sift through carefully, separating the chaff from the wheat. He also appears to have been the first to use periodicals extensively for literary history, citing systematically from twelve of the better known (London) periodicals in Dryden's day.

Malone tells us virtually all we have known about Dryden's earliest years, prior to the 1989 biography by James Winn, including his education at Westminster School and Trinity College, Cambridge and the poems he wrote there. Yet he was far from satisfied; he writes, 'The early history and first flights of every literary man naturally engage our curiosity and attention; but at the distance of a century and a half are involved in such obscurity as cannot be easily dispelled.'[47] He broke further new ground by examining public (not just parish) registers. He found the registers of schools and colleges particularly fruitful, as well as the Stationers' Register from which he was able to date accurately most of Dryden's writings. 'The chronology of a story is often of great service in ascertaining its authenticity', he writes.[48] 'If Malone had done nothing more for Dryden', one critic has remarked, 'than comb out these entries from the Stationers' Register, his name would still be mentioned with honor.'[49] Another innovative feature of his biography – and this is now, of course, an indispensable part of modern literary biography – was his combing through all Dryden's works, prose, poetry, and drama, for anything that could

---

[47] Ibid., p.23.   [48] Ibid., p. 505.   [49] See Osborn, *F&P*, pp. 39–53.

supply details of and insights into his life. He, moreover, contextualizes Dryden's achievements by comparing him to other playwrights. Malone establishes that Dryden was relatively diffident about correcting his manuscripts or revising for subsequent editions, and he divides the plays into four distinct periods that are still acceptable to critics.[50] 'A little attention to facts', he writes coolly, will overcome all obstacles.[51]

Further to place Dryden in his time and place, he discusses the ancestry of the Poet Laureateship, the character of literary criticism before Dryden, the role of London coffee-houses in Dryden's time, the history of St Cecilia's Day (in fifty pages) as a background to a discussion of Dryden's St Cecilia odes, the activities of London booksellers in the seventeenth century,[52] the progress of London theatres, an account of Jeremy Collier and the Puritans' hostility towards the stage, and an account of the manners and customs of Dryden's age. Even by his own standards, he had never been so thorough.

In contrast to his manner of overturning spurious stories about Shakespeare, Malone frequently becomes indignant when discrediting tales about Dryden because he perceives them to be, like forgeries, deliberate deceptions. They have 'confirmed and increased my distrust of traditional anecdotes, many of which, on a close examination, I have found, if not wholly false, yet greatly distorted by the ignorance, or inattention, or wilful misrepresentation, of those by whom they have been transmitted from age to age.' As the veteran from previous combats against forgers, he notes, 'we do not indeed always find pure and absolute falsehood; but many a plausible and well-attested story, when thoroughly sifted, has too often proved what Dryden has denominated *a sophisticated truth with an allay of lie in it.*'[53] He singles out Thomas Shadwell, who he says stained Dryden's reputation by claiming, among other things, that Dryden was sent down from Cambridge for insulting a nobleman. He censures Curll's sensational and fraudulent account of Dryden's funeral with a thirty-seven-page rebuttal, based on contemporary newspaper accounts.[54] His also extremely long sections on Dryden's wife and sons[55] – full of new information – appear to result from his determination to discredit elaborate tales about the poet's use of an astrologer. As for Dryden's income and real estate, he consults wills, deeds, and accounts that Lady Elizabeth Dryden sent him; the poet's writings and correspondence; Jacob Tonson's papers; Spence's *Anecdotes*; and much more in order to put to rest stories from which he had found it impossible to 'elicit truth.' He cannot resist adding irritably that times had not changed, that there was as much literary foul play in his

[50] His editorial practice, consistent with his methods in the Shakespeare edition, was to follow the first editions of all the works, except for the 'Essay of Dramatick Poesy' where he followed Dryden's revised copy (*DPW*, I:i, p. 122).   [51] Ibid., p. 122.
[52] For Malone on booksellers, see ibid., pp. 126, 523–40.   [53] Ibid., p. 148.
[54] Ibid., pp. 347–82.   [55] Ibid., pp. 393–430, 436–61.

own day as in Dryden's: 'In our own time we have seen the most flagitious calumnies published by the basest of mankind against the purest characters.'[56] He lashes out at these 'dealers in fiction' who regard such offences as 'light and venial'; the public, however, is 'too well acquainted with the value of integrity and truth, in all human dealings, not to hold the whole tribe of impostors and forgers of every kind in abhorrence' – 'detection and disgrace will assuredly at last overtake them.'[57]

In one of his bulkiest sections, eighty-seven rambling pages, he presents new material on Dryden's personal qualities and domestic manners.[58] Unfortunately, he had to tack it on to the end of the *Life*, after reaching the poet's death, because he acquired much of it after the relevant sheets had gone to the printer. This section manages to destroy whatever structural unity the narrative had managed to preserve. Its digressive character is epitomized by a five-page, 'python-length' footnote on Dryden's iconography that he added at nearly the last moment.[59] With his interest in literary iconography of any kind, this was a natural subject for him. No one had ever looked into the subject of Dryden's portraits before. Early eighteenth-century editors and commentators were as little interested in Dryden's appearance as in Shakespeare's. 'Dr. Johnson conceived', he writes, 'that no description of Dryden's person had been transmitted to us; but, on the contrary, there are few English poets, of whose external appearance more particulars have been recorded.'[60] His conclusions about extant pictures and their provenance, at a time when they were being moved around unpredictably from house to house and were in danger of being lost, have contributed valuably to Dryden scholarship.[61]

In spite of all he found, Malone remained unsatisfied. He had exhausted virtually all his sources, he tells the reader, but much about Dryden probably has been permanently lost. 'It is to be regretted that the history of his life was not undertaken at an early period, while some of his contemporaries were yet living, who might have supplied us with memorials which would have precluded the necessity of sometimes exploring our way by the glimmering twilight of uncertain tradition.'[62] He had said the same many times about Shakespeare, Pope, and even as recent a figure as Reynolds. It was time, he thought, for a change of heart about the great figures of the English past.

3

Dr Johnson occupies a special place of honour in the *Life of Dryden*, partly because he was the most recent biographer of Dryden and partly because Johnson was Johnson. As has already been suggested, Malone faced the

---

[56] Ibid., p. 27.   [57] Ibid., pp. 348–52.   [58] Ibid., pp. 461–548.
[59] Ibid., pp. 432–37; Osborn, *F&P*, p. 62.   [60] Ibid., p. 430.
[61] For Malone's correspondence relating to the whereabouts, dates, and identity of Dryden's portraits, see Ms. Malone 27.   [62] *DPW*, I:i, p.18.

delicate task of superseding Johnson without implying that Johnson's biography was inadequate. If he takes pot-shots at Dryden's biographers, he makes it clear Johnson is not one of his targets. He repeats that Johnson recoiled from tedious research, that he therefore originally gave up entirely the idea of writing a *Life* of Dryden, and that when he reconsidered he had no alternative but to rely on earlier biographies and accounts. Malone also explains that Johnson's idea was always to write the biography of the poet, not the man. All this amounted to a defence of Johnson, not a contest, because one can compete with such excellence 'only if one is actuated by a degree of confidence in himself, which I beg leave most strenuously to disclaim.'[63]

It may strike the reader, however, that he applies a double standard here. He is willing to forgive Johnson for uncritically perpetuating several of the traditional stories about Dryden, but is indignant when anyone else has done so. He exempts Johnson, but only Johnson, from the new standards of scholarship he has been promoting. 'When I mention these slight inaccuracies of Dr. Johnson', he writes, 'I hope not to be misunderstood. Such trivial errours [*sic*] can diminish little from the value of his incomparable Lives of the Poets, and ... are merely specks in the finest body of criticism extant in any language.'[64] George Hardinge, the MP and barrister on whom Byron later based his mock sketch of Jefferies Hardsman, the Welsh judge in *Don Juan*, was not alone in spotting this ambiguity. In his pamphlet, *The Essence of Malone* (1800), he doubts whether Malone, 'doughty as he is, would have written these comments [on previous biographers] (like a wasp's tail in the nose of a giant) upon so irritable a superior in literature if Johnson were still alive.'[65] But as Malone saw it, although Johnson openly admitted he was no scholar and had not examined 'the sepulchres of literature', he did not resent those who were genuine scholars.

Malone gets around the problem of citing Johnson's factual errors without criticizing him directly by censuring the unreliable sources which he claims misled Johnson. On the dating of Dryden's plays, for example, he notes Johnson's mistakes but observes that the real culprit was Gerard Langbaine who led Johnson into many errors with his *Account of the English Dramatick Poets* by adopting 'a very absurd method, that of arranging them

---

[63] Johnson told Malone that he 'made no preparation' for research, 'not being in the habit of extracting from books and committing to paper those facts on which the accuracy of literary history in a great measure depends, and being still less inclined to go through the tedious and often unsatisfactory process of examining ancient registers, offices of record, and those sepulchres of literature, publick repositories of manuscripts, he was under the necessity of trusting much to his own retentive memory ... '(*DPW*, I:i, pp. 1–2).

[64] *DPW*, I:i, p. 139.

[65] Hardinge, *The Essence of Malone, or, The 'Beauties' of that Fascinating Writer, Extracted from his immortal work, in Five hundred Sixty-nine Pages, and a Quarter Just Published, and (With his accustomed felicity) entitled, 'Some Account of the Life and Writings of JOHN DRYDEN!!'*, p. 63.

[the works] alphabetically; and frequently annexed to the several pieces the date of a late, instead of the earliest, edition.'[66] Langbaine, Malone argues, cannot always be trusted since for personal reasons he set out to damage Dryden's reputation by distorting much about his character and writings, though he knew little enough about his life.

Malone also avoids potential disagreements with Johnson by staying clear of any critical analysis of Dryden's writing. He considers when Dryden composed and published his works, why he wrote them, their effects on his reputation, how much money he earned from them, and so on, but he virtually never ventures into literary criticism. Instead, he cites Johnson's criticism, as well as Burke's and others'. 'A critical examination of the merits and defects of his [Dryden's] various productions', he writes, 'formed no part of the present undertaking; and indeed may be well dispensed with, after Dr. Johnson's elaborate and admirable disquisition on his writings; than which a more beautiful and judicious piece of criticism perhaps has not appeared since the days of Aristotle.'[67] One of the benefits of such an approach was that it served his self-appointed role as 'Johnsonianissimus' – a role that seems at times patriotic. Johnson bore the standard of national literary pride. By deferring to him, celebrating him, he could underscore the greatness of English literature.

4

'Why[,] the lovers of fine Printing and Paper will become readers of Dryden!', Burney rejoiced when he saw how beautiful the new edition was.[68] He was pleased especially with Malone's treatment of English musical history in the *Life*, indebted as it was to his own *History of Music*. 'Mr. Malone's Dryden must give great pleasure to true lovers of that excellent poet', he wrote to Joseph Cooper Walker. 'It is perhaps too minute for others, but for myself, I never can have enough to satisfy my craving love & curiosity ... '[69] Percy complained that there was no index.[70] 'I was aware that an *Index* would be of great use', Malone replied, 'but I had not time for it: however, I hope to add one hereafter'[71] – in a second edition, whenever that would be.

Lady Elizabeth Dryden sent him a haunch of venison from Canons Ashby to show her appreciation.[72] Andrew Caldwell was more conventional in his praise, writing to Percy, 'No writer I think ever took more pains to establish facts and detect errors: when he offers himself to the public it seems to be his aim to employ the utmost diligence of research, to

[66] *DPW*, I:i, p. 56.   [67] Ibid., pp. 548–49.

[68] 30 April 1800, Ms. Malone 27, fol. 151.

[69] Burney to J. C. Walker, 2 February 1801, (Maggs catalogue 365, no. 122).

[70] 8 September 1800, *P–M Letters*, p. 76.   [71] 13 September 1800, *P–M Letters*, p. 82.

[72] Malone to Hattie, 27 August 1800, Ms. Malone 37, fols. 3–5.

be useful, and to merit favour.'[73] He told Malone, whom he regarded as England's leading literary historian, that his diligence and learning as an editor created 'a noble example of what an Historian ought to do & what he may accomplish if he takes pains, but that is what the mob of Writers will never forgive.'[74] Such private acclamation was well and good, but Malone wanted to be praised publicly. Unaccountably, there were no long reviews, only short notices, which was galling since good reviews encouraged sales and the edition was selling slowly.

To make things worse, Caldwell was right about the 'mob of Writers.' Thomas Green, in his *Diary of a Lover of Literature*, on 13 May put his finger on the public's main objection. After deriding the 'drudgery' of Malone's labours, Green remarked that most of Malone's facts were 'of very little consequence though they regard so great a character' and might instead have been slipped into an appendix to Johnson's *Life of Dryden*: 'What a contrast between these two pieces of biography!'[75] Malone admits, indeed, that his is 'the life of the *man*, and Johnson's of the *poet*.' Green's soundest criticism, one acquiesced in by many others, was that the mass of factual detail in the notes, much of it relating to Dryden's descendants or others who only peripherally played a part in his life, tends to bury the text. When the *Critical Review* eventually got around to reviewing the edition in January 1801, it censured him similarly for excessive antiquarian enthusiasm: 'While we acknowledge Mr. Malone's merit in this collection, and his industry in discovering several inedited letters of this great author, we must arraign his taste in preserving every fawning dedication which necessity wrested from his [Dryden's] pen. No author would wish every careless or temporary production to be solemnly handed down to posterity.' As for the letters, they 'are in truth of little moment.'[76]

The main attack came from Hardinge's *The Essence of Malone*, an amusing parody in one hundred and sixteen pages. Unfortunately for Malone, it is quite readable and went into a second edition in November 1800. Hardinge tellingly focuses on Malone's fondness for antiquarian rubble. 'I have read [the book] with avidity', he remarks, 'and feel the same rapture in its charming *details* that I felt when *I heard Voltaire cough* ... ' He mocks the accounts of the Laureateship, St Cecilia's Day, and the 'discoveries' of the value of Dryden's Northamptonshire estate. Of the fifty pages on St Cecilia's Day, he writes: 'If any person dropt upon these passages of the work, he would fancy himself in *Burney's* delightful *History of Music*, especially as most part of it is copied from him.' He then elaborates four 'Canons' by which the public may recognize Malone the biographer.

---

[73] 16 September 1800, Nichols, *Illustrations*, VIII, p. 26. See also Malone to Percy, 4 March 1801, Nichols, *Illustrations*, VIII, p. 32.   [74] 4 April 1801, Ms. Malone 38, fol. 171.
[75] Green, *Extracts from the Diary of a Lover of Literature* (1810), p. 221. Green attacked Malone's anti-Jacobinism (*DPW*, I:i, pp. 38–42).   [76] *Critical Review* (January 1801), 36.

The first is: 'A *Biographer* should not only be correct in *trifles*, and *copious* in their *details*, but he should reform his own frequent inaccuracies backwards and forwards, till the reader is left as much in the dark as ever.' The several examples Hardinge gives are supposed to illustrate Malone's art of 'differing with himself.' Here he makes another telling point because he notices that there are contradictions between the notes to Dryden's prose and the *Life*; these resulted from Malone's failure to go back and revise the notes after writing the *Life*. The second canon describes how 'Malonianicus', who is Malone's own private devil, tempts him into supplying a host of other biographies in addition to Dryden's: 'The Life of A should be the lives of B, C, D, &c. to the end of the alphabet; for which the reader is to pay in the additional size of the volume.' The third and fourth canons read, 'A Biographer cannot be too minute in what relates to his Hero', and 'A Biographer should refute errors, and especially if they are trivial.'

In a letter to a friend, Hardinge explained that he had written *The Essence of Malone* as 'a little comic attack upon gossiping & minute historians', with Malone as the hero, 'who is like Mr Pitt or Mrs Siddons in his literary character which I have thrown into ridicule (but with no asperity) because I really thought it was due to him as Dryden's historian.' He denied having any malicious purpose.[77] Malicious or not, the attack acknowledges Malone's stature as the leading literary historian of his age by singling him out from the crowd. If he had been able to rise above resentment and irritation, he might have found himself flattered by the attention. Many like Ritson and Chalmers were doubtless delighted to see him cut down to size, but he had his defenders. One review of the second edition of *The Essence* in the *Gentleman's Magazine* for January 1801, remarked, 'Carping criticks will never be wanting, whether T. Warton or E. Malone be their object. They are little wrens that pick the teeth of the lordly crocodile...'[78]

But Malone as always wanted revenge. He told Percy he would answer Hardinge's 'sneaps' in a dialogue 'in which he is to sustain a part under a feigned character, and to defend all his absurdities.'[79] At first, his friends encouraged him to reply, but Blakeway wondered if it would be more prudent 'quietly to permit that worthy gentleman to fulfill his destiny – vendentem thus et odores [selling frankincense and spices] ... while you go down to posterity, in company with Shakspeare & Dryden.'[80] By then Malone had decided he would save his ammunition for the second edition of the *Dryden* edition, and to this end he made notes in his own copy.[81]

While Malone was debating his reply, Hardinge unexpectedly struck again, late in 1801, with *Another Essence of Malone, or, The 'Beauties' of*

[77] 5 November 1800, Bodleian, Ms. Eng. Let. e.1, fol. 129.
[78] *Gentleman's Magazine*, LXXI, January 1801, 58.
[79] 6 December 1800, *P–M Letters*, p. 87.   [80] Arthur O'Neill Collection.
[81] Bodleian, Malone E. 61–63.

Shakspeare's Editor. As the title suggests, this time he burlesqued his adversary's Shakespeare work, sarcastically calling him 'The Giant' among commentators. There was nothing timely about this pamphlet since Malone's last edition had appeared more than a decade earlier, but he was obviously encouraged by the success of the first *Essence.* And it was every bit as witty, if often obscure. 'Having, to illustrate the Historian of *Dryden's Life*', he begins, 'made a passing bow to the most brilliant of *Shakspeare's* editors ... I have delineated, with more accuracy, the interesting features of *Edmond* the *Editor of Shakespeare* ... ' If the public liked the first *Essence*, he says, it will '*hang over me enamoured*' for the attractions of *Edmond* the *Second.*' He offers additional Malonian canons, more malicious than the first set but making roughly the same points: (1) 'An Editor should prove that what a former Editor asserts, is false, – and should prove the falsehood by a counter-assertion'; (2)'An Editor should be the *Columbus* of *truisms*, of *self-evident* propositions'; and (3) 'An Editor of a Poet who was noted for the melody of his rhithm [*sic*], should make the verse as harsh as he can ... ' Hardinge is especially caustic when he censures Malone for stealing from Capell by putting these words in his mouth: 'Let *Capel* [*sic*] – my aversion – that *pedant* in *conceit* – that professed imitator of *Shakspeare's* clown in style – that *nocticide* of the longest night in *Russia*, (as I call him;) – that *separator of black hairs from white*, as *Johnson* called him, (*but never called me*) – let *him* be an exception – let me *use him* occasionally (with or without notice of the honor [*sic*] conferred upon *him*,) but let me ever *abuse him.*' There are amusing parodies, too, of a few of Malone's Shakespearean 'discoveries'; one of the cleverest, 'Malonian Revolution at Stratford', turns on Malone's repainting of the Stratford bust of Shakespeare in Holy Trinity Church.

In his copy of the pamphlet, Malone describes Hardinge as 'a crack brained Welsh Judge',[82] but he never evened the score. One of the reasons he did not was that sometime in mid-December 1800, he tripped and injured his leg on a 'horse block' at the British Museum getting out of a hackney coach. The philologist Robert Nares, Archdeacon of Stafford, told Percy about the accident on 19 January: 'Malone has been nearly destroyed by an accident, apparently insignificant, that of breaking his shin, in getting out of a coach in the [British] Museum. It has been very unwilling to heal, and sometimes has shown even a threatening tendency.'[83] Windham called on him on 23 December and noted in his diary that Malone 'had got downstairs and thought his leg much better',[84] but the next day Malone was in great pain when he wrote a short critical introduction to Blakeway's anti-Jacobin 'Letter' on John Pinkerton's surly Jacobin *Walpoliana*. In his own copy of that issue, Malone wrote: 'I wrote the little introduction ... in bed and in great pain, Dec. 24, 1800, being then

[82] Bodleian, Malone 150.   [83] Nichols, *Illustrations*, VII, p. 592.
[84] Windham, *Diary*, p. 435.

confined in consequence of a fall in coming out of a hackney coach, by which I rec[eive]d a hurt in my leg, that by neglect was near being attended with dangerous consequences.'[85] Convinced that Malone should not 'tease' himself by answering Hardinge's 'ribaldry', Michael Kearney suggested to him that he was scarcely up to a 'castigation' of Hardinge: 'Your long confinement has, I suppose, made exercise & relaxation necessary to your health; which ought not now to [be] risked by such disagreeable application.'[86] As in the case of Chalmers and the Ireland forgeries, that was certainly the best course. Malone's anger cooled, he grew less anxious about the sale of his edition, and it became easier to follow the Bishop of Killalla's advice, 'let those rascals prate on: they will never persuade people of taste out of their curiosity to know the minutest particulars of the story of eminent men.'[87]

But the *Dryden* did not sell well and Malone was left with a dilemma. He wanted a second edition, but naturally the booksellers shied away from one while there remained unsold copies of the first. A new edition, he explained to Percy on 2 June 1802, would include new letters and a newly organized *Life of Dryden*: 'I am at present trying to make some contract with the booksellers to accelerate their progress: but I find them very Jews.' He then thought of the expedient of collecting all of Dryden's poems, throwing in a few notes, and publishing what would certainly have been a rushed job: 'If his poetry were printed in four volumes they would immediately carry off all the remaining copies; and I have some thoughts of adding a few notes to the poems, and printing them, in order to attain this object.'[88] But he added as an afterthought, 'I have already too much on my hands, and rather wish it were done by another.' He admitted that the new edition would enable him to settle old scores as well as give him another chance to make the *Life* more readable: 'I have cast the Life into a much better form, by dividing it into sections, as I mean to do Shakspeare's also, and have made several corrections and additions to it; and I am very desirous to reprint it, both on this account and that I may have an opportunity of noticing some of Mr. Harding's cavils and impudent misrepresentations.'[89] As late as 1808, he still hoped in vain for a second edition.[90]

The deterrent to publication was the entirely new *Life* and complete edition of Dryden that Sir Walter Scott had had under way since 1805.

---

[85] Malone interleaved that issue of *The Porcupine* in his (Beinecke) copy of Pinkerton's *Walpoliana*. See his furious marginalia in his copy (Beinecke pd85); and Malone to Percy, 6 December, *P–M Letters*, pp. 86–87.   [86] 23 February 1801, Ms. Malone 38, fols. 41r-42v.
[87] Killalla to Malone, 25 September 1800, Ms. Malone 27, fols. 80–81; see also Malone to William Gifford, 25 March 1803 (Bodleian, Ms. Montagu, d.8, fols. 229–30).
[88] See Malone to Percy, 9 December 1802, *P–M Letters*, p. 128.
[89] *P–M Letters*, pp. 96–97.
[90] See Advertisement, *The Times* (11 October 1808). Malone's annotated vols. are in the Bodleian, Malone E. 61–63. Osborn published several of them (*F&P*, pp. 117–43).

Scott had long planned a complete edition with a full biography and was not put off by Malone's *Life of Dryden*. But he needed and hoped for Malone's assistance, who was disinclined to help because of his plans for a new edition. In the early stages of his work, on 29 March 1805, Scott acknowledged the problem to his collaborator, The Revd. Edward Forster, who later pulled out of the project: 'Malone in his Life of Dryden has pointed out some valuable sources & we must move heaven & earth to get at them ... I wish any means could be fallen upon to know what Malone proposes to [do] ... if he can be brought to look with a propitious eye on our undertaking it would be very agreeable.'[91] Although he respected Malone's research skills, Scott did not have a high regard for his abilities as a biographer, as he told Forster a month later: 'Malone's dates are very accurate & should be followed in arranging the plays – they differ considerably from those of Dr. Johnson & Congreve ... If Malone be tractable it will be a pleasant circumstance: he is a very laborious editor though I think confused and tasteless.'[92] By 'confused and tasteless', he meant that Malone had little idea of how to write a biography that the average reader would find entertaining as well as informative. Malone failed to realize that 'facts make fine servants but are poor masters.' Indeed, as he told his friend George Ellis on 17 October, 'I fear little can be procured for a Life beyond what Malone has compiled, but certainly his facts may be rather better told and arranged.'[93]

There are no surviving letters between Scott and Malone to clarify their attitudes towards one another, but so far as we know Malone did not offer Scott an ounce of help. Scott triumphantly published his very readable and sweeping biography of Dryden in 1808, on every third page mentioning his debts to Malone's *Life*, although he borrowed from him more heavily than that, virtually in every paragraph. In his introduction, he acknowledged that he could not have written his biography without Johnson and (especially) Malone:

In the Biographical Memoir, it would have been hard to exact, that the Editor should rival the criticism of Johnson, or produce facts which had escaped the accuracy of Malone. While, however, he has availed himself of the labours of both, particularly of the latter, whose industry has removed the cloud which so long hung over the events of Dryden's life, he has endeavoured to take a different and more enlarged view of the subject ...[94]

As a measure of his respect for Malone and gratitude for his pioneering scholarship on Dryden, if not for his assistance, Scott sent him his complete

---

[91] *The Letters of Sir Walter Scott*, ed. H. J. C. Grierson (1932), I, p. 247. Hereafter cited as *Scott Letters*. Without Malone's help, Scott did gain access to the Luttrell Collection (to George Ellis, 29 November 1805, *Scott Letters*, XII, p. 279). [92] 26 April 1805, *Scott Letters*, I, p. 250.

[93] *Scott Letters*, I, p. 262. Ellis replied that Scott would perform a great service by abridging Malone's 'very laborious compilation' (*F&P*, p. 73).

[94] Scott, *Life of Dryden*, pp. vi–vii.

eighteen-volume *Dryden* – 'because although he was churlish enough I have been so much obliged to his labours that I certainly owe him a tribute of respect.' 'Perhaps he also owes me something', he added later in a letter to Richard Heber, 'if I have succeeded in my attempt to make his lucubrations useful to the public at large.' He did not presume to write to him directly, though, 'as I think He always treated me rather drily.'[95]

It is a pity that Malone did not respond to Scott more positively, if for no other reason than that an acquaintance with Scott would have been one of the few contacts he might have made with the new generation of writers that replaced the Johnsonian world. He and Scott at least had Dryden in common as a bridge between the two literary generations. That he showed little desire to cross that bridge suggests that whatever portion of the new century he would live to see was for completing his Shakespeare work, keeping The Club going, and generally reflecting on the past.

[95] 5 April 1808, *Scott Letters*, XII, pp. 299, 301.

13

Signs of weariness

1

In late December 1799, Boswell's two sons, Alexander and James Junior, dined with Malone at his home while he was deep in his Dryden edition. At one point the conversation turned to Malone's determination to resume work on his Shakespeare edition once Dryden was out of the way. Alexander, who for some reason, perhaps jealousy of his brother James, resented Malone and others of his father's 'Gang', heard this without enthusiasm. To Forbes he commented, 'Stevens [*sic*] is to send forth another Edition of Shakspeare! Malone I understand has also another cargo of Notes ready – We shall surely understand him at last.'[1] James, on the other hand, devoted to Malone as he was, applauded his resolution. Malone, however, found it easier to talk about his Shakespeare work than get down to it. By the middle of 1800, well clear of Dryden, he was still trying to get going. In September, he informed Percy, rather limply, 'I contrive to amuse myself with the Life of Shakspeare, and fancy that I continue to make some new discoveries.'[2] Bindley, who felt himself ageing rapidly, urged him on: 'I wish you health & strength to perfect your great object, an entire Edition of your favorite Author. But don't forget Aubrey, in the meanwhile. I long to see it set about. I am growing an old gossip, and love to read all from and about people.'[3] Encouragements like this from a number of people over the next ten years would have little effect.

The summer of 1800 was excruciatingly hot and dry, especially in London, and Malone found it a trial to work. Few of his friends remained in the city and he drifted. He felt somewhat abandoned and even irrelevant, an old 'codger', as he called himself in a letter to Hattie. What he really needed was a change of scene, a holiday, but even for that he could not

---

[1] 26 December 1799, Fettercairn, Box 87, no. 67. For Alexander's apparent dislike of Malone, see Euphemia to Forbes, June 1800, Fettercairn, Box 88/F2. For his part, Forbes continued to have a high regard for Malone: 'I am much obliged to you for your mention of our London friends', he wrote to Euphemia on 19 June 1800, 'for all of whom & particularly Mr. Malone, I entertain a great respect' (Fettercairn, Box 88/F1).

[2] C. mid-1800, Ms. Malone 27, fols. 130–1. [3] 6 September 1800, *P–M Letters*, p. 75.

muster enthusiasm. It was more comfortable just to stay at home. 'How come you to be in town, you will say', he wrote to his sister in August, 'when not a mortal is in it but yourself? And I don't well know how to answer you.' Metcalfe had offered him the free use of a house in Brighton, 'but as I am afraid of Bathing, and when you have no object of that sort, *that* is but a paltry place, (not even a tolerably pleasant walk,) I refused ... I have not a crony of any sort in town, except a Mr. Bindley of the Stamp office, to whom I sometimes go of an evening, for the sake of some literary talk.' He sighed, 'I wish I could have transported myself for a couple of months to Baronston, without the journey by sea & land.'[4] In October, he wandered to Oxford, more to satisfy Catherine than for any compelling scholarly reason, 'for I had no particular business there; but I made some and did pretty well.' 'Day had passed away after day', he complained to her, '& week after week without my being able to give a good account of them, and without my doing much that I had intended and am bent on doing.'[5]

His ennui resulted partly from a sense of the ending of things. His impulse was to look back, not forward. The decline of The Club itself underlined the problem: attendance was poor, members were either dying at an alarming rate or felt too old to attend, many of them lived far from London, and even the venue for the weekly dinners had to be changed (on 26 February 1799) from Parsloe's to the so-called Thatched House in St James's Street.[6] In recent months, an average of only about five or six had been attending. 'Our brethren are dropping off very fast', he told Percy in June 1802. 'Death has made such ravages among us in a few years, that, even with ... acquisitions ... our total number is only 29; and of these, at least twelve are either out of the kingdom or never come among us; so that the attendance falls on about 16 or 17, which are too few to afford and supply a regular meeting.'[7] Eight or nine were as many as could be expected. Moreover, several of the young members 'seem to consider us as rather of the last age.' What was needed was a determined effort to fill vacancies 'to prevent a gradual decay.'[8] But what Malone did not then appreciate was that The Club was not for all time; it was not even for the nineteenth century.

His general feeling of abandonment was aggravated when several of his friends died near the turn of the century. In 1797, he lost Burke, Walpole, Farmer, and Mason. Then in August 1799, Charlemont died, before he

[4] 27 August 1800, Ms. Malone 37, fols. 3–5.   [5] 4 December 1800, Ms. Malone 37, fol. 6.
[6] Ms. Malone 36 contains correspondence about The Club, Malone's record of who attended, and his list of members with the dates of their election and death.
[7] 5 June 1802, *P–M Letters*, pp. 91–92. See also Malone to Bishop Douglas, 15 January 1799 (BL, Egerton 2186, fol. 105); and *DF*, VI, p. 2359.
[8] To Percy, 9 December 1802, *P–M Letters*, pp. 119–21.

could see the Dryden edition in print. This was a grievous loss, one
immediate effect of which was that he attended fewer book sales. For more
than twenty years he had entered into the excitement of the auctions,
competing for volumes to add to Charlemont's as well as his own library.
Four other links with the past disappeared between 1800 and 1802 with the
deaths of Steevens, Joseph Warton, Bennet Langton, and the Bishop of
Waterford. 'I have lost so many friends within a few years', he complained
to Windham, 'that I begin to fear that I shall at last stand single in the
world, – ultimus meorum [the last of my family]; the grievous price that we
are obliged to pay for life.'[9] When Reed died in February 1807, he felt that
at last he stood alone in one respect: 'I am become ultimus Remanorum,
– the last of the Shakspearians...'[10] How severely he felt the loss of old
friends is evident in a remark that slipped out one day at tea with
Farington: 'Malone said it was true that it [the acquisition of young
friends] was adviseable [sic], but it could not be expected that the vacancies
could to all intents be fulfilled; it could not be: that confidence & intimacy
which was formed at an early period of life can not be renewed at advanced
periods with new men. Agreeable intercourse is all that can be expected.'[11]

His response to Steevens' death on 22 January 1800 was mixed. He did
not even attend his funeral. Reed, Burney, and Windham were far more
moved. 'Poor Steevens!', Windham exclaimed; 'with all his faults, I was
sorry to hear of his having gone.'[12] Burney, who also had ambiguous
feelings about Steevens' character, esteemed his scholarly abilities highly,
as he remarked to Walker: 'He is a loss to the critical world. His learning
was considerable in the Latin Classics, his reading in old authors of our own
country, inferior to none... He was certainly an acute critic & seems to
have dedicated his whole life to Shakespeare, except what he bestowed
anonymously, on friends & foes in news-paper squibs & letters.'[13] Malone
could not allow himself any such praise. His recollections of his old rival did
not even improve with time. He rankled especially at the memory of how
Steevens had treated him in his last (1793) edition: 'The persevering
rancour and incessant malignity and animosity, with which Steevens... endeavoured to carp at and depretiate [sic] all my notes, on which any
sarcasm or cavil could be fastened, (even those which while I was only a co-
adjutor, he received as highly valuable and unobjectionable,) is known
probably only to myself.' He vowed to set the record straight – 'tho' I hate
controversy and studiously avoided it in my former edition, the Publick
certainly shall know it...'.[14] William Gifford, then the acerbic editor of the

[9] 9 July 1802, BL Add. Ms. 37854, fols. 150–51.
[10] To Burney, 14 February 1807, Folger, C.a.2 (12).   [11] 23 June 1804, DF, VI, p. 2359.
[12] Windham to Malone, c. 25 January 1800, Ms. Malone 39, fols. 281–82.
[13] 2 February 1800, cited from Maggs Catalogue 365, no. 122.
[14] P–M Letters, pp. 93–94.

Anti-Jacobin and later the first editor of the *Quarterly Review*, also got an earful:

> If, Sir, you had been acquainted with Mr Steevens, you would have had an easy clew [*sic*] to his controversy with me on the subject of Scenery in our ancient Stage. He had no relish for discoveries made by others. Hence his pertinacious adherence to that adulterated Copy of Shakspeare's plays, the Second Folio; his idle defence of old Macklin's forgery; and the unceasing asperity which pervades every part of his *last* edition; which I may say with confidence I had not at all deserved, having treated him throughout my book [the 1790 *Shakespeare*], with great civility & respect.[15]

These sentiments, however, did not spoil his appetite for Steevens' library auctioned in May 1802, on which he spent no less than two hundred pounds over the week of the sale. Young Boswell told his sister Euphemia that Malone attended the sale every day and bid for books that were going 'at a great price.'[16]

2

The large sum he spent on Steevens' books creates the impression that his finances were in good order,[17] but that was not the case. Malone had expensive domestic habits, such as keeping a large wine cellar and entertaining with expensive dinners, but even his wine cellar had declined by 1800: 'Never was my cellar in so wretched a state', he moaned in a letter to Catherine; 'I once had 120 dozen of all sorts in it: now not *five*', though he soon added a 'Pipe of Port', which when bottled would give him fifty-three dozen more.[18] That he could ill afford to buy extravagantly at Steevens' sale is borne out by his being rescued, just three months later, by an emergency two hundred pounds sent to him by Mr Forth, his land agent in Dublin. 'He has sent me £200 which will set me tolerably easy for some time', he informed Hattie. 'The greater part of it will fly in all directions in about a week; £90 for rent, 20 Coals, 20 Chandler, 20 Taylor, &c&c. I hope however to keep about £30 for Edmond himself.'[19] Because he continued to spend more on books than on anything else, his house looked neglected and untidy. Savings that he did not spend on books went into purchasing bonds and stocks instead of new furniture.[20]

[15] 19 March 1805, *P–M Letters*, pp. 165–66.

[16] See James Boswell Junior to Euphemia Boswell n.d., Fettercairn, Box 88/F1, no. 160.

[17] See Malone's 'Account of money laid out in the purchase of Books, and in Binding', 1777–1800 (Ms. Malone 34, fols. 177–80); and 'Account of money expended in Pictures and Drawings and Prints since I settled in London 1777' (1 August 1800). He valued at two hundred pounds two large portfolios containing 'near 1000' engraved portraits bought between 1780 and 1800 (Ms. Malone 34, fol. 176). His collection is lost.

[18] 4 December 1800, Ms. Malone 37, fol. 7.   [19] 27 August 1800, Ms. Malone 37, fol. 4.

[20] On the 'unlucky management' of his investments, see his letter to Catherine on 4 December 1800 (Ms. Malone 37, fols. 6–7). See also Ms. Malone 37, fol. 26; and Ms. Malone 38, fols. 296–99.

In spite of recurring remonstrations from his sisters, especially Catherine, he never curtailed his book purchases. In the second half of 1802, he briefly changed his diet in favour of more economical soups and broths, though he did this more to alleviate bouts of dyspepsia than to economize. 'I have been living upon nothing for a good while past', he told Catherine in January 1803; 'My butcher's bill for this whole year comes to but thirty-three pounds, and of that only seven guineas have been spent since July.'[21] Catherine became resigned to his expensive obsession with books. In 1807, after book purchases over a period of three years had totalled over eight hundred pounds: 'Mr. Forth told me he had sent you a pretty round sum of one thousand pounds. My answer to him was that I wished he had not sent you so much at a time; for that you would only be more profuse in buying *old* books, and think it would never be out. Is not this true enough?'[22] He had to admit it was.

3

When Malone visited Ireland in late summer and early autumn 1801, his family urged him again to do less scholarship and take more holidays, especially in the summer when London was deserted, hot, and unhealthy. In fact, with fewer friends in London during the summers, Malone reasoned that it was a good place and time to get some work done. 'Mr. Malone expressed to me His intention to remain in town the whole Summer except a slight excursion of a day or two', Farington noted, for 'the Summer was a Season to Him very agreeable for application.' Whereas most people would prefer to be outdoors on a fine summer's day, Malone at such times 'felt a chearfulness for application, & He the more felt the benefit of it, as in contrary weather, He is sometimes depressed and indisposed to study.'[23] He preferred spring and autumn for holiday excursions, to Cheltenham, Brighton, the several homes of friends, and the occasional English country house or cottage that his family rented. Since he would not leave London in the summer, his family often decided to come to him and try to ameliorate the physical side effects of his confining and sedentary life. In September 1803, after having spent a few weeks with him in London – during which he got little done – his sisters prevailed on him to join them for over a month of ruralizing at a 'villa' just outside Worcester. 'I did not think of leaving London this summer', he explained half-apologetically to Percy in late October, and 'meant to stick steadily to my work', but having been 'induced to break through my resolution, and having joined the ladies here, have been a complete idle gentleman for above a month.'[24]

---

[21] Prior, p. 272.   [22] Ibid., p. 300.   [23] *DF*, VI, p. 2360.
[24] 25 October 1803, *P–M Letters*, p. 155.

Through such visits, the ladies, who were with him again in London during the summer of 1804, could keep a closer eye on him, but they were powerless to care for him when they were not with him. His health was fragile and interfered with his work. Writing to Percy from London in July 1802, he complained, 'I have been for some time past molested with the gout, though I am not entitled to it hereditarily, nor have I earned it by any intemperance. This in some measure [has] disinclined me towards writing...'[25] There was also his recurring eye trouble which made him think back to Reynolds' eye problems and sympathize with Percy's failing vision.

After he published the fourth edition of Boswell's *Life of Johnson* in May 1804, however, he did rouse himself to do some work. He boarded the so-called 'Academic Coach' to Cambridge. 'Everybody is going out of town, & why should not I', he remarked to Catherine.[26] He stopped in Cambridge for seven days at the end of July to read 'the Matriculation and other Registers', from which, as he told Percy the following March, he 'obtained the ages and degrees of several of the poets of Shakspeare's time, who were bred there; of whom the common accounts are very unsatisfactory and erroneous; I mean, Marlowe, Nashe, Greene, France, &c.'.[27]

But by then Malone had contracted the most serious illness of his life. After he returned from Cambridge, the weather suddenly turned very hot. This made his daily routine unpleasant because for several weeks he walked every day to the Stationers' Hall near St Paul's where he was 'writing out old matters.'[28] He was desperate to get on with his account of the Elizabethan stage and manners between 1590 and 1620 – which he intended to include as part of his *Life of Shakespeare* – whatever the discomfort he had to endure. 'It takes me up three quarters of an hour to walk there & as much to return (a great waste of time)', he grumbled in a letter to Catherine on 8 September, 'and tho' I go out quite spruce, in about an hour I have not a crooked or dry hair on my head.' At home, for more air, he took to writing in his front room on the ground floor – 'a rare thing for me; & I do not feel myself at home in it.'[29] Day after day, for twenty days, at the Stationer's Hall and at home, he sat next to an open window in varying states of perspiration while the breezes cooled him. This 'great imprudence', he explained to Percy, 'laid the foundation... for the disorder which attacked me in October, when I had nearly completed my task. It was of the Erysipelas kind and I ought to be thankful that it was not a worse malady for it probably saved me from a dangerous fever.' He had been a 'poor invalid' ever since, suffering 'incessant pain for two

[25] 20 July 1802, *P–M Letters*, p. 101.   [26] 16 July 1804, Ms. Malone 34, fols. 8–10.
[27] 19 March 1805, *P–M Letters*, pp. 164–65.   [28] Ms. Malone 37, fols. 10–11.
[29] 8 September 1804, Ms. Malone 37, fols. 10–11.

months.'[30] Burney was dismayed: 'Poor Malone is seriously ill, suffers much, and I fear is in a dangerous state.'[31]

Malone fancied himself something of an amateur physician – 'I am you know', he remarked to Hattie, who had been suffering from stomach trouble, 'a little of a Doctor'[32] – and was, as we have seen, keenly interested in the illnesses from which Boswell, Reynolds, and Burke died. But he could not diagnose his own 'disorder.' His doctor, Henry Vaughan, later President of the Royal College of Physicians and member of The Club,[33] first diagnosed the ailment as shingles, but later decided it was a mild form of pneumonia. By early December, he had recovered enough to get around, though with 'a most irksome pain in my breast and shoulder which no physical aid has yet been able to alleviate.' He was ill well into the summer of 1805, unable to work or do much of anything else. The illness 'quite unfits me for any *solid* work', he admitted to Percy, 'so that for several months I have been able to do little more than to arrange and correct my papers, and have not composed a dozen pages.'[34] Kearney chimed in with some familiar advice on 6 April 1805: 'shut your books, & take some country air & exercise' for a couple of months; 'Why might you not go to Clifton near Bristol?... A short intermission of your studies would give an acuter relish for them, and more vigour in their pursuit.'[35] Characteristically, Malone ignored the advice.

In spite of these trials, in the spring of 1805 he began 'laying the foundation for an Essay on Shakspeare's metre and that of his contemporaries by reading over several plays of his time with this particular view.'[36] The essay would be a rebuttal of Steevens. He argues that in his 1793 edition, Steevens forsook the editorial tenet central to all his earlier editorial work on Shakespeare, that an editor must be as faithful as possible to what Shakespeare wrote, by arguing that many of Shakespeare's 'anomalies', 'barbarisms', and 'depravities of language' ought now to be suppressed in favour of 'modern sophistications.' Malone's object is to demonstrate the 'integrity of the original text' by comparing Shakespeare's language with that of his contemporaries. The project satisfied his profound urge to attack Steevens, but it also raised his flagging spirits.

In June, he sought relief at Cheltenham, where he took the waters 'very moderately' for a month, then went directly to Brighton, on Dr Vaughan's

---

[30] *P–M Letters*, p. 165.

[31] Burney Family Autograph Correspondence, 1789–1876, no. 31 (first count), n.d. ('Monday morning'), Berg Collection, New York Public Library.

[32] 12 November 1802, Ms. Malone 39, fol. 45v.

[33] See 26 July 1804, Ms. Malone 34, fols. 8–10.

[34] To Percy, 19 March 1805, *P–M Letters*, p. 165.   [35] Ms. Malone 39, fols. 55–56.

[36] 19 March 1805, *P–M Letters*, p. 165.

advice, for two weeks 'of the warm saltwater baths.'[37] Kearney was optimistic: 'You will receive this letter when you have returned from Brighton with your health perfectly renovated and the uneasy sensation in your breast, I sincerely hope, forever removed.'[38] And to his own great surprise and delight, Malone came home in September healed.

During the summer, his spirits also were improved by his dramatic discovery of the first quarto (1593) of *Venus and Adonis*.[39] He had been searching for it for more than twenty years. No other copy of this edition has ever been found. William Ford, a bookseller in Manchester in whose 'country catalogue' Malone first saw the quarto advertised, told him the good news on 20 July: 'On receiving this you will be shewn the Vol. of Venus & Adonis, the lowest price of which will be Twenty five Pounds... Had I not been disposing of my Books, an offer of 30 guineas should not have induced me to have parted with it.'[40] It was 'so extravagant a price that I am ashamed to mention it', he confessed to Percy. 'However, I do not at all repent of my bargain. It is worth to me all the money I gave for it; for on collation, I obtained from 25 to 30 new readings, and most of them valuable.' He had advertised for it a quarter of a century earlier for two guineas, which he then thought a great price. The thought elicited one of his perennial complaints: 'The booksellers... now, taking advantage of the present *rage* for old English Poetry, do not confine themselves within that limit.'[41]

Malone now hoped to find 'some day or other the original edition of *Hamlet*... which I am persuaded was in 1602, though none earlier than 1604 has yet been seen.'[42] Petworth House occurred to him as one of the more promising places to look, so he wrote to George O'Brien Wyndham, third Earl of Egremont, from Brighton in September: 'It has always appeared to me extremely probable, that in many of the houses of our old Nobility, there are, among their ancient papers, several curious documents, which might with very little pains be easily discovered; and what house more likely to contain stores of this kind than Petworth?' He recalled that on a visit to Petworth in 1802 he was told of 'the *old* Library ... in one of the upper rooms' which he had not had time enough to visit. Perhaps the owner of Petworth in Shakespeare's time, Henry, Earl of Northumberland, who patronized Raleigh and other eminent men, did not 'wholly neglect the works of Shakspeare.' Would his lordship please look in the library for any early editions of Shakespeare, especially for 'an edition of the play of Hamlet in 1602, and one of his Venus and Adonis in 1593.' He had long ago

[37] To Percy, 6 August 1805, *P–M Letters*, p. 184. See also Boswell's letter to Forbes, 2 August 1805 (Fettercairn, Box 88/F1); and Kearney's to Malone, 7 September 1805 (Ms. Malone 39, fols. 57–58).   [38] 7 September 1805, Ms. Malone 39, fols. 57–58.
[39] This unique quarto is now Malone 325 in the Bodleian.
[40] Ms. Malone 26, fol. 156. See also Ford to Malone, 30 August 1805, Ms. Malone 26, fol. 157.
[41] 6 August 1805, *P–M Letters*, p. 186.   [42] Ibid., p. 186.

stated in print that 'both of these existed, and would sometime or other be found ... '. He needed them to establish a correct text of the plays – 'such is the estimable value of *first* editions.'[43] It was a long shot, and like most long shots, it failed. Egremont's secretary replied simply that the library contained 'only a small number of Books, most of them of little value.'[44] Malone never did find the earliest *Hamlet* quarto; no copy was found until 1823.

Although he recovered almost completely from his illness, he found it more difficult to overcome depression. Farington's remark that a sunny day supplied him with a 'chearfulness of application' while bad weather made him 'indisposed to study' suggests he was prone to sudden shifts of mood. In addition to his uncertain health and the demoralizing effects of the deaths of friends, fear gnawed away at him that he might never complete his life's work on Shakespeare. In April 1806, Farington admonished him 'not to postpone [the *Life of Shakespeare*] but to consider how time is passing', to which he replied he 'should be very sorry to die before He had completed a work so long upon His mind & for which He had made such preparations.' It also dejected him that 'several of his friends, Lord Macartney among the number, [were] gradually falling off, which lessened His prospect of pleasure arising from the publication of it, as He could not have the gratification of affording them some amusement and of receiving their opinions.'[45] Moreover, financial problems still troubled him, especially as he missed out at the end of 1804 on a political appointment that would have made him financially secure.[46]

On top of everything else, Hattie was going through a period of mental instability and Susanna Spencer was lapsing into derangement. It was the latter's 'vexation' that alerted his family in November to his need for constant companionship and impelled them to send Robert Jephson's nephew, The Revd. John Jephson, to stay with him in May and, again, in November 1805.[47] Susanna had been living in a house in Grosvenor Square, where if Malone ever visited her he was very secret about it; she was committed to an asylum towards the end of the year.[48] John Jephson's arrival in November was timely, for he was able to help Malone arrange for her removal to an institution in Hoxton. At first, however, Malone resented

---

[43] 13 September 1805, Petworth House archives, on deposit at the West Sussex Record Office, Chichester.

[44] Charles Dunster to Malone, 6 October 1805 (Arthur O'Neill Collection).

[45] 21 April 1806, *DF*, VII, pp. 2726–27.

[46] Windham and the Duke of Portland failed to obtain a public appointment for Malone. See Portland to Windham, 1 January 1805, Ms. Malone 39, fol. 208; and Windham to Malone, 10 January 1805, Ms. Malone 39, fol. 291.

[47] See Jephson's letters to his wife on 3 and 6 May 1805, cited in M. D. Jephson, *An Anglo-Irish Miscellany: Some Records of the Jephsons of Mallow* (1964), p. 314.

[48] Michael Kearney alluded to this recent 'vexation' of Malone's in a letter on 8 January 1807 (Ms. Malone 39, fol. 63) and again on 21 April 1807.

the visit. Jephson reported to his wife that initially Malone 'was kind, but not remarkably warm' and then 'began to smell a rat', suspecting 'that I had been sent over by the Baronston lord and ladies.' He denied this to Malone and immediately set about 'drawing off his thoughts from melancholy objects.' Several days later, after Malone learned from Catherine how much Jephson had been inconvenienced to be with him, 'he seized my hand, and rated me for not telling him how much he was my debtor.' From then on they were at ease with each other. 'I sit down (November 4th, 1805)', Jephson wrote to his wife, 'in Mr. M.'s study, after having sent off Miss Spencer without much difficulty to Hockston [*sic*], where she is to be received in an excellent establishment for persons in her situation. I think I am of use to Mr. M., and if so, my whole object has been attained. I have hitherto never stirred from him ... ' They had just been to Hoxton and 'sat with poor Miss S. for half an hour. She is much better, but still evidently deranged; she kissed us both on our going away.' By 30 November, Malone began to talk of letting his guest return home, but Jephson refused to go 'till I am quite convinced that he really wishes it.' Although Susanna Spencer is 'a great deal better', he told his wife, 'I know that this appearance is fallacious, and have tried to instil that opinion into Mr. M. that he would do nothing without precise directions from Dr. Willis. We shall go to see her together on Monday next.'[49] It sounds as if Jephson feared that Malone might take it into his mind to bring her home with him. This may have been the very reason his family asked Jephson to go – the 'rat' that Malone smelled.

In spite of his own problems, Malone helped others with their emotional troubles more than he was helped. From 1806 onwards Kearney gave him detailed accounts of his wife's deterioration into dementia, soliciting his advice, asking for his suggestions of good asylums in England, and generally seeking his sympathy. 'But why do I pour out on you my domestick concerns? why affect your feeling mind? And yet my knowledge of your heart, though it ought to check these effusions, that must give you pain, induce me to communicate them where I have such experience of their being attended to.'[50] Malone insisted that Kearney's wife did not need medical help, just 'proper management' with skill and gentleness.

Hattie's health, physical and mental, also worried him. She had suffered from stomach complaints for several years, for which from time to time he offered remedies, but when she began to speak and write to him irrationally, he responded with patience, gentleness, and firmness. She imagined she was

---

[49] Prior, pp. 286–91. See also Malone to Harriet and Catherine, 15 September 1806, Ms. Malone 37, fols. 14–15.

[50] 21 April 1808, Ms. Malone 39, fols. 77–78. See also Kearney to Malone, 12 August and 8 September 1807 (Ms. Malone 39, fols. 73–74, 75), and 28 July 1808 (Ms. Malone 39, fols. 79–80).

unloved and excluded from her brother's and sister's affections. 'I never supposed for a moment my dear H.', he reassured her, 'that you had not the same affection for us all that you used to have so put that quick out of your mind; & think only of the future.' His diagnosis of her ailment: 'It appears to me, that when you are so ill of your nervous complaint, your powers of digestion being weak ... you acquire a store of bile or some other evil ... that produces this lowness of spirits.' He prescribed a large breakfast and then later a moderate dinner so that she would always finish with an appetite.[51] He also prescribed little methods of keeping her spirits up, such as that she should 'write down half a dozen lines on a bit of paper & keep it by her & the purport of it to be – that she now finds herself well & happy & therefore has actual *experience* that she was mistaken last year when she thought there was something *peculiar* in her low spirits & uneasiness at that time, different from anything she had felt before; & that therefore she has good grounds for hoping.' 'Pray, dearest Hattie', he pleaded, 'put down something of this kind on paper & keep it by you, & then appeal to it hereafter. It may do you some good *then*, & can do no harm now, or at anytime.'[52] While she never succumbed to dementia, he continued to write to her in this vein for the rest of his life.

Dr Johnson had told Malone in his last hours, 'Do good to others.' Without sentimentalizing the idea, he now felt, after his efforts to help these women, that he understood it more deeply. 'You are right in your opinion of Mr. M.'s mind', Jephson told his wife, 'and of the excellence of his heart. His kindness to me is unbounded, and the unqualified confidence in which we live together, with our many hours of talk which our mode of life induces, have certainly strengthened those bonds of amity that before subsisted between us.'[53] Malone confided to Catherine, 'Indeed my dear [I] agree with you entirely, that quiet, & content, and a disposition to oblige & to make others happy, are the greatest blessings this world affords, and that without them all the riches & grandeur it can give, are utterly worthless.'[54]

4

Through these years of personal anxiety, Malone's scholarship faltered, but his social life did not. Percy called him the 'great Corner Stone, or connecting cement' of The Club, which more than anyone else he helped revive.[55] He also dined regularly with Windham, Burney, Courtenay, young Boswell, Bindley, Metcalfe, and (when he was in London) Caldwell.

---

[51] 26 July 1804, Ms. Malone 34, fols. 8–10.
[52] Ms. Malone 37, fols., 10–11. See also Jephson's letter to Malone about Harriet (Ms. Malone 38, fols. 277–78).   [53] Cited in Prior, p. 289.   [54] Ms. Malone 37, fols. 14–15.
[55] To Malone, 26 May 1808, *P–M Letters*, p. 239. On Malone's efforts to rescue The Club from its decline, see Malone to Percy, 17 October 1806 and 25 September 1807, *P–M Letters*, pp. 206–7, 234–36.

Windham, always energetic and full of fun, especially cheered him up, as when they watched a boat race together from a boat under one of the arches of Westminster Bridge. No sooner had the 'contending parties' appeared, he wrote to Catherine in August 1804, than Windham 'dashed in among a hundred boats, shouting, splashing, and pulling about to keep pace for a moment with the rivals ... It was delightful to see what interest W took in the sport, to prevent obstruction or interference with the boats engaged, totally regardless of the safety of his own.'[56] When Malone was not ill, it was at his own home that he now preferred to be with his friends. 'I am [to be] a wretched visitor', he once protested when contemplating a visit to Walpole's old friends, the Berry sisters, at Little Strawberry Hill.[57] He might complain about too many guests, as when he blamed Richard Jephson and his family for interrupting his work for a week in the autumn of 1806, on their journey from Gibraltar: '*Shakspeare* is at a stand. On his account alone, I shall not be sorry when they are settled in their own house. However, I have the pleasure of reflecting that though inconvenient in housekeeping details, I have done a kind thing.'[58] Nonetheless, Malone enjoyed guests. At least in his own home he did not have to endure anyone he did not like. At Windham's, he dreaded being trapped by a tiresome old woman, Mrs Cholmondeley, who always seemed to be there when he was. On one occasion, which he described for Catherine, having returned to Windham's house after the theatre, he was marooned when Windham suddenly retreated to his study and he 'stumbled, as usual, on that detestable Miss C----y who is I think always there, & my bane.' 'Have not you observed', he asked his sister in exasperation, 'that agreeable people & those we like the best, have very often either some followers or friends that entirely destroy the pleasure of their company?' This made him think of marriage – about which he was not exactly an authority – where 'I believe, this frequently happens, for tho' one may be in love with a woman, yet she may have a pack of disagreeable relations or friends that may plague one to death.'[59]

At the insistence of his sisters, he also took more of an interest in his house and in a few domestic pleasures, like shopping, fashion, and daily constitutionals in adjacent neighbourhoods, simple pleasures that an intensely scholarly career had fairly well denied him. An early morning walk before breakfast especially appealed to him. 'I pretended to make a parcel of errands this morning', he announced to Catherine, '& paraded down Bond St before breakfast, quite a desart [sic], every tenth house repairing & painting.' Another morning, again 'pretending' to go shopping, he walked over to St James's Street and Pall Mall for coffee and tea. As a gesture towards better housekeeping, in 1804 he even took on two

[56] Cited in Prior, pp. 277–78.   [57] Ibid., p. 293.
[58] C. autumn 1806, cited in Prior, p. 292.   [59] 4 August 1806, Ms. Malone 37, fols. 12–14.

additional live-in servants. He also saw to improving his furniture.[60] And although at first he resisted it, he redecorated his house again in the autumn of 1809.[61]

5

One of Malone's greatest comforts after 1800 was Burney. They had been friends since Burney was elected to The Club in 1784, but it was not until the late stages of Malone's Dryden edition that they became intimate. In 1798–99 Burney contributed notes to Malone's third edition of Boswell's *Life of Johnson* and information for the musical background to his account of Dryden's 'Song for St Cecilia's Day', *Alexander's Feast*, and other Dryden poems. There were more personal reasons than literature, however, for their intimacy. Since the tragic death of his daughter Susan in January 1800, Burney had shut himself off completely from society for three months, avoiding The Club as well as declining invitations to dinner, the theatre, and concerts. When he re-emerged, Malone was one of the first whose company he sought. They tended to commiserate over the same things: deaths of old friends, ill health, cramped finances, and fears that their productive scholarship was declining sharply.

Malone marvelled at, and perhaps envied, Burney's remarkable discipline and industry between 1800 and 1804, through his late seventies, in writing a series of articles on music for a new *Cyclopaedia* on the arts, sciences, and literature.[62] Burney was motivated partly by the need for money and partly by his desire to put the loss of his daughter out of his mind, but it was a mammoth task, the articles amounting to an encyclopaedia of music in their own right. Like Malone with his Shakespeare, he was awed by the scope of the project. 'I have 10 years' work on my hands', he complained, '& perhaps not 10 months to do it in.'[63] In order to complete the task, Burney adopted a strict regimen that would have served Malone well, too; he conserved his resources, focused his energies, and thought of little else. However, he also abused his health and, with the departure of his daughter Fanny for France in April 1802, and the loss of his housekeeper (who was also his amanuensis) in July 1803, led a depressed and lonely existence at home without much relaxation from social engagements, except for the occasional dinner or regular Club evening.

So Malone filled a void for him. Recalling his encouragement of Boswell, Malone invited Burney regularly for quiet dinners at his home. There was no one else so accessible who could give Burney the professional encouragement, human understanding, and even advice on health that he

---

[60] Letters to Catherine, 28 July and 8 September 1804 (Ms. Malone 37, fols. 10–11).
[61] See his letter to Percy, 23 November 1809, *P–M Letters*, pp. 257–58.
[62] See Malone to Burney, 8 June 1808, Folger, C.a. 2 (14).
[63] To J. W. Callcot, 16 July 1800, OFB 46.58.

needed. At these 'little parties', Burney told Malone early in 1802, playing with musical imagery, he generally felt 'in perfect tune', in spite of a persistent cough: 'But, alas! my corporeal instrument has been very much out of tune, and greatly below con*sort* pitch for ... a fortnight.' As soon as he could 'get about again by daylight', he hoped for 'a little literary chat'[64] about Johnsoniana, new information for Malone's fourth edition of Boswell's *Life of Johnson* (1804), old ballads, and the reception of the Dryden edition.[65]

After Burney suffered a mild stroke in September 1806, that left his hand temporarily paralysed, he seldom saw Malone. They had to settle for writing to each other. They wrote about their health, Malone's Shakespeare work, book auctions,[66] music, The Club, Malone's eyesight,[67] Dr Johnson, their mutual friends, and so on. 'I find it impossible to let you off with a short letter', Burney admitted in July 1808, 'which I intend when I begin ... yet I have never said half of what I want & wish to say.'[68]

If Burney's example did not sufficiently inspire Malone to finish Shakespeare, neither did his occasional remark about how much he hoped to see the edition in print before he died. Wrapped up in flannels and blankets on a cold February day in 1808, he scribbled: 'Old, infirm, & almost bed-ridden, as I am during this Spitzburg in Weather, I cannot help hoping to live to see your *2d Edit*[*ion*] ... '[69] With a touch of irony, as he was searching for some madrigal music with which to write a note for Malone's edition, Burney remarked to his friend in November 1810, 'You are not in the press, yet, I presume.'[70]

[64] 23 (no month), 1802, Ms. Malone 38, fol. 129. [65] See *P–M Letters*, pp. 171–72.
[66] At Reed's sale in December, Malone spent one hundred and eighty pounds (*DF*, VIII, p. 3183).
[67] See Burney's letters to Malone, 8 and 10 June 1808 (Ms. Malone 38, fols. 143–44, 155).
[68] 9 July 1808, Ms. Malone 38, fols. 146–47.
[69] 24 February 1808, Ms. Malone 38, fol. 141.
[70] 21 November 1810, Beinecke, Tinker 447.

14

'The last of the Shakspearians'

1

When Isaac Reed died early in 1807, Malone called himself 'the last of the Shakspearians',[1] but by then he had little Shakespeare or any other kind of scholarship left in him. He would publish only three more works: *An Account of The Incidents From Which The Title and Part of the Story of Shakspeare's Tempest Were Derived; and Its True Date Ascertained* (1808); an edition of William Gerard Hamilton's works, together with a biographical sketch, under the title, *Parliamentary Logick* (1809); and *A Biographical Memoir of the Late Right Honourable William Windham* (1810). The first was a pamphlet privately printed and circulated, the result of a little original research. But the latter two, which were very time-consuming, had nothing to do with Shakespeare. At a time when he needed to conserve his weak eyesight and the little strength he had left in order to finish his *magnum opus*, they led him in the wrong direction. Most of his labour on them, honouring the memory of two recently deceased friends, was biographical, as was his similarly distracting contribution to *An Essay on the Earlier Part of the Life of Swift* by Dr John Barrett that appeared in John Nichols' third edition of Swift in 1808.

Not having heard from him since October 1806 – when Malone told him, 'I am creeping on slowly with my work, but my eyes are growing extremely weak' – Percy wrote on 10 April 1807 that he 'would not ... defer writing any longer, to enquire how Mr Malone's Studies are directed, and when the World may hope to see the completion of his Labours.'[2] Malone tried to be optimistic, but he sounded overwhelmed: he was trying to do something every day and although he was making 'a very slow progress', he had hopes of doing 'great things' and 'getting to press' that summer when the town emptied and he had more time to himself. He had 'abundant materials' for enlarging his history of the stage and essay on the order of Shakespeare's plays, 'many of which I have newly arranged', and he had collected materials for the essay on Shakespeare's versification 'in

---

[1] 14 February 1807, Folger, C.a. 2 (12).   [2] 10 April 1807, *P–M Letters*, pp. 212, 214.

order to support my former observations on this subject, and to refute some of Mr Steevens [*sic*] sarcastick remarks respecting it.' But his greatest ambition, his 'favourite object', was still the *Life of Shakespeare*, 'of which about a third part remains to be written: but all the materials for it are ready.' He even had three hundred pounds' worth of paper 'lying ready in the Printing House.'[3] All was in a state of readiness, but nothing galvanized him to start writing.

Another year passed, Malone published his pamphlet on *The Tempest* in January 1808, and Percy (after seeing it) wondered still more about his studies, 'especially on the subject of our great Dramatic Poet': had he completed his research for the *Life* and various essays and dissertations, 'which if the B[isho]p understood him right, were to precede or accompany his new Edition, and when will this be committed to the press?'[4] If 'the Great Giver of all good shall spare me life to execute it', Malone replied in June 1808, he intended to publish all of Shakespeare's works in twenty-three volumes, the first eight in a first installment and the remaining fifteen 'at a future time, in one other delivery.' As for his research, he had 'got together all that I probably shall ever get: but I have much still to *write*; – about one third of the Life; an Essay on the Metre and phraseology of Shakspeare, &c – and I have much yet to do to the History of the Stage, for which I have got several new materials.' Disburdening himself to Percy with resolutions that a number of his friends had heard before, he added, 'A thousand interruptions and avocations have retarded my work; but I mean to stay in town all this summer, and hope to do a great deal between this time and Christmas, and to go to the press early in next year.'[5]

That summer, though, was again very hot and it wore him out. The 'languor of the hot weather', he complained to Catherine in early August, made him 'quite unfit for any exertion.'[6] Not even The Revd. Mark Noble's 'Fresh Researches into the History of Shakespeare', published in the October–December 1808, issues of the *Monthly Mirror*, announcing that his corrections would place in doubt 'the authority of Mr. Malone, and other voluminous Commentators', could rouse him. Malone merely interleaved copies of these articles into his 1790 *Shakespeare* and wrote on them comments like 'no proof of this', 'all wrong', 'sad stuff', and 'blockhead.'[7] He did not even mention the articles to Percy, though he did raise with him another irritant, a facsimile publication of the First Folio (1807) that Percy thought he may have 'advised' or 'sanctioned.'[8] Not only had he had nothing to do with it, but he resented it because it tempted 'the idle gentlemen of the town' to think, 'Ay, now we shall have the true

[3] 6 May 1807, ibid., pp. 218–19.   [4] 26 May 1808, ibid., p. 238.
[5] 28 June 1808, ibid., pp. 241–42.   [6] Ms. Malone 37, fol. 22.
[7] The interleaved copy is in Beinecke, Malone 746; see *PP* (*1790*), I: ii, pp.1–96.
[8] 26 May 1808, *P–M Letters*, pp. 238–39.

thing, and perfectly understand this great author, without being bewildered by the commentators.' 'I would like to see a paraphrase by some of these gentlemen', he continued indignantly, 'on six pages of the first folio, after having been shut up for 12 hours in a room with this volume, and without any other book. It would probably be a very curious performance.'[9]

Nine months later, he still had not published any volumes of his edition, although he had somehow found time and energy for 'avocations', as he called them: a search for Swiftiana for Nichols' new edition; a twenty-page appendix to his pamphlet on *The Tempest* printed in January 1809; annotations of Dr Johnson's *Dictionary*; and considerable research on Hamilton and his writings. 'I continue to work on Shakspeare daily', he assured Percy on 21 March 1809, 'but, as I have told you, with several interruptions.' He cherished 'a hope that I shall live to finish the Life of Shakspeare', which remained only two-thirds written.[10] But what did his literary 'avocations' add up to? Did they compensate for the precious time lost on Shakespeare?

2

His pamphlet on *The Tempest* presents new information that he believed clarified how and when Shakespeare came to write the play. In the Advertisement he states that these pages made up part of a revised and enlarged essay on the order of the plays which would appear in 'a second edition of that great poet's works; which has been too long delayed by various causes, not necessary to be here stated, but will, I hope at no distant period, be committed to the press.' Citing passages from some 'scarce tracts' published in 1610 that described the shipwreck of Thomas Gates and Sir George Somers on Bermuda in 1609, he declares that no longer need he conjecture about when *The Tempest* was written and first acted. Arguing convincingly that Shakespeare took part of the story and imagery for his play from these accounts, he maintains that the play could not therefore have been written before the middle of 1610 and that it was probably not acted until the winter or spring of 1611. It owed its popularity to its action having been 'the subject of discourse during an entire year preceding its representation.'[11]

The pamphlet demonstrated how quickly Malone could still write when his competitive instinct was roused. Francis Douce provided the competition with his *Illustrations of Shakspeare and Ancient Manners* (1807), in which he suggests the same thesis about *The Tempest* as Malone does, though without careful documentation.[12] Michael Kearney reassured Malone, 'It was surely a proper measure to print the account of the

[9] 28 June 1808, ibid., p. 242. [10] 21 March 1809, *P–M Letters*, p. 253.
[11] *Account of The Tempest*, pp. 4, 35–36.
[12] See Malone's Advertisement (dated 12 January 1808) to the *Account*.

shipwreck illustrating the tempest; your discovery of which would otherwise have passed to another.'[13] Burney, who had always been troubled by the play's always 'being placed at the head of our dear Shakspeare's *Comedies*', was convinced that Malone had finally cleared up the confusion: 'no doubt can possibly remain in the readers of your narrative that the dreadful Tempest and Shipwreck at the Bermudas were the foundation of this most exquisite drama.'[14]

In each of the presentation copies of the *Account* that he sent friends and acquaintances, Malone carefully wrote: 'Not published; only eighty copies having been printed. It is requested, that this pamphlet may not be inadvertently put into the hands of any person who may be likely to publish any part of it.' The last thing he wanted was a competing Shakespeare editor to use his findings before he could include them in his own edition; nor did he wish his ideas to be brought to the public's notice in a review. In light of that, it was a risky business to circulate so many copies. Inevitably, the pamphlet was reviewed behind his back in the December 1808 issue of *The British Critick*[15] by his old acquaintance Robert Nares, formerly Assistant Librarian in the British Museum, to whom he had sent a copy. After summarizing all Malone's evidence and thereby spoiling its impact in his forthcoming edition, Nares claims that Capell had beaten him to this discovery decades before. Malone did not take this lying down. He promptly wrote a twenty-page *Supplement* to the *Account*, had it printed, and sent it to all the recipients of the original pamphlet. After reviving the old joke about Capell's inability to write, he explains that neither Farmer, Percy, nor Steevens was 'acquainted with the disaster of Somers ... ; it is manifest, that neither they nor Mr. Capell had the slightest suspicion that the storm which dispersed Somers's fleet, and wrecked his vessel on these islands, gave rise to the play.' As for himself, he 'certainly had no notion of the true origin of the comedy, till in the year 1800 or 1801 I read Jourdan's narrative of the disaster that befel [*sic*] his Admiral: when the passage in THE TEMPEST, in which an account is given of the dispersion of Alonzo's fleet ... struck me so forcibly, that I thought Shakspeare must have had the incidents attending Somers's voyage, immediately in view, when he wrote his comedy.'[16] There the matter rested, but the cat, nonetheless, was out of the bag.

The ease with which he wrote the *Account* ought to have encouraged him to write the last third of the *Life*, but he still found other things to do in the

---

[13] 21 April 1808, Ms. Malone 39, fols. 77–78.

[14] 24 February 1808, Ms. Malone 38, fol. 141.

[15] Pp. 630–33. See Malone's explanation of Nares' behaviour, to Percy, 21 March 1809, *P–M Letters*, pp. 250–51.

[16] In 1815 George Chalmers published *Another Account of the Incidents, from which the Title, and a Part of the Story of Shakspeare's Tempest, were Derived*, denying any discovery by Malone and urging 1613 as the date of the play but declining any interest in a 'mad-brain'd war' over it.

autumn of 1808, 'passing two works of other writers through the press, which occupied a great deal of my time and much obstructed my own more immediate pursuits.'[17] One of these was his editorial revision of Barrett's *Essay on the Earlier Part of the Life of Swift* that appeared in the autumn of 1808 in Nichols' edition, *The Works of the Rev. Jonathan Swift DD.* A few months after Nichols published his second edition of Swift in 1803, Malone began to think, with Nichols' encouragement, of adding biographically to the work for a third edition. Hence he made some enquiries of John Kearney, then Provost of Trinity College, concerning Swift's early academic training. This material appeared in the third edition and 'in some measure', Malone told Percy, gave rise to Barrett's account of Swift's education.[18] But he thought little more about Barrett, whom he did not know personally, or his biography, until April when the two men began to correspond; by June, Malone had the essay in hand for revisions and additions.[19] Burney, who got the wrong idea from Nichols, hoped the editor of the new edition and the author of the biography would be 'the English Aristarchus & friend of Shakespeare & Dryden'.[20] In his preface, Nichols makes it clear, however, that the essay had been merely revised by the 'friendly exertions' of Malone, 'a name respected by every literary man'; he adds that two new Swift letters were obtained by Malone's 'persevering attention.'[21] Nichols does not say so, but Malone was also responsible for persuading Nichols to reorganize Swift's letters in the edition. Just before publication, Malone remarked to Percy that 'the Letters (according to my suggestion in my Dryden[22]) are at last to be arranged in chronological order.'[23]

An ironic postscript to Malone's involvement in this Swift edition is Sir Walter Scott's appearance at about this time as the new self-declared biographer of Swift. Although Malone was not centrally or deeply involved in this Swift project, he was piqued to see Scott again moving in. Just before Nichols' edition was published, Michael Kearney, who appeared to be aware of Malone's irritation, reassured him: 'W. Scott will not be able to collect any anecdotical [*sic*] circumstances relative to Swift in Ireland; his contemporaries are all dead – The gossiping stories that may remain in memory are worthless.' Then after publication, Kearney reported that a woman, 'the harbinger of Walter Scott; who menaces a biographical

[17] To Percy, 21 March 1809, *P–M Letters*, p. 246.
[18] To Percy, 21 March 1809, *P–M Letters*, p. 246.
[19] See Barrett to Malone, 22 June 1808, South Kensington Museum, Ms. Forster 371, item 4; there are twelve letters in all from Barrett to Malone, from 18 April 1808 to 7 April 1809, items 1–12, in this repository. Malone's revised manuscript copy of Barrett's piece is in the Ms. Malone 37, fols. 70–92. See Malone to Percy, *P–M Letters*, p. 247.
[20] 23 June [1808], Ms. Malone 163.
[21] See Nichols' *Illustrations*, V, p. 396; and Malone to Percy, 21 March 1809, *P–M Letters*, p. 247.
[22] See *DPW*, I:ii, introductory note opposite the first letter.
[23] 28 June 1808, *P–M Letters*, p. 245.

invasion', was roaming around Dublin digging up facts. She found Barrett and interviewed him, but the latter 'fought shy & fled the ground. He is engaged to Nicolls [*sic*].'[24] Scott, however, was not about to be put off by such evasive tactics. He persevered and in 1814 published his own triumphant edition of Swift with a popular new *Life*.

Back in 1806, Malone decided it was time to honour his old friend, the statesman William Gerard Hamilton – 'Single-speech Hamilton', as he came to be known since after his brilliant and celebrated maiden speech in the House of Commons in 1755 he scarcely ever spoke there again. Hamilton, who died in 1796, had been a member of The Club and long an intimate friend of Dr Johnson's. Johnson respected his conversational powers and once remarked to him, 'I am very unwilling to be left alone, Sir, and therefore I go with my company down the first pair of stairs, in some hopes that they may, perhaps, return again. I go with you, Sir, as far as the street-door.'[25] It will be recalled that Hamilton had also retained Burke as his personal secretary when he was Chief Secretary for Ireland and Chancellor of the Irish Exchequer in the 1760s, and then had taken on Johnson briefly for a similar reason at just the time Malone was getting to know Johnson. Hamilton's promise remained unfulfilled, a fact that perplexed both his friends and the public. When he suffered a small stroke in 1792, Charlemont told Malone, 'There was a man whose talents were equal to every undertaking, and yet from indolence, or from a too fastidious vanity, of from what other cause I know not, he has done nothing.'[26] Malone remained his steadfast friend until his death.

In a letter to Lord Egremont in November 1806, Malone mentioned he had just been given access to Hamilton's papers: 'I spent several hours ... looking over the numerous volumes and papers and [have] selected such as seemed to promise anything worthy of being preserved.' There were two trunks of Hamilton's manuscripts, fifty-four volumes in all, 'great and small, some filled with writing, others containing only a few pages of manuscript.' Although he found little to interest the public, just a few speeches in the English and Irish Parliaments, several odes, and, above all, a treatise on parliamentary oratory, he decided to make a 'curious, little volume' out of the material.[27] Egremont acquired more papers for him, looked into a portrait of Hamilton that 'was taken at Goodwood [House] about thirty years ago with mine & many others, at a Christmas Party', and generally smoothed the way towards publication.[28]

Malone proceeded at a leisurely pace until an unexpected discovery

[24] 20 August and 25 November 1808, Ms. Malone 39, fols. 81, 83. On Scott, see Kearney to Malone, 9 December 1809 (Ms. Malone 39, fols. 85–86).   [25] Hill-Powell, I, p. 490.

[26] 20 August 1792, *HMC*, XIII, 8, p. 198.

[27] 14 November 1806, Petworth House Archives, 55.

[28] See Egremont's letters to Malone, 24 August, 3 September, and 17 October 1807; and 3 or 7 March 1808, Ms. Malone 38, fols. 220, 224, 226, 228.

in the summer of 1808 hastened publication. On 8 June, he told Burney about this 'dead secret', a 'new *scrap* of our friend Dr Johnson, that now first will see the light', entitled 'Considerations on Corn.' He was appending it to *Parliamentary Logick*, to which 'I do not mean to put my name, as editor; as I suspect some of the rhetorical precepts will be attacked. Johnson's paper is written with his usual vigour; and explains one of his prayers, – "On engaging in politicks with Mr. H.".'[29] Malone rounded up biographical data[30] and came to press in the autumn at the same time as the Swift edition.

Malone's memoir is a hotchpotch of fifty pages of elaborate praise, chiefly of Hamilton's speaking and writing, his criticism of books, and his friendship with Johnson. There are also four pages on Hamilton's friendship with Robert Jephson, the relevance of which probably escaped most of his readers, which he intended as a tribute to Jephson more than to Hamilton. There was also a ten-page argument against Hamilton as the author of the anonymous, politically partisan 'Letters of Junius' (1769–72), about the authorship of which people had speculated and gossiped for decades since their publication. For years, Hamilton had been, along with Burke, suspected as the author; Malone dismisses the possibility with convincing even-handedness.[31]

The book's reception justified Malone's decision not to place his name on the title page, for about a year after publication Francis Jeffrey attacked it in a scathing, politically motivated review in the *Edinburgh Review*, mocking it for (among other things) its perishability: 'This is all that remains of the famous Single-Speech Hamilton', he writes; it 'seems pretty well advanced in its voyage to oblivion.' After agreeing that Hamilton could not have been Junius because he could not write well enough, Jeffrey rebukes the editor, whose identity he appears not to have known in spite of a broad hint in the *Gentleman's Magazine* the previous June,[32] for justifying 'the personal politics of the author' and 'that cold-blooded indifference... which prevented him from entering with zeal into the views of any party.' 'This', Jeffrey adds, 'is a far more dangerous heresy than the mere idolatry of his abilities, and requires to be denounced with somewhat greater severity.'[33] Ever since the *Edinburgh Review* (with some bias) attacked his *Dryden* as an 'undistinguishing collection of rubbish', Malone expected the worst from it. He even imagined himself attacked for his contribution to Nichols' Swift edition: 'I suppose [the edition] has been abundantly abused, according to their usual method of depreciating whatever they do not understand.'[34]

---

[29] 8 June 1808, Folger, C.a. 2 (14).

[30] See Anthony Hamilton to Malone, 24 June 1808, Ms. Malone 38, fols. 263–64.

[31] See Malone's journal for 1792, Prior, 'Maloniana', pp. 418–24.

[32] The volume was reviewed positively in *Gentleman's Magazine*, LXXIX (June 1809), 529–35.

[33] *Edinburgh Review*, XV, 163–75.

[34] To Percy, 21 March 1809, *P–M Letters*, pp. 247, 254.

Another public show of respect towards Johnson that Malone planned was a new, correct, and expanded edition of the *Dictionary*. Towards this, beginning in November 1808, he systematically annotated all three volumes. He did it to counter the steady corruption of the *Dictionary* by greedy booksellers since Johnson's death. On the flyleaf of the first volume of the fifth edition (1775), the last one that in his view was correctly printed, he wrote (in 1810) that all the editions since Johnson's death had 'accumulated errors of the press; and the booksellers, whose chief object is profit, have rendered abridgement or suppression, in order to bring this work into a smaller compass.' Malone's annotations are very detailed; he combed through the three volumes, examining each definition and its illustrations and writing corrections and additions in margins and on slips of paper that he glued to the pages, keyed to words. He even counted his own annotations in each of the volumes – 360, 2,261, and 283 respectively – and made lists of 'Moderns Quoted' and 'English Idioms.' This astonishing effort cost him dearly in time and energy.[35] He never published a revised *Dictionary*, nor have his annotations ever been published.

Since he did not take on any of these projects to promote his own reputation, it is perhaps superfluous to note that they won him little or no credit. While it was valuable to Hamilton's friends to have biographical facts about him collected into a single narrative, and even more valuable to have Johnson's essay on the Corn Laws published, the fact remains that these literary 'avocations' brought him a year or more closer to the end of his days without his having written notably more about Shakespeare.

3

Malone's family were less interested in whether he would ever complete his *Shakespeare* than in his health and general well-being. Knowing he would now never leave London unless he had to, they continued to spend their summers there with him. Unfortunately, virtually no correspondence between them after 1808 has survived over this period. There is a rare glimpse of Malone's domestic life in the autumn of 1809 when his landlord forced him to have the interior of his house completely painted.[36] He retreated to Brighton to stay with Metcalfe but resented even this brief dislocation. The painting took three long months, but after it was over he was able to see its value, as he told Percy: 'I was obliged about three months ago, to give my house a thorough repair. Indeed it wanted painting so much in particular, that it could not be endured any longer; yet I was extremely unwilling to undergo the inconvenience which it induced, as it was necessary to take down all my books, and to scatter my Manuscripts

---

[35] Malone's annotated copy of the 1775 *Dictionary* is in the BL C.45.
[36] The name of Malone's street had recently been changed to Foley Place.

and various papers in such unaccustomed places, that I feared I should have mislaid many of them, and have never got them together again. – However matters have turned out better than I expected, and I think I have got up all my books, nearly in the very places where they stood before, which is a great help to the memory.'[37] The redecorating gave him a sense of renewal, but this did not transfer to his work. His family's visits did not help either. 'The truth is', he grumbled in the spring of 1810, 'my Brother and his family arrived in London ... and I entertained them for a fortnight, till they found a house in Upper Harley Street ... where I have since been much engaged with them.'[38]

He was 'overpower'd' on 4 June 1810 by the sudden death of Windham. It was hard for him to tell Percy the 'calamitous' news: 'the impression it then made on me, is almost as strong and vivid now, as when he was snatch'd from us.' His 'brief sketch of his private and publick life' appeared in the June issue of the *Gentleman's Magazine*,[39] but because it was so sketchy he decided to turn it into pamphlet form, to include the circumstances leading to Windham's death, 'not for publication, but for dispersion among his friends and my own.' He completed it in one month, although it took him 'more time than might have been expected, which to your lordship, who are well acquainted with the difficulty of ascertaining minute facts, will not seem surprizing [*sic*].' He sent out one hundred copies.[40]

As Malone acknowledges in his preface, he wrote *A Biographical Memoir of the Late Right Honourable William Windham* to do justice to his own 'feelings and conceptions.' Its style is unashamedly panegyric, as is evident in this passage: at Eton, Windham was 'the best cricketer, the best leaper, swimmer, rower, skaiter [*sic*]; the best fencer, the best boxer, the best runner, and the best horseman of his time.' He arrives at this judgment: 'As some centuries will probably pass away before a Johnson and a Burke shall appear among us, so neither is it to be expected, that for a long series of years another Windham shall arise. He was unquestionably the most distinguished man of the present time.'[41] Malone concludes with a moving account, setting the record straight (as he is careful to tell the reader), of how Windham incurred the wound that eventually killed him, how he endured painful operations, and how he finally succumbed.

The *Memoir* offered little that was biographically new or objective, but its preparation helped Malone over a loss that emptied his remaining days of much of their meaning and pleasure. Nothing would ever be the same, not The Club 'nor indeed London itself: for I had lived so long in such close

[37] 23 November 1809, *P–M Letters*, pp. 257–58.
[38] To Percy, 30 April 1810, *P–M Letters*, p. 262.
[39] *Gentleman's Magazine*, LXX (June, 1810), 588–93.
[40] 11 September 1810, *P–M Letters*, p. 267.
[41] *Biographical Memoir of ... William Windham*, pp. 8, 13.

intimacy with him, that the loss of his society and friendship will be deeply felt during the short period of life than now remains for me ... But God's will be done, in this, as in all other human events!'[42]

For a time, partly at others' urging, Malone considered expanding the pamphlet, perhaps into a full Life of Windham, for which he explored several sources, especially Burney.[43] As late as the middle of 1811, he was still considering it, but on 3 July he wrote to George Ellis, good friend to Windham and co-founder of the *Anti-Jacobin*, suggesting he write it instead, not merely because his own studies for too long had been 'out of the line of politicks', but because 'it is wholly incompatible with the work in which I am engaged, the second edition of my Shakspeare, which, together with his Life, I would fain execute, before I am taken away from literary & every other kind of labour.' Ellis was well qualified, he felt, because 'I have always thought that it is of great importance in biography, that the writer should have been well acquainted with the person of whom he treats.'[44] Ellis accepted but died before he could write it.

For literary 'chit-chat', Malone now had only Bindley and Burney in London and Percy and Kearney in Ireland. He maintained an interest in The Club, but even that was waning although Percy, ever sensitive about his reputation and still irritated over the way Boswell had described members of The Club in his *Life of Johnson*, was worried that he was contemplating a book containing biographical vignettes of all the members in The Club's history. He urged Malone in April 1811, either to send him anything he had written about him for vetting or 'to commit to the flames whatever he has collected on this Subject, for nothing could be more unfriendly and injurious than to leave among his papers incorrect Statements, which might afterwards ... wound the feelings of *his* surviving family.'[45] Of course, he quickly added, someone of Malone's 'integrity and honour' could not be that careless, but in his reply Malone sounds irritated:

I never had a thought of writing any [such memoirs] ... nor ever collected a single material for such a work, or wrote a single line on the subject, excepting only the biographical memoir of ... Mr Windham. I have indeed collected *prints* of many of our Members, and had drawings from pictures made of some others, of whom there were no engraved portraits; but my scheme never went further.[46]

Percy did not have much time left to worry about such matters because he died only five months later, on 30 September. While Malone was always

[42] To Percy, 11 September 1810, *P–M Letters*, p. 269.
[43] 27 July 1810, Folger, C.a.2 (18). See Malone's letters to Burney, 3, 13, and 28 August 1810, Folger, C.a.2 (18, 20, 21); and Burney's reply on 23 August 1810 (Add. 44–45).
[44] This letter is in the F. W. Hilles collection. See also Malone to H. Legge, 10 July 1811, BL Add. Ms. 37854, fols. 178–79.   [45] 16 April 1811, *P–M Letters*, p. 274.
[46] 14 May 1811, *P–M Letters*, p. 275. Percy apparently misunderstood or forgot what Malone wrote on 11 August 1807, *P–M Letters*, p. 228.

grateful for Percy as a correspondent, especially after Charlemont died, there had never been the warmth between them that he enjoyed with several others. He scribbled last comment on Percy, accurate except for the date of Percy's death, informative but without much emotion, on the latter's last letter: 'He had been blind from about the year 1806, and died at his house at Dromore in Ireland Oct. 1811, at the age, I think, of 83. We had been acquainted from about the year 1775; and corresponded for near 20 years.'[47] This is accurate but unemotional. Bindley's remark on Percy's death in a letter to Malone probably captured Malone's own feelings: 'Poor Man! What apprehension he had about what would be said of him; he needed not to have been afraid. Our friend Nichols will embalm him richly I dare say in the next Gentlemans [Magazine], and as Thersites [Ritson] is gone before him, there is no danger of any injury's being done to his memory.'[48]

The final literary task that Malone performed was to bring out the sixth edition of Boswell's *Life of Johnson* in April 1811. It contains a few new letters of Johnson's as well as some new information on his friendship with James Compton, whom Boswell ignored and who was at this time living in Islington.[49] He still gave Michael Kearney the impression of literary industriousness, 'not ... unpleasant, and I am sure beneficial to your health and spirits. Your old friend Shakspeare is inexhaustible and yet I rejoice that you are pushing towards a termination, that I may see your work before my departure from life.'[50] Kearney here struck an appropriately discreet note, for by now Malone had grown brittle about his Shakespeare work. When Nichols casually asked him, in January 1810, for help with the edition of Thomas Fuller's *Worthies* he was preparing, Malone replied tetchily: 'I am sure you are perfectly sensible that as an author and now actually engaged in a very important literary work, I stand in a different situation from a mere idle gentleman who amuses himself by collecting literary curiosities. If my second edition of Shakspeare were published, I should have no difficulty at all.'[51] But with Shakespeare he did little more. He served notice in a letter of 13 June 1810 that his research was finished: 'I conceive by various researches during these last twenty years I have obtained all that I am ever likely to find on this subject.'[52] Nor would he do any more writing of the *Life* or his history of the stage, both of which were incomplete when he died in 1812. It would fall to young Boswell to complete his edition for him.

In the opening of his Advertisement to Malone's second edition, the so-

[47] *P–M Letters*, p. 274.   [48] 9 October 1811, Ms. Malone 38, fol. 45.
[49] See Malone to Burney Junior, 11 October 1810, on the sixth edition (Folger).
[50] Michael Kearney to Malone, 8 April 1811, Ms. Malone 39, fols. 107–8.
[51] See Nichols' letter, Ms. Malone 39, fol. 150; and Malone's reply on 24 January 1810 (Folger).
[52] To R. B. Wheeler, Shakespeare's Birthplace Trust, Ms. 33, fols. 6–7.

called third variorum of 1821, Boswell explains the circumstances that led to his taking on the huge task of 'superintending' the edition. He had always loved Malone, he writes, ever since infancy, but 'when more advanced years had rendered me less unworthy of his society, I was permitted to enjoy it in the most unreserved and confidential manner, and was made a partaker of his literary views and sentiments.' So 'when he was finally preparing the result of his researches on that subject for the press' – probably in the last two or three years of his life – 'he availed himself of my assistance in the collection and arrangement of his scattered materials, which the gradual failure of his eyesight made every day more irksome and difficult to himself.' Boswell adds that during this time Malone would sometimes 'in a half-jocular tone' say to him, 'if any thing should prevent him from bringing [the edition] to a conclusion, that task must devolve upon me; but in his last illness he made this request to me in such terms, that I must have felt ashamed of myself for ever after, if I had hesitated for a moment ... '. Boswell never said so, though he must have thought it, but his acceptance of the editorial mantle was a splendid and fitting way for him to express his gratitude for Malone's love for his father. He affectionately concludes the Advertisement by referring to him as 'MINE OWN AND MY FATHER'S FRIEND.' His work thus was cut out for him, though he did not then know the half of it, and in his last days Malone was relieved of the deep anxiety that his labour of many years might never reach the public.[53]

4

The physical deterioration that ended Malone's life came swiftly and unexpectedly. At the end of January 1812, as he told a close friend of the family in Ireland on 17 April, he was suddenly struck by a dramatic loss of strength and flesh due to the failure of his digestive system. For ten weeks he had suffered mightily and kept the news from his family because Kate, to whom 'from my earliest years I have been accustomed to communicate ... every sentiment of my heart', was already distraught over the illness of Catherine and 'it would quite break her heart to learn how ill I have been, and indeed am.' He rejected the idea of a spa or seaside resort for a change of air, 'as I have an abhorrence of public places', but on the advice of his doctor, Sir Henry Halford, royal physician, who 'tried the usual medicines, but with little effect', he took to the country. He 'borrowed' Taplow Court from Lady Thomond from mid-March to mid-April, 'on condition of being my own purveyor', but he did not enjoy 'one

---

[53] *PP (1821)*, I, pp. v-vi. Metcalfe told Farington that Malone left '£200 and the superintendence of his papers to James Boswell'. He also 'left £3000 to each of his two sisters; £500 to Jephson Junr.' (3 July 1812, *DF*, XII, p. 4153).

soft or genial day.' He tried everything, even some distraction with Shakespeare:

My course was half a pint of new milk in bed at half-past seven. About half-past eight I rose, dressed for the day, and walked about half an hour before breakfast. From eleven to half-past one I devoted to the newspapers and a letter or two, and a few pages of *Shakspeare*. Then appeared a bark draught; after that I walked two or three miles if the weather would at all permit; dinner at five; tea at eight; the bark again at ten; and so to bed.

Neither medicine, nor air, nor Shakespeare helped. He returned to London even weaker and was greeted by the doctor's prognosis that if he survived 'he could not promise me ever to be again as in times past, but that I might live some years with tolerable health and strength.' For good measure, before rushing off to Windsor, the doctor 'ordered a new course of medicines.'[54]

Malone rallied briefly, but by the last week of April, as he told Windham's widow, he was again 'tormented ... with an accidental malady, that had no connection with my original complaint; and it became so violent on Monday & Tuesday of this week that my Physician was evidently alarmed; but by midday on Wednesday he was able to relieve me; and since that a strong infusion of bitters has been tried, which made me miserably sick this morning and would not remain on the stomach.'[55] On 28 April, he received an urgent letter from Catherine with news of Harriet's excruciating pains in the hip and calling on him 'for all the comfort I can give her.' He now could keep his secret no longer to himself. To Lady Sunderlin he replied in desperation, 'But alas! I wanted comfort myself; and the concealment of my own illness for near three months was a sad and heavy weight on my own mind.' Even so, in his own suffering he was moved by Harriet's and recommended potions and salt water hot baths for her which he had tried twenty years earlier when he damaged his own hip and leg.[56] He wrote also to Catherine who arrived with his brother in a matter of days. Nothing could be done, however. He died on 25 May.

One of his doctors told Farington that nothing could help him: 'it was a breaking up of the Constitution. He had no local complaint; it was general weakness and gradual decay.'[57] His brother, who with his sister Catherine was with him in the final days and hours, wrote to Boswell at nine on the morning of his death: 'My poor and ever-dearest Brother drew his last breath this morning a few minutes after four o'clock, & died, we thank the goodness of Providence, exactly in the way that we cou'd have wished him,

---

[54] Prior, pp. 314–15. This letter has been lost.
[55] To Mrs Joseph Windham, 24 April 1812, OFB 25.127.
[56] Prior, pp. 316–17. The letter is lost.   [57] *DF*, XII, pp. 4320–21.

& without a single moan ... '[58] When she read about his death in the papers, Mrs Piozzi wrote simply but feelingly enough in her diary: 'Mr Malone dead in the Paper; poor Malone! last of the old set. Helas!'[59] Young Boswell wrote in his *Memoir* of Malone that Malone 'left no instructions about his funeral; but his brother, who was anxious, with affectionate solicitude, to execute every wish he had formed, having inferred from something that dropped from him, that it was his desire to be buried among his ancestors in Ireland, his remains were conveyed to that country, and interred at the family seat of Baronston, in the county of Westmeath.'[60]

---

[58] Sunderlin to Boswell Junior, 25 May 1812 (interleaved in the Beinecke 1st edn. of Boswell Junior's *A Biographical Memoir of the Late Edmond Malone*). See also Malone to Lady Sunderlin, 4 May 1812, on his final illness (Prior, pp. 316–17).

[59] Hester Piozzi's diary is owned by Mrs Evans Brynbella. Michael Kearney wrote the epitaph for Malone's tombstone (see Ms. Malone 37, fol. 203).   [60] *PP (1821)*, I, p. lxx.

Epilogue

The Malone–Boswell third variorum
edition (1821)

Lord Sunderlin wrote to Boswell on the morning of Malone's death asking him to come to Malone's house promptly, for there were immediate decisions to be made concerning his brother's unfinished work. Sunderlin was executor of the whole estate, but he needed Boswell urgently as the unofficial literary executor. The first thing Boswell did was write the obituary, in which (without stating he would have anything to do with it) he said this about Malone's unfinished edition:

From the careful habit which he had of entering every new acquisition in its proper place, and the accurate references which he made to the source of his information, we should apprehend there will be little difficulty in the carrying this design into effect. With such a stock of materials as perhaps no other man than Mr Malone could have collected, the executor of his critical will must have a delightful task.[1]

The reality was that it took him a decade to complete and publish the edition, in twenty-one volumes. It appeared almost thirty years later than Malone had originally planned.

In the Advertisement to the edition, Boswell admits that there were many people more qualified than he to have taken the edition in hand, but from 'constant communication' with Malone he 'was better able to ascertain his final judgment on many contested points which occur in the illustration of our author's text, which, without that guidance, might have been frequently doubtful.' Still, there had been problems. One was Malone's handwriting. 'I may add', he continues, 'that it is not every one that could have deciphered his notes', for although Malone had a good hand when he was not rushed, his not very 'tenacious' memory forced him into 'the habit of using the first scrap of paper which presented itself, and marking down his memoranda in a species of short hand, of which no one, who was not accustomed to his manner, could readily comprehend the meaning.' Another problem, an enormous obstacle in fact, related to the large gaps in Malone's *Life of Shakespeare*, 'a chasm ... which I am unable to supply', and innumerable scattered memoranda that Boswell tried to

---

[1] *Edinburgh Annual Register* (1 June 1812); the obituary also appeared, almost word for word, in *Gentleman's Magazine*, XXXII (June 1812), 606.

271

round up, complete, and insert in various places throughout the twenty-
one volumes. Malone had led people to believe that all that was wanting
was the last third of the biography, and in his mind that certainly was the
main task he had left – the culmination of his life's work – but he had much
more left to do than that. In retrospect, one feels he must have known at
least by 1808, when he published his pamphlet on *The Tempest*, that he
would not live to finish. As the recent historian of Shakespearean biography
has remarked, Boswell 'coped heroically with an impossible task.'[2] A
further critical problem for Boswell was his frequent disagreement with
Malone on the interpretation of Shakespeare's text; the reader must realize
he is not 'responsible for the erroneous opinions' in Malone's commentary,
'if such there be.'[3]

All the prefatory material is in the first three volumes. Volume one
contains all prefaces that had been prefixed to earlier modern editions,
including Rowe's *Life*, though without Malone's critical notes that in the
1790 edition discredited virtually everything Rowe had to say. Malone
incorporated these notes, and several new ones on Rowe, into his new *Life*.
The first volume also contains several critical dissertations by Malone and
others. One of these, the 'Essay on the Metre and Phraseology of
Shakspeare', Boswell himself wrote with notes of Malone's that he found.
Malone, as we have seen, planned the essay as an attack on what he saw as
Steevens' capricious textual emendations in his 1793 edition as he corrected
supposed corruptions in Shakespeare's phraseology and metre. Boswell
writes in his Advertisement:

They both professed to follow the old copies with scrupulous fidelity, except where
a clear necessity compelled them to depart from the readings which they supplied.
To this plan it will be found Mr. Malone has still steadily adhered, while his rival
critick has latterly adopted maxims directly contrary to the opinions which he
formerly maintained.[4]

While Malone continued to retrieve Shakespeare's historical context for
language and metre, Steevens manipulated the verse 'in order to make it
perfectly consonant to our modern notions of metrical harmony.'[5] In his
'Essay on the Metre and Phraseology of Shakspeare', Malone was
'determined to bring these topicks into one connected view', toward which
'he had made considerable progress, but which, I am sorry to say, he did
not live to complete.' So he has taken it upon himself to write it, adding 'the
result of my reading to what my friend has left behind him.'[6]

Boswell placed the *Life* in the second volume, together with 'explanatory
documents' that Malone collected, such as extracts from the Stratford
Register and the Stationers' books, and information on Shakespeare's coat
of arms, mortgage, and will. The *Life* runs to 525 pages, but only 287 of

[2] Schoenbaum, *Shakespeare's Lives*, p. 246.   [3] *PP* (1821), I, pp. vi–viii.
[4] Ibid., I, pp. x–xi.   [5] Ibid., p. 511.   [6] Ibid., p. xi.

these consist of Malone's completed narrative. Considering how much of himself he put into his research and how intensely he wished to complete the narrative, the fragment we have – two-thirds of what he planned – is disappointing. It does not take Shakespeare very far, just barely out of Stratford. Nor does it address his character as a poet or as a man. Boswell printed the completed section as he found it. Where the narrative breaks off – just after a brief account of Shakespeare as an actor and before he embarked on a London stage career – he inserted Malone's revised chronology of the plays, which had of course previously existed as a separate essay. He admits that Malone would not have liked this decision, but he defends it by observing, 'the life of a writer must be strangely defective which contained no account of his works.'[7] Following the chronology are several memoranda Boswell found among Malone's papers that he inserted as often as possible into Malone's narrative. He then tacked on a fifty-four-page Appendix containing various documents and notes pertaining to Shakespeare's family and the history of Stratford.

Malone planned to write a section on 'a History of the prevailing manners of the English World' to be inserted into the *Life* where his completed fragment ends – at the point Shakespeare arrived in London and began his stage career.[8] Boswell states that he found the materials for this history in 'so loose and disjointed a state, that I could not have ventured upon the labour of arranging them without protracting the publication of this work to a distant period.' He also notes that these materials did not appear to have anything to do with dramatic history, but 'are rather illustrative of the general political state of the country.' Although he did not use any of this, he assures his readers, 'I have scrupulously abstained from destroying a single scrap of his literary remains.'[9]

In addition to the fragmentation and disorder that Boswell found in the papers relating to the *Life*, the narrative part of the biography that Malone managed to finish suffers, like his *Life of Dryden*, from substantive flaws.[10] Over one-third is devoted to a protracted and fairly tedious consideration of two poems by Spenser, *The Tears of the Muses* and *Colin Clout's Come Home Again*. Hungry to find genuine allusions to Shakespeare in contemporary literature, Malone spends much time rejecting a supposed allusion to 'pleasant Willy' in *Tears* and accepting another to Aetion in *Colin Clout*. The problem with both these critical efforts is that as the references in the poems are very ambiguous, any efforts to pin down the allusions are reduced to reasoned guesswork. Modern scholarship has rejected both as

---

[7] Ibid., p. xx. [8] See his letter to Davenport in December 1794, *M–D*, pp. 81–82.
[9] *PP (1821)*, I, p. xx.
[10] See Schoenbaum's discussion of the disappointments and achievements of the *Life of Shakespeare* in *Shakespeare's Lives*, pp. 236–48.

allusions to Shakespeare. 'These sections of Malone's narrative would no
doubt deserve a place in a study of Spenser', writes one critic; 'here they
are irrelevant, and it is hard to believe that they would not have wrecked
the symmetry of the Life, had Malone lived to complete it.'[11] Another
imbalance is the ratio of narrative text to footnote text. As in the *Life of
Dryden*, the footnotes frequently smother the text and destroy its rhythm
and momentum. There is also, surprising coming from Malone, too much
conjecture, even if most of it is carefully thought out. He conjectures
wrongly that Shakespeare's wife did not belong to the Hathaways of
Shottery, that he was trained in the law, and that Davenant was his godson.

On the other hand, Malone discovered more about Shakespeare's life
than anyone before or since, and for this reason the *Life* must be highly
regarded for its content. His discoveries about Shakespeare's genealogy,
which he obtained from Davenport and (to a lesser extent) Jordan, the
Stratford Corporation books, parish registers, sundry documents in
Worcester, the Stamp Office, and the College of Arms, comprise a solid
body of knowledge. He also discovered much about Shakespeare's
immediate family: the Ardens, his father's limited finances and trade as a
glover (not as a wool dealer as had been thought), Anne Hathaway, the
poet's brothers and sisters, and his children and grandchildren. He was the
first to record aspects of the Elizabethan world of Stratford, from the names
of bailiffs and population figures to the education Shakespeare would have
received at the free school and the names of a few of his probable teachers.
He demolishes once more, with increased evidence, the deer-poaching
episode, as well as the story that Shakespeare held horses at the theatre
door; and he contends, with plausible evidence, that it is likely the poet
conceived his love for the theatre in Stratford from seeing Warwick's Men,
Leicester's Men, and the Queen's Men perform there, and that he left
Stratford for London with the idea of pursuing an acting career. Boswell
also rescued from Malone's papers innumerable notes on aspects of
Shakespeare's life that he introduced at propitious times in the *Life* and that
had the effect of reducing the fragmentary character of the work. He also
published that letter of 25 October 1598 from Richard Quiney to
Shakespeare, of the discovery of which Malone was justifiably proud and
excited.

In the third volume, Boswell printed Malone's corrected 294-page
Historical Account of The Rise and Progress of The English Stage. This he
followed with an Appendix and Additions extracted from Malone's notes
and Henslowe's account book, and with essays on theatrical history by
George Chalmers and James Markland. In his *Biographical Memoir* of
Malone, which he wrote in 1814, Boswell says of the history of the stage:

[11] Ibid., p. 243.

His History of the Stage has now been published upwards of twenty years, during which period the attention of literary men has been much more generally drawn to researches of this nature; but it is still the standard authority to which all refer, and the guide in all subsequent inquiries.[12]

To have written the 'standard authority' on the *Life* as well as stage history, Boswell insists, vindicated Malone's astonishing attention to documentary detail, even if in his lifetime this often exposed him to ridicule.

In the process of explaining in his Advertisement how and why he organized the edition as he did, Boswell offers a comprehensive defense of Malone as scholar and editor. None of this would have been necessary, he says, if Malone had completed his work, for in that event the edition would have spoken for itself and his name would have been 'a sufficient recommendation.' But in light of the several editions by rival editors like Steevens and not a few attacks that had appeared in that time and muddied the waters, the public needed to be reminded of his friend's editorial and scholarly principles.

Boswell must often have heard Malone say that in his edition he would settle the score with Steevens for deceptions and double-dealing, and he decided that the best defence was a good offence. Steevens became the chief target against whose duplicitous and derisory comments he advanced his assessment of Malone as a scholar. He knew this would have greatly pleased Malone, but maintained nevertheless a level-headed approach to the subject and managed in several pages to explain Malone's attitude towards the collation of early editions while also giving credit to Capell,[13] Reed, and Steevens. Malone is his hero in this arena, however, and he summarizes:

The text has been printed according to the principle laid down by Mr. Malone, of adhering as strictly as possible to the ancient copies; and wherever they are deviated from, the reader is apprised of the alteration, and of the reasons upon which it is founded. The numerous sophistications introduced by Mr. Steevens have been removed; but it has not been thought necessary to enter into a contest about each individual passage.[14]

Malone's appreciation of Boswell's achievement in publishing his work would have known no bounds. Feeling the arduousness of his task, Boswell felt that he had fulfilled Malone's deathbed request at least adequately: 'I now take leave of this part of my task, which I have undertaken with reluctance, and have executed with pain. If in any part of it I have been betrayed into undue warmth (of which I am unconscious), my sub-

---

[12] *PP (1821)*, I, p. lxi.

[13] Of Capell, Boswell writes, 'I can sincerely state that I have never wished to conceal his merits...' (*PP (1821)*, I, p. xxii).

[14] *PP (1821)*, I, p. xxi. One of Malone's critics whom Boswell was eager to censure even more thoroughly than Steevens was William Gifford, Malone's sometimes friend and editor of the *Quarterly Review*, who had sarcastically attacked him in his edition of Jonson (1816) for his view that Jonson persecuted Shakespeare; see *PP (1821)*, I, pp. xxx–l.

ject ... will plead my excuse.'[15] The influence of the edition would extend throughout the nineteenth century and into the modern era of Shakespearean scholarship, which while it has demonstrated that Malone made mistakes, has also confirmed his distinctions as a pioneer not simply in matters Shakespearean but in literary-historical scholarship as a profession.

[15] *PP (1821)*, I, p. l.

Appendix A

In a manuscript at the Bodleian that Malone wrote before 1805, the year he acquired his precious 1593 edition of *Venus and Adonis*, he assessed the importance of his collection of Shakespeare editions, comparing it to others' collections: 'The Collection of Shakspeare's Plays and Poems in seven Quarto volumes, (with which several pieces on which he constructed dramas, bound up among my *Shakspeariana*, must be considered as connected) forms perhaps the most complete Assemblage of the early editions of his productions that has ever been made. It wants only the *Hamlet* of 1604, *King Richard II* 1597, *King Henry IV, Part I* 1598, and *Venus and Adonis* quarto 1593, to make it complete; and of these three plays it contains very early copies, carefully collated with those original editions; and of the fourth piece (the *Venus and Adonis* of 1593) no copy was ever seen by any of the Collectors of these precious rarities, or is now known to exist, though I have no doubt that at some future time it will be discovered.' Having, as he said, amassed as many old Shakespeare editions as he was ever likely to procure, he proceeded to list the other great collections since Pope's, all of which he knew intimately. He specified: Capell's at Trinity College, Cambridge; Steevens', 'now dispersed'; Garrick's, by then at the British Museum; John Philip Kemble's; and Charles Jennens' at Gopsal in Leicestershire, then owned by Lord Curzon. Farmer's collection, he noted, which had been dispersed and contributed to his own, was 'not sufficiently perfect to require particular notice.' He added that while one or the other of these collections contained all three of the editions he lacked, they all lacked many more of those he owned.[1]

The Shakespeare editions were the pride of Malone's library but only the centrepiece of a vast collection of early English drama and poetry. After his death in 1812, Lord Sunderlin passed on most of his books and literary papers to James Boswell Junior, Malone's literary executor, who used them to prepare the 1821 third variorum edition. Once the edition was published, Boswell handed over the collection, by agreement with Sunderlin, to the Bodleian Library, where they remain today. A catalogue of the collection was eventually published in 1836,[2]

---

[1] Ms. Malone 32.

[2] *Catalogue of Early English Poetry and Other Miscellaneous Works Illustrating the British Drama, collected by Edmond Malone Esq. and now Preserved in the Bodleian Library* (1836). The unique strength of this collection in early English drama is illustrated by its containing: 123 Shakespeare items, 32 Thomas Middleton, 17 Thomas Nashe, 25 George Chapman, 18 John Fletcher, 39 Francis Beaumont, 24 Ben Jonson, 25 Philip Massinger, 15 John Marston, 13 Christopher Marlowe,

prefaced by the following letter Sunderlin wrote to the Vice-Chancellor of Oxford University on 7 July 1815 offering his brother's collection to the Bodleian:

My brother, the late Edmond Malone, has formed a very curious collection of old English literature, which, at his death, he bequeathed to me; but at the same time expressed a wish that it should not be dispersed, but either retained as an heir-loom [sic] in his family, or deposited in some public library. Knowing as I did the just and high respect which he felt for the University of Oxford and the sense that he entertained of the politeness and liberality which he was always met with from that body in his researches, I am convinced that I cannot guide myself in their disposal in a manner that would have been more agreeable to my late brother, than by presenting them to the Bodleian, while at the same time I feel no small pleasure in laying hold of such an opportunity of shewing my respect for a University, in which I myself had the honour of being bred.

The books intended to be given by me are at present in the hands of Mr. Boswell, of Brazen Nose [sic], for the purpose of enabling him to prepare for the press the MSS. relating to Shakspeare, which my late brother left to his care; but upon the completion of that work, I wish it to be considered, that such part of the collection as is not already in the Bodleian, shall become the property of that Library. I flatter myself you will excuse me the liberty I have taken in making known to you my intentions, and have the honour to be, Rev. Sir,

Sunderlin

London July 7, 1815
No. 76, Gloucester Place

In accepting the gift, the Curators of the Bodleian promised to preserve the collection 'in a manner most worthy of Mr. Malone's distinguished literary character.' A final note reads, 'The books were not received from Mr. Boswell till the year 1821.'

But the dispersal of Malone's books and literary papers was more complicated than that. In 1803 Malone himself disposed of part of his library because he needed the money;[3] and other parts, including 2,555 lots containing duplicates of many rare English books and a collection of 700 tracts in seventy-six volumes, were sold separately at auction by Sotheby's in 1818.[4] Over the eight days of the sale, 1,913 lots of octavo editions (about 3,600 volumes), 460 lots of quarto editions (about 2,000 volumes), and 192 lots of folio editions (about 212 volumes) went under the hammer – a total of almost 6,000 volumes requiring about 500 feet of shelf space. The seventy-six volumes of tracts came into the book market again in 1838 when they were sold by Thorpe to the Bodleian.[5] Young Boswell purchased many items at the Sotheby sale but the Bodleian acquired by far the largest number, about 2,500 titles. Boswell was also the happy recipient of a remarkable gift of many of Malone's papers by the latter's sisters, doubtless out of gratitude for his work on the

11 Colley Cibber, 31 Thomas Dekker, 31 John Dryden, 24 Thomas D'Urfey, 39 Robert Green, 34 Thomas Heywood, 45 James Shirley, and 184 editions of anonymous plays.

[3] Thomas Thorpe in his Sale Catalogue I for 1841 included this item (no. 765): 'MALONE – Catalogue of a Collection of English Poetry &c., part of the Library of Edmund [sic] Malone, sold by Mr. King, 8vo. h.b., neat, with prices and purchasers' names. 1803".'

[4] See A Catalogue of the Greater Portion of the Library of Edmond Malone, Esq ... which will be sold by auction sold by Mr. S. Sotheby ... beginning Thursday, Nov. 26, 1818, for eight days.

[5] See Prior, pp. 470–71. The tracts were an extraordinarily rich collection on a multiplicity of literary and historical subjects assembled over Malone's thirty-five-year career. In a memorandum to himself, Malone specified the titles for seventy of these volumes, 'to be lettered & vamped, & in some cases tooled'. He tells for each what needs to be done. Bacon's essays, for example (vol. 24) were 'to be lettered on blue; and the title page neatly pasted on the paper in the book & at the bottom MDCXII' (Bodleian, Ms. Malone 37, fols. 29–35).

third variorum. His own library and papers, including the gift of the Malone material, came up for sale in 1825, after Boswell's death in 1822, and included almost 300 letters to Malone from many of his eminent friends such as Kemble, Burke, Steevens, Tyrwhitt, Farmer, Windham, and so on.[6]

Malone's collection of prints and engravings stayed in his family and was eventually bequeathed to The Revd. Thomas Rooper of Brighton, a relative of Malone's sister-in-law. The collection has now disappeared, although James Prior saw them in Hove, Sussex.[7] It is almost certainly this collection that is described in a small manuscript catalogue, now in the Folger Shakespeare Library,[8] in Malone's hand titled, 'English Poets.' Malone lists them under letters, with a few notes on the portraits but mostly with 'W' meaning 'Wanted by E.M.', or 'N' meaning 'never engraved.' He marked about one-fifth of the portraits 'W.' At the end he wrote: '355. Of the above 36 never engraved[;] queries 10. The number [of] engraved portraits therefore in this catalogue is 309.' Rooper also owned Reynolds' portrait of Malone, which the family presented to the National Portrait Gallery in 1883.

[6] See Prior, p. 327.

[7] Rooper left all his possessions to his wife and son William, whose son Godolphin eventually inherited them. When he died in 1903, they were divided between his five daughters. Whether or not Malone's collection of engravings and prints remained intact is not known. It is likely that the Roopers also inherited a cache of Malone's manuscripts. Henry Crabb Robinson in his *Diary, Reminiscences and Correspondence* (ed. Thomas Sadler, 1869) mentions seeing Rooper's Malone manuscripts on 13–14 December 1831.   [8] Folger 287.

Appendix B

In his memoir prefixing the 1821 variorum, Boswell wrote the following full description of Malone's character and physical appearance:

Mr. Malone, in his person, was rather under the middle size. The urbanity of his temper, and the kindness of his disposition, were depictured in his mild and placid countenance. His manners were peculiarly engaging. Accustomed from his earliest years to the society of those who were distinguished for their rank or talent, he was at all times and in all companies easy, unembarrassed, and unassuming. It was impossible to meet him, even in the most casual intercourse, without recognizing the genuine and unaffected politeness of the gentleman born and bred. His conversation was in a high degree entertaining and instructive; his knowledge was various and accurate, and his mode of displaying it void of all vanity or pretension. Though he had little relish for noisy convivial merriment, his habits were social, and his cheerfulness uniform and unclouded. As a scholar, he was liberally communicative ... His heart was warm, and his benevolence active. His charity was prompt, but judicious and discriminating; not carried away by every idle or fictitious tale of distress, but anxious to ascertain the true nature and source of real calamity, and indefatigable in his efforts to releive it. His purse and his time were at all times ready to remove the suffering and promote the welfare of others. As a friend he was warm and steady in his attachments; respect for the feelings of those whose hearts are still bleeding for his loss, prevents me from speaking of him as a brother.[1]

[1] *PP (1821)*, I, p. viii.

280

Bibliography

I. Manuscripts

The following are the principal repositories of manuscripts pertaining to Malone used in this book (smaller collections of manuscripts are cited in the notes):

Additional Manuscripts, British Library

Burney Family Autograph Correspondence, 1789–1876, Berg Collection, New York Public Library.

Charlemont Papers, *Reports of the Historical Manuscript Commission*

Fettercairn Papers, National Library of Scotland

Folger Shakespeare Library

Ms. Malone, Bodleian, Oxford University

Osborn Files, Beinecke Rare Book and Manuscript Library, Yale University.

II. Edmond Malone's publications

An Account of The Incidents, From Which The Title and Part of The Story of Shakspeare's Tempest Were Derived; and Its True Date Ascertained. 1808.

An Attempt to Ascertain the Order in which the Plays Attributed to Shakespeare Were Written. 1778. First published in the *Johnson–Steevens* Shakespeare, 2nd edn. 1778. Vol. I, pp. 269–346.

An Inquiry Into the Authenticity of Certain Miscellaneous Papers and Legal Instruments, Published Dec. 24, MDCCXCV. and Attributed to Shakspeare, Queen Elizabeth and Henry, Earl of Southampton, 1796

A Biographical Memoir of the late Right Honourable William Windham 1810.

(Editor) Boswell's *The Life of Samuel Johnson,* 3rd edn. 1799; 4th edn. 1804; 5th edn. 1807; 6th edn. 1811; 7th edn. 1811.

Conjectures Concerning the Date of ... Macbeth in *The Hibernian Magazine.* October, 1786.

The Correspondence of James Boswell with David Garrick, Edmund Burke, and Edmond Malone. Edited by Peter S. Baker, Thomas W. Copeland, George M. Kahrl, Rachel McClellan, and James M. Osborn. *The Yale editions of the private papers of James Boswell, research edition: Correspondence,* vol. 4. London, 1986.

The Correspondence of Thomas Percy and Edmond Malone. Edited by Arthur Tillotson. Baton Rouge, Louisiana, 1944.

The Correspondence of Edmond Malone, the Editor of Shakespeare, with the Rev. James Davenport, D.D., Vicar of Stratford-on-Avon, 1864.

281

(Editor) *The Critical and Miscellaneous Prose Works of John Dryden ... and An Account of the Life and Writings of the Author ...* 3 vols. 1800.

Cursory Observations on the Poems Attributed to Thomas Rowley (1782), ed. James M. Kuist, *The Augustan Reprint Society*, no. 123. Los Angeles, 1966.

A Dissertation on the Three Parts of Henry VI, tending to shew that those plays were not written originally by Shakspeare. 1787.

The Hibernian Journal (Dublin), letters by Malone 11 and 13 February 1775.

A Historical Account of the English Stage, in The Plays and Poems of William Shakspeare, ed. Edmond Malone, vol. I:i. 1790.

Letter to the Rev. Richard Farmer, D.D. Master of Emmanuel College, Cambridge; relative to the edition of Shakspeare, published in MCCXC, and some late criticisms on that work. 1792.

The Life of William Shakspeare ... And An Essay on the Phraseology and Metre of the Poet and His Contemporaries, ed. James Boswell Junior. 1821. (Extracted from Malone's 1821 edition; twenty-one copies privately printed.)

'Ode on the Royal Nuptials', in *Gratulationes: Nuptials. A Collection of Poems ... on the late Royal Nuptials by Students of the University of Dublin.* Dublin, 1761.

Original Letters from Edmond Malone, the Editor of Shakespeare, to John Jordan, the Poet, now first printed from the autograph manuscripts preserved at Stratford-upon-Avon. Edited by J. O. Halliwell, Esq. 1864. (Only ten copies printed.)

(Editor) *Parliamentary Logick,* with a biographical preface of William Gerard Hamilton. 1809.

The Plays and Poems of William Shakspeare, ed. Edmond Malone, 10 vols. in 11. 1790.

The Plays and Poems of William Shakspeare, eds. Edmond Malone and James Boswell Junior, 21 vols., 1821.

The Plays of William Shakespeare, Accurately Printed from the Text of Mr. Malone's Edition, with select explanatory notes [edited by John Nichols]. 7 volumes. London, 1790–96.

The Life of Oliver Goldsmith, in *Poems and Plays by Dr. Oliver Goldsmith, to which are prefixed, Memoirs of the Life and Writings of the Author.* Dublin, 1777; London edition, 1780.

(Editor) *Roman Portraits, A Poem, in Heroick Verse,* by Robert Jephson. 1794.

A Second Appendix to Mr. Malone's Supplement to the Last Edition of the Plays of Shakespeare. 1783.

'Shakspeare and Jonson', *Plays and Poems of William Shakspeare,* ed. Edmond Malone. I:ii. 1790.

A Supplement to the Edition of Shakespeare, Published in 1778 by Samuel Johnson and George Steevens, ed. Edmond Malone. 2 vols. 1780.

(Editor) *Works of Sir Joshua Reynolds ... [with] An Account of the Life and Writings of the author,* 2 vols. 1797; 3 vols. 1798.

III. Other sources

Unless otherwise indicated, place of publication is London. Eighteenth-century editions of Shakespeare are listed under the names of their editors.

Adams, John Quincy. *Dramatic Records of Sir Henry Herbert.* 1917.

Alexander, Peter. *Shakespeare's 'Henry VI' and 'Richard III'.* Cambridge, 1929.

Studies in Shakespeare. 1964.

Alumni Dubliniensis, 1756.

Amory, Martha Babcock. *The Domestic and Artistic Life of John Singleton Copley, R. A.* Boston, 1882.

Arnold, Matthew. *On the Study of Celtic Literature.* 1867.

Aubrey, John. *Brief Lives*, ed. Oliver Lawson Dick. 1949; rev. edn. 1958.

Lives of Eminent Men, ed. A. Clarke. 2 vols. 1898.

Baker, Peter S. and Thomas W. Copeland, George M. Kahrl, Rachel McClellan, and James M. Osborn, eds., *The Correspondence of James Boswell with David Garrick, Edmund Burke, and Edmond Malone. The Yale editions of the private papers of James Boswell, research edition: Correspondence*, vol. 4. London, 1986.

Baratariana. Volume of satirical papers, contributed to by Malone. Dublin, 1772; 2nd edn., 1773.

Bate, Jonathan. *Shakespeare Constitutions: Politics, Theatre, Criticism 1730–1830.* Oxford, 1989.

Bate, Walter Jackson. *Samuel Johnson.* New York, 1977.

Beechey, Henry William, ed. *The Literary Works of Sir Joshua Reynolds.* 2 vols. 1846.

Bennett, Josephine Waters. 'Benson's Alleged Piracy of *Shakespeare's Sonnets* and of Some of Jonson's Works', *Studies in Bibliography*, 21 (1968), 235–48.

Boaden, James. *An Inquiry into the Authenticity of Various Pictures and Prints ... Offered to the Public as Portraits of Shakespeare.* 1824.

Boswell, James. *Boswell's Life of Samuel Johnson, LL.D., together with Boswell's Journal of a Tour to the Hebrides*, eds. George Birkbeck Hill, rev. and enl. by L. F. Powell. 6 vols. Oxford, 1934–50.

Boswell's Life of Johnson, ed. and intro. by Sir Sydney Roberts. 2 vols. New York and London, 1960.

Journal of a Tour to the Hebrides with Samuel Johnson, LL.D. 1773 (first published in 1785), eds. F. A. Pottle and C. H. Bennett. New York, 1961.

Letters of James Boswell, ed. Chauncey Brewster Tinker. 2 vols. 1924.

The Private Papers of James Boswell from Malahide Castle, in the Collection of Lt.-Colonel Ralph Heyward Isham, eds. Geoffrey Scott and Frederick A. Pottle. 18 vols. Mount Vernon, 1928–34.

Boydell, John, and Josiah Boydell. *Collection of Prints, from Pictures Painted for the Purpose of Illustrating the Dramatic Works of Shakspeare, by the Artists of Great Britain.* 2 vols. 1803.

Brady, Frank. *James Boswell: The Later Years, 1769–1795.* New York, 1984.

and Marlies K. Danziger, eds. *Boswell: The Great Biographer 1789–95.* London and New York, 1989.

Bronson, Bertrand H. 'Thomas Chatterton', *The Age of Johnson: Essays presented to Chauncey Brewster Tinker*, ed. Frederick W. Hilles. New Haven, 1949; 2nd printing, 1964.

Joseph Ritson, Scholar at Arms. 2 vols. Berkeley, 1938.

Brown, Arthur. 'Edmond Malone and English Scholarship', an inaugural lecture delivered at University College London, 21 May 1963. London, 1963.

Bryant, Donald C. *Edmund Burke and His Literary Friends.* St Louis, Missouri, 1939.

Buchanan, David. *The Treasure of Auchinleck: The Story of the Boswell Papers.* 1975.

Butt, John. *The Mid-Eighteenth Century*, ed. Geoffrey Carnall. Oxford History of
English Literature, VIII, 1979.

Byng, the Hon. John (later 5th Viscount Torrington), *The Torrington Diaries*, ed. C.
Bruyn Andrews. 4 vols. 1934–38.

Caldecott, Thomas [under the name of Samuel Ireland]. *An Investigation of Mr.
Malone's Claim to the Character of Scholar, or Critick; being an Examination of his
Inquiry into the Authenticity of the Shakspeare MSS.* 1798.

Capell, Edward. *William Shakespeare, His Comedies, Histories, and Tragedies.* 1768.
Notes and Various Readings to Shakespeare, ed. John Collins. 3 vols. 1779–83.

Capell's Ghost, to Edmund [sic] Malone, esq., editor of Shakespeare. A parody. Anonymous.
1799. Reprinted in *School for Satire*, 1802, pp. 401–7.

*A Catalogue of Early English Poetry and Other Miscellaneous Works Illustrating the British
Drama, collected by Edmond Malone Esq. and now Preserved in the Bodleian Library.*
Oxford, 1836.

*A Catalogue of the Greater Portion of the Library of the Late Edmond Malone, Esq ... sold by
S. Sotheby ... beginning Thursday, Nov. 26, 1818.* 1818.

Caulfield, James. *An Enquiry Into the Conduct of Edmond Malone Esq. Concerning the
Manuscript Papers of John Aubrey, F.R.S in the Ashmolean Museum, Oxford.* 1797.
The Oxford Cabinet. 1797. (An attack on Malone, who bought up the entire 250
print run.)

Chalmers, George. *Another Account of the Incidents, from which the Title, and a Part of the
Story of Shakspeare's Tempest, were Derived.* 1815.
An Apology for the Believers in the Shakspeare-Papers, 1797.
*A Supplemental Apology for the Believers in the Shakspeare-Papers, Being a Reply to
Malone's Answer Which was Early Announced, but Never Published.* 1799. (Dedicated
to George Steevens.)

The Collection of Autograph Letters and Historical Documents formed by Alfred Morrison,
2nd ser., 1896, privately printed.

The Confessions of W. H. Ireland. 1805.

Copeland, Thomas W., ed. *The Correspondence of Edmund Burke.* 9 vols. Cambridge,
1958–70.

Cotton, William. *Sir Joshua Reynolds' Notes.* 1859.

Courtenay, John. *Poetical Review of the Literary and Moral Character of the Late Samuel
Johnson.* 1786, intro. by Robert E. Kelley, *Augustan Reprint Society*, no. 133.
1969.

Crossley, Ceri, and Ian Small, eds. *The French Revolution and British Culture.* Oxford,
1989.

Davis, Bertram H. *Johnson Before Boswell: A Study of John Hawkins' Life of Samuel
Johnson.* New Haven, Connecticut, 1960; reprinted 1973.
Thomas Percy: A Scholar-Cleric in the Age of Johnson. Philadelphia, 1989.

de Grazia, Margreta. *Shakespeare Verbatim: The Reproduction of Authenticity and the 1790
Apparatus.* Oxford, 1991.

Derry, Warren. *Dr. Parr: A Portrait of the Whig Dr. Johnson.* Oxford, 1966.

Douce, Francis. *Illustrations of Shakespeare and of Ancient Manners, With A Dissertation
on the Clowns and Fools of Shakespeare.* 1807.

Drake, Nathan. *Shakespeare and His Times.* 2 vols. 1817.

Duff, Monstuart E., ed. *Annals of The Club, 1764–1914.* 1914.
  The Club. 1905.
Eliot, Sir Gilbert. *The Life and Letters of Sir Gilbert Eliot 1751–1806,* ed. the Countess
  of Minto. 2 vols. 1874.
Evans, G. Blakemore. 'Shakespeare's Text', *The Riverside Shakespeare.* Boston, 1974.
  'Shakespeare's Text: Approaches and Problems', in *A New Companion to
  Shakespeare Studies,* ed. Kenneth Muir. Cambridge, 1971.
Fairer, David. *The Correspondence of Thomas Warton.* Athens, Georgia, 1994.
George Faulkner's Dublin Journal, 28 August 1759.
Freeman, Arthur, gen. ed. *Inquiry Into the Authenticity of Certain Miscellaneous Papers
  and Legal Instruments ... Attributed to Shakspeare ...* (1796) by Edmond Malone,
  in *Eighteenth-Century Shakespeare,* vol. 22. 1970.
Fuseli, Henry. *Lectures on Painting, delivered at the Royal Academy.* 1820.
Ganzel, Dewey. *Fortune and Men's Eyes: The Career of John Payne Collier.* New York,
  1982.
Garlick, Kenneth and Angus Macintyre, eds. (vols. I–VI); Kathryn Cave, ed.
  (vols. VII–XVI continuing). *Diary of Joseph Farington.* New Haven and
  London, 1978.
Garrick, David. *Letters,* eds. D. M. Little and G. M. Kahrl. Cambridge, 1963.
Gibbon, Edward. *The History of the Decline and Fall of the Roman Empire.* 4 vols.
  1776–88.
Graves, Robert and Laura Riding. *Survey of Modernist Poetry.* 1927.
Grebanier, Bernard. *The Great Shakespeare Forgery: A New Look at the Career of William
  Henry Ireland.* New York, 1965.
Green, Thomas. *Extracts from the Diary of a Lover of Literature.* 1810.
Greene, Edward B. *Strictures Upon a Pamphlet Intitled, 'Cursory Observations on the Poems
  Attributed to Rowley'.* 1782.
Greene, Robert. *A Groatsworth of Wit.* 1592.
Greg, W. W. *The Editorial Problem in Shakespeare: A Survey of the Foundations of the
  Text.* 3rd edn., Oxford, 1967.
  'Editors at Work and Play,' *Review of English Studies,* 2 (1926).
Halliwell-Phillipps, James O. *A Few Words in Defence of the Memory of E. Capell.* 1860.
Hardinge, George. *The Essence of Malone, or, The 'Beauties' of that Fascinating Writer,
  Extracted from his immortal work, in Five hundred Sixty-nine Pages, and a Quarter Just
  Published, and (With his accustomed felicity) entitled, 'Some Account of the Life and
  Writings of JOHN DRYDEN!!'.* 1800.
  Another Essence of Malone, or, The 'Beauties' of Shakspeare's Editor. 1801.
Harington, Sir John. *Brief Apologie of Poetrie.* 1591.
Haslewood, Joseph. *Some Account of the Life and Publications of the Late Joseph Ritson,
  Esq.* 1824.
Hawkins, Sir John. *Life of Samuel Johnson.* 1787.
Hill, George B., ed. *Johnsonian Miscellanies.* 2 vols. 1897; reprinted 1967.
  The Literary Career of Sir Joshua Reynolds. Hamden, Connecticut, 1967.
Hoper, Winifred, ed. 'Some Unpublished Windham Papers', *The 19th Century and
  After,* 86, 673–74.

Hurdis, James. *Cursory Remarks Upon the Arrangement of the Plays of Shakespeare*; *Occasioned by... Malone's Essay...* 1792.

Hyde, Mary. *The Impossible Friendship: Boswell and Mrs. Thrale.* Cambridge, 1972.

Ireland, Samuel. *Miscellaneous Papers and Legal Instruments under the Hand and Seal of William Shakspeare: including the Tragedy of King Lear and a Small Fragment of Hamlet, from the Original MSS in the Possession of Samuel Ireland, of Norfolk Street.* 1795.

 Mr. Ireland's Vindication of His Conduct, Respecting the Publication of the Supposed Shakspeare MSS, being a preface... to a reply to the critical labours of Mr. Malone in his Enquiry into the authenticity of certain papers. 1796.

Jephson, Maurice Denham. *An Anglo-Irish Miscellany: Some Records of the Jephsons of Mallow.* Dublin, 1964.

Jephson, Robert. *Roman Portraits.* 1794.

Johnson, Samuel and George Steevens, eds. *The Plays of William Shakespeare, with Notes by Samuel Johnson and George Steevens.* 2nd. edn., 10 vols. 1778; ed. Isaac Reed, 10 vols. 1785; 15 vols. 1793; 21 vols. 1803; 21 vols. 1813.

 The Rambler, in *The Yale Edition of the Works of Samuel Johnson*, eds. W. J. Bate and A. B. Strauss. Vol. III. 1969.

Kahrl, George M. and George Winchester Stone , *David Garrick: A Critical Biography.* Carbondale and Edwardsville, Illinois, 1979.

Kemble, J. P. *Macbeth Reconsidered; An Essay.* 1786. (Dedicated to Malone.)

Keynes, Geoffrey L. *The Complete Writings of William Blake.* 3 vols. 1957.

Landry, Hilton. 'Malone as Editor of Shakespeare's Sonnets', *Bulletin of the New York Public Library*, 67:7 (1963), 435–42.

Langbaine, Gerard. *An Account of the English Dramatick Poets.* 1691. Malone's annotated copy is in the Bodleian Library, Malone 129.

Lecky, William Edward Hartpole, *The History of Ireland in the Eighteenth Century.* 5 vols. 1896.

Leslie, C. R. and T. Taylor. *The Life and Times of Sir Joshua Reynolds.* 2 vols. 1865.

Lewis, Wilmarth S. 'Edmond Malone, Horace Walpole, and Shakespeare', in *Evidence in Literary Scholarship: Essays in Memory of James M. Osborn*, eds. Rene Wellek and Alvaro Ribeiro. Oxford, 1979.

 Ed. *The Yale Edition of Horace Walpole's Correspondence*, New Haven, 1937–81.

 The Life and Correspondence of David Garrick, extra-illustrated volume, Harvard Theatre Collection, Harvard College Library (TS 937.3).

Lintot, Bernard. *A Collection of Poems.* 2 vols. 1711.

Lipking, Lawrence. *The Ordering of the Arts in Eighteenth-Century England.* Princeton, 1970.

Lodge. John. *Peerage of Ireland*, ed. M. Archdall. Dublin, 1789.

Lustig, Irma L. and F. A. Pottle, eds. *Boswell: The Applause of the Jury 1782–85.* 1982. *Boswell: The English Experiment 1785–89.* 1986.

McCarthy, William. *Hester Thrale Piozzi: Portrait of a Literary Woman.* Chapel Hill, 1985.

McKerrow, Ronald B. 'The Treatment of Shakespeare's Text by his Earlier Editors, 1709–1768', in *Library of Shakespearean Biography and Criticism.* 1933; reprinted, Freeport, New York, 1970.

Mair, John. *The Fourth Forger: William Ireland and the Shakespeare Papers*. 1938.

Markham, Sarah. *A Testimony of Her Times*. 1991.

John Loveday of Caversham 1711–1789: The Life and Times of an Eighteenth-Century Onlooker. 1984.

Martin, Peter. 'Edmond Malone, Sir Joshua Reynolds, and Dr. Johnson's Monument in St. Paul's Cathedral', in *The Age of Johnson*, ed. Paul Korshin, III. 1989, pp. 331–51.

Mathias, Thomas James. *The Pursuits of Literature, or What You Will: A Satirical Poem in Dialogue. Part the First*. 1794.

Murray, John, ed. *Observations, Anecdotes, and Characters of Books and Men Arranged with Notes by the Late Edmund [sic] Malone Esq.* 1820.

Nichols, John. *Illustrations of the Literary History of the Eighteenth Century*. Vol. V. 1817–58.

Nicols, John. ed. *The Works of the Rev. Jonathan Swift DD*. 3rd edn. 19 vols. 1808. (Malone assisted Nichols with this edition and revised Barrett's *Essay on the Earlier Part of the Life of Swift* for it.)

Northcote, James. *Memoirs of Sir Joshua Reynolds*. 1813.

Osborn, James M. '"By Appointment to His Majesty Biographer of Samuel Johnson, LL.D."', For the Annual Dinner of The Johnsonians in celebration of *Dr. Johnson's* two hundred and fifty-fifth birthday, 18 September 1964.

'Dr. Johnson and the Contrary Converts', published for the Ninth Annual Dinner of The Johnsonians in celebration of *Dr. Johnson's* two hundred and forty-fifth birthday, 18 September 1954.

'Edmond Malone and Baratariana,' *Notes & Queries*, 27, January, 1945.

'Edmond Malone and Dr. Johnson', *Johnson, Boswell, and Their Circle*, ed. Mary Lascelles. Oxford, 1965, pp. 1–20.

'Edmond Malone and Oxford', in *Eighteenth-Century Studies in Honor of Donald F. Hyde*, ed. W. H. Bond. The Grolier Club, New York, 1970.

'Edmond Malone: Scholar–Collector', *Transactions of the Bibliographical Society*, XIX (1964), 11–37.

'Horace Walpole and Edmond Malone', in *Horace Walpole: Writer, Politican, and Connoisseur*, ed. W. H. Smith. New Haven, 1967, pp. 299–324.

John Dryden: Some Biographical Facts and Problems. 1940; rev. edn., Gainesville, Florida, 1965.

Joseph Spence: Observations, Anecdotes, and Characters of Books and Men. 2 vols. Oxford, 1966.

'Dr. Johnson on the Sanctity of an Author's Text', [as reported by Malone], *PMLA*, 50 (September 1935), 928–29.

'Ritson, Scholar at Odds', in *Modern Philology*, 37, no. 4 (1940).

Patterson, Remington T. 'Edmond Malone and "some curious Manuscripts" relative to the stage' (forthcoming).

Percy, Thomas. *Reliques of English Poetry*. 1765.

Pinkerton, John. *Walpoliana*. 1800.

Piozzi, Hester Thrale. *Anecdotes of the Late Samuel Johnson*. 1786.

Piper, David. *The Image of the Poet: British Poets and Their Portraits*. Oxford, 1982.

'*O Sweet Mr. Shakespeare I'll have his picture*': *The Changing Image of Shakespeare's Person 1600–1800*. Washington, 1964.

Pope, Alexander. *The Twickenham Edition of the Poems of Alexander Pope*, gen. ed. John Butt. New Haven and London, 1939–69.

Pottle, F. A. *The Literary Career of James Boswell, Esq.* Oxford, 1929.
  Pride and Negligence: The History of the Boswell Papers. New York, 1982.

Pottle, F. A. ed. *Boswell's Journal of a Tour to the Hebrides with Samuel Johnson, LL.D.* 1961; new edn., 1973.

Pottle, F. A. and J. W. Reed, eds. *Boswell: Laird of Auchinleck 1778–82*. 1977.

Pottle, F. A. and Geoffrey Scott, eds. *Private Papers of James Boswell from Malahide Castle, in the Collection of Lt.-Colonel Ralph Heyward Isham*, 18 vols. 1974.

Prior, Sir James. *Life of Edmond Malone*. 1860.

Prown, Julius David. *John Singleton Copley in England 1774–1815*. Cambridge, Mass., 1966.

Reed, Isaac, ed. David Erskine Baker, *Biographia Dramatica, or a Companion to the Playhouse: a new edition*. 2 vols., 1782.
  The Reed Diaries 1762–1804, ed. Claude E. Jones. University of California Publications in English, vol. 10. Berkeley, 1946.

Reynolds, Sir Joshua. *The Letters of Sir Joshua Reynolds*, ed. Frederick W. Hilles. 1929.
  Works – [with] An Account of the Life and Writings of the author, ed. Edmond Malone. 2 vols., 1797; 2nd edn., 3 vols., 1798.

Ritson, Joseph. *Bibliographia Poetica: a Catalogue of English Poets, of the 12th, 13th, 14th, 15th, and 16th Centuries*. 1802.
  Cursory Criticism of the Edition of Shakespeare published by Edmond Malone. 1792. (Malone bound up a number of Ritson's works and other criticisms of himself in a volume titled *Shakspeariana*; it is in the Bodleian Library, Malone 150.)
  The Letters of Joseph Ritson, Esq., ed. Joseph Frank, with a *Memoir* by Sir Harris Nicolas. 2 vols. 1833.
  The Quip Modest. 1788.
  Remarks, Critical and Illustrative, on the Text and Notes of the Last Edition of Shakspeare. 1783. New York, 1973.

Robinson, Henry Crabb. *The Diary, Reminiscences and Correspondence of Crabb Robinson*, ed. Thomas Sadler. 3 vols. 1869.

Rollins, Hyder Edward, ed. *The Sonnets*. 2 vols. Philadelphia and London, 1944.

Schoenbaum, Samuel. *Internal Evidence and Elizabethan Dramatic Authorship: An Essay in Literary History and Method*. Evanston, 1966.
  Shakespeare's Lives. Oxford and New York, 1970; rev. edn. 1991.
  William Shakespeare: A Compact Documentary Life. Oxford, 1977.

Scott, Sir Walter. *The Letters of Sir Walter Scott*, ed. Sir Herbert J. C. Grierson. 12 vols. 1932–37.

Seary, Peter. *Lewis Theobald and the Editing of Shakespeare*. Oxford, 1990.

Sen, Sailendra Kumar. *Capell and Malone, and Modern Critical Bibliography*. Calcutta, 1960.

Sherbo, Arthur. *The Birth of Shakespeare Studies: Commentators from Rowe (1709) to Boswell–Malone (1821)*. East Lansing, Michigan, 1986.

'George Steevens' 1785 Variorum *Shakespeare*', *Studies in Bibliography*, 32 (1979), 241–46.

Isaac Reed, Editorial Factotum. Victoria, British Columbia, 1988.

Sill, R. (pseudonym Charles Dirrill). *Remarks on Shakespeare's Tempest, containing an Investigation of Mr. Malone's Attempt to Ascertain the Date of that Play.* 1797.

Simpson, Frank. 'New Place: The Only Representation of Shakespeare's House, from an Unpublished Manuscript', in *Shakespeare Survey*, 5 (1952), 55–57.

Smith, D. Nichol. 'Edmond Malone', *Huntington Library Quarterly*, III:i (October 1939), 23–36.

Eighteenth Century Essays on Shakespeare. 2nd. edn., Oxford, 1963; first published, 1903.

Shakespeare in the Eighteenth Century. Oxford, 1928.

Spence, Joseph. *Observations, Anecdotes, and Characters of Books and Men.* With notes by Malone. 1820.

Spielmann, M. H. 'Shakespeare's Portraiture', in *Studies in the First Folio*. 1924.

Steevens, George. *Catalogue of Mr. Capell's Shakespeariana*, presented by him to Trinity College Cambridge, 1779 (privately printed), ed. W. W. Greg. Cambridge 1903.

Strong, Roy. '*And When Did You Last See Your Father?': TheVictorian Painter and British History.* 1978.

Swift, Jonathan. *The Works of the Rev. Jonathan Swift DD.*, ed. John Nichols. 1808.

Taylor, Gary. *Reinventing Shakespeare: A Cultural History From the Restoration to the Present.* London and New York, 1989.

Taylor, John. *Records of My Life.* 2 vols. 1833.

Taylor, W. J. A. *History of Dublin University.*

Thornton, R. D. 'The Influence of the Enlightenment upon Eighteenth-Century British Antiquaries, 1750–1800', in *Studies on Voltaire and the Eighteenth Century*, XXVII (1963), 1601ff.

Tillotson, Arthur, ed. *The Correspondence of Thomas Percy and Edmond Malone.* Baton Rouge, Louisiana, 1944.

Tyrwhitt, Thomas. *Observations and Conjectures upon Some Passages of Shakespeare.* 1766.

Poems, supposed to have been written at Bristol, by Thomas Rowley and Others, in the Fifteenth Century. 1777.

A Vindication of the Appendix to the Poems, called Rowley's. 1782.

Waingrow, Marshall, ed. *Correspondence and Other Papers of James Boswell Relating to the Making of the Life of Johnson.* 1969.

Walker, Alice. 'Edward Capell and his Edition of Shakespeare', in *Studies of Shakespeare*, ed. Peter Alexander (1964), pp. 132–48.

Walpole, Horace, *The Yale Edition of Horace Walpole's Correspondence*, ed. W. S. Lewis. New Haven, 1937–85.

Anecdotes of Painting in England (and A Catalogue of Engravers). 3rd edn., 5 vols., 1782.

Walton, J. K. 'Edmond Malone: An Irish Shakespeare Scholar', *Hermathena*, XCIX (1964), 5–26.

Warton, Joseph. *An Essay on the Genius and Writings of Pope.* 1782.

Warton, Thomas. *The History of English Poetry, From the Close of the Eleventh to the Commencement of the Eighteenth Century.* 3 vols., 1774–78.

The Life and Literary Remains of Ralph Bathurst. 1761.

An Enquiry into the Authenticity of the Poems attributed to Thomas Rowley. 1782.

Wendorf, Richard. *The Elements of Life: Biography and Portrait-Painting in Stuart and Georgian England.* Oxford, 1990.

Wilson, F. P. *Shakespeare and the New Bibliography*, rev. and ed. Helen Gardener. Oxford, 1970.

Wilson, John Dover, ed. 'Malone and the Upstart Crow', in *2 Henry VI* (1952), section II, (a) 'Back to Malone'. Cambridge, 1952.

Wilson's Dublin Directory. 1792.

Wimsatt, William K. 'Images of Samuel Johnson', *Journal of English Literary History*, 41 (1974), 356–74.

Windham, William. *The Diary of the Right Hon. William Windham 1784–1810*, ed. Mrs Henry Baring. 1866.

The Windham Papers, ed. Rosebery, the Earl of. 2 vols., 1913.

Woods, James. *Annals of Westmeath.* Dublin, 1907.

Woodson, W. C. 'The Printer's Copy for the 1785 Variorum Shakespeare', *Studies in Bibliography*, 31 (1978), 208–10.

Wooll, John. *Biographical Memoir of the Late Rev. Joseph Warton.* 1806.

Wyatt, John. *A Comparative Review of the Opinions of Mr. James Boaden.* 1796.

Index

Addison, Joseph, 56
Alexander, Peter, 122
Alleyn, Edward, 126
Analytical Review, 199
Annual Register, 214
Ashmolean Library, 81
Astle, Thomas, 196
Aubrey, John, 117, 124, 131–33, 165, 173, 174, 176–77, 190, 191 *see also* Malone

Bacon, John, 61
Baker, David Erskine, 75
Baker, William, 225
Baldwin, Henry, 98, 157
Banks, Joseph, 52, 61, 62, 65, 95, 208
Baratariana, 14
Bardolatry, 25–8
Barnard, Thomas (Bishop of Killaloe), 99
Baronston, Malone estate, Co. Westmeath, 1, 15, 93, 185, 244, 252, 270
Barrett, Dr John, 257, 261
Barrington, Daines, 136
Beauclerk, Hon. Topham, 29, 52, 73
Beechey, Henry, 216
Betterton, Thomas, 26, 91
Bindley, James, 224, 225, 226, 227, 243, 261, *see also* Malone
biography, eighteenth-century taste for, 23–5
Blackstone, Sir William, 37
Blakeway, Rev. John Brickdale, 226–27, 238, 239
Blake, William, 217–18
Boaden, James, 90, 93, 181, 192, 195
Bodleian Library, 57, 81, 117, 127, 128, 166, 173–74, 232, 277–8 *see also* Malone
Bolingbroke, Viscount (Henry St John), 2, 13
Boswell, Alexander, 162, 227, 243
Boswell, Euphemia, 161
Boswell, James, 5–6, 8, 52, 53, 54, 55, 56, 63, 82, 95–111, 130, 135, 138, 144, 149, 150–51, 152, 153, 154–57, 158, 161–62, 184, 189, 190, 207, 208, 211, 212

anxiety at Malone's absence, 156; cannot write in Scotland, 151; death of, 160; denigration of Piozzi's *Anecdotes*, 145; depressed over *Life*, 155–57; fears duel with Macdonald, 106; honorary degree mentioned by, in *Life of Johnson*, 7; kneels before forgeries, 191; manuscripts of, 161–64; on reception of *Plays and Poems* (1790), 135; post-publication depression, 160; reports Burke's praise of *Plays and Poems* (1790), 138; temperance of, 150–51
Life of Johnson, 32
  begins writing, 149; 2nd edn, 158; 3rd edn, 144; published, 158; returns to London to complete, 153; worries over, 149
Tour to the Hebrides
  concern over Macdonald's hostility to, 105; offends friends in, 103–5; public criticism of, 101; reviews of, 103; 2nd edn, 109; sells well, 102
  see also Malone
Boswell, James Junior, 127, 162, 164, 243, 246, 249, 267, 269, 270, 271–3, 275, 277, 280
  describes his editorial problems in PP (1821), 271–73; explains his editorship of PP (1821), 267–68, 271–72, 275–76; sales of his books and papers at auction, 278
  see also Malone
Boswell, Mrs James (Margaret), 106, 108, 153
Boswell, Veronica, 108, 161
Bover, Maria, 183–85
Bowles, William Lisle, 223–24
Boydell, Alderman John, 114–15
Boydell, Josiah, 141
British Museum, 21, 22, 23, 35, 42, 56, 66, 73, 84, 95, 118, 232, 239, 260
  and Johnson letters, 164; Musgrave, Sir William, retired Curator of, 227

291

CAMBRIDGE STUDIES IN EIGHTEENTH-CENTURY
ENGLISH LITERATURE AND THOUGHT

Printed in the United Kingdom
by Lightning Source UK Ltd.
103299UKS00002B/273